Biosocial Interrelations in Population Adaptation

World Anthropology

General Editor

SOL TAX

Patrons

CLAUDE LÉVI-STRAUSS
MARGARET MEAD
LAILA SHUKRY EL HAMAMSY
M. N. SRINIVAS

MOUTON PUBLISHERS · THE HAGUE · PARIS
DISTRIBUTED IN THE USA AND CANADA BY ALDINE, CHICAGO

Biosocial Interrelations in Population Adaptation

Editors

ELIZABETH S. WATTS
FRANCIS E. JOHNSTON
GABRIEL W. LASKER

MOUTON PUBLISHERS · THE HAGUE · PARIS
DISTRIBUTED IN THE USA AND CANADA BY ALDINE, CHICAGO

General Editor's Preface

This book symbolizes, in the words of J.S. Weiner, "a remarkable and notable stage in the history of ... physical anthropology" as it has come to be thought of as human population biology. Since World War II, physical anthropology has become ever more biological and ever more international, movements climaxed by the organization of the International Association of Human Biologists, which at the 1973 International Congress in Chicago affiliated with the International Union of Anthropological and Ethnological Sciences. Human biology, like medicine, draws upon the knowledge and methods developed in many of the biological sciences. Unlike medicine, it goes beyond individual differences relating to health to discover the biological characteristics of the species itself as they are affected by evolutionary and ecological circumstances. Moreover, since our species biology is intimately related to the historical, social, and cultural differences which affect individual populations, human biology is uniquely part of general anthropology. It is hardly surprising therefore that it must, like the rest of anthropology, draw its scientists from every part of the world.

The IXth Congress was planned from the beginning not only to include as many of the scholars from every part of the world as possible, but also with a view toward the eventual publication of the papers in high-quality volumes. At previous Congresses scholars were invited to bring papers which were then read out loud. They were necessarily limited in length; many were only summarized; there was little time for discussion; and the sparse discussion could only be in one language. The IXth Congress was an experiment aimed at changing this. Papers were written with the intention of exchanging them before the Congress, particularly in extensive pre-Congress sessions; they were not intended to be read aloud at the Congress, that time being devoted to discussions — discussions which were simultaneously and professionally translated into five languages. The method for eliciting the papers was structured to make as representative a sample as was allowable when scholarly creativity — hence self-selection — was critically important. Scholars were asked both to propose papers of their own and to suggest topics for sessions of the Congress which they might edit into volumes. All were then informed of the suggestions and encouraged to re-think their own papers and the topics. The process, therefore, was a continuous one of feedback and exchange and it has continued to be so even after the Congress. The some two thousand papers comprising *World Anthropology* certainly then offer a substantial sample of world anthropology. It has been said that anthropology is at a turning point; if this is so, these volumes will be the historical direction-markers.

As might have been foreseen in the first post-colonial generation, the large majority of the Congress papers (82 percent) are the work of scholars identified with the industrialized world which fathered our traditional discipline and the institution of the Congress itself: Eastern Europe (15 percent); Western Europe (16 percent); North America (47 percent); Japan, South Africa, Australia, and New Zealand (4 percent). Only 18 percent of the papers are from developing areas: Africa (4 percent); Asia-Oceania (9 percent); Latin America (5 percent). Aside from the substantial representation from the U.S.S.R. and the nations of Eastern Europe, a significant difference between this corpus of written material and that of other Congresses is the addition of the large proportion of contributions from Africa, Asia, and Latin America. "Only 18 percent" is two to four times as great a proportion as that of other Congresses; moreover, 18 percent of 2,000 papers is 360 papers, 10 times the number of "Third World" papers presented at previous Congresses. In fact, these 360 papers are more than the total of ALL papers published after the last International Congress of Anthropological and Ethnological Sciences which was held in the United States (Philadelphia, 1956).

The significance of the increase is not simply quantitative. The input of scholars from areas which have until recently been no more than subject matter for anthropology represents both feedback and also long-awaited theoretical contributions from the perspectives of very different cultural, social, and historical traditions. Many who attended the IXth Congress were convinced that anthropology would not be the same in the future. The fact that the next Congress (India, 1978) will be our first in the "Third World" may be symbolic of the change. Meanwhile, sober consideration of the present set of books will show how much, and just where and how, our discipline is being revolutionized.

The reader of this volume will be interested in many others of the series, especially those dealing with the evolution and prehistory of man and adaptations to environments in different areas of the world; demography and migration; physical, medical, and psychological anthropology; nutritional, regional, and sex differences; and physiological and social problems, as these are examined cross-culturally.

Chicago, Illinois   SOL TAX
September 3, 1975

Table of Contents

Introduction

ELIZABETH S. WATTS, FRANCIS E. JOHNSTON, and
GABRIEL W. LASKER

The papers included in this volume were presented at a conference entitled "Biosocial Interrelations in Population Adaptation," held on August 29–31, 1973, at Wayne State University in Detroit, Michigan. The sponsorship, purpose, and significance of this conference are admirably summarized by Professor Weiner in his opening remarks. It is only left to the editors to make a brief statement concerning the content and organization of the volume.

The twenty-three papers have been grouped into several sections according to their principal focus for the convenience of those readers whose interest is confined to a particular area of human biology. Those who read the entire volume will appreciate the difficulty of grouping interdisciplinary papers of this sort whose subjects overlap to such a great degree.

Part 1, Adaptation and Adaptive Strategies, begins with theoretical and general considerations and proceeds to particular cases. Mazess discusses and organizes a theoretical framework for studying adaptation, on both population and individual levels. Stini carries this forward by considering both population size and individual body size in relation to environmental adaptation. Lasker and Womack's calculations show the importance of considering population differences in body composition as well as size in assessing adaptive relationships. Frisancho, et al. investigate the question of whether small body size is adaptive in a specific population. Kennedy adds the time dimension and traces past adaptations within a particular region.

The papers in Part 2, Genetics, Society, and Population Dynamics, explore several different points of interaction between social, demographic, and genetic processes — the continuing usefulness of genetic traits and frequencies in assessing population histories (Crawford, and Schanfield and Fudenberg), the social cost of certain genes (Roberts), the genetic effects of certain social preferences and practices (Hiernaux) and demographic patterns (Salzano), and the influence of sociocultural variables on population structure (Clegg, Beaubier).

Part 3, Nutrition, Health, and Disease, demonstrates the inseparable nature of cultural and biological adaptations of human populations to their environments, so that any consideration aimed at improving health and nutrition must always include a thorough knowledge of existing behavioral patterns and their consequences.

Part 4, Growth and Development, shows the continuing value of using the copious existing growth data on American children to test hypotheses which may give new insights into the mechanics of the growth process (Frisch, Roche, et al.), and the importance of studying and comparing non-Western populations in order to assess the impact of socially and genetically mediated variables on child growth (Fiawoo, Malcolm, Johnston, et al.).

Considered as a whole this volume is a representative definition of the field of human biology. It transcends both national boundaries and those of traditional academic disciplines. It studies both past and present human populations. It is not restricted to a single approach or set of methods. Rather, it involves choosing a particular problem to explore and seeking its solution wherever it may lead. The latter point is well illustrated in the present volume where one sees the work of a group of researchers who began from many different starting points — anthropology, genetics, medicine, and parasitology, to name only a few — and pursued problems concerning various aspects of human adaptation, achieving complementary and often mutually enlightening results. For these reasons there are few areas of research today which are as exciting or as intellectually rewarding as the study of human population biology.

Opening Remarks: The Significance of this Symposium

J. S. WEINER

I would like to say something about the form and the content of the Symposium on "Biosocial Interrelations in Population Adaptation." In form and content this symposium symbolizes a remarkable and notable stage in the history of the subject we variously call physical anthropology, anthropological biology, human biology, or simply *anthropologie* on the Continent, but I have personally always preferred the term human population biology. A future historian of our discipline has available in this meeting a "package" as it were of all the major features that have reshaped and now characterize this discipline as a result of the developments since World War II.

Let us look first at the organizational features of this symposium. As participants, some of us may not realize the many different roles which can be assigned to us. We are here first of all under the all-embracing global polydisciplinary sponsorship provided by the long established Congress and Union of Anthropological and Ethnological Sciences. It is right and proper that our symposium should figure as one of the satellites in the orbit of this parental body for the relationship of human biological sciences to the non-biological disciplines of anthropology has an importance which all of us fully appreciate. The title and contents of our symposium make this abundantly clear.

There is in this symposium another supranational component represented by the contribution, direct and indirect, from the Human Adaptability project of the IBP. In its ten-year program, the Human Adaptability Section has operated on a truly supranational basis because the research projects, the methodology, and many of the research teams have largely transcended national boundaries. Many of the participants in this symposium were, or still are, engaged in the human adaptability program, and I think they will agree with me that this represents the greatest effort made so far for achieving a world wide coordinated study of the biology of man in an ecological setting. The HA has in many different ways given a strong momentum to our discipline, and we are determined, I am sure, that this impetus will not be lost.

As the HA programme draws to its end officially in October 1974, we witness the arrival on the scene of the International Association of Human Biologists, of which many of us here are members. The IAHB represents the major organized international component in this symposium. The IAHB was founded with the help of the Wenner-Gren Foundation to consolidate and perpetuate the international contact amongst physical anthropologists brought about largely by the foundation itself and also by the HA section of the IBP. Appropriately this new union or association has already achieved recognition by the IUBS which is a major segment of ICSU. The IAHB is therefore of the family of international unions which sponsors the IBP. The IAHB should now bring together not only individual physical anthropologists but also, for the good of our discipline, the existing national societies in a strong international federation. In getting recognition from IUBS and ICSU and in many other ways, Jean Hiernaux, the retiring secretary-general, and Sir Macfarland Burnet, Nobel Laureate, the retiring president, have given the IAHB an all-important basis for its future development.

In the organization of our symposium we have of course a number of national bodies deeply involved since the holding of the satellite was entrusted (as it were) to the Society for the Study of Human Biology, and the SSHB in its turn was glad of an opportunity of holding its first scientific meeting in the United States (though some years ago Professor Lasker held a successful teaching summer school at Wayne State in association with the SSHB). This present symposium in fact ranks as No. 13 in the series held by the Society. Fortunately the SSHB has an enthusiastic North American membership and the Symposium Committee drawn from them, with benevolent support from our sister society, the American Association of Physical Anthropologists, has brought this symposium successfully into being. Francis Johnston, Elizabeth Watts, and Gabriel Lasker and the local committee have between them shouldered the burden of the organizing, and we give them our deepest thanks.

At this point I feel, as the outgoing Chairman of the SSHB, that I should refer frankly to a development which has afforded the Society deep concern and which has now been resolved. I refer to the discontinuation of *Human Biology* as the Society's official journal. The SSHB, after much heart searching and discussion, has decided that the time is ripe for launching its own journal *The Annals of Human Biology* with editors, Dr. Harrison, Professor Tanner, and Dr. Edholm. We are confident that *Human Biology* and the *Annals* can co-exist happily, and that our discipline is now mature enough to accommodate both these two journals along with several other newcomers (in English), namely *Human Evolution* and *Human Ecology, Human Biology in Oceania* while the *American Journal of Physical Anthropology* continues to flourish. I am pleased to serve as a member of the Editorial Boards of *Human Biology, Human Ecology* and *The Annals of Human Biology*, and I see no conflict in this arrangement.

When all is said and done I hope that this symposium will be remembered as one which signalled the definitive advent of the IAHB on the world scene of anthropology as representing the international body of physical anthropologists and human biologists. In the future, symposia of this sort, held in association with the International Congress of Anthropology, should undoubtedly be the responsibility of the IAHB and not of any single national body. Indeed, Professor Hiernaux and I have already proposed to the Permanent Council of the International Union of Anthropological and Ethnological Sciences, that the IAHB in future should be given responsibility (along with the local national committee) for organizing all sessions, symposia and satellites on human biology and physical anthropology, so as to ensure meetings as up-to-date and well attended as possible. In the same way the international role and responsibility of IAHB should be extended to co-sponsorship of the two other major international congresses in our field, namely those on human genetics and on ecology. Both of these are under the aegis of the IUBS and in fact at the First International Congress on Ecology next year in Holland the IAHB will be organizing one session on human ecology in association with IBP.

These activities show that the IAHB, given support from all working physical anthropologists and human biologists, is in a position to play a strong international role, and can do many more things with such a role; for example, it could set up commissions to advise UNESCO, UNEP, WHO, and so on, and ensure a proper role for human biology in major international activities such as the UN Environmental Programme and in MAB.

To turn briefly now to the content of our symposium. The title and the papers to be presented reflect in many different ways the developments which I have outlined above in institutional and organization terms. The symposium stresses the sociological factors in human biology. When we consider the two great themes of our subject, the evolutionary differentiation of the human species and the ecological adaptiveness of the human species, we know that the major processes involved, whether they are developmental, genetic, or physiological are, among the hominids, inevitably set within a social and cultural framework. Evolutional differentiation and population affinities have proceeded under the powerful social and cultural agencies of isolation, migration, and hybridization. Biological adaptation takes place in an ecological setting which has a predominantly cultural and technological component. In man Darwinian fitness and physiological fitness are in many ways sociological phenomena.

Our links with social anthropology, with general ecology, with demography and with evolutionary studies are all implicit in the proceedings of this symposium, and I now leave it to our distinguished contributors to amplify this in convincing detail, as I am sure they will do.

PART ONE

Adaptation and Adaptive Strategies

Biological Adaptation: Aptitudes and Acclimatization

RICHARD B. MAZESS

Perhaps no term in the biological and social sciences has such varied, vague, and equivocal meanings as ADAPTATION. Part of this difficulty has been one of nomenclature and definition. Dubos (1965a: 56) indicated "acclimatization, acclimation, adaptation, and habituation are often used interchangeably because the processes these words are supposed to denote usually overlap and because the fundamental mechanisms involved are poorly understood." Prosser (1958, 1964) was among the most prominent in providing a conceptual framework for dealing with adaptation, and in particular "physiological adaptation." Eagan (1963) and Folk (1966) examined the problems of nomenclature, and both suggested that adaptation be kept as a generic (note not genetic) term. There has been a widespread tendency, especially in physical anthropology, to consider adaptation as genetic adaptation, with the implication that natural selection is involved. Dobzhansky (1968) attempted to clarify the concept of "adaptedness." He recognized that adaptation could refer to both individuals and populations, and he delineated adaptedness, fitness, and persistence; all were applied at the population level. Most nongeneticists and nonanthropologists do not consider adaptation primarily as populational but rather as individual, although it is recognized that individual adaptation can contribute to population adaptation (McCutcheon 1964). I have recently proposed a conceptual framework in which adaptation is used in a generic sense to apply to all levels of the biological and social hierarchy (Mazess i.p.). This report will outline some aspects of that framework and will discuss two aspects of individual adaptation, aptitudes and acclimatization, which are often confused with population adaptation.

THE MEANING AND REFERENCES OF ADAPTATION

Adaptation is usually defined as the ability to survive, function, and reproduce (McCutcheon 1964; Prosser 1958, 1964; Dobzhansky 1968; Baker 1966), without really noting, as does Lasker (1969), that the term is relative. Survival, maintenance of functioning, and reproduction, however, are mere existence; adaptation, if it is not to be teleological, must mean more than this. The essence of environmental adjustments deemed adaptive seems to be that they are considered RELATIVELY advantageous, beneficial, or meritorious, or that they are to a degree necessary. Survival is somewhat equivalent to necessity, and maintenance of function and reproduction are examples of relatively beneficial properties; necessity and relative benefit are, however, more general categories than those of the conventional definition of adaptation, and they are particularly useful if one is to deal with adaptation at suborganismic levels, for example, molecular adaptation.

Adaptive significance, in terms of relative benefit or necessity, can be applied to all levels of biological and social hierarchies, but the notions of what is beneficial and what is necessary will vary with the referential level. A great deal of confusion in biological anthropology has resulted from trying to apply notions of population adaptation, such as selection, to individual adaptation or from extrapolating from individual adaptation to populations. The biological hierarchy to which adaptive evaluations might be applied can be conceived as increasing in organizational complexity:
1. Physicochemical
2. Cellular
3. Organ systems
4. Organisms (individual)
5. Population
6. Ecosystem

Each succeeding level of this hierarchy forms the dominant environmental focus of the preceding level; the environment of the cell is the organ, and that of the population is the ecosystem.

At each referential level different criteria, or "adaptive domains," are used in assessing benefit and necessity. At the physicochemical, cellular, and organ system levels, the major emphasis is on homeostasis. For individual organisms several major aspects of living are considered adaptive domains:
1. Reproduction — survival, reproductive advantage
2. Health — morbidity, mortality, disease resistance

3. Nutrition — nutrient requirements, utilization, and efficiency
4. Nervous system — sensory, motor, and neural function
5. Growth and development — physical and mental progression in rate and attainment
6. Resistance and cross-tolerance — generalized stress resistance
7. Physical performance — exercise and motor abilities; skills
8. Affective function — happiness, tolerance, sexuality
9. Intellectual ability — learning, expression

Traits or responses that are beneficial to one or more of these domains are usually considered adaptive to the individual. These domains are also pertinent to the definition of a "stress." Stress is not merely a large deviation of an environmental factor but a deviation that has a significant actual or potential effect on one or more adaptive domains. Much of the study of human adaptability consists of extrapolation from individual to population adaptation, and hence these domains are of primary import to that study. At the population level the emphasis is upon assessing benefit and necessity in relation to size, density, distribution, composition, and organization of the population. Selective advantage, fitness, and persistence (Dobzhansky 1968) become important at this level, at least for the genetically oriented biologist. Unfortunately, population adaptedness is almost impossible to evaluate directly in human populations, and many of our inferences are based on individual adaptation.

Acclimatization Responses

Folk (1966) has presented an extensive discussion of the term ACCLIMATIZATION and has shown its varying and often disparate usages. There has been a tendency by some ecologists and others to use acclimatization to describe adjustments made by a species over the course of several generations, or in a way nearly synonymous with "genetic adaptation," with the assumption of evolution and adjustment through natural selection. However, Folk showed that this is a quite restricted and unusual use of the term, and that an earlier and more frequent use of acclimatization is in a general sense to denote the adjustment of an organism to its environment. It is this general sense of the term, common to physiology, that is supported here.

Eagan (1963), following Prosser (1958) and Hart (1957), proposed that acclimatization refer to adjustments to an environmental complex, presumably a multistress environment, and included seasonal and climatic changes. The term ACCLIMATION was reserved to deal with adjustments to a single environmental factor, as might be the case in controlled experiments, or even presumably in a natural environment with a single dominant stress (that is, a natural experiment). As Folk (1966: 24) indicated, there is no real priority for this distinction — and more often than not, the terms ACCLIMATE and ACCLIMATIZE are used interchangeably. However, the distinction may be worth maintaining — if only to demonstrate some respect for attempts at systematizing nomenclature. In the following I will use the term ACCLIMATIZATION, but the content applies equally to ACCLIMATION.

It is fairly clear that the widest use of acclimatization is in reference to the adjustments of individual organisms to the environment. It is usually neither organ systems nor populations that are thought to acclimatize, but rather the individuals within a population. The acclimatization responses of a population are aggregates of the adjustments of individuals. Moreover, acclimatization refers to responses, and hence to phenotypically plastic adaptive traits — that is, to those characteristics of an individual that change in response to environment. It is rather unfamiliar to talk of phenotypically stable characteristics when dealing with acclimatization. For example, adult stature or eye color would not be considered acclimatizational, but adjustments of heart rate, skin color (tanning), or even attention span would.

Phenotypic characteristics can be usefully categorized as structural (morphological), functional (physiological), and psychobehavioral. Acclimatization can be described using these modifying terms where appropriate, or using some equivalent terms such as HABITUATION and ACCOMMODATION.

1. STRUCTURAL ACCLIMATIZATION: changes of histology, anatomical relationships, morphology, and body composition. An example would be muscle hypertrophy, or change of fiber type, in response to exercise.

2. FUNCTIONAL ACCLIMATIZATION: changes in organ system function, which may be further subdivided into:

a. PHYSIOLOGICAL ACCLIMATIZATION: this is the most common meaning of acclimatization. Examples are shivering in cold and sweating in heat.

b. NEUROLOGICAL ACCLIMATIZATION OR HABITUATION: changes of sensory function and neural control. Habituation has usually meant diminutions of normal neural responses, for example, decreases of sensation such as pain. Other pertinent subcategorizations of neurological acclimatization include peripheral versus central and specific versus generalized (Eagan 1963).

3. PSYCHOBEHAVIORAL ACCLIMATIZATION: changes of complex neural functioning involving control and alteration of activity, and of affective and cognitive states. Several subclasses are useful:

a. AFFECTIVE ACCLIMATIZATION, OR ACCOMMODATION: the latter term, while often used more generally to specify adjustments, frequently has the connotation of an affective shift. Examples might be sublimation or personality changes.

b. COGNITIVE ACCLIMATIZATION, OR LEARNING: changes in complex perception and cognition, with obvious direct influences on behavior.

c. BEHAVIORAL ACCLIMATIZATION: shifts in sets of behavioral correlates, or activity patterns.

Within this framework, acclimatizational responses are systematically classified. Regardless of acclimatizational categorization, however, the adaptive significance of the response must be demonstrated if an assessment of acclimatization is really to have purchase. It is not enough to demonstrate that a response occurs in relation to a single or multiple stress environment; it is mandatory to show that the response is of at least potential benefit. Because acclimatization deals essentially with responses of individual organisms, assessment of benefit is made in adaptive domains at the individual level.

APTITUDES

In the previous section it was pointed out that acclimatization and acclimation refer to responses of individuals, and hence to phenotypically plastic characteristics. The examination of adjustments to the environment must also deal with traits having stable phenotypic expression; there has been no scientific term in general use to describe these traits. APTITUDE, in the sense of suitability, ability, or capacity in relation to environment, is an appropriate term, and I believe that it would prove useful if accepted. One of the great misunderstandings and sources of equivocation in adaptability studies derives from the hiatus in terminology for relatively fixed individual characteristics. The terms ADAPTATION and PREADAPTATION are sometimes used to describe these aptitudes; as a consequence, there has been a tendency to mistake them for genetic adaptations. Aptitudes, like acclimatizational responses, are phenotypic characteristics, and the genetic basis and heritability of both must be determined prior to ascription of genetic adaptation.

Just as acclimatization may be categorized as structural, functional, and psychobehavioral, so may aptitudes.

1. STRUCTURAL APTITUDES: histological, anatomical, morphological, and body composition characteristics. An example would be large muscle mass in relation to exercise or dark skin color in relation to insolation.

2. FUNCTIONAL APTITUDES: organ system functions.

a. PHYSIOLOGICAL APTITUDES: an example would be a high cardiac output in exercise above the level associated with training (which is acclimatizational). Environmental physiologists who have compared different ethnic groups have tried to define the functional aptitudes of these populations.

b. NEUROLOGICAL APTITUDES: differences of sensory function and neural control, for example, visual acuity.

3. PSYCHOBEHAVIORAL APTITUDES: differences in behavioral patterns, activity levels, and affective and cognitive states. For example, a high intelligence quotient could be considered a cognitive aptitude, in contrast to the process of learning, which is cognitive acclimatization.

As is the case with acclimatization, the adaptive significance of aptitudes must be shown in terms of potential benefit or necessity at the individual level of adaptive domains.

Information and Misinformation

The study of adaptation, and in particular of human adaptation, often has been denigrated as error-prone and speculative, and unfortunately this opprobrium is frequently appropriate. Three striking problems are immediately evident.

First, there is confusion with regard to the concepts and nomenclature of adaptation. There has been lack of specificity as to the level of organization referred to when examining adaptation, and in human studies there has been egregious equivocation between individual and populational adaptation. One consequence of this equivocation has been the tendency to view genetic and even aptitudinal differences among populations as being not only genetic adaptation but evidence of the operation of natural selection. Aptitudinal differences among populations may, of course, not have a firm genetic basis. As should be clear from preceding sections, aptitudinal or acclimatizational differences among populations which do have a firm genetic basis can be considered genetic adaptions regardless of the evolutionary mechanism by which they arose. Not all evolutionary changes are adaptive, and not all adaptive evolutionary changes arise through natural selection.

Second, the study of adaptation has been marred by the postulation of erroneous relationships between characteristics or responses and environmental factors. For example, alterations of growth may be ascribed to a climatic stress, but they may actually be due to nutrition; metabolic alterations may be due to climatic factors rather than the nutritional stress to which they are ascribed. Many of these speculative relationships have been postulated on the basis of eco-geographical character gradients, or clines (Mayr 1956). In anthropology such relationships have been taken as evidence of man's climatic and nutritional adaptation (Newman 1953; Baker 1960; Schreider 1964). Eco-geographical gradients are useful for suggesting lines of investigation but should not be taken as evidence of an environmental relationship, and certainly not as evidence of adaptive import.

The third problem is in fact that of adaptive import. One of the fundamental errors is the ascription or denial of adaptive benefit without investigation or demonstration of a relationship with any adaptive domain. It is in this area that teleology appears to encroach on scientific caution. One could argue that mere survival, especially in a stressful environment, is evidence of adaptation (Baker 1966), and hence the variations among populations, especially the differences existing in stressed populations, might be taken as adaptive. For example, barrel-chestedness at high altitude and a low ratio of surface area to weight in cold have been broadcast as adaptive for certain human populations without any real evaluation of their functional import. I have previously criticized the tendency to deal with high-altitude populations in this way (Mazess 1970), and the same criticisms apply to other stressed populations.

APTITUDES, ACCLIMATIZATION, AND HUMAN ADAPTABILITY

The description and categorization of characteristics and responses providing adjustment to environmental stress, with consequent benefit, are indeed formidable tasks. Comparisons among individuals, and among populations, are needed to delineate the nature and extent of environmental adjustments. Among the parameters of interest are:

1. TIME COURSE: period of exposure requisite to development of the adjustment, and also the effects of rate of exposure and of intermittent exposure.
2. REVERSIBILITY: many responses to stress, particularly those occurring during the developmental period, may be irreversible or only partially reversible (Brauer 1965). This also raises the possibility that a

beneficial characteristic developed during childhood may prove maladaptive yet irreversible in the adult.

3. CRITICAL AGES: are there critical times, for example, during growth,
when certain characteristics or responses may develop in response to
stress? Developmental physiological acclimatization seems to be very
important in determining peripheral responses to cold and in exercise
and ventilatory performance in hypoxia.

4. GENETIC BACKGROUND: the heritability of aptitudes and acclimatizational responses needs elucidation so that inferences with regard to
genetic adaptation may be made. Are there genetic differences within
populations and among populations?

Examination, in detail, of aptitudes and acclimatization will provide
one basis for more general formulations with regard to adaptability.
The type of individual adaptation to different stresses, as well as population differences, will then become much clearer. For example, with
regard to human climatic adaptations, it seems that short-term reversible physiological acclimatization is of paramount importance in
the sense that such acclimatization provides the primary adjustment
for individuals within any population or within the species. This is
followed by long-term and developmental physiological acclimatization.
Differences among individuals, and populations, of comparable age and
sex may be in part attributable to the large variance in aptitudes. The
genetic basis for differences in aptitudes and acclimatization appears
minimal, and genetic adaptation does not appear to account for much
of the adjustment of humans to climatic stresses. A somewhat different
pattern appears evident with regard to human adaptation to other
stresses, such as disease.

In addition to such generalization with regard to adaptive strategies,
there is a need for examination of and generalization about the relationships among adaptive domains. Because adaptive significance is
relative to operationally defined domains, it becomes important to
achieve some precision in this area, specifically, in the formulation of
a relatively coherent set of priorities among the domains. The construction and elaboration of a theory of human adaptability depends upon
both the biological documentation and the social-psychological documentation of valuational criteria.

Adaptation and the Optimal Environment

Adaptation is essentially valuational, despite all disclaimers to the contrary, and assessment of adaptation involves judgments and decisions

as to benefit, good, or necessity. The contemporary revival of interest in adaptation over the past decade is occurring, interestingly enough, after almost a century of eschewing valuation in science, and at a time when there is widespread acceptance of the notion of an "objective reality." There are implications of this apparent contrast for the study of human adaptability, and vice versa. If human adaptability is to remain viable, we must ask to what extent valuation of environmental adjustments may be dealt with objectively. Success in this area will depend upon the operational precision and accuracy in exploring adaptive domains and assessing adaptation. Dubos (1965b) has pointed out the importance of viewing models and scientific knowledge as describing regularities rather than realities, and there is every reason to presume that the regularities in valuation of environmental adjustments may be studied scientifically.

But is the study of human adaptability of any value? Dubos (1965b) suggests that the role of biology is to provide the essential information, describing biological potentials and limitations, within which man formulates goals and makes personal decisions. Adaptation provides analogous information on the valuation of biology in relation to environment; it is not mere description of the regularities of response, but of the regularities in how men value these responses. Human goals with relation to environment have been variously expressed, from a Garden of Eden to Utopia. The formulation and creation of an optimal environment requires more than a listing of environmental likes and dislikes; it is the knowledge of human adaptability that forms the basis for this task.

REFERENCES

BAKER, P. T.
   1960   Climate, culture and evolution. *Human Biology* 32:3–16.
   1966   Human biological variation as an adaptive response to the environment. *Eugenics Quarterly* 13:81–91.
BRAUER, R. W.
   1965   "Irreversible effects," in *The physiology of human survival.* Edited by O. G. Edholm and R. Bachrach. London: Academic Press.
DOBZHANSKY, T.
   1968   "Adaptedness and fitness," in *Population biology and evolution: Proceedings of an International Symposium.* Edited by R. Lewontin, 109–121. Syracuse, New York: Syracuse University Press.
DUBOS, R.
   1965a *Man adapting.* New Haven: Yale University Press.

1965b Humanistic biology. *American Scientist* 53:4–19.

EAGAN, C. J.
1963   Introduction and terminology. *Federation Proceedings* 22:930–932.

FOLK, G. E., JR.
1966   *Introduction to environmental physiology*. Philadelphia: Lea and Febiger.

HART, S. J.
1957   Climatic and temperature induced changes in the energetics of homeotherms. *Revue canadienne de biologie* 16:133–141.

LASKER, G. W.
1969   Human biological adaptability. *Science* 166:1480–1486.

MAYR, E.
1956   Geographic character gradients and climatic adaptation. *Evolution* 10:105–108.

MAZESS, R. B.
1970   Cardiorespiratory characteristics and adaptation to high altitudes. *American Journal of Physical Anthropology* 32:267–278.

i.p.   *Adaptation: a conceptual framework*.

MCCUTCHEON, F. H.
1964   "Organ systems in adaptation: the respiratory system," in *Handbook of physiology*, volume four: *Adaptation to the environment*. Edited by D. B. Dill, E. F. Adolph, and C. G. Wilber, 167–191. Washington, D.C.: American Physiological Society.

NEWMAN, M. T.
1953   The application of ecological rules to the racial anthropology of the aboriginal New World. *American Anthropologist* 55:311–327.

PROSSER, C. L.
1958   "General summary: the nature of physiological adaptation," in *Physiological adaptation*. Edited by C. L. Prosser, 167–180. Washington, D.C.: American Physiological Society.

1964   "Perspectives of adaptation: theoretical aspects," in *Handbook of physiology*, volume four: *Adaptation to the environment*. Edited by D. B. Dill, E. F. Adolph, and C. G. Wilber, 11–25. Washington, D.C.: American Physiological Society.

SCHREIDER, E.
1964   Ecological rules, body heat regulation, and human evolution. *Evolution* 18:1–9.

Adaptive Strategies of Human Populations under Nutritional Stress

WILLIAM A. STINI

It has long been recognized that average body size has been increasing in most human populations. This secular increase in stature and weight has been accompanied by a trend toward earlier maturation in these same populations (Tanner 1968). Interpretations of these concurrent events implicate improvement in nutritional state and in the quality of medical care as contributory factors. Support for this point of view is found in the variations in body size observed in different socioeconomic groups in contemporary (Mendez and Behrhorst 1963; Ashcroft, Heneage, Lovell 1966; Sabharwal, Morales, Mendez 1966; Dellaportas 1969; Villarejos, et al. 1971) and past human populations (Tanner 1964). There appears to be a general pattern in which individuals respond to stress by altered growth trajectories. Because such alterations improve the chances for survival in the face of potentially lethal stresses, they may properly be called adaptive. The capacity to adjust individual metabolic demand avoids or defers the cost of natural selection and, as a result, retards the process of genetic change that would qualify as true adaptation. However, it must be kept in mind that the ability to make the necessary adjustment is a variable trait that will in itself be subject to natural selection. The existence of the ability to make nongenetic adjustments in body size may be inferred from current increases in body size which reveal the retention of genetic programs for larger body size although these programs have not been expressed to their maximum for many centuries. The most attractive explanation for this phenomenon is that body size *per se* is not being subjected to the full force of natural selection in most human populations. Instead, there exists a high degree of developmental plasticity. As a result, certain aspects of the genome of the population are "buffered." Slobodkin (1968) has argued for the existence of hierarchical response systems to environmental stressors. Through such graded responses organisms undergo slow, deep–seated physiological changes which permit continued exploitation of more rapid, short–term adjustments in the most flexible manner. Slowing of growth and its termination before the attainment of full genetically programmed adult size would be an example of such a mechanism.

Living organisms are successful competitors in the game of evolution and therefore have accrued adaptations to a host of environmental challenges. A well–adapted population would be, as Slobodkin argues, one that enjoys a relatively high probability of survival under conditions highly likely to occur. Since man has become an agriculturist and a dweller in cities in increasing numbers, two regularly encountered stressors have been nutritional imbalance and disease. Adaptation to one of these conditions necessarily affects the degree of adaptation to the other. Diseases account for most mortalities of protein–deficient children. These children are unable to satisfy their anabolic amino acid requirements and simultaneously synthesize adequate quantities of antibodies essential to combat infection. Selection for adaptability in human populations would tend to favor physiological mechanisms that would deal with these problems synergistically. One such mechanism involves a shift in adrenocortical function which simultaneously affects anabolic processes and antibody synthesis. Such general stress responses produce profound changes in growth and maturation which, if suitably prolonged, will be reflected in late maturation and reduced adult body size. From the standpoint of the population's genetic constitution, such reductions relax the pressure on food resources available to each individual and thereby allow a larger number of individuals to coexist. Relaxation of one form of mortality permitting an increase in population size allows maintenance of genetic variability and reduces the likelihood of extinction. It may be convincingly argued that such nongenetic adaptations possess great importance in influencing the nature of genetic adaptations capable of surviving in a population and must therefore be taken into account whenever the process of adaptation is considered. It is in this context that the following discussion of human adaptive strategies under conditions of nutritional stress will be undertaken. It is hoped that the importance of the interaction of individual body size and population size will attain increased significance when viewed in this way.

METABOLIC DEMAND AND BODY SIZE

Although tissues vary in their metabolic demands, thereby making precise estimates of caloric requirements for a given total body weight difficult, there is a direct relationship between lean body mass as found in skeletal muscle and metabolic rate. Certain constants may be consulted when estimations of metabolic demand are attempted. For instance, speed of shortening of particular muscles is similar from species to species. When the generality of the mechanism of muscle contraction and sarcomere structure is considered, it can be seen why this similarity exists. Also, the power output of any muscle and the metabolic variables involved in maintaining energy flow to that muscle all depend upon its cross–sectional area (McMahon 1973). Of course, there are muscles with varying functions which contract at different rates and thereby differ in metabolic cost of maintenance. Broadly, differentiating between tonic and phasic muscles makes possible prediction of differing metabolic costs of contraction. Although the sharp distinction between red and white fibers has been criticized recently (Goldspink 1970), there is good reason to think that the energy requirement of white fibers is greater than that of red fibers, and the tonic muscles bear a greater proportion of red fibers than do the phasic muscles. It might be anticipated, then, that tonic muscles are metabolically less demanding than phasic ones. There is also evidence that fibers can shift from white to red characteristics during their lifetimes (Goldspink 1970). Such shifts may make possible the reduction of metabolic demand while allowing a full complement of fibers to survive during periods of nutritional deficiency. It also appears that metabolizing tissue may be replaced by inert collagen (Scrimshaw 1964).

While acknowledging the potential effects of the above-mentioned factors, it must be stressed that there is a close relationship between the amount of skeletal muscle present and the metabolic requirements of the individual. Activity levels will certainly affect caloric requirements as well, and the work performed by an organism includes the function of moving its own mass from one place to another. As that mass increases, the energy cost of work increases, creating additional caloric demand. If standards for metabolic cost of activity are consulted (Consolazio, Johnson, Pecora 1963), it is possible to estimate the magnitude of difference in energy requirements for individuals of different body size. An example of such estimation may be seen in Table 1. The quantities used in Table 1 are drawn from United States standards (Consolazio et al. 1963) and data collected in a South Amer·

ican Caucasian population living in an area of endemic protein-caloric deficiency (Stini 1968).

Table 1.   Comparison of caloric requirements of males of mean body weight in United States and Colombian populations at various activity levels

	United States	Heliconia, Colombia
Mean body weight (kilograms)	70	60
Caloric costs (kilocalories)		
Resting (8 hours)	570	480
Sedentary activity (6 hours)	492	266
Light labor (8 hours)	1,527	1,123
Moderate labor (2 hours)	654	482
Total	3,243	2,351

As may be seen from comparison of the total energy requirement of the males shown in Table 1, the 70–kilogram man requires about 3,200 kilocalories per day in the performance of a normal round of activities. The 60–kilogram man performs the same round of activities at a cost of approximately 2,300 kilocalories. The difference between these two daily requirements, about 900 kilocalories per day per man, is about one–third of the daily requirement of the 60–kilogram man. Stated another way, four 60–kilogram males may be supported on a resource base capable of supporting three 70–kilogram men. Size differences between females in United States and South American populations are not as pronounced, a point that will be discussed below.

Differential protein requirements also emerge when individuals of different body size are compared. According to the somewhat generous daily recommendations published by the Food and Nutrition Board of the National Research Council (1958), a 70–kilogram man should ingest 70 grams of protein per day, while a 60–kilogram man would require 60 grams. A 58–kilogram woman would need 58 grams of protein, while a 51–kilogram woman would need 51 grams. All of the above figures apply to the adult segment of the population and take into account the lower metabolic rate prevailing in females. Energy but not protein requirements are reduced in later years in both sexes. Requirements for both protein and calories are higher during the adolescent growth spurt in well–nourished populations where the characteristic sigmoid curve of values for both attained height and weight makes its abrupt upward deflection. However, this pattern of growth and development may be altered so that both attained height and weight follow a more linear and prolonged trajectory. Later attainment of adult body size and less explosive growth both tend to be more economical in terms of caloric requirements of the individual. In this manner further reductions in caloric demand supplement those made possible through reduced adult body size.

When the yield of agricultural land is considered in the light of energy requirements of the human population, the significance of some of the reductions in individual caloric requirements becomes more apparent. For instance, maize culture as practiced in much of South America may be expected to yield 3500 kilocalories per acre per day, while wheat yields 2,000 kilocalories per acre per day (Weiner 1972). By bringing additional land under cultivation, it is possible to support a larger population, and the benefit of a large family of immature, metabolically inexpensive workers is more practical than philosophical. If a population's division of labor is arranged to maximize the labor input of children under such circumstances, the biological advantages of a broad–based demographic profile, with many young people and relatively few in the higher age categories, can be seen (Thomas 1972). In terms of maximization of population number, this advantage holds even when no additional land remains to be brought under cultivation. However, when population density attains a level where all land is exploited to the limit, Malthusian factors will assert themselves and the buffering effect of nongenetic adaptations will rapidly diminish under continued population pressure. Ultimately, the action of natural selection would favor adaptations of the genetic variety. More will be said on this point in another section of the present study.

MECHANISMS CONTROLLING BODY SIZE

Growth and development in man is a lengthy process made up of a number of stages. Intrauterine life is characterized by an early period of hyperplastic growth wherein the cell population increases from one to over two and one–half trillion. Before birth, hyperplastic growth has given way to hypertrophic growth in most tissues. Increase in cell size rather than number will characterize future growth. This is particularly true of functional cells of the nervous system and of skeletal muscle. Much has been written concerning the early termination of skeletal muscle hyperplasia. Some early discussions of this topic date from over a hundred years ago (Olivier 1869; Hayern 1875; Bompar 1887; MacCallum 1898; Durante 1902; Bramwell and Muir 1907; Bablet and Normet 1937), while experimental work pursuing the precise mechanisms involved continues today. Although there is some disagreement concerning the time when hyperplasia ceases (Cheek 1968), as well as evidence that in some species limited amounts of muscle fiber replacement occur (Cheek, Brasel, and Graystone 1968), there is abundant evidence that few if any new skeletal muscle fibers appear in humans after the sixth month postpartum. As a result of this early shift from hyperplastic to hypertrophic muscle growth, factors preventing the formation of a full complement of muscle fibers before the sixth month postpartum and those resulting in destruction of fibers after that time will permanently reduce the number of fibers present in the adult. Such reductions might be viewed as a "resetting" of the individual's future caloric demand. By what means are these reductions obtained? At this point all the evidence available must be drawn from nonhuman species, which may or may not react in a manner identical to human subjects.

It has been convincingly demonstrated by a number of researchers using several mammalian species that the stress of protein–caloric deficiency evokes a response from the adrenal cortex. The level of this response may be monitored by determination of the concentration of anti–inflammatory glucocorticoids in the serum (Kinsell, et al. 1953; Castellanos and Arroyave 1961; Hamwi and Tzagournia 1970). It is believed that the presence of increased concentrations of these hormones effects a shift in liver function resulting in the cycling of essential amino acids through synthetic pathways which reduce the likelihood of damage to that vital organ (Waterlow 1955). The diversion of amino acids from anabolic pathways results in their loss to the maintenance and growth processes of skeletal muscle. Because skeletal muscle is constantly exchanging amino acids with the surrounding interstitial fluid, the cutoff of supply results in a net loss to the muscle, sometimes referred to as a reduction in "protein stores" (Clark 1953; Waterlow 1955; Leon 1966; Goldberg 1969; Korner 1960). Administration of adrenocorticotrophic hormone (ACTH) and hydrocortisone have both been shown to cause reductions in muscle mass in experimental animals (Sidransky, Wagle, and Verney 1969; Sidransky and Verney 1970). In addition, presumptive evidence of adrenocortical hyperactivity under prolonged stress of malnutrition may be found in the enlargement of the cortices and in some cases their breakdown under extended periods of stress (Newman 1973). The latter observation would be expected if the "exhaustion phase" of the general adaptive syndrome of Selye (1950) had been reached. It is significant that high serum concentrations of hydrocortisone have the additional effect of suppressing antibody synthesis (Dean 1964). This somewhat maladaptive concomitant of the general adaptation syndrome may be interpreted as furnishing additional evidence for the high priority of the preservation of liver function.

The foregoing discussion, though by no means exhaustive, provides a consistent explanation for several elements of the reduction in lean body mass occurring during prolonged protein–calorie malnutrition. Perhaps a fuller understanding of all the mechanisms involved will be possible in the near future, but many aspects of the process occurring in man are still unknown. Nevertheless, observations of reduction in human muscle fiber populations under severe protein–calorie malnutrition have been published (McFie and Welbourne 1962; Montgomery 1962). Detection of reduced muscle fiber population has been accomplished by means of total fiber count performed on a cross–section of the sartorius muscle. Muscles from adults who had suffered severe malnutrition as children were compared with those of individuals having no record of malnutrition and were found to contain significantly fewer fibers. In an attempt to ascertain whether such early losses of muscle fiber could be induced in a relatively short time and still be permanent, the author examined sartorii from a sample of domestic hogs subjected to protein deficiency for three months after birth. These were compared with muscles from animals fed continuously high–protein diets. Despite the fact that all the animals were provided with high–protein diets for six months following the experimental period, the protein–deficient category showed significant reductions in body weight, sartorius cross–section, and fiber count. The results of this study are shown in Tables 2 through 5. It is not known whether this permanent reduction in fiber population reflects an interruption in hyperplastic growth soon after birth or a destruction of fibers that had already formed. Whichever process (or possibly both) determined the final fiber population, the reduction in lean body mass and associated metabolic demand is impressive (Stini 1972b). Other studies have pointed out the permanence of size reductions associated with malnutrition during critical stages of growth (Sidransky and Verney 1970), while in some cases arguing that metabolic efficiency, at least in anabolic processes, may be somewhat impaired by early protein deficiency, particularly during nursing (Barnes, et al. 1973).

Table 2.   Weights of pigs in four nutritional categories

N n	Category	Weight at 3 weeks (kilograms)	Slaughter weight (kilograms)	Dietary intake during experimental period
5	Control			
	11–2	6.9	285	18 percent casein
	11–4	6.5	319	protein diet
	10–6	5.8	313	*ad libitum*
	16–5	5.1	319	x̄ = 307
	16–13	3.3	299	
6	Restricted			
	9–1	4.8	248	18 percent casein
	10–3	4.8	272	protein limited
	11–1	6.1	292	to 2 kilograms
	14–1	6.0	263	total intake
	16–3	4.8	271	per day
	16–7	4.6	282	x̄ = 271
6	Intermediate protein			
	10–1	6.9	287	5 percent casein
	9–6	6.5	237	protein diet
	11–7	5.8	272	*ad libitum*
	14–6	5.5	302	x̄ = 272
	14–10	6.4	290	
	16–9	3.4	245	
6	Low protein			
	9–2	4.1	234	3 percent casein
	10–7	5.1	255	protein diet
	11–9	5.5	244	*ad libitum*
	14–3	6.9	240	x̄ = 243
	16–4	5.0	233	
	16–12	4.2	251	

Table 3.   Analysis of variance: slaughter weights of four nutritional categories

	Category Controls (n = 5)	Restricted (n = 6)	Intermediate (n = 6)	Low protein (n = 6)	Total
Σx	1,535	1,628	1,633	1,457	6,253
x̄	307	271	272	243	
Σx^2	472,117	442,886	447,851	354,207	1,717,061
			Correction term		1,700,000
			Total sum of squares		17,061

Sources of variation	d.f.	Sums of squares	Mean square
Total	23	17,061	
Groups means	3	11,232	3,744
Within group	20	5,829	291
$F = 3,744/291 = 12.86; p < .001$			

Table 4. Mean corrected cross-sectional areas and fiber counts from sartorius muscles of four nutritional categories of pigs

	Category Controls	Restricted	Intermediate	Low protein
Area (square millimeters)	200.5	206.9	190.0	176.4
Count/ square millimeter	29.7	31.2	32.6	32.0
Total fibers	5,934	6,395	6,155	5,562

Table 5. Analysis of variance for mean total muscle fiber populations within and between four nutritional categories of pigs

Sources of variation	d.f.	Sums of squares	Mean square
Total	89	103,644,166	
Group means	3	8,969,257	2,989,752
Within group	86	94,674,969	1,100,872

$F = 2,989,752/1,100,872 = 2.72$, d.f. $= 3.86$; $p \sim .05$

Evidence of Lean Body Mass Reduction in Living Humans

There are several methods for estimating the lean body mass of human subjects. An underlying principle of most techniques involves differences in the specific gravity of muscle and that of fat. Most of the elaborate techniques, such as underwater weighing, are impractical under most field conditions. Field studies attempting to make such estimates generally rely on less precise but more feasible procedures. Among the latter category are such readily applicable procedures as measurement of muscle shadows on radiographic plates or the derivation of muscle circumference of the limb from measurement of its outer circumference minus skinfold thickness. Use of upper arm muscle circumference in the estimation of relative lean body mass has yielded much useful information in field studies and has been the subject of a long and active debate concerning its predictive value (for discussion and description of technique, see Stini [1972c]).

A reasonable position is that whatever the difficulties in extrapolating from upper arm muscle circumference to a precise estimate of total lean body mass, comparisons of population means for upper arm muscle circumference and mean body weight allow estimation of the relative amounts of lean body mass present in the respective populations. When a comparison of the values for upper arm muscle area is made between the adults of a protein–deficient Caucasoid population in South America and those of the United States, the figures shown in Table 6 are obtained.

Table 6. Comparison of Heliconia, Colombia, and United States values for upper arm muscle area (square millimeters)

	Heliconia		United States		Heliconia percent of United States	
	area (mm²)	weight (kg)	area (mm²)	weight (kg)	area (mm²)	weight (kg)
Male	4,267	60	6,464	70	66	(85)
Female	3,450	51	4,272	58	81	(88)
Percent female of male	81	85	66	83		

The comparison shown in Table 6 clearly indicates the tendency for adults in Heliconia, Colombia, to attain significantly lower values for this measure of lean body mass. This observation lends support to the assertion that the difference in adult body weights observed in the two populations bears a sizable component of lean body mass and hence might reasonably be expected to affect relative caloric requirements to at least the extent calculated in Table 1. It is therefore possible that the difference in caloric requirements is greater than indicated by application of standard values, as was done in the preparation of Table 1. This observation would support the suspicion, held by many researchers, that the recommended values for both protein and caloric intake (National Research Council 1958), having been developed through the study of well (or excessively) fed populations of industrialized countries, may be highly inaccurate when extrapolated to populations adapted to much lower nutrient intake. Additional support for this point of view may be found in comparison of actual versus recommended caloric and protein intakes in areas of endemic nutritional stress, as in Heliconia, Colombia (Vitale and Velez 1967). When such comparisons are made, it is found that actual nutritional intake is considerably lower than recommended with respect to both protein and calories.

Reductions in lean body mass (more accurately, total protein; for discussion see Waterlow and Alleyne [1972]) are directly associated with reductions in caloric and protein requirements but cannot be sustained without other morphological adjustments. An important component of the adjustment is the alteration in the pattern of skeletal growth (Bartley 1968). The end result of the pattern observed in nutritionally stressed populations is a reduction in the size of the skeleton. The skeleton grows more slowly, particularly in males, with respect to both appearance of ossification centers and epiphyseal growth and closure. Termination of epiphyseal growth in males may not occur until the second half of the third decade of life. This attenuated and prolonged growth pattern under endemic nutritional stress, while associated with size reduction, appears to have little effect on allometric relationships. General proportionality is seldom affected to any appreciable degree. The most striking examples of this phenomenon may be seen in cases of "nutritional dwarfism" wherein statures 60 to 70 percent of normal for the local population occur in individuals whose body proportions are in every way normal (Stini 1968).

Despite the overall tendency to maintain normal proportions, one clearly discernible difference between populations living under conditions of nutritional stress and better–fed populations is the greater linearity of nutritionally stressed adults. This linearity, as measured by ponderal index scores, is most pronounced in males. As seen in Table 7, ponderal index scores are higher in males than in females of even well–fed populations, but the difference grows larger as the nutritional state becomes more marginal. Although fat is clearly implicat-

Table 7. Comparisons of adult mean values for stature, weight, and ponderal index in various parts of the world ranked by male ponderal index (from Stini 1972a)

	Male			Female			
	Stature	Weight	Ponderal index	Stature (cm.)	Weight (kg.)	Ponderal index	Rank
India	163.0	48.2	13.43	150.7	45.2	12.69	(1)
Burma	161.5	49.9	13.15	150.7	45.2	12.69	(2)
Thailand	161.0	53.2	12.83	151.0	45.8	12.65	(3)
Vietnam	157.6	49.1	12.82	147.6	63.5	12.59	(4)
Malaya	161.8	55.1	12.75	149.8	47.8	12.28	(9)
Japan	163.2	56.8	12.71	151.9	49.1	12.42	(6)
Nuñoa, Peru	160.7	55.6	12.68	148.8	52.6	11.89	(15)
Heliconia	162.0	57.1	12.59	151.3	50.7	12.24	(10)
Sweden	175.9	75.1	12.49	164.0	65.2	12.22	(11)
United States	175.5	77.6	12.45	161.8	61.7	12.39	(7)
Northeast Brazil	160.6	58.0	12.43	150.4	48.8	12.34	(8)
Colombia	160.1	59.6	12.28	152.2	49.4	12.44	(5)
Bolivia	161.3	61.0	12.28	151.0	54.0	11.97	(13)
Ecuador	157.7	57.5	12.25	146.3	51.3	11.81	(16)
Uruguay	168.1	70.0	12.23	155.5	60.0	11.90	(14)
Chile	162.8	64.3	12.18	151.9	56.4	11.98	(12)

ed in the observed lower ponderal indices of well–fed populations as well as in those of the female members of poorly fed ones, reduction in lean body mass is the more important variable producing the greater linearity of poorly fed males. It is noteworthy that populations exhibiting this tendency toward reduction of sexual dimorphism for total body mass, and by implication protein and calorie requirements, show little if any difference with respect to sexual dimorphism for stature (Stini 1972a). The world range of male/female stature ratios is a fairly narrow one (approximately, from 1.04 to 1.09), and poorly fed populations show no systematic tendency to cluster near either end of this range. Values for a number of populations are shown in Table 8.

Table 8.   Male stature as percent of female stature (within populations) ranked in descending order (adapted from Stini 1972a)

Macedonia	109.0	Costa Rica (Urban)	106.9
Sweden	109.0	Bolivia	106.8
Lera (Africa)	108.8	Brazil	106.8
Venda (Africa)	108.8	Vietnam	106.8
Yugoslavia	108.5	Germany (North)	106.7
United States	108.5	Thailand	106.6
Bulgaria	108.4	Germany (South)	106.4
Portugal	108.2	Costa Rica (Rural)	106.3
India	108.2	Norway	106.2
Wales	108.2	Ukraine	106.2
Uruguay	108.1	Switzerland (Geneva)	106.1
Gypsy	108.0	Bassari (Africa)	106.1
Peru (Highland)	108.0	Switzerland (German)	106.0
Malaya	108.0	Poland	105.8
Ecuador	107.8	Highland Swiss	105.7
Czechoslovakia	107.8	Bisago (Africa)	105.5
Estonia	107.7	Gondar (Africa)	105.2
Baka-Bayaka (Africa)	107.6	Colombia (Lowland)	105.2
Japan	107.4	Mbuti (Africa)	105.1
Chile	107.2	Mangisi (Africa)	104.7
Burma	107.2	Lari (Africa)	104.6
Heliconia (Colombia)	107.1		

The Significance of Reductions in Sexual Dimorphism

The tendency for the male members of malnourished human populations to experience greater reductions in adult lean body mass than do females may well be adaptive for the population. Because most tasks are performed well below the maximum capacity of the smaller males and because division of labor may make possible the utilization of labor of slowly growing adolescents and young adults without serious loss of productivity, larger body size in males would raise the cost of their maintenance while providing little or no gain in terms of resource capture. It has been shown in several populations that smaller size may be combined with an equal (Viteri as cited by Waterlow and Alleyne 1972) or superior functional efficiency in the performance of a number of tasks (Parizkova and Merhaustova 1970). There is a real advantage, then, in developmental adjustments producing smaller but well–proportioned and functionally unimpaired males. The problem is not as easily resolved in the case of females. While work performance is important for women in populations where endemic nutritional stress occurs, the capacity to reproduce successfully would be more directly subject to the action of natural selection.

From the standpoint of fitness, fertility and fecundity are all–important factors. Even so, success in conceiving, bearing, and giving birth to normal infants is genetically meaningless if the infants themselves do not mature and reproduce. One critical period in the formation of a viable organism occurs early in embryological development when differentiation gives rise to the organs and tissues essential to independent life. Damage occurring in this early period will result in a defective infant or, in many cases, early loss as an aborted fetus. The human mother is remarkably capable of shielding the developing embryo and fetus from nutritional stress during early gestation. It has often been said that the fetus parasitizes the maternal organism. Although there are differences of opinion on the degree to which the host–parasite analogy may be accepted, there can be little doubt that malnourished mothers provide essential nutrients to their fetuses even when they themselves receive inadequate quantities of them. This is particularly true with respect to protein. In most malnourished human populations, the recommended intake of essential amino acids, most readily obtained from animal protein, is not available. As mentioned earlier, adult protein requirements are frequently estimated as being on the order of one gram per kilogram body weight per day. To satisfy this requirement, a 50–kilogram woman would need 50 grams of protein every day, an amount she probably never receives. It is clear that physiological adjustments allow survival in the face of this persistent deficiency. The situation is severely exacerbated during the second half of pregnancy, when protein requirements are thought to rise by 20 grams per day. Even more severe is the stress occurring during lactation when a milk flow of 850 milliliters per day requires 40 grams of protein above the baseline requirement. Energy requirements also rise, by about 1,000 calories per day, during lactation. It is during the months following birth, when the mother is nursing her infant, that a second and possibly most critical threat to survival occurs. If the mother is incapable of providing sufficient milk, the infant will be unlikely to survive because of both nutritional and immunological factors. A reduction of the quantity of milk might, within limits, be tolerated and does appear to occur. Alterations in the quality of mother's milk are seldom if ever seen and would be more destructive to the infant's welfare if they did occur.

The maintenance of something near the normal quantity of flow of high–quality mother's milk can only be accomplished at the expense of the maternal organism. Because the most serious imbalance occurs with respect to protein, it is carcass protein that must supply the difference. The mechanisms by which maternal tissue are caused to give up amino acids which ultimately supply the needs of a growing fetus and a nursing infant have been studied in experimental animals. It appears that the maternal adrenal cortex and placental hormones are capable of evoking this response (Aschkenasy–Lelu and Aschkenasy 1959; Kinzey and Srbnik 1963; Berg, Siggs, Greengard 1967; Kinzey 1968). The possession of such a mechanism allows survival of the infant through depletion of the reserve of essential amino acids maintained in maternal tissue, particularly skeletal muscle. Such capability would be rendered useless if there were no maternal reserve. Therefore, reduction in the number of muscle fibers possessed by the female members of a malnourishd human population to the degree occurring in males would be maladaptive.

The end result of this combination of selective forces is the tendency for males to reduce lean body mass to a greater extent than do females in the same population, thereby reducing the degree of sexual dimorphism for this trait. Here we see demonstrated the capacity of populations to exploit physiological adjustments to soften the impact of natural selection. Evidence that nonhuman primate mothers are capable of resorbing significant quantities of tissue to maintain their fetuses has recently been discussed by Watts and Riopelle (1973). The results observed in controlled experiments with rhesus macaques appear consistent with those observed in humans. It appears that delay of skeletal growth is not as great among females as among males in these same populations. This provides further evidence that females are better buffered against the effects of nutritional stress, with the likelihood that the preservation of the reproductive potential of the population is the biological factor involved.

The Limits of Physiological Adaptation

One view of the role of physiological adaptations in the process of evolution is that stated by Waddington (1957), i.e. such adaptations allow the population to survive and remain in an area characterized by a particular stress until such time as the proper genetic events occur to allow truly adaptive change. When more adaptive genes or gene combinations arise in the population, their superior fitness would result in a shift in gene frequencies producing a restructuring of the population's genome — an event that could properly be called adaptation *sensu strictu*.

What are the indications that natural selection might be altering gene frequencies in nutritionally stressed human populations? A number of studies have pointed out greater survivorship of smaller newborns in areas where maternal nutrition is inadequate. These studies include a sampling of lower socioeconomic categories in the city of Aberdeen, Scotland (Baird as cited by Drillien 1964), where lower birth weights and a higher percentage of stillbirths occur than in higher socioeconomic categories. Other studies conducted in India reveal that survivorship of very small infants (1,600– to 2,000–gram birth weights) is higher among individuals of lower socioeconomic strata than among their more prosperous neighbors. This is true despite the fact that superior medical attention, including in–hospital births, is available to members of the higher socioeconomic categories (Jayant 1964). Similar observations have been made in Africa (Hollingsworth 1965) and England (Karn and Penrose 1951). Frisancho, in discussing Peruvian data (Frisancho, et al. 1973), provides evidence of higher rates of survival for infants born of smaller parents. In all of these studies, however, it is difficult to ascertain whether higher survivorship of smaller infants may, in some cases, reflect early loss of less viable embryos and fetuses, excluding them from calculation in the categories of neonatal and infant mortalities. Future demographic studies of malnourished populations will gain considerable value through increased attention to these categories of conceptus loss.

One line of evidence concerning the mechanism of conceptus loss is revealed by the frequent observation of reduced adrenal weights in stillborn infants of poor parents in developed countries (Newman 1973). Such reductions may reflect increased adrenocortical activity on the part of stressed mothers. The genetic implications of whatever mechanisms affect the survivorship of infants could, over an extended period, be profound. It is unlikely, however, that simple genetic mechanisms will be sufficient to explain the form of selection occurring. The traits involved are polygenic and the interaction of the changes which might be anticipated under various forms of stress would make the most acceptable model the one that involved "multiple adaptive peaks" as proposed by Sewell Wright (1948), rather than "a single best type" model which would lend itself to straightforward deterministic treatment. In short, there is evidence that natural selection is at work in populations under nutritional stress. Although it is not possible at this time to produce a predictive model that could be tested in these populations, it seems warranted to assume that the cultural, behavioral, physiological, and developmental buffers which modify the intensity of natural selection under conditions of long-term nutritional stress have limits to their effectiveness. When the stress is severe, intense, and prolonged enough, the price of natural selection must be paid. The cost of the loss of a conceptus rises with each day it survives, so that early loss of embryos would be the most effective adaptive strategy for populations under severe stress. Loss of third–trimester fetuses would be more costly, and loss of neonates and infants would, of course, be increasingly more maladaptive from the standpoint of the population's survival. Whether human populations employ adaptive strategies in a series that effectively minimizes the cost of natural selection during gestation and early postnatal life is not clear from the available evidence. It is unquestionably an important area for future research.

SUMMARY AND CONCLUSIONS

Using an analogy introduced by Slobodkin, it might be said that adaptation restores flexibility to physiological responses much as learning restores flexibility to behavior. Taking the analogy a step further, we might compare genetically determined response patterns to a particular stress to stereotypic behavior in a given circumstance. Both are extremely effective and economical in the absence of drastic change in conditions. But both bear the potential of being severely disadvantageous when conditions are sufficiently altered. Because the adaptedness of a population might be stated in terms of the probability of its survival under conditions that are very likely to occur, it might be anticipated that there would be a high value associated with the possession of a sequence of adaptive responses of increasing cost for frequently encountered stressors. The most costly response would involve the loss of an adult individual before that individual contributed either to the energy capture function or to the gene pool of the population.

Because nutritional stress is a frequently encountered and potentially lethal stressor, it might be anticipated that human populations would possess a variety of adaptive responses to it. Evidence for a number of physiological and developmental adjustments occurring in human populations makes it possible to discern the outline of a graded response sequence to this significant form of stress. There are obviously many gaps in the account presented here. There are also important lines of evidence excluded, such as a variety of behavioral alterations and cultural practices observed in areas of persistent nutritional deficiency. The reader is directed to such works as those by Jelliffe (1968) and Geertz (1970) for treatment of some of these factors. It is hoped that the present account will alert others to the importance of considering the variety of ways a population may adapt to a severe stress before genetic change occurs. Genetic adaptation alone would frequently result in a stereotypic and potentially maladaptive and rigid response.

The evolutionary importance of a multiplex and graded response systems should not be underestimated merely because it is difficult to quantify. If a flexible array of adaptations allows populations to survive and reproduce in the face of environmental fluctuations of large magnitude, persistent exposure to stress will allow beneficial mutations and recombinations to occur and spread through the population. This process makes possible the sort of genetic change that can rightly be called evolution.

Interesting questions arise from any attempt to reconstruct human evolutionary history using adaptive strategies in response to nutritional stress as an example. One question involves the probable size of our ancestors. If the current secular trend of increase in body size is indeed revealing the genetic potential possessed by the species before agriculture and urbanization created conditions favoring reduced body size, is there not the possibility that selection favored larger size at some earlier date? There is little evidence for large body size in early *Homo sapiens* populations. However, the amount of evidence available is not adequate to exclude the possibility that early hunters and gatherers possessed mean body size resembling our own more than those of our more recent ancestors.

Another question arises from consideration of adaptive strategies of human populations under nutritional stress: is it desirable to induce larger adult body size by nutritional practices stressing excessively high animal–protein consumption? There is evidence that high–protein diets may have undesirable side effects, including greater susceptibility to cardiovascular diseases. From the standpoint of human populations throughout the world, it should be pointed out that the effects of the current population explosion are amplified by the human biomass explosion that is accompanying it. This is particularly true of the increased consumption of organisms of high trophic level, i.e. beef cattle and fattened hogs. Also, if the adaptive strategy of poorly fed populations involves reduced adult body size, it may well be that dietary supplementation stressing animal–protein intake in the early stages of life may inactivate one level of adaptation and force the population to fall back on its next line of defense. In most cases, the next line of defense involves the payment of the cost of natural selection through increased mortality rates. It is necessary, then, to be certain that early dietary supplementation can be followed by the supply of sufficient nutritional resources to satisfy the inevitable increase in both protein and calorie requirements.

REFERENCES

ASCHKENASY-LELU, P., A. ASCHKENASY
 1959 "Effects of androgens and estrogens on the metabolism of protein and the growth of tissues," in *World review of nutrition and dietetics*. Edited by G. H. Bourne, 33–60. Philadelphia: Lippincott.
ASHCROFT, M. T., P. HENEAGE, H. G. LOVELL
 1966 Heights and weights of Jamaican school children of various ethnic groups. *American Journal of Physical Anthropology* 24:35–44.
BABLET, J., L. NORMET
 1937 *Les lésions histopathologiques de la bouffissure d'Annam*. Bulletins of the Academy of Medicine 117:242.
BARNES, R. H., E. KWONG, L. MORRISSEY, L. VILHJALMSDOTTIR, D. LEVITSKY
 1973 Maternal protein deprivation during pregnancy or lactation in rats and the efficiency of food and nitrogen utilization of the progeny. *Journal of Nutrition* 103:273–284.
BARTLEY, M. H., JR.
 1968 "Structural activities of the anti-inflammatory steroids and their relationship to osseous tissue." Unpublished doctoral dissertation, University of Utah.
BERG, B. N., E. B. SIGGS, P. GREENGARD
 1967 Maintenance of pregnancy in protein-deficient rats by adrenocortical steroid or ACTH administration. *Endocrinology* 80:829–839.

BOMPAR, F.
1887   Etude sur l'atrophie des muscles thoraciques chez les tuberculeux. *Journal of Medicine of Bordeaux* 17:121–130.

BRAMWELL, F., A. MUIR
1907   A remarkable muscular lesion occurring in sprue with notes of a case of peculiar (myopathic) muscular atrophy in which somewhat similar changes were pictured. *Quarterly Journal of Medicine* 1:1.

CASTELLANOS, H., G. A. ARROYAVE
1961   Role of adrenal cortical system in response of children to severe protein malnutrition. *American Journal of Clinical Nutrition* 9: 186–195.

CHEEK, D. B.
1968   "Muscle cell growth in normal children," in *Human growth, body composition, cell growth, energy and intelligence*. Edited by D. B. Cheek, 337–351. Philadelphia: Lea and Febiger.

CHEEK, D. B., J. BRASEL, J. E. GRAYSTONE
1968   "Muscle cell growth in rodents: sex difference and the role of hormones," in *Human growth, body composition, cell growth, energy and intelligence*. Edited by D. B. Cheek, 306–325. Philadelphia: Lea and Febiger.

CLARK, I.
1953   The effect of cortisone upon protein synthesis. *Journal of Biological Chemistry* 200:69–76.

CONSOLAZIO, C. F., R. E. JOHNSON, L. J. PECORA
1963   *Physiological measurements of metabolic functions in man*. New York: McGraw-Hill.

DEAN, R. F. A.
1964   "Kwashiorkor," in *Recent advances in pediatrics*. Edited by D. Gardner, 234–265. London: Churchill.

DELLAPORTAS, G. J.
1969   Growth of school children in Gondar area, Ethiopia. *Human Biology* 41:218–222.

DRILLIEN, C. M.
1964   The growth and development of the prematurely born infant. *Journal of Pediatrics* 7–8:73–95.

DURANTE, G.
1902   "Anatomie pathologique des muscles," in *Manuel d'histologie pathologique*. Edited by A. V. Cornil and L. A. Ranvier. Paris: Alcan.

FRISANCHO, A. R., J. SANCHEZ, D. PALLARDEL, L. YANEZ
1973   "Adaptive significance of small body size under poor socioeconomic conditions in Southern Peru." Paper delivered at the annual meeting of the American Association of Physical Anthropologists, Dallas, Texas, April 12-14.

GEERTZ, CLIFFORD
1970   *Agricultural involution: the processes of ecological change in Indonesia*. Berkeley: University of California Press.

GOLDBERG, A. L.
1969   Protein turnover in skeletal muscle, II: Effects of denervation and cortisone on protein catabolism in skeletal muscle. *Journal of Biological Chemistry* 244:3223.

GOLDSPINK, G.
1970   "Morphological adaptation due to growth and activity," in *Physiology and biochemistry of muscle as food*. Edited by D. Brisky, L. Casseus, and D. Marsh, 521–536. Madison: University of Wisconsin Press.

HAMWI, J. J., M. TZAGOURNIA
1970   Nutrition and diseases of the endocrine glands. *American Journal of Clinical Nutrition* 23:311–329.

HAYERN, M. G.
1875   Note sur les maladies musculaires qu'on observe dans les maladies chroniques. *Comptes Rendus Sociologiques et Biologiques* 1:69.

HOLLINGSWORTH, M. J.
1965   Observations on the birthweights and survival of African babies: single births. *Annals of Human Genetics, London* 28:291–300.

JELLIFFE, D. B.
1968   *Infant nutrition in the subtropics and tropics.* Geneva: World Health Organization.

JAYANT, K.
1964   Birthweight and some other factors in relation to infant survival: a study in an Indian sample. *Annals of Human Genetics, London* 27:261–267.

KARN, M. N., L. S. PENROSE
1951   Birthweight and gestation time in relation to maternal age, parity and infant survival. *Annals of Eugenics, London* 16:147–164.

KINSELL, L. W., J. W. PARTRIDGE, L. BOLERIG, S. MARGEN
1953   Dietary modification of the metabolic and clinical effects of ACTH and cortisone. *Annals of Internal Medicine* 37:921–929.

KINZEY, W. G.
1968   Hormonal activity of the rat placenta in the absence of dietary protein. *Endocrinology* 82:266–270.

KINZEY, W. G., H. H. SRBNIK
1963   Maintenance of pregnancy with short-term injections of ovarian hormones. *Proceedings of the Society for Experimental Biology and Medicine* 114:158–168.

KORNER, A.
1960   The role of the adrenal gland in the control of amino acid incorporation into protein of isolated rat liver microsomes. *Journal of Endocrinology* 21:177.

LEON, H. A.
1966   Early effects of corticosteroids on amino acid incorporation by rat liver systems subsequent to its in vitro injection. *Endocrinology* 78:481.

MAC CALLUM, J. B.
  1898 On the histogenesis of the striated muscle fiber, and the growth of the human sartorius muscle. *Johns Hopkins Hospital Bulletin* 90–91:208–215.

MC FIE, J., H. F. WELBOURNE
  1962 Effect of malnutrition in infancy of the development of bone, muscle and fat. *Journal of Nutrition* 76:97.

MC MAHON, T.
  1973 Size and shape in biology. *Science* 179:1201–1204.

MENDEZ, J., C. BEHRHORST
  1963 The anthropometric characteristics of Indian and urban Guatemalans. *Human Biology* 35:457–469.

MONTGOMERY, R. D.
  1962 Muscle morphology in infantile protein malnutrition. *Journal of Clinical Pathology* 15:511–521.

NATIONAL RESEARCH COUNCIL
  1958 *Recommended daily dietary allowance.* National Academy of Sciences Food and Nutrition Board, Publication 589. Washington, D.C.

NEWMAN, M. T.
  1973 "Unsolved problems in human nutrition." Paper delivered in symposium "What we need to know but do not know about ecology and adaptation in man" at the annual meeting of the American Association of Physical Anthropologists, Dallas, Texas, April 12–14.

OLIVIER, A.
  1869 "Des atrophies musculaires." Unpublished thesis, Paris.

PARIZKOVA, J., J. MERHAUSTOVA
  1970 The comparison of somatic development, body composition and functional characteristics in Tunisian and Czech boys of 11 and 12 years. *Human Biology* 42:391–400.

SABHARWAL, K. P., S. MORALES, J. MENDEZ
  1966 Body measurements and creatine excretion among upper and lower socio-economic groups of girls in Guatemala. *Human Biology* 38:131–140.

SCRIMSHAW, N. S.
  1964 Ecological factors in nutritional disease. *American Journal of Nutrition* 14:112.

SELYE, H.
  1950 *The physiology and pathology of exposure to stress.* Montreal: Aetna Medical Publishers.

SIDRANSKY, H., E. VERNEY
  1970 Skeletal muscle protein metabolism changes in rats force-fed a diet inducing an experimental kwashiorkor-like model. *American Journal of Clinical Nutrition* 23:1154–1159.

SIDRANSKY, H., D. S. WAGLE, E. VERNEY
  1969 Hepatic protein synthesis in rats force-fed a threonine-devoid diet, and treated with cortisone acetate or threonine. *Laboratory Investigation* 20:364.

SLOBODKIN, L. B.
1968   "Toward a predictive theory of evolution," in *Population biology and evolution.* Edited by R. C. Lewontin. Syracuse: Syracuse University Press.

STINI, W. A.
1968   "Physiological and morphological correlates of kwashiorkor in Colombia." Unpublished doctoral dissertation, University of Wisconsin.
1969   Nutritional stress and growth: sex difference in adaptive response. *American Journal of Physical Anthropology* 31:417–426.
1972a   Malnutrition, body size and proportion. *Ecology of Food and Nutrition* 1:121–126.
1972b   Lean body mass reductions in domestic hogs subjected to protein-deficient diet. (Abstract.) *American Journal of Physical Anthropology* 37:451.
1972c   Reduced sexual dimorphism in upper arm muscle circumference associated with protein-deficient diet in a South American population. *American Journal of Physical Anthropology* 36:341–352.

TANNER, J. M.
1964   "Hormonal, genetic and environmental factors controlling growth", in *Human biology.* Edited by G. A. Harrison, J. S. Weiner, J. M. Tanner, and N.A. Barnicot, 340–354. New York: Oxford University Press.
1968   Earlier maturation in man. *Scientific American* 218:21-27.

THOMAS, R. B.
1972   "Human adaptation to a High Andean energy flow system." Unpublished doctoral dissertation, Pennsylvania State University.

THOMPSON, A. M., W. Z. BELEWICZ
1963   Nutritional status, maternal physique and reproductive efficiency. *Proceedings of the Nutrition Society* 22:55–60.

VILLAREJOS, V. M., J. A. OSBORNE, F. J. PAYNE, J. A. ARGUEDAS
1971   Heights and weights of children in urban and rural Costa Rica. *Journal of Tropical Pediatrics and Environmental Child Health* 17:32–43.

VITALE, J. J., H. VELEZ
1967   *Estudio Socio-económico del Municipio de Heliconia.* Investigacion Upjohn. Medellin, Colombia, February 1967, pages 8-10.

WADDINGTON, CONRAD
1957   *The strategy of the genes.* London: Allen and Unwin

WATERLOW, J. C.
1955   *Protein malnutrition.* A symposium held under the auspices of FAO, WHO, and the Josiah Macy Foundation. London: Cambridge University Press.

WATERLOW, J. C., G. A. O. ALLEYNE
1972   Protein malnutrition in children — advances in knowledge in the last ten years. *Advances in Protein Chemistry* 26:117–241.

WATTS, E. S., A. J. RIOPELLE
1973 "The effects of maternal protein deprivation on size and skeletal maturity of newborn Rhesus monkeys." Paper delivered at the annual meeting of the American Association of Physical Anthropologists, Dallas, Texas, April 12-14.

WEINER, J. S.
1972 "Tropical ecology and population structure," in *The structure of human populations*. Edited by G. A. Harrison and A. J. Boyce. London: Oxford University Press.

WRIGHT, S.
1948 On the roles of directed and random changes in gene frequency in the genetics of natural populations. *Evolution* 2:279–294.

An Anatomical View of Demographic Data: Biomass, Fat Mass, and Lean Body Mass of the United States and Mexican Human Populations

GABRIEL LASKER and HENRY WOMACK

When anatomists are asked to look at human populations they see them in a somewhat different light than do demographers. We cannot report definitive results of anatomical studies of populations here, but we will introduce some partial figures that will allow extrapolated conclusions useful chiefly for heuristic purposes. We had anticipated that the International Biological Program's Human Adaptability Project (IBP/HAP) would have developed representative data of just the kind needed, but if it has, the results are not readily available, and we have found it easier for the time being to rely on older and very limited data.

When demographers look at populations they tend to emphasize numbers. The census is their most accurate tool. Even when population counts are broken down into age and sex subgroups, one purpose is still to help project future numbers. Without belittling other demographic objectives (actuarial, economic, and sociological considerations), we do note that the growing concern with human ecology has not led to much examination of the anatomy of populations by either demographers or human biologists. Those who have examined populations have all too easily accepted the postulate that peoples are demographically equivalent. On the other hand, those who have examined anatomical differences have usually been concerned with standards for judging individual health and physiological performance.

We do not know of published accounts of any efforts to estimate

We thank Dr. Bernice Kaplan for assistance with the collection of data in Peru, Dr. Marcus Goldstein for past access to his protocols, and Drs. Stanley Garn, A. R. Frisancho, and F. E. Johnston for their personal communications and helpful criticisms.

the biomass of the world population of *Homo sapiens* and to "dissect" it into the biomasses of his various tissues. We shall therefore indicate what one would try to do to evaluate the biomass and its components in two national populations, and we shall discuss some obligatory assumptions. The actual figures on the biomass of the populations of the United States and Mexico and on the mass of metabolically inactive (fat) and active tissues for these national populations remain tentative, and data on the whole human species are not yet available.

However, one may consider the world as made up of two kinds of populations: those having had reasonably ample food resources for the last several generations and those that have had relatively restricted amounts of food for their population. In a general way these populations correspond to "Western" versus "non-Western"; i.e., Europe and northern North America versus the rest of the world. It will be readily apparent that there are other areas where food may have been scarce but which now are prosperous (such as Japan), and others such as Israel, Australia, New Zealand, and Siberia which are, from this point of view, "Western." Data on the U.S. on the one hand, and Mexico, Guatemala, and Peru on the other, may stand for the two ecological types and hence be used to give at least a crude picture of the world population from an anatomical perspective.

The distinction between consistently well fed areas and those populations which have often gone through "bottlenecks" of food shortages is not seen primarily in population density. The U.S. had an estimated population of 209,166,000 in 1972 for 3,675,911 square miles or 57 persons per square mile. Mexico has an area of 761,602 square miles with a population estimated at 54,253,000 in 1972 or 71 persons per square mile. But if one discounts Alaska's 586,412 square miles, the population densities of the two countries are nearly equal and are about the world average (72 per square mile). Prosperous areas of the world have densities ranging from 4 per square mile for Australia to 162 per square mile for Europe.

What we shall do is to take the average weight of Mexicans of various age and sex groups, multiply by the number of individuals in each group, respectively, and then sum all of the weights to get a figure for the total biomass of *Homo sapiens* in Mexico. When the same is done for the United States, the figure obtained will be compared with that of Mexico and the ratio will be compared with the corresponding ratio of population numbers.

An effort will then be made to estimate the amount of human fat in these populations. For our purposes we will use data from the 10-State

Nutrition Survey (Garn, personal communication). These data include triceps skinfolds and age- and sex-specific constants which allow estimates of fat weight. Unfortunately, we know of no corresponding data for Mexico. However, one of us measured the triceps skinfolds of adult Peruvians of both sexes in three towns of the north coast of Peru. Like the national populations of Mexico, the origins of these Peruvians include a major indigenous element (usually in Mestizo form), a European element (rarely unmixed with Amerindian), and a very minor African element (Kaplan and Lasker 1953; Lasker and Kaplan 1965). For younger ages (one to eighteen years) data on triceps skinfolds are from the Instituto de Nutrición de Centro América y Panamá (INCAP) (1969) for six Latin American countries. We use those of rural Guatemala as being most similar ethnically and environmentally to Mexico. Once the biomass and fat mass of a population are known, the difference between them (body weight minus fat mass) gives the lean body mass (LBM), which is of great importance because of its relationship to the food needed by that population.

Since metabolically active tissues do not have equal levels of metabolism in different countries either in basal or habitual circumstances, one cannot directly equate the ratio of LBM of two countries with their relative food use, let alone their food needs. Of the edible portion of foods utilized, only part is consumed and, of that consumed, only part is absorbed and metabolized. The magnitude of both these fractions probably depends to some extent on the amount of food available, and there may well be human adaptations to the amount that has been available: (1) in the immediate past (influencing psychological hunger and some biological "hunger"); (2) during development (influencing body size and hence caloric needs) and (3) over generations (influencing the survival of those with genetically lower caloric needs or those with a genetically higher capacity to supply caloric needs under very complex biocultural conditions of natural selection).

RESULTS

The average body weights of the white population of each age and sex in the United States, as reported by Stoudt, et al. (1960), were converted into kilograms and accepted for the total population without correction for the minor nonwhite elements. These weights are given in Table 1. For the Mexican population, Table 2 shows weights at birth and one and two years of age averaged from two sources reported by Meredith and Goldstein (1952). Weights of Mexicans three to seven-

Table 1. Data on weight and triceps skinfold thickness of United States population samples by age, estimated body fat, lean body mass (LBM), and the constants by which these are derived

Age	Weight (kg.)[a]	Triceps (mm.)[b]	Constant[c]	Fat (kg.)[d]	LBM (kg.)[e]
Males					
1–4	11.5	9.7	–	2.9	8.6
5–9	24.4	9.3	–	6.1	18.3
10–14	41.2	11.7	.869	10.2	31.0
15–19	64.4	11.5	.971	11.2	53.2
20–24	71.7	12.0	.971	11.7	60.0
25–34	74.7	13.4	.829	11.1	63.3
35–44	75.5	14.1	.887	12.5	63.0
45–59	75.1	14.2	.924	13.1	62.0
60–64	73.5	13.2	.962	12.7	60.8
65–74	72.4	12.7	.962	12.2	60.2
75 up	69.8	12.1	.962	11.6	58.2
Females					
1–4	11.1	9.6	–	3.2	7.9
5–9	23.4	10.8	–	6.8	16.6
10–14	41.8	14.8	.815	12.1	29.7
15–19	55.0	17.5	.911	15.9	39.1
20–24	56.7	18.0	.911	16.4	40.3
25–34	58.3	20.3	.984	20.0	38.3
35–44	63.5	22.9	1.057	24.2	39.3
45–59	65.8	24.0	.965	23.2	42.6
60–64	66.2	23.1	.873	20.2	46.0
65–74	65.8	21.8	.873	19.0	46.8
75 up	65.3	19.0	.873	16.6	48.7

[a] Data for U.S. whites from Stoudt, et al. (1960).
[b] Weighted averages of triceps fatfolds of U.S. white population from Garn (1972).
[c] Constants based on data from Garn (1972). The constants for calculating body fat from triceps fatfolds are for ages 10, 20, 30, 40, and 60, respectively. The age 20 constant is used for the 15–19 year old group. For ages 45–59 the constants for ages 40 and 60 are averaged.
[d] Body fat is determined by multiplying the triceps fatfold thickness by the constant. For ages 1–4 and 5–9 fat is taken to be in the same ratio as for 10–14 years of age.
[e] Lean body mass (LBM) is weight minus fat.

teen years old are given from one source by the same authors (and they cite similar figures for Mexicans in the United States). For ages eighteen and up, data for Mexicans measured by Goldstein and tabulated and graphed by Lasker (1953) have been utilized in Table 2. The Mexican population was measured some time ago (most of it in 1941), and it is possible that more recent data would indicate a secular trend to increased weights and earlier growth (as has been noted in most countries

Table 2.   Data on weight and triceps skinfold thickness of Latin American samples by age, estimated body fat, lean body mass, (LBM) and the constants by which these are derived

Age	Weight (kg.)[a]	Triceps (mm.)[b]	Constant[c]	Fat (kg.)[d]	LBM (kg.)[e]
Males					
1–4	10.6	8.6	–	1.8	8.8
5–9	21.2	7.0	–	3.7	17.5
10–14	33.9	6.7	.869	5.9	28.0
15–19	53.2	8.8	.971	8.5	44.7
20–24	57.5	11.3	.971	11.0	46.5
25–34	59.8	10.0	.829	8.3	51.5
35–44	63.6	11.9	.887	10.6	53.0
45–59	63.6	8.6	.924	7.9	55.7
60–64	62.0	8.3	.962	8.0	54.0
65–74	62.0	6.8	.962	6.5	55.5
75 up	62.0	4.9	.962	4.7	57.3
Females					
1–4	10.1	9.3	–	2.5	7.6
5–9	20.3	8.7	–	5.1	15.2
10–14	35.2	10.8	.815	8.8	26.4
15–19	48.0	15.7	.911	14.3	23.7
20–24	51.6	14.0	.911	13.6	38.0
25–34	52.7	15.2	.984	15.0	37.7
35–44	55.5	16.3	1.057	17.2	38.3
45–59	59.1	16.4	.965	15.8	43.3
60–64	57.3	12.8	.873	11.2	46.1
65–74	57.3	16.1	.873	14.1	43.2
75 up	57.3	11.7	.873	10.2	47.1

[a]   Ages 1–17 for Mexican children in Mexico from Meredith and Goldstein (1952); ages 18 and up from Mexican data of Goldstein (graphed by Lasker 1953).
[b]   Ages 1–18 for Guatemala from INCAP (1969: Volume 25); ages 18 and up for Peru from unpublished data of Lasker (see Lasker 1962 for description of subjects).
[c]   See Footnote c, Table 1.
[d]   See Footnote d, Table 1.
[e]   See Footnote e, Table 1.

studied). For the United States, Hamill, et al. (1972) have published weight data for children aged 6 to 17¾. These figures are slightly higher than those here, but being more recent they are even less comparable to the Mexican data.

The triceps skinfold measurements for the white population in the United States (Table 1) were provided by S. M. Garn from unpublished data collected for the 10-State Nutrition Survey. For the Latin American population (Table 2), ages one to eighteen are for Guatemalans from the INCAP studies (1969). Ages eighteen and over are for Peruvians from unpublished data of Lasker. In an effort to calculate the factors of metabolizing and nonmetabolizing tissues, we have estimated the total body fat from these skinfold measurements. This was done by multiplying the skinfold thickness by a specific constant for each age-sex group. The constants were derived by Garn from data of the 10-State Nutrition Survey, and he has kindly permitted us to use these unpublished constants. The values for skinfold thickness and total body fat for the Latin American population (Table 2) are well below those for the United States (Table 1). A. R. Frisancho and S. M. Garn (personal communications) confirm the same finding for Latin American populations with which they have worked. The INCAP (1969) studies also show, in general, smaller triceps skinfolds in boys under eighteen in rural populations of six Central American countries, and similar or smaller values in girls, compared to English standards. Because the average skinfolds in England are below those in the United States, the same can be said of all six Central American countries studied.

Lean body mass was determined by substracting the total body fat from total body weight. The values for United States individuals are shown in Table 1 and those for Latin American individuals in Table 2. The values for total biomass, fat, and lean body mass for the entire United States and Mexican populations are shown in Tables 3 and 4, respectively. These values were obtained by multiplying the individual values by the total number of individuals as abstracted from United Nations Demographic and Statistical Reports for the 1970 decennial censuses of the United States and Mexico.

Table 5 summarizes these total values and shows the various ratios between the two populations. The 1970 population of Mexico (48,377,200) is 23.8 percent of that of the United States (203,165,700). The biomass of the Mexican population is estimated here to be 17.2 percent of that of the United States. The fat mass of the people of Mexico as calculated here (409,058,800 kg.) is 14.7 percent of the fat mass calculated for the people of the United States (2,781,028,100 kg.). The LBM of the Mexican population (1,528,224,800 kg.) is 18.0 percent of the LBM estimated for the population of the United States (8,483,111,600 kg.).

DISCUSSION

It is not easy to evaluate the quality of data on weight and fat until repeated estimates have been made. A preliminary (and independent) estimate of body fat in the United States was extrapolated on the basis

Table 3. Estimates of the number, biomass, and constituency of that biomass in non-metabolizing (fat) and metabolizing lean body mass (LBM) fractions of the United States population by age and sex

Age	Number	Biomass (kg.)	Fat (kg.)	LBM (kg.)
United States males				
1–4	8,744,700	100,564,100	25,359,600	75,204,500
5–9	10,166,300	248,057,700	62,014,400	186,043,300
10–14	10,589,200	436,275,000	108,009,800	328,265,200
15–19	9,633,900	620,423,200	107,899,700	512,523,500
20–24	7,920,100	567,871,200	92,665,200	475,206,000
25–34	12,217,000	908,944,800	135,608,700	773,336,100
35–44	11,223,100	847,344,100	140,288,800	707,055,300
45–59	15,952,700	1,198,047,800	208,980,400	989,067,400
60–64	4,027,000	295,984,500	51,142,900	244,841,600
65–74	5,431,400	393,233,400	66,263,100	326,970,300
75 up	2,976,500	207,759,700	34,527,400	173,232,300
United States females				
1–4	8,422,300	93,487,500	26,951,400	66,536,100
5–9	9,788,600	229,053,200	66,562,500	162,490,700
10–14	10,198,400	426,293,100	123,400,600	302,892,500
15–19	9,435,700	518,963,500	150,027,600	368,935,900
20–24	8,451,600	479,205,700	138,606,200	340,599,500
25–34	12,691,500	739,914,500	253,830,000	486,084,500
35–44	11,848,600	752,386,100	286,736,100	465,650,000
45–59	17,216,200	1,132,826,000	399,415,800	733,410,200
60–64	4,589,200	303,805,000	92,701,800	211,103,200
65–74	6,993,300	460,159,100	132,872,700	327,286,400
75 up	4,648,400	303,540,500	77,163,400	226,377,100
Totals	203,165,700	11,264,139,700	2,781,028,100	8,483,111,600

of data from Brožek (1952), Škerlj, et al. (1953), Newman (1956), Garn (1957), Lee and Lasker (1958), and Forbes and Amirhakimi (1970). The constants Garn has supplied yield slightly less body fat at ages one to twenty and slightly more at ages twenty-five and above. The total fat estimated is essentially the same, 2,802 versus the 2,781 million kilograms estimated in Table 3, a difference of 0.76 percent. The corresponding difference in LBM is 0.24 percent. Only further data from large samples of randomly selected and carefully measured populations can provide really "good" estimates, however, especially for non-western nations.

To the extent that one can accept the assumptions concerning the equivalency of Guatemalan, Peruvian, and Mexican populations in respect to triceps skinfolds as a measure of total body fat, the LBM of Mexicans is calculated as 18.0 percent of that of the population of the United States (Table 5). In fact, the lean body mass of Mexicans is

Table 4.   Estimates of the number, biomass, and constituency of that biomass in non-metabolizing (fat) and metabolizing lean body mass (LBM) fractions of the Mexican population by age and sex (fat and LBM) estimated by analogy using data from Guatemala and Peru

Age	Number	Biomass (kg.)	Fat (kg.)	LBM (kg.)
Mexican males				
1–4	4,164,400	44,142,600	7,496,000	36,646,600
5–9	3,947,300	83,682,800	14,605,000	69,077,800
10–14	3,281,400	111,239,500	19,360,300	91,879,200
15–19	2,497,900	132,888,300	21,232,200	111,656,100
20–24	1,935,100	111,268,300	21,286,100	89,982,200
25–34	2,870,200	171,638,000	23,822,700	147,815,300
35–44	2,202,000	140,047,200	23,341,200	116,706,000
45–59	1,927,000	122,557,200	15,223,300	107,333,900
60–64	452,600	28,061,200	3,620,800	24,440,400
65–74	589,300	36,536,600	3,830,500	32,706,100
75 up	273,100	16,932,200	1,283,600	15,648,600
Mexican females				
1–4	4,029,800	40,701,000	10,074,500	30,626,500
5–9	3,801,600	77,172,500	19,388,200	57,784,300
10–14	3,134,900	110,348,500	27,587,100	82,761,400
15–19	2,570,200	123,369,600	36,753,900	86,615,700
20–24	2,107,400	108,741,800	28,660,600	80,081,200
25–34	3,005,600	158,395,100	45,084,400	113,310,700
35–44	2,257,500	125,291,300	38,829,000	86,462,300
45–59	1,925,900	113,820,700	30,429,200	83,391,500
60–64	468,400	26,839,300	5,246,100	21,593,200
65–74	605,400	34,689,400	8,536,100	26,153,300
75 up	330,200	18,920,500	3,368,000	15,552,500
Totals	48,377,200	1,937,283,600	409,058,800	1,528,224,800

Table 5.   The relative size of the human population of Mexico and the United States and the relative biomass, fat mass, and lean body mass of the two populations (in kilograms)

Population of Mexico (1970)	48,377,200	
	———————	= .238
Population of United States	203,165,700	
Weight of people of Mexico	1,937,283,600	
	———————	= .172
Weight of people of United States	11,264,139,700	
Fat mass of people of Mexico	409,058,800	
	———————	= .147
Fat mass of people of United States	2,781,028,100	
Lean body mass of people of Mexico	1,528,224,800	
	———————	= .180
Lean body mass of people of United States	8,483,111,600	

slightly larger than that since Mexicans are, on average, smaller in body size (as measured by stature, for instance) than Americans, and the same triceps skinfold no doubt represents less total weight of fat in a Mexican. Since we used the same constants for Mexican and American populations we have no doubt overestimated the fat component in Mexico and hence underestimated lean body mass. In any case, both because of the greater proportion of children in the population and because of slower growth and maturation and smaller adult size, the average amount of metabolizing tissue per Mexican is much less than that per American.

Brožek and Grande (1955) have shown that components of the lean body do not metabolize equally. Liver is the most active tissue and we know next to nothing about the relative size of the liver and other organs in various parts of the world. During severe weight loss all tissues are known to be reduced in mass and the best assumption, for present purposes, is that various metabolizing tissues represent more or less constant proportions of lean body mass and that amount of mass is linearly correlated with measures of metabolism.

Data on metabolism are usually reported as Basal Metabolic Rate (BMR). Some early studies apparently indicated scores above the United States in at least some Latin American people. On the other hand, studies in China and other parts of the non-Western world usually show a BMR of less than one hundred. Unfortunately, the BMR is standardized for persons of equal surface area. If actual O_2 utilization or heat production were reported, inferences could be made directly relevant to the total populations as we have presented them. In any case, surface area (usually estimated from height and weight) is highly correlated with LBM since both reflect the size of the body frame. If the BMR is not elevated in such peoples as Mexicans (and there is every reason to believe that it is not), the bodily utilization of food as calories per individual must, like lean body mass, be considerably lower than in the United States. In life, of course, it is not basal conditions that count but the metabolism during the actual daily round of activities and at rest. Anecdotes about the long periods of siesta in Mexico have no basis in fact. Many Mexicans work through the day, and our best guess would be that the energy actually expended per individual in the United States and Mexico is probably more or less proportional to their respective mean lean body weights.

To the extent that this kind of finding can be generalized to Western versus non-Western countries, what are the policy implications of such studies? Do they demonstrate a lower per capita need for food in underdeveloped countries and hence justify less concern for their scarcity of food or less generous response to it? Concern and generosity are moral questions beyond the scope of a biological study; all one can say is that food needs at present may be less PER CAPITA in some countries than in others but that these differences may be the result of adaptation to past food shortages. The more abundant resources now available, through equality of opportunity for growth in the immediate future, open the possibility of equality of nutritional needs later.

The problems of hypercaloric nutrition, obesity, and their morbid consequences in the United States make it uncertain just what level of caloric intake and what type of adaptation are desirable. The fact remains, however, that without food surpluses there is no choice of response. With the access to food which wealth permits the individual can — to the extent his culture allows — make a voluntary choice of the level of caloric intake which he considers desirable for his immediate comfort and pleasure or for his long-term health.

The extension of studies on population anatomy may lead to an understanding of the probable effects of various population policies and may help eventually to inform decisions so as to extend "freedom from hunger" to a wider freedom of choice.

REFERENCES

BROŽEK, J.
  1952   Changes of body composition in man during maturity and their nutritional implications. *Federation Proceedings* 11:784–793.
BROŽEK, J., F. GRANDE
  1955   Body composition and basal metabolism in man: correlation analysis versus physiological approach. *Human Biology* 27:22–31.
FORBES, G., G. AMIRHAKIMI
  1970   Skinfold thickness and body fat in children. *Human Biology* 42: 401–418.
GARN, S. M.
  1957   Roentgenogrammetric determinations of body composition. *Human Biology* 29:337–353.
  1972   "A preliminary analysis of anthropometric, radiographic and dental data for the 10-State Survey." Unpublished manuscript.
HAMILL, P., F. JOHNSTON, S. LEMESHOW
  1972   Height and weight of youths 12–17 years. *U.S. National Center for Health Statistics*, series 11, number 124. Washington, D.C.: U.S. Government Printing Office.

INSTITUTO DE NUTRICIÓN DE CENTRO AMÉRICA Y PANAMÁ
1969 *Evaluación Nutricional de la Población de Centro América y Panamá*, volumes twenty-five to thirty. Guatemala City, Guatemala.

KAPLAN, B., G. LASKER
1953 Ethnic identification in an Indian Mestizo community. *Phylum, the Atlanta University Review of Race and Culture* 14:179–190.

LASKER, G.
1953 The age factor in bodily measurements of adult male and female Mexicans. *Human Biology* 25:50–63.
1962 Differences in anthropometric measurements within and between three communities in Peru. *Human Biology* 34:63–70.

LASKER, G., B. KAPLAN
1965 The relation of anthroposcopic traits to the ascription of racial designation in Peru. Homenaje a Juan Comas en su 65 aniversario, Mexico, 2:189–220.

LEE, M., G. LASKER
1958 The thickness of subcutaneous fat in elderly men. *American Journal of Physical Anthropology* 16:125–134.

MEREDITH, H., M. GOLDSTEIN
1952 Studies on the body size of North American children of Mexican ancestry. *Child Development* 23:91–110.

NEWMAN, R.
1956 Skinfold measurements in young American males. *Human Biology* 28:154–164.

ŠKERLJ, B., J. BROŽEK, E. HUNT
1953 Subcutaneous fat and age changes in body build and body form in women. *American Journal of Physical Anthropology* 11:577–600.

STOUDT, H., A. DAMON, R. MCFARLAND
1960 Heights and weights of white Americans. *Human Biology* 32:331–341.

UNITED NATIONS
1970 *Demographic and statistical report, 1970 Census.*

Possible Adaptive Significance of Small Body Size in the Attainment of Aerobic Capacity Among High-Altitude Quechua Natives

A. ROBERTO FRISANCHO, TULIO VELASQUEZ, and JORGE SANCHEZ

There is fairly extensive information available on the effects of high altitude on aerobic capacity of sea-level and high-altitude natives (Balke 1964; Buskirk, et al. 1967; Dill, et al. 1966; Elsner, Bolstad, and Forno 1964; Baker 1969; Kollias, et al. 1968; Velasquez 1964; Mazess 1969; Frisancho, et al. 1973). However, little is known of the relationship between variations in body size and the attainment of aerobic capacity at high altitude. According to studies conducted at sea level, variations in body size and morphology affect the attainment of aerobic capacity (Astrand 1952; Buskirk and Taylor 1957; McArdle and Magel 1970; Von Dobeln 1956; Wilmore 1969; Wyndham, et al. 1963). For this reason, and as part of an investigation concerned with the developmental processes of functional adaptation to high altitude (Frisancho, et al. 1973), we have studied, during maximal exercise, the aerobic capacity of high-altitude Quechua natives characterized by small and large body size. This study presents evidence indicating an enhanced oxygen intake, measured in milliliters per kilogram per minute (ml/kg/min), associated with small body size, high hemoglobin concentration and increased residual lung volume among high-altitude Quechua natives tested at 3,840 meters of altitude in Southern Peru.

The authors gratefully acknowledge the facilities and cooperation provided by the Instituto de Biología Andina, Universidad Nacional Mayor de San Marcos; the Hospital Regional and Area de Salud of Puno; and the cooperation of the Peruvian Army Headquarters at Puno, Peru.

Research was supported in part by Grant HE-13805 of The Heart and Lung Institute of The National Institutes of Health.

METHODS AND MATERIALS

Sample

Because the attainment of maximal aerobic capacity can be influenced by variation in age, physical activity, and health status of the subjects, the sample for this study was selected with these factors in mind. It consisted of two subgroups of high-altitude young adult Quechua natives: twenty-two subjects characterized by small body size and eighteen subjects characterized by large body size. The stature of the small body size group ranged from 150 to 159 centimeters, and the stature of the large body size group ranged from 162 to 174 centimeters. The age in both groups ranged from eighteen to twenty-five years. These subjects were serving as soldiers at the Army Headquarters of the city of Puno (3,840 meters). They were under the same training program and their length of service in the Army ranged from 0.9 to 1.9 years. Their nutritional and health status was good, as judged by both the anthropometric measurements and the reports of the medical officers. They all were of blood type 0 and Rh+.

Measurements

Following the same procedure as in a previous study (Frisancho and Baker 1970), standard anthropometric measurements were obtained from all subjects. These included measurements of height, weight, chest circumference at maximum inspiration and maximum expiration, skinfold thickness at the upper arm, chest juxtanipple, chest midaxillary, and subscapula. The difference between chest circumference at maximum inspiration and maximum expiration was used as an index of thoracic elasticity (TE). In addition, employing standard techniques, peripheral values of hemoglobin, hematocrit, and red blood cells were obtained (Wintrobe 1972), as well as measurements of forced vital capacity and residual lung volume (Frisancho, Velasquez, and Sanchez 1973). From these measurements the: (1) mean hemoglobin concentration in red blood cells

$$\text{M Hb C} = \frac{\text{Hemoglobin in gm/100 ml}}{\text{Red Blood Cells in Millions/cu mm}} \times 10$$

and (2) the Percent Residual Volume as:

$$\text{PRV} = \frac{\text{Residual Volume (RV) in ml}}{\text{Total Lung Capacity (TLC) in ml}} \times 100$$

were calculated.

Direct measurements of work capacity were carried out in the physiology laboratory of the Instituto de Biología Andina, located at 3,840 meters above sea level ($P_B = 486$ mm Hg, $P_{O_2} = 101$ mm Hg) in the city of Puno, Peru. The experimental procedures were the same as those indicated in our previous investigation (Frisancho, et al. 1973). They consisted of two replicate work capacity tests conducted with the Monark bicycle ergometer, on which work load was changed by altering the calibrated frictional resistance of the pedal. The frictional resistance of the pedal is measured in kilopond meters per minute (kpm/min). The test was designed to exhaust a man within twelve minutes. The pedaling frequency was maintained at about sixty revolutions per minute (rpm) with the aid of a metronome. During the first five minutes, or until the heart rate reached 180 beats per minute, the resistance of the bicycle pedal was maintained at a moderate work load of 2-3 kp or 720-1,080 kpm/min. After the heart rate passed over 180 beats per minute, the resistance of the pedal was increased gradually by 0.5 kp (180 kpm) every minute thereafter until the subject could not continue (Buskirk, et al. 1967; Kollias, et al. 1968). Subjects were encouraged to continue as long and as forcefully as possible. Oxygen intake and corresponding ventilation and heart rate data obtained during these two tests were recorded as the maximal oxygen intake, maximal ventilation, and maximal heart rate.

Each subject breathed monitored room air through a low-resistance Collins triple-J valve and a short length of large-bore and low-resistance tubing. Expired air was collected in Douglas bags each minute period after the heart rate reached over 180 beats per minute, until exhaustion. A Scholander micrometer gas analyzer was used to examine gas samples for oxygen, carbon dioxide, and nitrogen concentration. The volume of expired air was determined with a Tissot gasometer. Temperature and pressure were recorded to correct gas volumes BTPS (body temperature, ambient pressure, saturated) and STPD (standard temperature and pressure, dry). Heart rate was measured by stethoscopic auscultation for fifteen- and thirty-second periods during each minute of work.

Each subject was tested twice. Work loads were the same in both tests. The intertest correlation for maximal oxygen intake in all four groups was greater than 0.95 and in maximal ventilation varied from 0.75 to 0.85, and from 0.90 to 0.95 in maximal heart rate. Maximal values for oxygen intake, ventilation, and heart rate were reached either in the penultimate or final minute of work.

RESULTS AND DISCUSSION

Table 1 shows the mean and standard deviation of the anthropometric characteristics of the two groups. These data indicate that the tall and short samples had the same proportion of subcutaneous fat. Further, the lung volumes (FVC, RV, and TLC) expressed as milliliters per centimeter (ml/cm) of height are similar in the short and tall subjects. In the same manner, the peripheral values for hematocrit, hemoglobin, and red blood cells appear to be similar in both short and tall groups.

Table 1. Physical characteristics of high-altitude Quechua natives tested at 3840 meters in southern Peru

	Body size group					
	Small			Large		
	N	Mean	S.D.	N	Mean	S.D.
Age (years)	22	21.3	2.4	18	20.2	1.6
Height (cm)	22	156.7	2.9	18	166.8	2.3
Weight (kg)	22	59.5	3.8	18	66.2	4.3
Chest Circumference						
Maximum Inspiration (cm)	22	93.7	3.0	18	97.5	4.0
Maximum Expiration (cm)	22	84.6	2.8	18	87.7	3.2
Fat-Free Weight (kg)	22	51.2	2.8	18	56.7	3.1
Percent of Fat (%)	22	13.8	2.1	18	14.2	2.5
Forced Vital Capacity (ml/ht)	22	29.6	2.3	18	30.1	2.9
Residual Volume (ml/ht)	21	9.5	2.0	15	10.4	2.0
Total Lung Capacity (ml/ht)	21	39.0	3.8	15	40.7	3.3
Hematocrit (%)	22	52.0	1.9	18	50.4	3.5
Hemoglobin (gm/100 cc)	22	17.7	1.3	18	17.6	1.2
Red Blood Cells (million/mm³)	22	5.7	.6	18	5.7	.6
Hemaglobin Concentration						
(Hb × 10/RBC)	22	31.0	2.5	18	30.7	2.3

Table 2 presents the minute-by-minute data derived during maximal work. As illustrated in Figure 1, during each minute of maximal work (nine to twelve minutes), the short subjects attained a significantly ($p < 0.05$; $p < 0.01$) greater oxygen intake (ml/kg/min) than their tall counterparts in both the first and second test. However, the ventilation rate ($\dot{V}_E$max) and maximal workload in the short subjects were comparable to those attained by the tall natives. Similarly, the ventilation equivalent ($\dot{V}_E$) and maximal heart rate did not show any significant difference between the short and tall groups (not shown here).

The increased maximal oxygen intake (ml/kg/min) associated with short stature of the high-altitude natives differs from that reported for sea-level subjects. Studies at sea level indicate that the $\dot{V}o_{2max}$ (lit/min) is directly proportional to body size so that large and small individuals

Table 2. Physiological data of high-altitude Quechua natives during maximal work on a bicycle ergometer tested at 3840 meters of altitude in southern Peru (Short: n = 22, Tall: n = 18)

Group-Variable	8–9 min		9–10 min		10–11 min		11–12 min	
	Mean	S.D.	Mean	S.D.	Mean	S.D.	Mean	S.D.
First test								
Short — $\dot{V}_E$ max (lit/min)	101.7	13.6	121.3	16.9	123.8	19.9	133.7	18.8
Tall — $\dot{V}_E$ max (lit/min)	107.9	19.0	131.0	23.6	130.1	22.1	142.4	26.8
F	1.41		2.23		0.90		1.41	
Short — $\dot{V}_{O_2}$ max (ml/kg/min)	41.7	5.0	46.3	4.4	46.6	4.5	48.8	6.4
Tall — $\dot{V}_{O_2}$ max (ml/kg/min)	38.6	5.7	43.2	5.0	43.2	4.7	44.1	4.1
F	3.34		4.33[a]		5.46[b]		7.65[b]	
Short — Workload (kpm/min)	1092.2	175.1	1134.0	155.6	1182.6	146.9	1186.2	145.2
Tall — Workload (kpm/min)	1092.6	124.3	1108.0	140.1	1124.6	155.2	1124.6	175.8
F	0.01		0.31		1.47		1.46	
Second test								
Short — $\dot{V}_E$ max (lit/min)	106.8	10.7	123.7	15.5	130.1	14.6	142.0	18.3
Tall — $\dot{V}_E$ max (lit/min)	111.9	20.0	130.8	23.3	134.5	23.9	143.5	26.2
F	1.01		1.29		0.49		0.04	
Short — $\dot{V}_{O_2}$ max (ml/kg/min)	43.3	5.3	46.2	5.2	47.2	4.2	49.8	7.9
Tall — $\dot{V}_{O_2}$ max (ml/kg/min)	40.7	7.7	43.0	2.4	44.0	4.3	45.4	3.6
F	2.23		5.31[b]		5.67[b]		5.14[b]	
Short — Workload (kpm/min)	1157	116	1173	111	1196	121	1195	121
Tall — Workload (kpm/min)	1147	105	1156	106	1183	135	1189	149
F	0.09		0.26		0.09		0.03	

[a] Significant at 0.05 level
[b] Significant at 0.01 level

attain the same oxygen intake per kilogram of body weight (Wyndham, et al. 1963). In an attempt to test the extent to which variations in body size are reflected in variation in $\dot{V}_{O_{2max}}$ at sea level, we have analyzed the individual data of Von Dobeln (1956). We selected this study because it includes a large sample of young subjects (college students) and the $\dot{V}_{O_{2max}}$ was measured on a bicycle ergometer. Of the thirty-five male

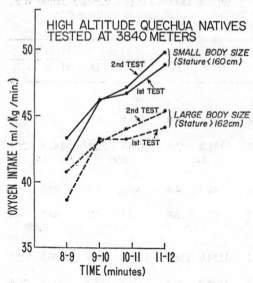

Figure 1. Increased aerobic capacity associated with small body size among high-altitude Quechua natives

subjects, we selected eleven short subjects (stature: 167-175 cm) and fifteen tall subjects (stature: 177-188 cm) who were under thirty years of age.

Analyses of those results indicated that the short subjects attained a $\dot{V}o_{2max}$ of 57 ml/kg/min which was not significantly different from the mean values attained by their tall counterparts (56 ml/kg/min). Comparing the $\dot{V}o_{2max}$ in terms of fat-free weight, the short and tall subjects attained a mean $\dot{V}o_{2max}$ of 62 ml/kg/min. Thus, it would appear that among young sea-level subjects, variations in body size are not reflected in concomitant differences in maximum O_2 intake per kilogram of body weight.

In order to study the role of hemoglobin concentration $\dfrac{Hb}{RBC} \times 10$ on the attainment of aerobic capacity, we have separated the whole sample into either (1) high hemoglobin concentration, or (2) low hemoglobin concentration groups, depending upon whether the hemoglobin concentration was greater than or less than the mean hemoglobin concentration (30.9 ± 2.4). In the same manner, the subjects were separated into either (1) high residual lung volume, or (2) low residual lung volume groups, depending upon whether their residual lung volume was greater than or less than the mean residual lung volume (1585.1 ± 338.4). These groupings, through a one-way analysis of covariance, were tested for differences in maximum oxygen intake.

As shown by the analyses of covariance presented in Table 3, the subjects characterized by high hemoglobin concentration and high residual lung volume attained significantly ($p < 0.05$; $p < 0.07$) greater aerobic capacity (ml/kg/min) than their counterparts of low hemoglobin concentration and low residual lung volume.

Table 3. Covariance adjustment of $\dot{V}O_2$ max among high-altitude Quechua natives tested at 3840 meters in southern Peru

| | | $\dot{V}O_2$ max (ml/kg/min) | | | |
| | | Original | | Adjusted for age and height | |
	N	Mean	S.E.	Mean	S.E.
High hemoglobin concentration	21	52.61	4.60	52.60	0.96
Low hemoglobin concentration	15	49.50	4.98	48.51	1.14
F-test			1.91	4.31	$p < 0.05$
High residual lung volume	16	52.84	4.81	52.88	1.12
Low residual lung volume	20	50.10	4.82	48.82	1.33
F-test			1.89	3.32	$p < 0.07$

In order to test the possibility of predicting the $\dot{V}O_{2max}$ (ml/kg/min) from the physiological and anthropometric measurements, the data of the Peruvian subjects were analyzed by stepwise multiple regression techniques. The results indicate that $\dot{V}O_{2max}$ (ml/kg/min) is negatively related to body height (Ht), positively related to mean hemoglobin concentration (HbC), thoraxic elasticity (TE), and Percent of Residual Lung Volume (PRV). The multiple correlation coefficient equalled $r = 0.61$ and the multiple regression equation was:

$$\dot{V}O_{2max} \text{ (ml/kg/min)} = 93.76 - 0.44 \text{ (Ht)} + 0.49 \text{ (HbC)} + 0.38 \text{ (TE)} + 0.35 \text{ (PRV)}$$

$N = 36$; S.E. $= 4.12$.

Davis, et al. (1973) recently pointed out that among sea-level samples the $\dot{V}O_{2max}$ is positively related to leg volume. Since we have no measurements of leg volume, it is difficult to ascertain whether the enhanced $\dot{V}O_{2max}$ of the short Peruvian subjects is related to a greater leg muscle. In any event, and inasmuch as the $\dot{V}O_{2max}$ is considered to measure both the capacity of the working muscles to utilize ozygen and the ability of the cardiovascular system in transporting and delivering oxygen to the tissue cells, the findings in the present study would suggest that small subjects at high altitude have an enhanced functional adaptation. According to Thomas (1972), high-altitude Quechua natives of small body size under submaximal work have a significantly lower oxygen intake than those of large body size. Thus, it would appear that among high-altitude natives, small body size may be adaptive under maximal and submaximal work. The extent to which these findings are applicable to sea-level subjects acclimatized to high altitude cannot be determined at present.

In view of the importance of hemoglobin (Reynafarje et al. 1964) and lung function (Frisancho, et al. 1973) in the process of adaptation to high altitude, it is not surprising that the attainment of $\dot{V}o_{2max}$ is related in multiple fashion to mean hemoglobin concentration, and to enlarged residual lung volume.

SUMMARY AND CONCLUSIONS

The physiological responses of forty high-altitude young adult Quechua natives were measured during maximal exercise on a bicycle ergometer in Puno, situated at 3,840 meters above sea level in southern Peru. The result of this study indicated:

1.   The level of functional adaptation at high altitude, as measured by the maximum oxygen intake per unit of body weight (ml/kg/min) in the short subjects is greater than that of the large subjects. The biological mechanisms that result in an increased aerobic capacity associated with small body size await clarification through further investigation.

2.   The residual lung volume, thoracic elasticity, and mean hemoglobin concentration are positively related to the attainment of maximum oxygen intake. These results confirm the adaptive significance of the morphological and physiological characteristics of high-altitude natives.

REFERENCES

ASTRAND, P. O.
  1952   *Experimental studies of physical working capacity in relation to sex and age.* Copenhagen: Munksgaard.
BAKER, P. T.
  1969   Human adaptation to high altitude. *Science* 163:1149–1156.
BALKE, B.
  1964   "Work capacity and its limiting factors at high altitude," in *The physiological effects of high altitude.* Edited by W. H. Weihe. Oxford: Pergamon Press.

BUSKIRK, E. R., H. L. TAYLOR
1957 Maximum oxygen intake and its relation to body composition, with special reference to chronic physical activity and obesity. *Journal of Applied Physiology* 11:72–78.

BUSKIRK, E. R., J. KOLLIAS, R. F. AKERS, E. K. PROKOP, E. PICON-REATEGUI
1967 Maximal performance at altitude and on return from altitude in conditioned runners. *Journal of Applied Physiology* 23:259–266.

DAVIS, C T. M., D. MBELWA, G. CROKFORD, J. S. WEINER
1973 Exercise tolerance and body composition of male and female Africans aged 18–30 years. *Human Biology* 45:31–40.

DILL, D. B., L. G. MYHRE, D. K. BROWN, K. BURRUS, G. GEHLSEN
1967 Work capacity in chronic exposures to altitude. *Journal of Applied Physiology* 23:555–560.

DILL, D. B., L. G. MYHRE, E. E. PHILLIPS, JR., D. K. BROWN
1966 Work capacity in acute exposures to altitude. *Journal of Applied Physiology* 21:1168–1176.

ELSNER, R. W., A. BOLSTAD, C. FORNO
1964 "Maximum oxygen consumption of Peruvian Indians native to high altitude," in *The physiological effects of high altitude*. Edited by W. H. Weihe. Oxford: Pergamon Press.

FRISANCHO, A. R., P. T. BAKER
1970 Altitude and growth: a study of the patterns of physical growth of a high altitude Peruvian Quechua population. *American Journal of Physical Anthropology* 32:279–292.

FRISANCHO, A. R., C. MARTINEZ, T. VELASQUEZ, J. SANCHEZ, H. MONTOYE
1973 Influence of developmental adaptation on aerobic capacity at high altitude. *Journal of Applied Physiology* 34:176–180.

FRISANCHO, A. R., T. VELASQUEZ, J. SANCHEZ
1973 Influences of developmental adaptation on lung function at high altitude. *Human Biology* 45:583–594.

KOLLIAS, J., E. R. BUSKIRK, R. F. AKERS, E. K. PROKOP, P. T. BAKER, E. PICON-REATEGUI
1968 Work capacity of long-time residents and newcomers to altitude. *Journal of Applied Physiology* 24:792–799.

MC ARDLE, W. D., J. R. MAGEL
1970 Physical work capacity and maximal maximum oxygen uptake in treadmill and bicycle exercise. *Medical Science Sports* 2:118–123.

MAZESS, R. G.
1969 Exercise performance at high altitude (4000 meters) in Peru. *Federation Proceedings* 28:1301–1306.

REYNAFARJE, C., J. RAMOS, J. FAURA, D. VILLAVICENCIO
1964 Humoral control of erythropoietic activity in man during and after altitude exposure. *Proceedings of the Society for Experimental Biology and Medicine* 116:649.

THOMAS, R. B.
1972 "Human adaptation to a high Andean energy flow system." Unpublished doctoral dissertation, Pennsylvania State University.

VELASQUEZ, T. M.
1964 "Response to physical activity during adaptation to altitude," in *The physiological effects of high altitude*. Edited by W. H. Weihe. Oxford: Pergamon Press.

VON DOBELN, W.
1956 Human standard and maximal metabolic rate in relation to fat-free body mass. *Acta Physiologica Scandinavia* 37:1–79.

WILMORE, J. H.
1969 Maximal oxygen intake and its relationship to endurance capacity on a bicycle ergometer. *Respiration Quarterly* 40:203–210.

WINTROBE, M. M.
1972 *Clinical hematology*. Philadelphia: Lea and Febiger.

WYNDHAM, C. H., N. B. STRYDOM, J. F. MORRISON, C. G. WILLIAMS, G. BREDELL, J. PETER, H. M. COOKE, A. JOFFE
1963 The influence of gross body weight on oxygen consumption and on physical working capacity of manual laborers. *Ergonomics* 6:275–286.

Biological Adaptations of Prehistoric South Asian Populations to Different and Changing Ecological Settings

KENNETH A.R. KENNEDY

Important to a study of biosocial interrelations of ancient human populations are investigations of extinct ecological settings, prehistoric cultures, and the skeletal record by paleoecologists and paleodemographers. Population densities, rates of fertility and mortality, morbidity factors, and related aspects of health, nutrition, and energy levels are all aspects of a biosocial profile which have been defined already for some earlier populations from Europe, Western Asia, and North America. These projects have been undertaken only recently in the South Asian countries of Afghanistan, Pakistan, India, Bangladesh, Sri Lanka (Ceylon), and the Himalayan principalities of Nepal, Sikkim, and Bhutan. Tibet and Burma will be treated here as border regions of Central Asia and Southeast Asia respectively. Geological and archeological studies were initiated over a century ago in the subcontinent, and contributions to our knowledge of the prehistory of man in this part of the world have been significant. However, the history of paleontological discoveries of Pleistocene hominids in South Asia is a less impressive story. This paper discusses some aspects of our present knowledge about the biosocial interrelations of earlier human populations with particular attention to (1) the nature of the hominid skeletal record presently available from sites in South Asia, (2) some possible explanations which may account for the low rate of recovery of fossil hominids in this part of the world, given the higher measures of success attained in regions beyond the Himalayas, (3) an outline of major paleoecological changes during the South Asian Pleistocene and post-Pleistocene periods, (4) a comparative summary of paleodemographic situations studied in ancient sites in Africa, Europe and Western Asia, and (5) an analysis of paleodemographic circumstances which may be peculiar to South Asia itself. These issues are relevant to investigations into adaptive ways of life of prehistoric populations in South Asia and in particular to the success of ongoing efforts of paleontologists to recover the skeletal record of Pleistocene man.

THE HOMINID SKELETAL RECORD FROM SOUTH ASIA

The most ancient trace of hominid occupation in South Asia is attributed to *Ramapithecus punjabicus*. Teeth and gnathic fragments have been recovered from several Miocene–Pliocene deposits in the Siwalik Hills of northern India and Pakistan. Although recognized as a hominid by Simons (1964a), other students question this claim (Yulish 1970). *Gigantopithecus indicus* is represented by a mandible found by Simons (1969) and his Indian colleagues in a Middle Pliocene savanna-type faunal deposit in the Siwaliks. The species *blacki* of the same genus had been known earlier from dental evidence found in Chinese pharmacies and from two mandibles from a cave in Kwangsi Province. There is general agreement among paleontologists that *Gigantopithecus* is a fossil pongid which may have been a contemporary of early hominids. Artifacts are not present in the deposits with which either of these hominids is associated. No fossil or lithic record has been found to indicate the distribution of australopithecines into South Asia.

The period from the time of the *Ramapithecus* settlement in the Siwaliks to the date assigned to a probable Neanderthal skeleton from eastern Afghanistan represents a temporal hiatus of some eleven million years in the South Asia fossil record. However, evidence of hominid settlement of the subcontinent during a Middle Pleistocene climatic phase of some 270,000 years ago is well established by the archeological presence of crude chopper–type tools made of large flakes. These have been given the label of Pre–Soan artifacts. Such tools have been associated with the Boulder Conglomerate deposits which mark the Second Glacial of the Middle Pleistocene sequences of the Himalayan foothills. Their affinity to the Early Soan and Abbeville–Acheulian or Chelles–Acheul industries which became dominant during the Second Interglacial stage is by no means well established. Apparently, a chopper–chopping tool (Soan) tradition and a hand-axe-cleaver (Acheulian) tradition existed side by side in some parts of India throughout the archeological period of the Indian Early Stone

Age (Lower and Middle Paleolithic). The subsequent archeological period is called the Indian Middle Stone Age (Upper Paleolithic) and it is recognized by a technological shift to smaller tools, namely burins, borers, awls, and scrapers. These appear in Upper Pleistocene geological contexts. Although blade tools are rare in peninsular India, Levalloisian techniques were practiced in South Asia. Also certain features of the Eurasian Mousterian tradition are recognizable. It is in association with a Mousterian site at Darra–I–Kur in eastern Afghanistan that a Pleistocene fossil hominid has been discovered.

Prehistoric research in Afghanistan between 1959 and 1966, under the direction of Dupree (1972), led to the finding of a broken right temporal bone at Darra–I–Kur. This bone was found in a cultural deposit dated to 30,000 ±1900 to 1200 years B.P., as determined by radiometric assay. The bone was carefully described in Dupree's report by J. Lawrence Angel who concluded, after a comprehensive comparison of the temporal bone with skulls from series of Neanderthals and modern–type men, that the Darra–I–Kur temporal would fit into a partly Neanderthal population, such as Skhul in Israel, as well as into a modern population. The bone's most unusual feature is a very massive vascular foramen on the medial wall of the pyramid where the large cavern of the internal acoustic meatus has almost three times the size of a normal cross–sectional area: 160.6 millimeters as compared to 62.5 millimeters using πr^2. It is tempting to suggest, as Angel has done with caution, that the increased size of the vascular foramen may have a connection with the slight vascular hypertrophy which is an adaption to high altitudes. Darra–I–Kur is situated in the foothills of the Hindu Kush.

From Indian Late Stone Age (Mesolithic) industries the paleodemographer is rewarded with a number of individual specimens and small skeletal series. Tools of this archeological complex are microlithic, and they occur in deposits dated from the terminal part of the Pleistocene to the historic period. Indeed, in some parts of India, Late Stone Age stone-chipping methods using bottle glass were practiced by tribal groups as late as the eighteenth century A.D. At Sarai–Nahar–Rai near Allahabad in north-central India, a subfossil human burial complex was found three years ago. Bone samples from the deposit have been dated by radiocarbon methods to 10,345 ±110 years B.P. The associated cultural remains consisted of microliths and crude pottery, all assignable to the Late Stone Age. The geological evidence has been interpreted to indicate a dry post–Pleistocene climatic phase. The complete skull of one male adult specimen has been described in a brief report which appeared in *Nature* (Dutta 1971). In all anatomical features this specimen falls within the normal range for *Homo sapiens*. A third series of human skeletal specimens of some antiquity are from the Late Stone Age site of Bellanbandi Palassa in Sri Lanka. At the time of the description of these specimens several years ago, dating was based upon samples of charcoal provided from the upper levels of the open–air site (Kennedy 1965). The occupation was assumed to date to the second century B.C. Recently Wintle and Oakley (1972) published the results of their thermoluminescent dating of fired rock crystal directly buried in the matrix of one of the skeletons. A date of 6500 ±700 years B.P. was obtained.

At present these are the most ancient specimens of prehistoric man known from South Asia. With the exception of the "Neanderthal" fragment from Darra–I–Kur, all of these skeletons are of post–Pleistocene date. Individual specimens and cemetery series from archeological deposits of more recent Late Stone Age date, as well as from Neolithic, Chalcolithic, Harappan (Indus Valley Civilization or Bronze Age), and Iron Age sites, have been anthropometrically described (Ayer 1960; Ehrhardt and Kennedy 1965; Guha and Basu 1938; Gupta, Dutta, and Basu 1962; Kennedy and Malhotra 1966; Rao and Malhotra 1965; Sarkar 1960). The paleodemographic significance of some of these series has been discussed elsewhere (Kennedy 1969, 1972a, 1973b). However, analysis of these later prehistoric series lies outside the scope of this paper. It is the problem of continued failure to recover human skeletal remains from Middle and Upper Pleistocene contexts that is examined here. Traditional explanations to account for this hiatus in our record of fossil man are not satisfying.

QUALIFYING FACTORS IN PALEONTOLOGICAL RESEARCH

Failure to recover the skeletal remains of early man in South Asia cannot be blamed on the presence of any peculiar conditions causing deterioration of bone in geological deposits. A kind of Eastern fatalism is sometimes implicit in the claim that inevitable destruction lies in store for organic materials buried in the Indian soil whose dissolving capabilities are deemed remarkable. Obvious to paleontologists working in South Asia is the fact that the bones of extinct organisms, both large and small, have accumulated into what is a very extensive paleontological record in the subcontinent. This notion that human bone is especially vulnerable to deterioration in the ground may have its origin in the excavation of Iron Age megalithic tombs in peninsular India where local conditions of preservation are poor and human skeletons do literally turn to dust when disturbed by the archeologist's spade.

Nor can one accept the old saw that searching has not been extensive enough to uncover the remains of ancient man in South Asia. But it is certain that many exploratory efforts have been carried out in unsuitable places. Any suggestion that early man's habitation of the subcontinent was marginal can be refuted immediately with reference to the abundant archeological evidence from almost all regions and covering a time span of hundreds of millennia. Rather the explanations would appear to rest elsewhere, and some attention to the following considerations may enhance future efforts to add South Asian hominid material to the picture of man's evolution which is still best known from discoveries made beyond the Himalayas.

First of all, many early man sites which have been reported in India since 1863, when Robert Bruce Foote collected a handaxe near Madras, are no longer recognizable. Excessive collecting of surface finds and a dearth of records about exact localities of find sites has meant that many rich loci of prehistoric human activity are lost to us forever. One primary factory site which has been carefully excavated is Chirki on the Pravara River (Corvinus 1970). Another is Adamgarh Hill in the Narbada River area which has yielded a sequence of Early Stone Age to Middle Stone Age tool assemblages (Joshi 1966). But the tens of thousands of stone tools which are preserved in museum collections in South Asia and abroad are seldom documented as to their provenance. If bones from the manufacturers of these paleoliths were deposited near these collecting areas, traces of their burial remain unknown to us.

A second reason for the lack of specimens may be that incorrect assumptions have been made as to the best places to look for the bones of Pleistocene man. What was so innovative about the work carried out by the late Theodore D. McCown and his colleague, George Shkurkin, was that the search for new sites was conducted along the tops and sides of the more ancient terraces cut by the river. The paleolithic stone tools which occur in the lower beds have been washed there from above and do not represent true samples of integrated and specific industries. Collecting along the earlier–formed terraces produced some pristine assemblages where the degree of disturbance to the deposit had been less severe. Here is the type of situation where undisturbed skeletal remains of ancient man are likely to be encountered.

The successful cave research that has characterized prehistoric investigations in Europe does not have a parallel in South Asia. Limestone caves are few in India, and those which have been explored do not contain the bony remains of Pleistocene man, save for Darra–I–Kur. Since the 1880's when Foote (1884) began excavations of the magnificent caverns of Billa Surgam in Kurnool District in southern India, teams of archeologists have paid visits to the caves, transporting tons of earth from the interiors to the outside (Khatri 1963). But continued digging has revealed that the earliest occupancy of the caves dates to Neolithic times. We visited Billa Surgam and other caves in the vicinity during a field trip last year when we had the opportunity to observe excavation in progress by a team of archeologists from Deccan College, Poona. Neither my coworker, Güdrun Corvinus, who is a geologist, nor I encountered a single piece of evidence at these caves to convince us that they had been occupied by man before the time when agriculture and herding were introduced into this part of India around 2000 B.C. Neolithic–type pottery of wheel–made pattern is present in the deeper parts of one of the caves we investigated. Yet there is a persistent bias that the Kurnool caves must have been the abode of hominids of much greater antiquity, a bias born perhaps of the awareness that natural shelters of this sort were the favored habitations of prehistoric men of Europe during the Würm and into early post–Pleistocene times. In South Asia, rock shelters and cliff ledges with overhangs occur more frequently than do limestone caves. These, too, were neglected as habitation sites by Pleistocene hominids, but the post–Pleistocene people practicing the microlithic technology associated with Late Stone Age industries did occupy these rock shelters, especially those in central and southern India. Paintings of animals and anthropomorphic figures often appear on the surface rock of these shelters, and their floors may contain burials.

Related to this matter of looking for the osteological evidence of early man in inappropriate places is the continuing practice of turning to those remote hill and jungle areas still occupied by hunting–gathering tribal populations as promising places to find the remains of their ancient ancestors. Surely with these aboriginal groups must lie the solution to knowing more about the earliest hunters and gatherers of the subcontinent! Our own visits to these relict hilly tracts has led us to conclude that it was not until relatively recent times that many of these jungle areas were settled by man, an opinion earlier expressed by Subbarao (1958). The ancestors of living tribal peoples occupied the lowland plains which were once rich in game and various edible vegetable products, but with the pressure from agricultural communities moving into their fertile areas, the hunters and gatherers of the aboriginal populations migrated to marginal and less desirable forested regions in the hills. Archeological evidence indicates an abundance of lithic industries in the river valleys now inhabited by the agricultural communities, but there is very little if any prehistoric artifact material to be found in regions occupied by most of the marginal tribal groups.

Another facet of this problem is the sad fact that in those few cases where the actual skeletal vestiges of fossil man have been discovered in this part of the world, the bones have not always been recognized. The result has been the loss of valuable specimens both at the places of their discovery and subsequently in museums in South Asia and Europe. It is quite probable that Upper Pleistocene hominid skulls were found at Gorakhpur during the middle of the last century. In the 1830's human bones in a Pleistocene geological context appear to have been encountered along the banks of the Ganges, for the published records describing the deposits in which the bones were found indicate these circumstances. Similar tragedies are associated with provocative discoveries at other places, and the most notable cases are described in the literature (Rajaguru and Kennedy 1964, Kennedy 1972b).

PALEOECOLOGY OF THE SOUTH ASIAN PLEISTOCENE PERIOD

Paleobotanical and paleozoological studies have demonstrated that there was a gradual cooling of warm climates that had prevailed since the close of the Permocarboniferous Ice Age. Eocene isotherms of the temperate zone were displaced poleward by some fifteen to twenty degrees of latitude, and this reduction of temperature gradient, coupled with a lower geographical relief in the Paleogene, appears to be related to broad zones of aridity in middle latitudes. Equatorial temperatures were not significantly higher at this time, however. A series of brief but severe cold phases began during the latter part of the Pliocene. The successions of final major cold–climate complexes were associated with the accumulation of continental glacial masses and ice build-up in higher altitudes due to a general decline of world temperatures. Also related to these climatic phenomena were fluctuations of sea level by some 100 to 150 meters and significant faunal changes. Stratigraphic sequences of Pleistocene events have been determined for some nine major geographical regions of the world of which two — the Indo–Pakistan side of the Himalayas and the Irrawaddy Valley of Burma — are relevant to paleoecological problems under consideration here.

The geological and archeological surveys of the Yale–Cambridge expedition to northern India in 1935 have come to assume the status of a model for Pleistocene glacial and tectonic events applicable to both northern India and the peninsular reaches of the subcontinent. More correctly however, the efforts of DeTerra and Paterson (1939) to correlate geological and archeological data with Himalayan sequences do not have obvious implications toward an understanding of ecological settings and artifact sequences beyond the borders of their very specific regions of study. Their desire to correlate river terraces of the Narbada with glacial advances and recessions in the North, a project carried out in the limited scope of a fortnight and only within a narrow extent of the Narbada, was not completely satisfied. Subsequent attempts by other workers to correlate Pleistocene events in peninsular India with Himalayan glacial events have been equally frustrating both geologically and because of the problems presented by the archeological data (Movius 1944, 1949, 1969).

Overlooked in these exercises in geological–archeological correlation are two factors which have emerged from more recent research. First, the profound changes brought about by cold–climate conditions in one sector of the Himalayas are not always associated in any obvious way with situations existing in immediately adjacent areas. The presence of glacial ice in one valley does not mean that other valleys of the vicinity were choked with ice, nor could a geologist easily make the orogenic patterns coincide by simply investigating different parts of the mountain chain. The attempts to relate particular strata in northern India or the peninsula to specific glacial sequences from more remote areas, such as the Alpine or North American glaciations, have been even less satisfactory. Second, the ancient ecological picture for peninsular India can be interpreted most directly from a very different set of conditions than those related to Himalayan ice, namely the influence of the monsoonal rain cycles. Since the Pliocene, rain–bearing winds of the Indian Ocean monsoon belt have contributed the greatest precipitation along the Western Ghats and in Assam. Periodic shifts of wind direction because of low pressure areas in central India and Gujarat contribute heavy rainfall to these areas from time to time. Given the continuation of these monsoonal conditions throughout the Pliocene and the Pleistocene to the present day, attempts to relate wet and dry climatic phases in the peninsula to glacial events in the north assume no real foundation. Nor can wet cycles be regarded as analogous or related to African pluvial periods, a climatic theory of great complexity and one which has been by no means well established for that continent. Where glacial events did affect peninsular Indian climate the consequences were indirect. Certainly the lowering of sea levels during the periods of glacial optima caused acceleration of water flow and a faster rate of downcutting in river valleys.

The climatic shifts to warmer temperatures which are geologically documented for post–Pleistocene deposits in Europe, Africa, and western Asia do not precisely coincide with the South Asian geological evidence either. It was to examine terminal Pleistocene and early Holocene ecologies in South Asia that Zeuner (1950) visited Gujarat and central India in 1949. He has described a number of dry–humid climatic cycles in the Sabarmati Valley and has explained the considerable amount of aeolian deposition throughout northwestern India and sub–Himalayan Pakistan as a consequence of an extension of an eastern arm of the Saharo–Arabian desert during the final phases of the Pleistocene (Zeuner 1963). The wind–borne sands extended as far south as the banks of the Godavari River in the Deccan Plateau of western India. To Zeuner this phenomenon represented a dry climatic period in the northwestern and Deccan Plateau portions of the subcontinent during a time when a final glacial advance was underway in the Himalayas. From other investigations it can be established that there were arid localities in Orissa during the final part of the Pleistocene. More recently Allchin and her colleagues (Allchin, Hegde, and Goudie 1972) have determined that the arid phase in Rajasthan and adjacent desert regions came to an end about 9000 years B.P. Thereafter, dunes became established in Rajasthan and climates prevailed, such as those present today in this part of India.

The tropical humid belt became established at its present limit by around 10,000 years B.P., but during the Pleistocene it had extended some eight to ten degrees further north. But apart from the changes to drier conditions in some areas of northern and central India, most of the subcontinent has remained within the tropical humid belt from Pliocene times to the present. The erosional damage that is observable in India today is the result of excessive pastoral and agricultural practices which began with the Neolithic economies in the second and third millennia B.C. The rain forests which exist today in Kerala and the Western Ghats, in upcountry Sri Lanka, and in Bengal and Assam were formerly more extensive. No single ecological zone has ever been typical of South Asia, and it is this regional complexity of snow–covered highlands, tropical rain forests, semiarid plains, waterless deserts, well–watered valley systems, and forested hill country which is so essential to bear in mind when searching for archeological evidence for the food resource base, settlement pattern, and population density of South Asia's prehistoric inhabitants.

PALEODEMOGRAPHIC STUDIES IN AFRICA, EUROPE, AND WESTERN ASIA

If we accept the findings of contemporary geological and archeological investigations that the South Asian subcontinent underwent some geological and climatic changes during and after the Pleistocene and that these changes are not directly correlated with others which took place beyond the Himalayas at the same time, then the question of distinctive paleodemographic patterns of South Asia arises. Were the adaptive aspects of subsistence base, settlement pattern, population density, and other elements of man's biosocial interrelations markedly similar or distinct from what the paleodemographer finds in the theater of prehistoric hominid activity in Africa, Europe, and western Asia? Furthermore, what bearing might these paleodemographic data concerning man in South Asia have upon expanding our knowledge of his evolution in this part of the world? Lastly, can the data help us formulate a new strategy in our search for man's skeletal remains?

Archeological data about economic areas and habitation centers are derived from the contents of caves and rock shelters, factory sites, open-air camps which may be recognized by surface finds, and pristine or redeposited and disturbed stratigraphic deposits. While caves may provide optimum conditions for preservation of bones and perishable artifactual materials, they are seldom ideal sources of stratigraphic information, save where the faunal criteria are good. Less well protected habitation areas are more vulnerable to erosional damage. Factory sites, which are the easiest to recognize, represent only the technological aspects of an extinct culture, and a highly specialized cultural element at that. Yet from study of the contents of such places the prehistorian has been able to draw in broad outline some important demographic facts which are critical to an understanding of earlier biosocial patterns.

During the Pleistocene, African hominids had adapted to life in grassy woodlands or in open savanna country where game was most abundant, avoiding the dense tropical rain forests and the high altitude regions of intense cold. Middle latitudes where drier conditions prevailed were marginal areas of settlement. But in Europe, hominids of the Middle Pleistocene had adapted to cold glacial conditions, although preferred habitation areas were in the loess grasslands. During the Pleistocene, open vegetation cover extended to the shores of the Mediterranean. The cold steppes of Asia were marginal areas of occupation. On both continents life was nomadic, selection of temporary campsites being determined by ready access to water, favorable circumstances for protection from predators and perhaps from hostile hominid bands as well, proximity to food resources, and, in the case of factory sites, availability of raw materials for tool manufacture. Transition to new and seasonal camps must have been easy, and these appear to have ranged from makeshift open–air shelters to caves and rock shelters whose entrances could be shielded by construction of overhanging branches and mats of grass. M.D. Leakey (1967) describes a circle of loosely piled lava blocks which were artificially arranged at Bed I at Olduvai. At Terra Amata, an Acheulian site at Nice, de Lumley (1967, 1969) reported the imprints of stakes driven into sand to form walls for shelters, lines of stone paralleling the stake imprints, and impressions of thick posts along the central axis of these structures. An arrangement of elephant bones and rocks is known from Ambrona (Howell 1966). J. Desmond Clark (1960) has described the crescent of stones at the Kalambo Falls site in Zambia. Caves did not predominate as habitation sites during most of the Pleistocene period in Africa and Europe, but toward the close of the glacial epoch they were in vogue in Europe and in western Asia. Hominid skeletal remains and artifacts are frequently encountered in caves, even when these did not serve as habitations. The Lower Pleistocene sites of Sterkfontein and Swartkrans afford good examples of this situation, for they appear to have been leopard lairs used over many millennia, as well as natural depositories for lithic material transported there by flood waters. To be sure, Sterkfontein and Swartkrans may have served as temporary refuges for australopithecines, as they did for other creatures contemporary with these hominids, but there is no good evidence to indicate that these caves were permanent habitation sites (Brain i.p.).

Butzer (1971: 407–408) estimates these primitive hunting settlements to have consisted of from four to twenty-four families composed of from twenty to one hundred individuals. Aggregates of twenty–five to fifty persons to a band would afford a population density of four to one hundred individuals per 1000 square kilometers, according to an estimate by Lee and DeVore (1968) based on studies of unspecialized hunting groups. They suggest that a stable long–term situation would be a hunting population established at 20 to 30 percent of the carrying capacity, an estimate that fits well with paleodemographic evidence from a number of archeological sites (Howell 1966; Howell and Clark 1963: 458–533). Issac's study (1968) of an Acheulian camp at Olorgesailie indicates the presence of a group of four to thirty adults with small splinter groups forming as the frequency of adults exceeds that rate within a given community. It seems obvious that Pleistocene hunters and gatherers survived in an ecological balance within their natural environments, affecting it in ways which were not essentially different from the activities wrought by the animals they hunted. Australopithecine and *Homo erectus* populations were not dominant members of their ecological communities in the sense of being able to displace and eliminate other large predators. By terminal Pleistocene times this way of life was undergoing profound changes in some areas of hominid habitation: the best evidence of this comes at the present time from archeological and paleodemographic studies in Europe and western Asia.

Some exploitations of the food resource base had already begun by Middle Pleistocene times through the development of more efficient hunting skills. This was a matter of superior technological control of toolmaking habits as well as a product of improved biosocial relationships within and beyond the limits of the hunting–gathering community. The development of the elaborate tool kit of the Mousterian hunters who were entering the "last frontier" of cold steppe and forest tundra marks this shift to the establishment of a broader food resource base, more efficient use of territory through gaining access to sources of raw material necessary to a more advanced technology, and a maximization of the potential of the community energy budget. Tailored clothing and well–built shelters enhanced the survival success of these hominids adapting to cold climate conditions. The low latitude Pleistocene tundras provided as favorable a foundation for subsistence as had the warmer grassland environments enjoyed by pre–Würm populations — and perhaps they were even more advantageous. One result of improved environmental control was an increase in population density, although community size may have remained stable under normal circumstances. It should be emphasized that the technological and biosocial advances relevant to this more efficient exploitation of the food resource base did not take place in the forested regions of the tropical belt. An "improvement" in climatic conditions to warmer, drier, or more stable phases does not appear to be a direct cause here, the Würm glaciation being essentially a continuation of that series of intense cold–climate oscillations that had prevailed in Eurasia for some half million years. Furthermore, these changes may be unrelated to the knowledge of the control of fire with which hominids in both Europe and the Far East had been familiar since the Middle Pleistocene. However, new uses of fire may have been discovered, such as the burning off of land to drive game to kill sites or to promote the growth of vegetation in regions where certain plant foods were collected. Such a practice would have had the effect of converting forests into grasslands.

Among specialized hunters, as Mousterian men certainly were, summer camps may have been temporary in the open tundra, but winter settlements were more permanent as protection from cold became more critical to survival during periods of glacial optima. Emiliani (1968) has written that the European summers during the glacial ages were even colder than the European winters of today, thus the Pleistocene winters of this part of the world must have been dreadful indeed! Submerged dwellings were built, and caves, formerly occupied sporadically, now became favored habitations. Mousterian Neanderthals of southwestern France occupied caves year round and did not practice the seasonal migratory customs of their kin living as nomads within the margins of the tundra. Traces of open–air camps are recognized at Salzgitter–Lebenstedt in northern Germany (Tode, et al. 1953) and at Molodona in the Soviet Union Southwest (Klein 1969). Settlement patterns became more complex during the period of the final phase of the Würm when the Mousterian traditions were replaced by the blade-tool industries of the Eurasian Upper Paleolithic. Regional variations of habitation practices occurred, both caves and open–air campsites with tents being occupied within a single locality and used either seasonally or permanently.

Population size of European and western Asian Upper Paleolithic communities may not have been larger than was the case for Mousterian bands (Vallois 1961: 214–235; Narr 1963), but Butzer (1971: 480–481) suggests that the density of settlements and the accumulation of faunal remains from kill sites may be interpreted to mean a larger overall population, one increasing by as much as a factor of ten in Europe between early and late Würm times. For contemporary groups of specialized hunters, 10 to 250 square kilometers per person is one estimate of population density which has been suggested (Butzer 1971: 407). This is based upon the assumption of shifting campsites rather than stable communities. Some regional variations of population density must have been present due to seasonal fluctuations of food supply and cultural shifts in food–procuring activity. However, the increase in population density does not appear to have effected any change in Mousterian mortality rates, according to Vallois (1961) who examined European and western Asian skeletons from terminal Pleistocene sites. He reports that less than 50 percent of some seventy–six Upper Paleolithic skeletons in his sample are those of individuals who lived to the age of twenty–one years, while only 12 percent passed age forty. Almost no females survived beyond their third decade.

By the end of the Pleistocene, man had settled into all habitable environments save for the high arctic barren wastes and the most arid deserts. Physiological adaptions to habitats well beyond the tropical regions of his origins were possible because of the successful buffering of selective pressures by a multiplicity of technological, social, and philosophical (ethical?) innovations that marked the beginnings of new ways of life in certain global regions. Excessive forest clearance, increasing domestication of captured animals, a great dependence in some areas upon vegetable products whose yield could be increased through cultivation of the soil, striking faunal changes resulting perhaps from overkill of megafaunas, and the invention of new craft skills, such as the making of pottery, are all aspects of the Mesolithic which adumbrated the food–producing subsistence pattern which followed. A "cultural landscape" with higher population densities and a greater degree of labor specialization to meet new technological and trading demands was rapidly replacing the more balanced ecological setting of earlier populations. According to Braidwood and Reed (1957), population densities of village farming communities reached 2500 persons per hundred square miles in southwestern Asia by around 5000 B.C. Their estimates of urban communities for this region and period are 5000 persons per square mile. Thus the paleodemographer passes from estimates of population densities of Pleistocene skeletal series assembled from a vast geographical region to estimates of "closed system" series, defined by Cook (1972: 37) as those in which there is some certainty that the skeletal remains studied are of individuals who

died in a specific locality which is being excavated, the so–called cemetery populations whose paleodemographic implications have been
studied to great advantage by Angel (1969), Cook (1972), and other
pioneers of paleodemography.

PALEODEMOGRAPHIC FEATURES SPECIFIC TO
SOUTH ASIA

South Asian data concerning prehistoric food resource bases, settlement patterns and population densities resemble the paleodemographic picture from Africa, Europe, and western Asia more nearly
for the Middle and early Upper Pleistocene periods than they do for
late Upper Pleistocene and Holocene. The manufacturers of the Acheulian and Soan tools in the subcontinent favored watered and grassland
areas as did their contemporaries beyond the Himalayas. As noted
above, much of the distribution of these Middle Pleistocene artifacts
lies today in arid portions of India due to severe erosional changes
wrought by man's pastoral and agricultural activities over the course
of the past four to five millennia, but before Neolithic times the region
from the Himalayan foothills to the tip of the peninsula was covered
with grasslands and jungle. Acheulian industries do not occur north
of the Caucasus, Elburz, and Hindu Kush and Himalayan mountains. Quite probably, the cold steppe country of the Iranian Plateau, the Ukraine, and central Asia was uncongenial to Acheulian
hominids in this period. The discovery of handaxes in upper Sind
and in the lower Indus Valley and the distribution of Mousterian flake
tools in northern Afghanistan – Middle Paleolithic industries well
known from the archeological record of western and central Asia —
has been interpreted by Fairservis (1971: 72) to mean that the northwestern portion of the subcontinent marked a transitional zone between Eurasian and South Asian Paleolithic industries. Here was
the main corridor of diffusion of certain cultural elements from these
western regions into the Indian landmass. Peninsular India was the ter-
minus in this diffusionary range.

   The Soan tradition in India is a western arm of the chopper–
chopping tool complex which prevailed in Southeast Asia and parts of
the Far East from Middle Pleistocene times until much later. Its distribution in the subcontinent is concentrated in the northern and eastern portions of the landmass, and it does not appear in as high a frequency in the far south as do Acheulian tools. Both traditions fade

with the onset of Middle Stone Age cultures by the close of the Pleistocene. After 10,000 years B.P., Late Stone Age industries predominate in most parts of South Asia and continue in some areas to Neolithic, Iron Age, and even into historic periods. Elements of Late Stone
Age traditions are not obvious among isolated tribal groups, save for
special practices like manufacturing microliths from bottle glass and
for particular elements of a hunting–gathering way of life which these
primitive groups still practice in remote areas. It would not be true,
however, to regard tribal populations in India and Sri Lanka as the
survivors of a prehistoric Late Stone Age tradition. The aboriginal population of Sri Lanka — the Veddas — have depended upon iron tools
which were procured from Sinhalese and Tamil neighbors by trade
for many centuries and they are unaware of any traditions of chipping
stone to make tools.

In South Asia the only direct sources of information about food
resource bases and settlement patterns for Early Stone Age hominids
are factory sites, stratified and often disturbed river gravels, and boulder spreads which may also bear signs of redistribution. Evidence
of regular occupation of caves is essentially absent, save for a few
notable cave settlements dating to later Pleistocene times when Middle Stone Age industries were replacing those of the Acheulian and
Soan traditions. The cave deposit of Darra–I–Kur has been mentioned above. Sanghao is a cave site in the region of the Northwest Frontier Province near Pakistan. It has ten feet of occupational levels
which are indicative of several periods of occupation by Middle Stone
Age people (Dani 1964). Both of these cave sites are much more
a part of a central Asian archeological context than they are typically
South Asian, representing a transitional zone with Mousterian cultures
to the west. The rock shelter at Adamgarh on the Narbada (Joshi
1966) and the Gudiyam cavern near Madras provide evidence of casual occupation by both Early and Middle Stone Age people, but indications of continuous or extended occupation are lacking in the archeological record. This striking absence of regular occupation of caves
by Early and Middle Stone Age communities in South Asia during those
periods of the Pleistocene when cave habitation was in vogue in Europe and western and central Asia goes far to suggest that a nomadic
life with the pitching of temporary camps in open regions of grassland along watercourses was the usual practice. Such open–air settlements are not well represented in the archeological annals of South
Asia. They are elusive particularly in the vicinity of large factory sites,
as at Chirki on the Pravara, although they must have existed close to

these ancient working areas. The essential absence of Early Stone Age sites in Sri Lanka may mean that the dense forest cover of the island was too inhospitable to Pleistocene hominids who had adapted to the open grasslands of the Indian mainland. The existence of a Middle Stone Age culture on the island is debated at the present time, although S. Deraniyagala and I have collected lithic material there which does not fit easily into present definitions of Late Stone Age technologies. Forested regions of the Western Ghats in Mysore and Kerala do not provide the archeologist with the wealth of artifactual materials gathered in other parts of India.

Cave and rock shelter occupation came into practice in South Asia at the time that Late Stone Age cultures were developing toward the very end of the Pleistocene. The Vindhyan sandstone formations of central India lent themselves to cavern and rock shelter formation, and these became the favored campsites, their walls often decorated by the hunters who painted the animals they sought, their ritual symbols, and representations of themselves. Many of these protected campsites served as cemeteries as well as shelters, and human skeletal remains are well preserved from the floors of the shelters of Baghai Khor, Lekhahia, and Mohana Pahar, all in central India (Misra 1965). Barapedi cave in Belgaum in the Western Ghats served as a factory site and as a living area. Hunter (1935, 1936) located human burials and habitation floors at caverns in the Mahadeo Hills near Nagpur. Caves in Sri Lanka have yielded Late Stone Age tools and evidence of continuous occupation, even into the time of the ethnographic present when the Sarasin cousins (1892–1893) and the Seligmans (1911) visited rock shelters in the eastern portion of the island which was then inhabited by tribal Veddas. But the preference for cave habitation was a regional phenomenon in South Asia, and impressive cave complexes, such as Billa Surgam, did not become regular habitations until Neolithic and later times. Even in regions where caves were available for shelter or were occupied only occasionally, the establishment of open–air camps might exist. In this part of the world these open camps assume a great variety of forms, if one can judge from a study of posthole and support structures which have survived. At Birbhanpur in West Bengal, postholes for hut construction have been observed by Lal (1958). The teri sites at the southern tip of the peninsula were camps sheltered by sand dunes (Zeuner and Allchin 1956). Headlands and islands as well as promotories overlooking the sea served as camps in the vicinity of Bombay (Todd 1939). Hillocks, coastal ridges, stream banks, and natural lakes remained favored open–air sites in many regions. Langhnaj in northern Gujarat is a Late Stone Age site established upon fossil sand dunes which became covered with a holding vegetation cover (Karve-Corvinus and Kennedy 1964; Sankalia 1946). Here and at the open–air sites of Bellanbandi Palassa (Deraniyagala 1971), Sarai Nahar Rai on the flood plain of the Ganges (Dutta 1971), and Bagor in Rajasthan (Misra et al. 1972) human skeletal material has been preserved in stratigraphic deposits.

Unlike the primitive hunters of the Indian Early Stone Age, men of the Middle and Late Stone Age traditions were specialized hunters whose subsistence base was as successful as that of the Mousterian and Upper Paleolithic peoples of Europe and Western Asia. The evidence of greater population density and continuity of occupation of certain territories is seen in the tremendous size of some of the Late Stone Age factory sites. The distribution of hunters into the cold–climate reaches of the Himalayan highlands and into the heavy evergreen forests of the peninsula had its beginning in this period. It is tempting to explain this trend towards transcendence of the selective pressures of the natural environment by looking to the influence of altering climatic conditions in the subcontinent following the retreat of the last glacial movement. Some scholars have made this kind of interpretation (Allchin and Allchin 1971; Zeuner 1963). Certainly evidence for the existence of climatic cycles of dry and humid phases is well documented from Langhnaj, Birbhanpur, Pushkar, and the teri sites. But the significance of these oscillations as critical causative factors in the determination of human behavior must be viewed with a certain degree of temperance. In theory the issue is not HOW did climatic changes affect post–Pleistocene man in South Asia but rather TO WHAT DEGREE did these shifts of dry–humid phases influence the resource food base, settlement pattern, population density, technology, etc. But, in fact, the real significance of these climatic factors remains unknown. At best we can conclude that climatic cycles were of regional influence and should be so considered by the interpreter of the archeological record. They varied in their timings, intensities, and spheres of influence in the subcontinent. Post–Pleistocene temperature changes in the Sabarmati Valley cannot account for human responses to analogous changes along the course of the Narbada. Far more important are the cultural changes that increased man's capacity to control more effectively his food resource base in South Asia and meet the stresses of this natural environment.

Late Stone Age societies continued in some parts of South Asia in symbiotic relationships with Neolithic communities. As these food-producing communities expanded into the fertile valley regions of the peninsula, the hunting–gathering people sought refuge in areas of isolation in the wooded hilly tracts. Some of their rock shelter habitations were taken over by the Neolithic communities. Prehistoric research among the descendants of these refugees has not been rewarding because their prehistoric record rests in regions from which they had been displaced. Even the large game still present in these jungle retreats does not have a long period of adaptation there, for earlier natural habitats were occupied by sedentary communities or by populations associated with these human groups.

Detailed studies of population densities of South Asian prehistoric populations remain to be carried out, although Fairservis (1967) has prepared estimates of urban populations for the Harappan centers. The richness of Neolithic, Chalcolithic, and Iron Age prehistoric materials in South Asia offer a challenge and a reward to the paleodemographer.

DISCUSSION AND CONCLUSIONS

Wherever Pleistocene hominids had adopted settlement patterns of permanent or temporary occupation of caves, the probability of the preservation of their artifactual and skeletal remains is enhanced. Cave habitations were of significant survival value to the Pleistocene inhabitants of Europe and western Asia during times of glacial optima, and prehistorians have been successful in collecting the cultural and biological remains of those communities who had adapted to the harsh cold-climate conditions. Of those settlements established in open areas, archeological and skeletal traces have been recognized, but conditions of favorable preservation are quite different under these circumstances than in cases of protected cave environments. Therefore it is not surprising that the fossil hominid record for Europe and western Asia is best represented for the periods of the Pleistocene when cave habitation was in vogue, particularly during the time of the Würm glaciation and continuing throughout much of early post–Pleistocene times.

In South Asia cave habitation was infrequent during the Pleistocene, except in the northwestern corner of the subcontinent which bordered on the western and central Asian Mousterian cultures and where cold–climate conditions prevailed as a part of the glacial activity of the Himalayan and Hindu Kush chains. Caves and rock shelters were occupied by post–Pleistocene communities of Late Stone Age hunters and gatherers, as of about 10,000 years B.P. From these protected habitation deposits a skeletal record of prehistoric man in South Asia has been assembled.

Archeological studies of Late Stone Age cultures have not yet been able to explain why caves and rock shelters were favored by post–Pleistocene communities in South Asia. But paleoecological investigations have demonstrated that the severe cold–climate conditions which rendered cave occupation so important to survival for men of Europe and western Asia during the Würm advance were not present in South Asia. Apart from local areas of the Himalayan chain, the subcontinent did not undergo radical climatic and faunal modifications during the Pleistocene. It is doubtful if cave settlement had ever been a critical factor in the survival of large numbers of hominid groups here. As noted above, Gujarat and adjacent regions were experiencing a dry climatic phase and the formation of desert conditons at the height of the final glacial advance in the Himalayas. It was possible for Pleistocene man in South Asia to continue to live in open–air camps and occupy caves only sporadically. Since the Pliocene, climatic conditions in peninsular India had been relatively stable, and the annual cycle of monsoonal rains had made a more significant mark on the resource food base, settlement pattern, and population density than had phases of Pleistocene glacial advances in the regions to the North.

For these reasons it seems probable that those ideal conditions of preservation of skeletal remains in protected cave and rock shelter environments which are encountered in habitation sites outside the subcontinent will be found less often in this region. The settlement patterns of Pleistocene hominids of South Asia were such that opportunities for eventual discovery of corporeal remains are likely to be in the exploration of natural rock fissures, in the vicinity of factory sites, and in stratified beds containing evidence of open–air habitation camps. This search for early man in South Asia continues and its importance to a fuller knowledge of human evolution is simply and engagingly expressed in 1949 by one of the early students of this quest, Helmut De Terra:

But India holds a key position for all future work, and the human paleontologist will one day have a field day here which will reveal vital facts without which the riddle of human ancestry cannot be solved. The equivalents to Java and Pekin Man remain to be found in the Narbada and adjoining alluvial tracts of Central India.

Table 1. Chronology of South Asian prehistoric cultural periods

Archeological Period	Baluchistan	Northern India	Deccan Plateau	Southern India	Sri Lanka
Historic	350 B.C.–	350 B.C.–	300 B.C.–	300 B.C.–	500 B.C.–
Iron Age	800–500	800–400	800–300	600 B.C.–100 A.D.	300
Bronze Age	(2,800)	2,500–1,700	/////	/////	/////
Chalcolithic	3,100–1,650	1,700–800	2,000–800	/////	/////
Neolithic	4,000–3,100	(3,000)	2,800–1,000	2,100–1,000 ?	
Late Stone Age (Mesolithic)	8,000–4,000	8,000–10,000	5,000–1,600	8,000–500	8,000 B.C.–100 A.D.
Middle Stone Age (Upper Paleolithic)	—	40,000–8,000	—	—	?
Early Stone Age (Lower & Middle Paleolithic)	—	?–40,000	—	—	?

Note: B.C. dates are given unless otherwise indicated
    (   ) = Range of period is unknown; focal date.
    ///// = Little or no evidence of culture of a specific period.
    ?   = Possible existence of culture of a specific period.

REFERENCES

ALLCHIN, B., R. ALLCHIN
   1971   *The birth of Indian civilization: India and Pakistan before 500 B.C.* Baltimore: Penguin Books.

ALLCHIN, B., K. T. M. HEGDE, A. GOUDIE
   1972   Prehistory and environmental changes in western India: a note on the Budha Pushkar Basin, Rajasthan. *Man: Journal of the Royal Anthropological Institute* 7:541–564.

ANGEL, J. L.
   1969   The basis of paleodemography. *American Journal of Physical Anthropology* 30:427–438.

AYER, A. A.
   1960   "Report on human skeletal remains excavated at Piklihal near Mudgal," in *Piklihal excavations.* Edited by R. Allchin, 143–154. Andhra Pradesh Government Archaeological Series 1.

BRAIDWOOD, R. J., C. A. REED
   1957   The achievement and early consequences of food-production: a consideration of the archaeological and natural-historical evidence. *Cold Spring Harbor Symposium on Quantitative Biology* 22:19–31.

BRAIN, C. K.
i.p.   The South African australopithecine bone accumulations. *Transvaal Museum Memoirs*.

BUTZER, K. W.
1971   *Environment and archaeology: an ecological approach to prehistory* (second edition). Chicago: Aldine.

CLARK, J. D.
1960   Human ecology during the Pleistocene and later times in Africa south of the Sahara. *Current Anthropology* 1:307–324.

COOK, S. F.
1972   *Prehistoric demography*. McCaleb module in anthropology. Reading, Mass.: Addison-Wesley.

CORVINUS, G.
1970   "The Acheulian workshop at Chirki on the Pravara River, Maharashtra," in *Studies in Indian archaeology*. Edited by S. B. Deo and M. K. Dhavalikar, 13–22. Indian Antiquary 4.

DANI, A. H.
1964   Sanghao cave excavation, the first season, 1963. *Ancient Pakistan* 1:1–50.

DE LUMLEY, H.
1967   Découverte d'habitats de l'Acheuléen ancien, dans des dépôts mindéliens, sur le site de Terra Amata (Nice). *Comptes Rendus Académie Scientifique* 264:801–804.
1969   A paleolithic camp at Nice. *Scientific American* 220:42–50.

DERANIYAGALA, S.
1971   Prehistoric Ceylon: a summary. *Ancient Ceylon* 1:3-46.

DERANIYAGALA, S., K. A. R. KENNEDY
i.p.   Report of the sixth archaeological expedition to the Late Stone Age site of Bellan Bandi Palassa, Ceylon: 1970. *Ancient Ceylon* 2.

DETERRA, H., T. T. PATERSON
1939   *Studies on the Ice Age of India and associated human cultures*. Carnegie Institution of Washington 493.

DUPREE, L.
1972   Prehistoric research in Afghanistan: 1959–1966. *Transactions of the American Philosophical Society* 62(4).

DUTTA, P. C.
1971   Earliest Indian human remains found in a Late Stone Age site. *Nature* 233:500–501.

EHRHARDT, S., K. A. R. KENNEDY
1965   *Excavations at Langhnaj: the human remains*. Deccan College Building Centenary and Silver Jubilee Series 7.

EMILIANI, C.
1968   The Pleistocene epoch and the evolution of man. *Current Anthropology* 9:27–47.

FAIRSERVIS, W. A.
1967   The origin, character and decline of an early civilization. *American Museum Novitiates* 2302:1–48.
1971   *The roots of ancient India: the archaeology of early Indian civilization*. New York: Macmillan.

FOOTE, R. B.
    1884   Rough notes on Billa Surgam and other caves in the Kurnool
            District. *Records of the Geological Survey of India* 17:27–34.
GUHA, B. S., P. C. BASU
    1938   "Report on the human remains excavated at Mohenjo-daro in
            1928–29," in *Further excavations at Mohenjo-daro, being an
            official account of archaeological excavations carried out by the
            government of India, etc.*, volume one. Edited by E. J. H. Mackay,
            613–638. New Delhi: Government Press.
GUPTA, P., P. C. DUTTA, A. BASU
    1962   *Human skeletal remains from Harappa.* Memoirs of the Anthro-
            pological Survey of India 9.
HOWELL, F. C.
    1966   Observations on the earlier phases of the European Lower Pa-
            leolithic. *Special Publications of the American Anthropologist*
            68(2):88–201.
HOWELL, F. C., J. D. CLARK
    1963   *Acheulian hunter-gatherers of sub-Saharan Africa.* Viking Fund
            Publications in Anthropology 36.
HUNTER, G. R.
    1935   Interim report on the excavations in the Mahadeo Hills. *Nagpur
            University Journal* 1.
    1936   Final report on the excavation in the Mahadeo Hills. *Nagpur
            University Journal* 2.
ISSAC, G. L.
    1968   "Traces of Pleistocene hunters: an East African example," in *Man
            the hunter.* Edited by R. B. Lee and I. DeVore, 253–261. Chi-
            cago: Aldine.
JOSHI, R. V.
    1966   Acheulian succession in Central India. *Asian Perspectives* 8:150–
            163.
KARVE-CORVINUS, G., K. A. R. KENNEDY
    1964   Preliminary report on Langhnaj: the preliminary report of the
            1963 archaeological expedition to Langhnaj, northern Gujarat.
            Bulletin of the Deccan College Research Institute 24:71–76.
KENNEDY, K. A. R.
    1965   Human skeletal material from Ceylon, with an analysis of the
            island's prehistoric and contemporary populations. *Bulletin of the
            British Museum (Natural History), Geology* 11:135–213.
    1969   Palaeodemography of India and Ceylon since 3000 B.C. *American
            Journal of Physical Anthropology* 31:315–320.
    1972a   "The palaeodemography of Ceylon: a study of the biological
            continuum of a population from prehistoric to historic times," in
            Perspectives in palaeo-anthropology. Edited by A. K. Ghosh. Cal-
            cutta.
    1972b   "The search for fossil man in India," in *Physical anthropology
            and its expanding horizons.* Edited by A. Basu, 25–44. Calcutta.
    1973a   "The physical anthropology of the megalith-builders of South
            India, Sri Lanka and Ceylon." (In press.)

1973b Biological anthropology of prehistoric South Asians. *The Anthropologist* 17:1–13.

KENNEDY, K. A. R., K. C. MALHOTRA
1966 *Human skeletal remains from Chalcolithic and Indo-Roman levels from Nevasa: an anthropometric and comparative analysis.* Deccan College Building Centenary and Silver Jubilee Series 55.

KHATRI, A. P.
1963 Recent exploration for the remains of early man in India. *Asian Perspectives* 7:160–192.

KLEIN, R. G.
1969 The Mousterian of European Russia. *Proceedings of the Prehistoric Society* 35:77–111.

LAL, B. B.
1958 Birbhanpur, a microlithic site in the Damodar Valley, West Bengal. *Ancient India* 14:4–48.

LEAKEY, M. D.
1967 "Preliminary survey of the cultural material from Beds I and II, Olduvai Gorge, Tanzania," in *Background to evolution in Africa.* Edited by W. W. Bishop and J. D. Clark, 417–446. Chicago: University of Chicago Press.

LEE, R. B., I. DeVORE, *editors*
1968 *Man the hunter.* Chicago: Aldine.

MISRA, V. N.
1965 "Mesolithic phase in the prehistory of India," in *Indian prehistory: 1964.* Edited by V. N. Misra and M. S. Mate, 57–85. Deccan College Building Centenary and Silver Jubilee Series, 32.
1972 "Problems of paleoecology, paleoclimatology and chronology of microlithic cultures of north-west India." Paper presented at International Symposium on Radiocarbon and Indian Archaeology, Tata Institute of Fundamental Research, Bombay, March 6, 1972.

MISRA, V. N., K. A. R. KENNEDY, J. R. LUKACS
1972 *Archaeology and physical anthropology of prehistoric Bagor, Rajasthan.* (In preparation.)

MOVIUS, H. L.
1944 Early man and Pleistocene stratigraphy in Southern and Eastern Asia. *Papers of the Peabody Museum of Archaeology and Ethnology* 9:17–20.
1949 The Lower Paleolithic cultures of Southern and Eastern Asia. *Transactions of the American Philosophical Society* 38(4).
1969 "Lower Paleolithic archaeology in Southern Asia and the Far East," in *Early Man in the Far East.* Edited by W. W. Howells. Oosterhout, The Netherlands: Meeuwessa.

NARR, K. J.
1963 *Kultur, Umwelt und Leiblichkeit des Eiszeitmenschens.* Stuttgart: G. Fischer.

RAJAGURU, S. N., K. A. R. KENNEDY
1964 The skeletal evidence for Pleistocene man in India. *Bulletin of the Deccan College Research Institute* 24:71–76.

RAJAN, K. V. SOUNDARA
1952   Stone age industries near Giddalur, District Kurnool. *Ancient India* 8:64–92.

RAO, M. S. NAGARAJA, K. C. MALHOTRA
1965   *The Stone Age hill dwellers of Tekkalakota: preliminary report of the excavations at Tekkalakota.* Deccan College Building Centenary and Silver Jubilee Series 31.

SANKALIA, H. D.
1946   *Investigations into prehistoric archaeology of Gujarat, being the official report of the first Gujarat prehistoric expedition 1941–42.* Baroda: Baroda State Press.

SARASIN, P. B., F. SARASIN
1892–   *Ergebnisse Naturwissenschaftlicher Forschungen auf Ceylon.*
1893   Wiesbaden.

SARKAR, S. S.
1960   Human skeletal remains from Brahmagiri. *Bulletin of the Department of Anthropology, University of Calcutta* 9:5–26.

SELIGMAN, C. G., B. Z. SELIGMAN
1911   *The Veddas.* Cambridge: Cambridge University Press.

SEWELL, R. B. S., B. S. GUHA
1931   "Human remains," in *Mohenjodaro and the Indus civilization, being an official account of archaeological excavations carried out by the government of India, etc.*, volume two. Edited by J. Marshall, 599–648. London: Probsthain.

SIMONS, E. L.
1964a   The early relatives of man. *Scientific American* 211:50–62.
1964b   On the mandible of *Ramapithecus. Proceedings of the National Academy of Sciences* 51:528–535.
1969   Recent advances of paleoanthropology. *Yearbook of Physical Anthropology* 1967:14–23.

SUBBARAO, B.
1958   *The personality of India* (second edition). Baroda: University of Baroda.

TODD, K. R. U.
1939   Paleolithic industries of Bombay. *Man: Journal of the Royal Anthropological Institute* 69:257–272.

TODE, A., F. PREUL, K. RICHTER, A. KLEINSCHMIDT
1953   Die Untersuchung der paläolithischen Freilandstation von Salzgitter-Lebenstedt. *Eiszeitalter und Gegenwart* 3:144–220.

VALLOIS, H. V.
1961   *The social life of early man: the evidence of skeletons.* Viking Fund Publications in Anthropology 31.

WINTLE, A. G., K. P. OAKLEY
1972   Thermoluminescent dating of fired rock-crystal from Bellan Bandi Pallassa, Ceylon. *Archaeometry* 14:277–279

YULISH, S. M.
1970   Anterior tooth reduction in *Ramapithecus. Primates* 11:255–263

ZEUNER, F. E.
1950   *Stone Age and Pleistocene chronology in Gujarat*. Deccan College Monograph 6.
1963   "Environment as inferred from fauna and flora: environment of Early Man with special reference to the tropical regions," in *The Maharaja Sayajirao Memorial Lectures: 1960–1961*, lecture three. Baroda: University of Baroda Press.

ZEUNER, F. E., B. ALLCHIN
1956   The microlithic sites of Tinnevelly District, Madras State. *Ancient India* 12:4–20.

PART TWO

Genetics, Society, and Population Dynamics

Genetic Affinities and Origin of the Irish Tinkers

MICHAEL H. CRAWFORD

For over fifty years serological evidence has been employed to resolve controversies surrounding the ethnogenesis and cultural affinities of various populations. Two Hungarian scientists, Verzar and Weszeczky (1921, 1922), utilizing the allelic frequencies at the ABO blood group locus attempted to test the linguistically derived hypothesis that the Hungarian Gypsies had originated from Northern India in the ninth century A.D. (Rex-Kiss, et al. 1973). They were able to demonstrate that the Gypsies do in fact resemble the Northern Indian populations in allelic frequencies at some loci. However, subsequent studies of Gypsy populations from Slovenia, France, England, and Hungary reveal considerable genetic variability between the Gypsy populations. Other ethnological questions of anthropological interest include the origins and affinities of the geographically widely distributed Pygmies, Negritos, Lapps, Bushmen, and Tinkers.

This study focuses upon the genetic affinities and ethnogenesis of an itinerant population of Ireland, known as the Tinkers. In addition to comparisons of allelic frequencies by inspection, the similarities and differences among the Irish Tinkers and other European populations are

I would like to thank the traveling people who participated in this study. In particular, I am indebted to Mr. Thomas (Bon) Connors, without whose effort this research could not have been possible. The help of Dr. Liam Connvery, Dr. Geoffrey Dean, Dr. George Gmelch, and Dr. Theodore Rebič is acknowledged. The Irish Heart Association kindly provided us with blood specimens from their survey of the Kilkenny population. Mr. Francis Lees aided in the analysis of the data and wrote the computer program for the Sanghvi X^2 measure of genetic distance.

This study was supported in part by grants from the Wenner-Gren Foundation for Anthropological Research, grant number 2647, and The University Center for International Studies, University of Pittsburgh.

quantified by the computation of genetic distances based upon allelic frequency distributions.

POPULATION

The roads of Europe are traversed by thousands of itinerants who are socially, genetically, and linguistically heterogeneous. The greatest concentration of those traveling people is in Hungary, with an official government count of 200,000, and England, where the itinerant population has been estimated at 100,000 individuals *(Report of the Commission on Itinerancy,* 1963). Genetically the most widely studied traveling people are the Romany Gypsies of Sweden, France, Hungary, Yugoslavia, and England. (Beckman, Takman, and Arfors 1965; Beckman and Takman 1965; Cazal, Graafland, and Mathieu 1952; Ely 1961, 1966; Nicoli and Sermet 1965; Rex-Kiss and Szabo 1971; Rex-Kiss, et al. 1973; Hočevar 1965; Galikova, et al. 1969; Fraser, et al. 1969; and Avcin 1969). This report examines an itinerant population from Ireland — the Tinkers, or the Traveling People. The Tinkers number approximately 6,000 individuals and are distributed throughout the Irish countryside, but with the greatest concentration in the counties of Galway, Cork, and Tipperary. Four population censuses of the Tinkers, taken by the Irish police *(Garda)*, registered a slight population decrease in recent years, from 7,148 in 1956 to 5,880 in 1961. This decrease in population size, according to the *Report of the Commission on Itinerancy* (1963), is primarily the result of emigration. In addition, seasonal fluctuations in population size are explained by the fact that some of the male Tinkers work in the mines or pursue seasonal agricultural labor in England.

Like the Romany Gypsies, the Tinkers are seminomadic, living in tents, horse-drawn wagons, and caravans. The Tinkers practice occupations similar to the Gypsies, namely tinsmithing, scrapmetal collecting, horse dealing, peddling, and begging. Traditionally, the Tinkers traveled regular circuits within the confines of one or two county areas, repairing pots and pans in exchange for food or money. The less affluent Tinkers who did not own a horse and cart followed shorter circuits on foot. The Tinkers are viewed with some suspicion and although they work for the settled farmers, the travelers are not welcome in the settled community once their work is done. This fear and suspicion of the Tinkers by the settled community maintains some of the social isolation and contributes to the endogamy (Crawford and Gmelch 1974). Tinkers usually camp on the outskirts of a town with an encampment consisting of three to six related, extended families. Since most social interactions experienced by the young or juveniles are with relatives it is not surprising that consanguineous marriages are frequent.

The Tinkers are highly fertile with the mean number of children per woman forty years of age and older of 10.43 and a variance of 22.39. The mean fertility of the Tinkers is one of the highest recorded in contemporary human populations, surpassed only by the highly prolific Hutterites. This high fertility can be explained, in part, by long reproductive careers of the females who, on the average, are married at eighteen years of age and continue reproducing until forty to forty-five years of age. There appears to be a new trend of younger marriages for females, a result of settlement! Contraception of any sort is rarely, if ever, used because of religious convictions and personal preference for large families. Reproductive wastage is high because of a lack of sanitation in highly crowded caravans and exposure to the elements after birth and during neonatal life. Close to 50 per cent of the children fail to survive until the age of reproduction — i.e. fifteen years of age. This population, with high fertility and mortality, has the potential for rapid genetic change through the action of natural selection.

Mate selection usually occurs within the confines of a county, with approximately 80 per cent of the marriages contracted between residents of the same county. Another 16 per cent of the matings are between individuals from different counties but within the same province. These matings are probably between members of the most mobile group of Irish Tinkers — the horse dealers or "blockers," who travel between county fairs selling and trading horses to the local farmers.

The Tinkers speak a distinct language, unintelligible to the Irish, called Gammin or Shelta. Although the origins of this language are historically uncertain, some scholars believe that it is related to the lost language of the medieval monasteries. MacMahon (1971) describes Shelta as mostly "jumbled Gaelic or Irish with a faint trace of Romany." He suggests that this language may have been "developed" by a dissolute priest or homeless monk who wandered astray as a result of England's suppression of the monasteries. It is highly unlikely that Gammin or Shelta would arise spontaneously and through the design or effort of a single, or even a group of monks. Most likely, the language evolved from early Gaelic which was spoken by the medieval craftsmen and artisans who traveled the roads of Ireland. However, because of social isolation and the incorporation of a specialized occupational jargon, the language diverged from the Irish or Gaelic spoken in the surrounding populations.

Recently, MacMahon (1971) has summarized some of the prevalent theories about the ethnogenesis of the Irish Tinkers. These are: (1) The Tinkers are the descendants of the outcasts who chose to live beyond the "circle of the Brehon Laws" — the ancient body of common laws of the prehistoric Irish Island. (2) The Tinkers are descendants of native chieftains and their families, who, dispossessed in the successive English plantations of Ireland, assumed an itinerant way of life. MacMahon claims that the Tinkers of today bear the names of some of the noblest Irish clans and are associated with the territories inhabited by their chieftain ancestors. (3) A more likely explanation is that the Tinkers are displaced farmers and laborers who were driven from their lands and occupations by severe famines and droughts. The potato famine of 1846, when almost the entire crop was lost and thousands of tenant farmers were evicted by the landlords, was particularly devastating. (4) While the skin, hair, and eye color of the Tinkers do not suggest an Indian origin, it is possible that the Tinkers' gene pool experienced some gene flow from the Romany Gypsies. MacMahon contends that some words of Gypsy vocabulary have been incorporated into Gammin. If linguistic borrowing has taken place, then gene flow is also likely. The Irish Tinker gene pool may be a hybrid of Irish and Romany Gypsy genes.

METHODS

The data upon which this analysis is based were collected during the summer of 1970 by a team of researchers from the United States and Ireland. A total of 238 Irish Tinkers were interviewed and tested; of these, 126 were travelers on the roads of Dublin, Wicklow, and Wexford, while the remainder of the sample came from three government settlements — LaBrea Park, Finglas, and Church Town.

Blood specimens were obtained from 127 Tinkers and 95 unrelated males from the town of Kilkenny, who were participants in a survey conducted by the Irish Heart Association. The sample from Kilkenny, although small, provides a comparison with the Tinkers because little published information is available on the red blood cell and serum polymorphisms in Irish populations. The blood specimens were collected into ACD preservative, centrifuged, and the red blood cells and sera were shipped in separate tubes, by air, to the National Institute of Dental Research, Bethesda, Maryland. The methods of analysis are described by Crawford et al. (1974). The samples were typed with standard antisera for the following antigens: A, A_1, B, H, M, N, S, s, P_1, C(Rh'), $C^w(Rh^w)$, c(hr'), D(Rhô), E(Rh"), e(hr"), K k, Kp^a, Le^a, Fy^a. As a check, reverse typing with red blood cells of known antigenetic specificity was used for the ABO blood group system.

The serum was subjected to high voltage electrophoresis using methods described by Brown and Johnson (1970). The red cell enzymes — adenylate kinase, acid phosphatase, and phosphoglucomutase were tested for electrophoretic polymorphism in starch gel slabs according to the modified methods of Hopkinson, Spencer, and Harris (1963) and Giblett (1969). Allelic frequencies are maximum likelihood estimates computed by the MAXLIK computer program of Reed and Schull (1968). The Rhesus chromosomal segment frequencies were determined by a method described by Mourant (1954). The use of Mourant's method was necessitated by the computer program's failure to converge because some of the phenotypic categories contained too few members.

Genetic distances between the Irish Tinkers, Kilkenny residents, and other European populations are based on Sanghvi's X^2 measure of distance between populations which was developed for discrete characters occurring in multiclass situations, and which provides a measure of divergence based on differences in frequencies over any number of loci, for pairs of populations (Sanghvi 1953).

RESULTS

The allelic frequencies of the blood groups, serum, and red blood cell proteins for the Tinkers, unrelated Kilkenny residents, and an Irish sample grouped by Pálsson, Walter, and Bajatzadeh (1970), are summarized in Tables 1 and 2. The allelic frequencies of the Irish Tinkers are similar to those of the Kilkenny, and the Irish composite.

According to Rex-Kiss, et al. (1973), the B (q) gene frequency of the Gypsies is higher than in any European populations and corresponds to the proportion found in East Indian groups. They point out that the frequency of the B allele in indigenous European populations varies from 0.09 to 0.15, while a range of 0.1924 to 0.3023 is observed among the European Gypsies. However, the frequency of the B allele in some Gypsy populations falls outside this range: British Gypsies, B = .0636 (Clark 1973); in the Swedish Gypsies, B = 0.05 (Beckman, Takman, and Arfors 1965); Yugoslavian Gypsies, from the Prekmurje region, exhibit a frequency of 0.0878; and French Gypsies have a gene frequency of 0.3084 for the B allele (Cazal, Graafland, and Mathieu 1952).

Both the Tinkers and the Kilkenny Irish populations exhibit a higher frequency of the B allele than do either the British or the composite Irish samples. However, these frequencies do fit within the range of indigenous

Table 1. Allelic frequencies of blood groups from Irish Tinkers compared to other Irish populations (after Crawford, et al. 1974)

System	Alleles	Tinkers	Kilkenny	Irish *	British Gypsies **
ABO	A_1	0.1675	0.1213	0.100	0.2004
	A_2	0.0411	0.0711	0.039	0.1093
	B	0.1203	0.1207	0.075	0.0636
	O	0.6739	0.6870	0.786	0.6268
MNSs	MS	0.2626	0.2705	0.277	
					0.7018 M
	Ms	0.2920	0.3155	0.340	
	NS	0.0736	0.0466	0.047	
					0.2981 N
	Ns	0.3718	0.3673	0.336	
Rhesus	cde	0.3801	0.4852	0.402	0.3348
	Cde	0.0441	0.0134	0.018	0.0133
	cdE	0.0000	0.0000	0.008	0.0133
	cDe	0.0278	0.0000	0.052	NT
	CDe	0.2760	0.3815	0.364	0.4894
	CDE	0.0000	0.0000	0.000	NT
	$CD^{u}e$	0.2190	0.0000	NT	NT
	cDE	0.0247	0.1197	0.156	0.1489
Kell	K	0.0379	0.0541	0.029	0.0463
	k	0.9621	0.9459	0.971	0.9537
Duffy	Fy^a	0.3519	0.4258	0.304	0.5043 [1]
	Fy^b	0.6481	0.5742	0.696	0.4057 [1]
P	P+	0.5509	0.4611	0.451	NT
	P—	0.4491	0.5388	0.549	NT
Lewis	$Le^{a}+$	0.2782	0.1878	NT	0.0917
	$Le^{a}-$	0.7218	0.8122	NT	0.9083

* From Pálsson, et al. (1970).
** From C. A. Clark (1973).
NT (not taken).
[1] (Phenotypic frequencies).

European populations cited by Rex-Kiss, et al. (1973). Published investigations of the distribution of the B allele in Ireland reveal a relatively narrow range of variability, with most populations ranging between 0.05 and 0.08 (Dawson 1952; Hackett, Dawson, and Dawson 1956; Mourant 1954; and Pálsson, Walter, and Bajatzadeh 1970).

Although the allelic frequencies of the Tinkers resemble those of the Irish, some significant differences are present. At the Rhesus blood group locus the cDE chromosomal segment has an exceptionally high incidence among the Tinkers — more than twice the frequency of the Kilkenny population. This chromosomal segment does not appear to have a high incidence in either the Gypsies or the East Indian and Pakistani populations, with the former frequencies ranging from 0.0236 to 0.1209 and the latter exhibiting a range of 0.0116 to 0.0878 (Rex-Kiss, et al. 1973;

Table 2. Allelic frequencies of serum and red blood cell protein polymorphisms of Tinker, Kilkenny, and Irish populations (after Crawford, et al. 1974)

Serum proteins

System	Alleles	Tinkers	Kilkenny	Irish*
Group Specific Component	Gc¹	0.6115	0.5965	0.755
	Gc²	0.3884	0.4034	0.245
Haptoglobins	Hp¹	0.3162	0.4340	0.378
	Hp²	0.6837	0.5659	0.622
Transferrin	Tf^B	0.0079	0.0105	NT
	Tf^c	0.0992	0.9895	NT
Albumins	Al^A	1.0000	1.0000	1.000

Red cell proteins

Acid Phosphatase (A.P.)	P^a	0.4049	0.3225	0.288
	P^b	0.5986	0.6774	0.676
	P^c	0.0000	0.0000	0.036
Phosphoglucomutase (PGM)	PGM$^1_1$	0.7438	0.7638	**0.864**
	PGM$^1_2$	0.2561	0.2315	0.136
Adenylate Kinase (AK)	AK¹	0.9791	0.9789	0.873
	AK²	0.0208	0.0210	0.127

* From Pálsson, et al. (1970).
NT — not taken.

Avcin 1969; Mourant 1954). The Tinkers also exhibit anomalous frequencies of the P^a allele, at the acid phosphatase locus, P+ phenotype at the P locus, and the Hp¹ gene has a relatively low frequency when compared with the Kilkenny and Irish samples (see Table 2).

While these comparisons of the allelic frequencies suggest that the Tinkers resemble the Irish more closely than they resemble any other populations, these observations are subjective. There is no quantification of the sum total of the similarities and differences between the various populations. As a result, in order to test the genetic affinities and the various theories of ethnogenesis of the Irish Gypsies, genetic distances were computed using Sanghvi's X² method. Computation of the genetic distances between the eight populations was based upon fourteen alleles and chromosomal segments from four genetic systems — ABO, Rh, MN, and Haptoglobin. Although allelic frequencies for fifteen systems were available for the Irish Tinkers and Kilkenny, there is an inverse relationship between the number of available alleles and the number of available populations. In other words, the greater the number of populations used in the analysis, the fewer the available allelic frequencies. Table 3 summarizes the computed genetic distances between eight populations or geographical groups. The allelic frequencies representing England and

Table 3.   Genetic distances based upon Sanghvi's X^2 measure

	Tinkers	Kilkenny	Ireland	England	Iceland	Hungarian Gypsies	Hungary	Punjab
Tinkers	0							
Kilkenny	1.150	0						
Ireland	1.446	0.674	0					
England	2.312	0.851	0.457	0				
Iceland	3.949	1.770	1.338	0.798	0			
Hungarian Gypsies	3.269	1.840	4.574	4.200	5.341	0		
Hungary	1.823	2.479	2.109	1.702	2.823	0.658	0	
Punjab	3.088	3.214	6.007	6.487	8.231	0.868	2.144	0

Iceland were compiled from Mourant (1954) and Giblett (1969); Hungarian Gypsy, Hungarian and Punjab frequencies were obtained from Rex-Kiss, et al. (1973). Ireland is represented by the Pálsson, Walter, and Bajatzadeh (1970) study. Although any attempt to characterize the entire population of Ireland with a sample of 295 individuals has little biological validity, this provides the only available data on a number of the red blood cell protein polymorphisms. Thus, the sample was utilized in this study.

Genetic distance measures support the serologically derived hypothesis that the Tinkers are closest genetically to the Irish populations. What is surprising is that Hungarians appear to be closer genetically to the Tinkers than to the English. The Tinkers differ most from the Icelandic sample, which is surprising considering the known historical relationship between Iceland and Ireland. This difference can be explained on the basis of the Tinkers' social isolation, which produced little gene flow from surrounding populations. The Kilkenny, Irish, and English samples are much closer to Icelanders than are the Tinkers. The Tinkers do not appear to be related to the Romany Gypsies and are closer to the Hungarians than to the Hungarian Gypsies, from whom they differ to the same degree as they do from the Punjab populations.

These genetic distance data support the hypothesis that the Gypsies originated in Northern India or Pakistan. The Hungarian Gypsies resemble the Punjab population more than does any other European group in this study. These results also suggest that gene flow between the Gypsies and surrounding Hungarian populations may have occurred in both directions. After the Gypsies, Hungary is genetically closer to the Punjab than is any other population in Europe. The Hungarian Gypsies closely resemble both the Hungarians and the Punjabi of Pakistan.

CONCLUSION

Judging from the allelic frequencies and the genetic distances, it appears that the Irish Tinkers constitute a social isolate that has differentiated from the surrounding Irish populations. The Tinkers are undoubtedly of Irish ancestry, as they resemble neither the Gypsy nor the Pakistan populations to any appreciable degree. It is possible that the Tinkers may have experienced some gene flow from Romany Gypsies, but probably of low magnitude.

Contrary to MacMahon's hypothesis that the Tinkers were forced to become travelers by the famines of the 1880's, the historical accounts suggest that the Tinkers predate the potato blights and the agricultural plantations of Cromwell. The literature of both Ireland and England contains numerous references to Tinkers. For example, in the late 1500's, Shakespeare referred to the Tinkers in several of his plays, most notably in *Henry IV*. In the early 1500's, legislation directed against the Tinkers was passed in Ireland. There is considerable documentation that the Tinkers were craftsmen and artisans during the medieval period. Some of the present-day Tinkers may be descendants of the original craftsmen who worked in the monastic settlements of sixth century A.D. However, with the Norman invasion of the twelfth century, the monasteries were closed and the Tinkers were forced into a traveling existence. Calamities and political upheavals forced additional people to take to the road and assume the Tinker way of life. The famines, the droughts, and the repression accompanying British occupation resulted in a constant recruitment of members from the surrounding populations. Presently, with the government settlement programs and the obsolescence of a number of traditional occupations, the Tinkers are gradually being assimilated into Irish society.

REFERENCES

AVCIN, M.
  1969   Gypsy isolates in Slovenia. *Journal of Biosocial Sciences* 1:221–233.
BECKMAN, L., J. TAKMAN
  1965   On the anthropology of a Swedish Gypsy population. *Hereditas* 53:272–280.
BECKMAN, L., J. TAKMAN, K. E. ARFORS
  1965   Distributions of blood and serum groups in a Swedish Gypsy population. *Acta Genetica,* Basel, 15:134–140.

BIRDSELL, J. B.

1941 A preliminary report of the trihybrid origin of the Australian aborigines (Abstract). *American Journal of Physical Anthropology* 28:6.

1951 "The problem of the early peopling of the Americas as viewed from Asia," in *Papers on the physical anthropology of the American Indian.* Edited by W. S. Laughlin, 1–69. Ann Arbor: Viking Fund, Edwards Brothers.

BOYD, W. C.

1963 Four achievements of the genetical method in physical anthropology. *American Anthropologist* 65:243–252.

BROWN, K. S., R. S. JOHNSON

1970 Population studies on Southwestern Indian tribes, III: Serum protein variations of Zuni and Papago Indians. *Human Heredity* 20: 281–286.

CASEY, A. E., K. HALE, J. CASEY, A. HOGG, B. R. KYNERD

1969 Distribution of Kell blood group in Slieve Lougher, Southwest Ireland. *Alabama Journal of Medical Science* 6:411–416.

CAZAL, P., T. GRAAFLAND, M. MATHIEU

1952 Les groupes sanguins chez les Gitans de France. *Montpellier Medicine* 41–42: 1058.

CLARK, V. A.

1973 "Genetic factors in some British Gypsies," in *Genetic variation in Britain.* Edited by D. F. Roberts and E. Sunderland, 181–196. London: Taylor and Francis.

CRAWFORD, M. H., *et al.*

1974 "Human biology of the Irish Tinkers: demography, ethnohistory and genetics." *Social Biology* 21:321–331.

CRAWFORD, M. H., W. C. LEYSHON, K. BROWN, F. LEES, L. TAYLOR

1974 Human biology in Tlaxcala, Mexico: II. Blood group, serum and red cell enzyme polymorphisms, and genetic distances. *American Journal of Physical Anthropology* 41:251–268.

DAWSON, G. W. P.

1952 The frequency of the ABO blood groups in Dublin. *Heredity* 6:243–246.

1964 The frequencies of the ABO and Rh (D) blood groups in Ireland from a sample of 1 in 18 of the population. *Annals of Human Genetics* 28:49–59.

ELY, B.

1961 Les groupes sanguins de 47 Tsiganes de la région parisienne. *Bulletins et Memoires de la Société d'Anthropologie* 11:233.

1966 Les Gitans d'Avignon. *l'Anthropologie* 70:103–112.

GALIKOVA, J., M. VILEMOVA, V. FERAK, A. MAYEROVA

1969 Haptoglobin types in Gypsies from Slovakia (Czech.). *Human Heredity* 19:480–485.

GIBLETT, E. R.

1969 *The genetic markers in human blood.* Philadelphia: F. A. Davis.

FRASER, G. R., P. GRUNWALD, F. D. KITCHIN, A. G. STEINBERG

1969 Serum polymorphisms in Yugoslavia. *Human Heredity* 19:57–64.

HACKETT, E., M. E. FOLAN
  1958   The ABO and Rh blood groups of the Aran Islanders. *Irish Journal of Medical Sciences* (June):257–261.
HACKETT, W. E. R., G. W. P. DAWSON, C. J. DAWSON
  1956   The pattern of the ABO blood group frequencies in Ireland. *Heredity* 10:69–34.
HOČEVAR, M.
  1965   "Die Verteilung der Blutgruppen bei einem Zigeunerisolat," in *Proceedings of the Tenth Congress of the International Society of Blood Transfusion, Stockholm, 1964.*
HOPKINSON, D. A., N. SPENCER, M. HARRIS
  1963   Red cell acid phosphatase variants: a new human polymorphism. *Nature* 199:969.
MAC MAHON, B.
  1971   A portrait of Tinkers. *Natural History* 80:24–35, 104–109.
MOURANT, A. E.
  1954   *The distribution of the human blood groups.* Springfield: Charles C. Thomas.
NICOLI, R. M., P. SERMET
  1965   Les Tziganes de France. *Transfusion,* Paris, 8:89–92.
PÁLSSON, J. O. P., H. WALTER, M. BAJATZEDEH
  1970   Sero-genetical studies in Ireland. *Human Heredity* 20:231–239.
POLLITZER, W. S.
  1964   Analysis of a tri-racial isolate. *Human Biology* 36:362–373.
REED, T. E., W. J. SCHULL
  1968   A maximum likelihood estimation program. *American Journal of Human Genetics* 20:579–580.
Report of the Commission on Itinerancy
  1963   Dublin: Stationery Office, Government Publications.
REX-KISS, B. L. SZABO
  1971   Results of haptoglobin types examinations in Hungary. *Human Genetik* 13:78–80.
REX-KISS, B. L. SZABO, S. SZABO, E. HARTMAN
  1973   ABO, MN, Rh blood groups, Hp types and Hp level, Gm (1) factor investigations on the Gypsy population of Hungary. *Human Biology* 45:41–61.
SANGHVI, L. D.
  1953   Comparison of genetical and morphological methods for a study of biological differences. *American Journal of Physical Anthropology* 11:385–404.
SOFAER, J. A., J. D. NISWANDER, C. J. MacLEAN, P. L. WORKMAN
  1972   Population studies on southeastern Indian tribes. *American Journal of Physical Anthropology* 37:357–366.
SPENCER, N., D. A. HOPKINSON, H. HARRIS
  1964   Phosphoglucomutase polymorphism in man. *Nature* 204:742.
VERZAR, F., O. WESZECZKY
  1921   Rassenbiologische Untersuchungen mittels Isohamagglutininen. *Biochemische Zeitschrift* 126:33–39.
  1922   Neue Untersuchungen über Isohamagglutinine. *Klinische Worchenschrift* 1:928–931.

The Anthropological Usefulness of the IgA Allotypic Markers

M. S. SCHANFIELD and H. H. FUDENBERG

The Gm allotypic markers on the heavy chains of human IgG have been very useful anthropologically because of the presence of either unique haplotypes in different populations or marked differences in the frequencies of the haplotypes. The Inv allotypic markers on the Kappa light chains of human immunoglobulin are not as useful because of the smaller number of alleles present; however, they can be used to discriminate between populations. The discovery of a polymorphic allotypic marker on the IgA_2 subclass of human IgA allowed additional information to be gained (Kunkel, et al. 1969; Vyas and Fudenberg 1970), but the major gain in information came with the verification that the IgA_2 allotypic marker was genetically linked to the Gm allotypic marker, creating a large Gm-Am haplotype (van Loghem, Natvig, and Matsumoto 1970). The ability to discriminate populations was further enhanced by the recent discovery of a second allotypic marker at the IgA_2 locus which appears to be allelic to the first (van Loghem, Wang, and Shuster 1973). To allow for a single, unified nomenclature, the allotypic markers on IgA_2 will be referred to as $A_2m(1)$ and $A_2m(2)$, after the suggested nomenclature of van Loghem, Wang, and Shuster (1973). In this paper we report the distribution of the Gm-A_2m haplotypes in the major races of man and

Supported in part by United States Public Health Postdoctoral Research Fellowship (HD-52597-1).

The authors would like to thank Drs. S. D. Litwin, J. Shuster and E. van Loghem for providing some of the reagents used; Drs. P. B. Booth, P. Herzog, J. Gergely, R. Hornabrook, P. Kwiterovich and E. Sutton for supplying some of the serum samples tested; and the Irwin Memorial Blood Bank for providing laboratory space during the course of this project.

the unique information presented by the Gm-A₂m haplotypes in answering questions that could not be answered by means of the Gm haplotypes alone.

METHODS AND MATERIALS

Immunoglobulin allotyping for Gm and A_2m allotypic markers was carried out in microtiter plates, using a standard three-drop technique (Schanfield 1971). Gm typing was done with red blood cells coated with incomplete Rh antibodies of defined specificities or with myeloma proteins coated onto red blood cells by means of chromic chloride. Chromic chloride was also used to coat IgA myeloma proteins onto red blood cells. Chromic chloride coating was done using a modification of the method of Vyas, et al. (1968), with all proteins coated at a concentration of 1 milligram/milliliter and using 0.05 percent chromic chloride, while the special TAP diluent of the original method was

Table 1.   Reagents used for immunoglobulin allotyping

Specificity		Agglutinator	Coat
Original	WHO		
Gm a	1	Hel	Dwi
x	2	Dev	Yap
z	17	Pon	Dwi
b², f	3, 4	Sta	Dan
b⁰	11	Har	Hun
b¹	5	Ble	Hun
b³	13	F841*	Hun
b³	13	Ams*	Hun
b³	13	Log*	Hun
b⁵	10	Ste*	Hun
c³	6	And	Bor[a] or Ada
c⁵	24	Hod	Bor[a] or Ada
g	21	B755[a]	Sul
g	21	Gha*	Sul
g	21	Leh	Sul
s	15	Gai	3068[a] or Puh
t	16	Ros	3068[a] or Puh
Ray	–	Ray	Sul
n	23*	K9547[b]	Jas
A₂m 1		Far	Her
2		Tay[c]	For

* Not all sample types with this reagent.
[a] Supplied by E. van Loghem.
[b] Supplied by S. Litwin.
[c] Supplied by J. Shuster.

replaced by 0.85 percent saline. All samples were tested at a dilution of 1/10 or 1/20 with the reagents listed in Table 1.

A total of 1,694 samples was tested for Gm (a, x, z, f, b, c^3, c^5, g, s, t, and Ray) and A$_2$m (1) and (2). Many of these samples were also tested for Gm(n). Included in these samples were 630 Caucasians, 58 Chinese, 53 Japanese, 587 Papuans, 207 Melanesians, 112 Afro-Americans, and 65 Mexican Indians of selected phenotypes. In addition, 119 nonhuman primates, including 59 chimpanzees, 19 orangutans, 6 gibbons, 15 baboons, 16 assorted macaques, and 4 patas monkeys, were tested for A$_2$m (1) and (2).

RESULTS

The approximate haplotype frequencies for the major human populations studied are presented in Tables 2, 3, 4, and 6, with the racial distribution summarized in Table 7. None of the 119 nonhuman primates were positive for either A$_2$m (1) or (2). Thus far, twenty-seven different haplotypes have been found; of these, twenty-two are found in a single racial group or in populations derived from or admixed with that racial group. Seven of the twenty-two racially unique haplotypes are rare, with frequencies less than 1 percent. The haplotypes presented in Tables 2, 3, 4, 5, 6, and 7 include the specificity Gm(Pa), which was not tested for but is presumed to be present from the known distribution of this marker (van Loghem and Grobbelaar 1971).

DISCUSSION

The simplest way to discuss the anthropology of the IgG, IgA allotypic markers is by population. Thus far, thirteen Gm-A$_2$m haplotypes have been observed in Caucasians, but only four of these have a frequency greater than 1 percent (Table 2). In contrast to its frequency among Negroes and Orientals, A$_2$m(2) appears to be very infrequent in Caucasians. Only 1.1 percent of 612 Caucasians with Caucasian phenotypes were A$_2$m(2) positive, however, 61.1 percent of 18 Caucasians with non-Caucasian phenotypes were A$_2$m (2) positive, supporting the observation originally put forth by van Loghem, Wang and Shuster (1973) that A$_2$m (2) was not present originally in Caucasians. The presence of A$_2$m (2) in Caucasians appears to be associated with either

Table 2.   Gm–A_2m haplotypes in Caucasians

Gm–A_2m haplotypes		Approximate frequency
Common haplotypes		
Gm (– b^1 Pa b^5 Ray b^3 b^0; f – –; n) A_2m (1)		0.484
(– b^1 Pa b^5 Ray b^3 b^0; f – –; –)	(1)	0.292
(g – Pa – Ray – – ; z a –; –)	(1)	0.175
(g – Pa – Ray – – ; z a x; –)	(1)	0.045
Uncommon haplotypes		
(g – Pa – Ray – – ; z a –; –)	(2)	0.005
(g – Pa – Ray – – ; z a x; –)	(2)	0.005
(– b^1 Pa b^5 Ray b^3 b^0; f – –; n)	(2)	0.005
(– b^1 Pa b^5 Ray b^3 b^0; z a –; –)	(1)	0.002
	(2)	0.003
(– – st b^5 Ray b^3 b^0; z a –; –)	(1)	0.003
	(2)	0.008
(g – Pa – Ray – – ; f – –; n)	(1)	0.005
(– b^1 Pa b^5 Ray b^3 b^0; f – x; ?)	(1)	0.002

the Oriental $Gm^{az,bst}$, A_2m^2 haplotypes or the Negro $Gm^{az,b}$, A_2m^2 haplotype. The most common one in the Central European populations studied is the $Gm^{az,bst}$, A_2m^2 haplotype. In general, the presence of A_2m(2) in Caucasians appears to be due to admixture with Orientals and Negroes. It is possible that the presence of A_2m(2) on the Caucasian $Gm^{f,b,n}$, A_2m^2 haplotype may be due to recombination between a non-Caucasian haplotype in the population and the very common $Gm^{f,b,n}$ haplotype.

Data are available thus far only on Negro populations from the Americas. In the present study, fifty-six Afro-American families from the United States were studied, while van Loghem, Wang, and Shuster (1973) studied thirty-one families from Surinam. It is evident that the Surinam Afro-Americans have less Caucasian admixture than the sample from the United States as indicated by the absence of Caucasian haplotypes in their study (Table 3). Nine haplotypes appear to be indigenous to Negroid populations, of which seven appear to exist in pure Negro populations in frequencies greater than 1 percent. The majority of haplotypes present in Afro-Americans are A_2m(2) positive (64.2 percent United States and 76.8 percent Surinam). This is in distinction to the Papuans (Table 4), who also show a high frequency of $Gm^{az,b}$ haplotypes. The differences are that the Papuan $Gm^{az,b}$ haplotype is usually Gm(n) positive, while the Negro one is Gm(n) negative, and the Papuan haplotype is almost always A_2m(1) positive, while the Negro haplotype is usually A_2m(2) positive. Thus, even without the use of Gm(n), it is possible to differentiate the $Gm^{az,b}$

Table 3. Gm–A_2m haplotypes in Afro-Americans

Gm–A_2m haplotypes		Texas N = 112	Surinam[a] N = 62
Gm (– b^1 Pa b^5 Ray b^3 b^0; z a –; –) A_2m	(1)	0.134	0.137
	(2)	0.455	0.476
(– b^1 Pa – c^5 c^3 b^0; z a –; –)	(1)	0.036	0.040
	(2)	0.143	0.234
(– b^1 Pa b^5 Ray c^3 b^0; z a –; –)	(1)	–	0.024
(– – s b^5 Ray b^3 b^0; z a –; –)	(1)	0.009	0.024
	(2)	0.027	0.057
(– b^1 Pa b^5 Ray b^3 b^0; z a x; –)	(1)	0.004	0.008
(g b^1 Pa b^5 Ray b^3 b^0; z a –; –)	(2)	0.009	–
(– b^1 Pa b^5 Ray b^3 b^0; f – –; n)	(1)	0.107	–
	(2)	0.004	–
(– b^1 Pa b^5 Ray b^3 b^0; f – –; –)	(1)	0.018	–
(g – Pa – Ray – –; z a –; –)	(1)	0.022	–
(g – Pa – Ray – –; z a x; –)	(1)	0.027	–
	(2)	0.004	–

[a] Taken from van Loghem, Wang and Shuster (1973).

Table 4. Gm–A_2m haplotypes in Papua New Guinea

Gm–A_2m haplotypes		Papuans N = 587	Melanesians N = 207
Gm (– b^1 Pa b^5 Ray b^3 b^0; f a –; n) A_2m	(1)	0.020	0.162
	(2)	0.084	0.403
(– b^1 Pa b^5 Ray b^3 b^0; f a –; –)	(1)	0.009	0.048
	(2)	0.005	0.017
(– b^1 Pa b^5 Ray b^3 b^0; z a –; n)	(1)	0.384	0.126
	(2)	0.003	0.010
(– b^1 Pa b^5 Ray b^3 b^0; z a –; –)	(1)	0.025	0.027
(g – Pa – Ray – –; z a –; –)	(1)	0.411	0.171
	(2)	0.031	0.027
(g – Pa – Ray – –; z a –; n)	(1)	0.001	–
(g – Pa – Ray – –; z a x; –)	(1)	0.027	0.010

Table 5. Comparison of selected Melanesians and Papuans

Gm–A_2m haplotypes		Papuans N = 189	Melanesians N = 129
Gm (g – Pa – Ray – –; z a –; –) A_2m	(1)	0.205	0.108
	(2)	–	0.023
(g – Pa – Ray – –; z a x; –)	(1)	0.011	0.008
(– b^1 Pa b^5 Ray b^3 b^0; z a –; n)	(1)	0.681	0.070
	(2)	–	0.015
(– b^1 Pa b^5 Ray b^3 b^0; z a –; –)	(1)	0.03	0.012
(– b^1 Pa b^5 Ray b^3 b^0; f a –; n)	(1)	–	0.190
	(2)	–	0.535
(– b^1 Pa b^5 Ray b^3 b^0; f a –; –)	(1)	–	0.023
	(2)	–	0.015

haplotypes found in Papuan and Negro populations by means of the A_2m allotypic markers.

Papua New Guinea consists of many genetically heterogeneous populations. Further marked differences in the distribution of Gm haplotypes have been observed by some investigators between the speakers of Papuan languages and those speaking Melanesian languages (Giles, Ogan and Steinberg 1965; Steinberg 1967; Curtain, et al. 1971; Curtain, et al. 1972; Schanfield 1971). These differences are magnified by the addition of the A_2m allotypic markers. It is evident that a certain amount of gene flow has existed between the two populations, and the marked differences may not be visible in the samples of Papuans and Melanesians presented here because they represent the pooled results of several different Papuan and Melanesian populations. The dichotomy is easily seen by looking at a subset of Melanesians from insular New Guinea who are characterized by the high frequency of the haplotype $Gm^{af,b,n}$, A_2m^2, while Papuans from the Fly River area are almost exclusively $Gm^{az,b,n}$, A_2m^1. The former haplotype is found predominantly in southern Asiatics, as reflected by the small sample of Chinese studied (Table 6). The marked differences between Papuans and Melanesians originally observed by Giles, Ogan, and Steinberg (1965) and magnified by Steinberg (1967) are further delineated through the use of the A_2m markers.

Table 6. Gm–A_2m haplotypes in Orientals

Gm–A_2m haplotypes		Chinese N = 58	Japanese N = 53	Japanese[a] N = 98
Gm (– b1 Pa b5 Ray b3 b0; f a –; n) A_2m	(1)	0.112	0.028	0.010
	(2)	0.672	0.151	0.141
(– – st b5 Ray b3 b0; z a –; –)	(1)	–	–	0.047
	(2)	0.026	0.226	0.214
(g – Pa – Ray – – ; z a –; –)	(1)	0.121	0.349	0.349
	(2)	–	0.047	0.057
(g – Pa – Ray – – ; z a x; –)	(1)	0.069	0.160	0.125
	(2)	–	0.038	0.026

[a] Taken from van Loghem, Wang and Shuster (1973).

In contrast to the random variation seen with Papuan populations, the heterogeneity observed in Oriental populations is present as a marked cline in the distribution of the Gm haplotypes in eastern Asia (Schanfield and Gershowitz 1973). To demonstrate the two extremes of this cline, A_2m typing was carried out on samples of southern Chinese and Japanese (Table 6). The Chinese are characterized by a high frequency of $Gm^{af,b,n}$, A_2m^2, which is found among the peoples of Southeast Asia and the South Pacific, while the Japanese are characterized by high frequencies of $Gm^{az,g}$ A_2m^1, $Gm^{xaz,g}$ A_2m^1, and $Gm^{az,bst}$ A_2m^2, which are found commonly in the Indian populations of the New World. The differences between the Chinese and Japanese are also reflected on the basis of the A_2m haplotypes: the Chinese are 30 percent A_2m^1 and 70 percent A_2m^2, while the Japanese are 64 percent A_2m^1 and 36 percent A_2m^2. Again, even without the use of the highly informative Gm allotypic markers, these two groups of Orientals can be differentiated by means of the A_2m

Table 7. Gm–A_2m haplotypes in the different populations studied

Gm–A_2m haplotypes		Populations
Gm ($- b^1$ Pa b^5 Ray b^3 b^0; f $- -$; n) A_2m	(1)	Caucasians
	(2)	Caucasians (rare)
($- b^1$ Pa b^5 Ray b^3 b^0; f $- -$; $-$)	(1)	Caucasians
($- b^1$ Pa b^5 Ray b^3 b^0; f $-$ x; ?)	(1)	Caucasians (rare)
(g $-$ Pa $-$ Ray $- -$; z a $-$; $-$)	(1)	All but pure Negroes
	(2)	Orientals, Papuans, Melanesians; Caucasians (rare)
(g $-$ Pa $-$ Ray $- -$; z a $-$; n)	(1)	Papuans (rare)
(g $-$ Pa $-$ Ray $- -$; z a x; $-$)	(1)	All but pure Negroes
	(2)	Only common in Orientals
($- b^1$ Pa b^5 Ray b^3 b^0; z a $-$; n)	(1)	Papuans, Melanesians
	(2)	Papuans (rare), Melanesians (rare)
($- b^1$ Pa b^5 Ray b^3 b^0; z a $-$; $-$)	(1)	Negroes, Caucasians (rare), Papuans (rare)
	(2)	Negroes, Caucasians (rare)
($- b^1$ Pa $-$ c^5 c^3 b^0; z a $-$; $-$)	(1)	Negroes
	(2)	Negroes
($- b^1$ Pa b^5 Ray c^3 b^0; z a $-$; $-$)	(1)	Negroes
($- -$ s b^5 Ray b^3 b^0; z a $-$; $-$)	(1)	Negroes
	(2)	Negroes
($- b^1$ Pa b^5 Ray b^3 b^0; z a x; $-$)	(1)	Negroes (rare)
(g b^1 Pa b^5 Ray b^3 b^0; z a $-$; $-$)	(2)	Negroes (rare)
($- b^1$ Pa b^5 Ray b^3 b^0; f a $-$; n)	(1)	Orientals, Melanesians, Papuans
	(2)	Orientals, Melanesians, Papuans
($- b^1$ Pa b^5 Ray b^3 b^0; f a $-$; $-$)	(1)	Melanesians, Papuans (rare)
	(2)	Melanesians, Papuans (rare)
($- -$ st b^5 Ray b^3 b^0; z a $-$; $-$)	(1)	Orientals
	(2)	Orientals
(g $-$ Pa $-$ Ray $- -$; f $- -$; n)	(1)	Caucasians (rare)

allotypic markers. When the Gm allotypic markers are added, the differences are more pronounced.

In an attempt to resolve several questions relating to the presence of different Gm haplotypes in American Indian populations, sixty-five Mexican Indians selected for their Gm phenotypes were tested for $A_2m(1)$ and (2). This was done in an attempt to shed some light on the controversy as to whether the southern Oriental haplotype $Gm^{af,b}$ exists in American Indian populations. This is discussed extensively in a paper by Szathmary, et al. (1974). Because it has been shown that the vast majority of $Gm^{af,b}$ haplotypes are also $A_2m(2)$ positive, while the Caucasian $Gm^{f,b}$ haplotype is almost exclusively $A_2m(1)$ positive, it would be expected that individuals who are Gm(f,b) positive and carrying the $Gm^{af,b}$ haplotype would be $A_2m(2)$ positive, while those carrying $Gm^{f,b}$ would be $A_2m(1)$ positive. Among thirty-seven Indians who were either Gm (a, z, g, f, b) or Gm (a, x, z, g, f, b) only three were positive for $A_2m(2)$. These three are explained by the presence of the infrequent Oriental haplotype $Gm^{az,g}$ A_2m^2, which was also found. Four individuals of the phenotype Gm(f,b) were negative for $A_2m(2)$ as expected. In contrast, out of sixteen individuals positive for Gm(st), only one was negative for $A_2m(2)$, indicating that the majority of the Indians studied had the $Gm^{az,bst}$ A_2m^2 haplotype. In addition, seven of ten $Gm^{az,b}$ haplotypes were A_2m^2, which is consistent with the distribution of $A_2m(1)$ and (2) among Negro $Gm^{az,b}$ haplotypes. Thus, again the A_2m allotypic markers give us additional information on the indigenous haplotypes present and the introduced haplotypes. In this case, the Indians appear to have $Gm^{az,g}$ A_2m^1, $Gm^{az,g}$ A_2m^2, $Gm^{axz,g}$ A_2m^1, $Gm^{az,bst}$ A_2m^2, and $Gm^{az,bst}$ A_2m^1 with the introduced Caucasian haplotype $Gm^{f,b}$ A_2m^1 and the Negro haplotypes $Gm^{az,b}$ A_2m^1 and $Gm^{az,b}$ A_2m^2.

CONCLUSIONS

The allelic allotypic markers of the A_2m system are quite informative in their own right and contribute substantially to the differentiation of human populations. However, when used in conjunction with the closely linked Gm allotypic markers, the amount of information gained is formidable. The number of racially exclusive Gm-A_2m haplotypes may possibly exceed the number of racially unique haplotypes of the HL-A system. If true, this would make the combined Gm-A_2m haplotypes the most polymorphic system in man. Though comparisons have not been made with regard to the increase in the amount of genetic distance gained by the new haplotypes generated by the Gm-A_2m

system, it should be substantial when compared with Gm haplotypes alone. It has been previously demonstrated that the contribution of the Gm haplotypes to genetic distance measurement is significantly more than the contribution of the ABO, Inv, MN, and Rh systems (Schanfield and Gershowitz 1971).

REFERENCES

CURTAIN, C. C., E. VAN LOGHEM, A. BAUMGARTEN, T. GOLAB, J. GORMAN,
C. R. RUTGERS, C. KIDSON
 1971   The ethnological significance of the gamma-globulin (Gm) factors in Melanesia. *American Journal of Physical Anthropology* 34: 257–272.

CURTAIN, C. C., E. VAN LOGHEM, H. H. FUDENBERG, N. B. TINDALE,
R. T. SIMMONS, R. L. DOHERTY, G. VOS
 1972   Distribution of the immunoglobulin markers at the IgG$_1$, IgG$_2$, IgG$_3$, IgA$_2$ and K-chain loci in Australian aborigines: comparison with New Guinea populations. *American Journal of Human Genetics* 24:145–155.

GILES, E., E. OGAN, A. G. STEINBERG
 1965   Gamma-globulin factors (Gm and Inv) in New Guinea: anthropological significance. *Science* 150:1158–1160.

KUNKEL, H. G., W. K. SMITH, F. G. JOSLIN, J. B. NATVIG, S. D. LITWIN
 1969   Genetic marker on the γA$_2$ subgroup of the γA immunoglobulins. *Nature* 223:1247–1248.

SCHANFIELD, M. S.
 1971   "Population studies on the Gm and Inv antigens in Asia and Oceania." Ann Arbor: University Microfilms.

SCHANFIELD, M. S., H. GERSHOWITZ
 1971   "The comparative efficiencies of blood group and immunoglobulin markers in the measurement of intra- and inter-population differences." Paper presented at the Fourth International Congress of Human Genetics, Paris, September 6–11, 1971.
 1973   Non-random distribution of Gm haplotypes in East Asia. *American Journal of Human Genetics* 25:567–574.

STEINBERG, A. G.
 1967   "Genetic variations in human immunoglobulins: the Gm and Inv types," in *Advances in immunogenetics*. Edited by T. J. Greenwalt, 75–98. Philadelphia: Lippincott.

SZATHMARY, E. J. E., D. W. COX, H. GERSHOWITZ, D. L. RUCKNAGEL,
M. S. SCHANFIELD
 1974   The northern and southern Ojibwa: serum proteins and red cell enzyme systems. *American Journal of Physical Anthropology* 40: 49–66.

VAN LOGHEM, E., B. G. GROBBELAAR
 1971   A new genetic marker of human IgG$_3$ immunoglobulins. *Vox Sang* 21:405–410.

VAN LOGHEM, E., J. B. NATVIG, H. MATSUMOTO
   1970   Genetic markers of immunoglobulins in Japanese. *Annals of Human Genetics* 33:351–359.
VAN LOGHEM, E., A. C. WANG, J. SHUSTER
   1973   A new genetic marker of human immunoglobulin determined by an allele at the a_2 locus. *Vox Sang* 24:481–488.
VYAS, G. N., H. H. FUDENBERG
   1970   Immunobiology of human anti-IgA: a serologic and immunogenetic study of immunization to IgA in transfusion and pregnancy. *Clinical Genetics* 1:45–64.
VYAS, G. N., H. H. FUDENBERG, H. M. PRETTY, E. R. GOLD
   1968   A new rapid method for genetic typing human immunoglobulins. *Journal of Immunology* 100:274–279.

Genes and Society: A Study of Biosocial Interactions

D. F. ROBERTS

The complex integration of biological abilities and cultural development that has brought man to his present unique and dominating
position in the animal kingdom, has given him the wherewithal to
withstand a variety of stresses. But, in particular, the rapid developments over the last few generations in technology controlling survival
have also brought a series of problems, which are relevant, indeed
critical, to man's future evolution. Such problems do not occur in
populations of simpler organisms unencumbered by culture. For them,
genetic fitness is defined in terms of survival and reproduction, because
in these terms it summarizes the advantages or disadvantages with
which a gene endows its carrier which, in turn, determine the frequency of the gene in the population.

In modern human society, deleterious genes assume an importance
beyond that which they confer on the life of the individual himself.
They present a far wider range of problems than mere survival and
reproduction imply, problems not only of treatment, often expensive
and long-continued, but also of day-to-day care and maintenance. The
aim of this discussion is to illustrate how far society itself is adversely
affected by the presence of deleterious genes.

In Britain, as in many other countries, little is known about the
burden that genetically determined disease imposes on our health
resources. Many assume it to be so slight as not to be worth mentioning. Yet the limited evidence suggests that the burden, assessed
in terms of morbidity and mortality, is considerable. Stevenson (1959),
in northern Ireland, endeavored to measure the genetic disease burden
in terms of demands on personnel. He found that approximately 6

percent of all consultations with family doctors and 8 percent of consultations with specialists were by patients with genetic disease, 26 percent of all institutional beds were occupied by patients with genetically determined illnessess, while two per thousand of the population were occupied fully in caring for these patients.

We therefore endeavored to estimate the contribution of genetic disease to the total child mortality in a group of Newcastle hospitals (Roberts, Chavez, and Court 1970). This it was hoped would complement the previous estimates of the genetic burden, provide a basis for comparison with a similar analysis at a later date, and be of some guidance in planning the future hospital service. The data were collected from the reports of deaths of children in five hospitals in Newcastle upon Tyne. All ill children admitted to hospital in Newcastle would come to one or another of these institutions. For the years 1960–1966, the total number of children's deaths in these hospitals was 1,067. For twenty-six of these information was insufficient for any classification to be possible, and these were discarded, leaving a total usable series of 1,041 cases. For each of these, the causes of mortality and details of associated conditions were reviewed and classified. The genetic disease was not necessarily the immediate cause of death; for instance, in children with fibrocystic disease of the pancreas the immediate cause of death may have been pneumonia, but there is little doubt that the fibrocystic disease was fundamental. The cases were classified into five categories:

1. Single-Gene Effects

It is very convenient for practical purposes to regard some diseases as due to a replacement of one allele by another at a particular point on a chromosome, showing the classical patterns of dominant or recessive or codominant inheritance. Some 600 conditions are well established as being due to such single-gene substitutions, and for some 900 more the evidence is strongly suggestive. Out of the present series of deaths eighty-eight cases with such simple genetic diseases could be identified. Of these, seventy-four were recessive, two dominant and three sexlinked, and nine neither (hemolytic disease of the newborn). Thus 8.5 percent of deaths in the series were associated with single-gene defects, and most (84 percent) of these were recessive in character.

2. Chromosomal Disorders

Disorders in which chromosomal irregularities appear as secondary phenomena, e.g. chronic myeloid leukemia, or are of doubtful relevance to the main disorders, were not included in this category. Twenty-five of the deaths in the series (2.5 percent) occurred where there was an associated numerical chromosomal aberration. The most frequent was Down's syndrome, with or without associated defects, which accounted for twenty-two of the cases. This total is a clear underestimate, because chromosomal examination was not at that time done routinely.

3. Disorders of Complex Genetic Etiology

Included here were (1) those diseases in which a genetic component is detectable by reason of their tendency to familial occurrence, but in which the pattern of hereditary transmission is not that observed in the case of single-gene effects; and (2) those in which a strong but complex genetic component seems likely, because of the specificity of the disorder of normal development in the absence of common extrinsic factors, and those due to persistence of some earlier embryonic stage of development again unassociated with any detectable maternal pregnancy disorder; both the latter may be interpreted as deriving from disorders of the genetic mechanisms controlling development. Diseases in this category can be regarded as due to a number of genes interacting with each other and with other factors of the milieu of development; hence the name multifactorial is applied to this type of inheritance. Altogether these cases numbered 326, the most frequent being disorders of the central nervous systems, closely followed by various congenital heart conditions. This category of genetic disease was associated with 31 percent of deaths in the series.

4. Diseases of Doubtful Etiology

These conditions were the most difficult to classify. In some a slight degree of genetic influence has been postulated, yet the evidence is not sufficiently consistent to accept; in others, the effects of environment seem predominant, though this specific factor is not identifiable. Others are clearly heterogeneous. The group was virtually composed of two broad categories: first, the various neoplasms, including leukemia, accounting for ninety-two deaths; and second, babies of low birth weight, accounting for fifty-one deaths. There were altogether 179 cases in this category.

5. *Nongenetic*

Finally a series of deaths was selected in which it seemed that genetic factors were not primarily responsible. There was no doubt about causes such as road accidents, burns, etc. In this environmental group were also included deaths from specific infections, among which respiratory and gastrointestinal predominated. Because almost every one of these deaths could have been prevented by not exposing the child to the infecting agent they are included under this heading, though it is possible that in some there was a genetic component in their susceptibility. The whole group accounted for 423 deaths.

The above series of hospital deaths cannot be used to quantitate the genetic component in child mortality in general; there is a degree of subjectivity in the classifications used; and, of course, there are no clear-cut distinctions among the five categories. There is a continuous spectrum of diseases — at one end those due to genes alone, at the other those due to environment alone, and a majority of disorders lying between these two extremes. But, making allowance for the evident limitations of this type of survey, the results are nonetheless striking. Deaths from simple genetic disease account for 8.5 percent and those from chromosomal aberrations for 2.5 percent, so that together these two categories make up 11 percent of identifiable deaths in the series. Then, 31 percent of the total deaths occur in disorders in whose etiology the genetic component is complex. The environmental end of the spectrum accounts for some 41 percent of the total, but here again there may well be some genetic component in resistance or susceptibility to infections which make up a considerable proportion of the total deaths in this large group.

Carter (1956) examined the causes of death in three groups of children coming to necropsy at Great Ormond Street Hospital, London, one in 1914, one in 1934, and the third in 1954. In 1914 two-thirds of all deaths were from diseases such as pneumonia, tuberculosis, and various infections particularly intestinal, which are preventable by well-known public health measures and can therefore be regarded as primarily of environmental origin; only 16 percent of the deaths were attributable to genetic or partly genetic causes. By 1954, however, the environmental proportion had dropped to 15 percent, over one-third were due wholly or partly to genetic causes, while almost a half were classified as of unknown etiology, and these mainly included various congenital malformations and cancers of childhood. While the different nature of the two hospital populations, and the new knowledge of the fifteen intervening years, impede close comparison of our findings with those of Carter's 1954 series, there is quite good correspondence of his total of wholly and partly-genetic with the total of our first three categories (Table 1).

Table 1. Causes of childhood deaths

Newcastle 1960–1966 survey (1041 deaths)			Carter's 1954 results (200 deaths)		
Single-gene defects	8.5%	11.0%	Wholly genetic	12.0%	
Chromosomal disorders	2.5%		Partly genetic	25.5%	
Probable but complex genetic	31.0%		Unknown	48.0%	62.5%
Disease of unknown etiology	17.0%	58.0%	Environmental	14.5%	
Non-genetic	41.0%				

The results of this survey show the heavy genetic contribution to present-day child mortality in Newcastle. It is a reasonable conclusion from comparison with earlier surveys that this burden is probably increasing. The study says nothing of the genetic contribution to adult mortality or to morbidity, but it is reasonable to assume that genetic morbidity is pursuing a parallel course. Direct evidence is slight, but in 1922 the Board of Education made a survey of the causes of blindness in schoolchildren, and found that 37 percent of blindness in the school population was due to congenital and hereditary anomalies. A similar survey in 1950 showed that whereas the total rate of blindness had been halved, there had been no reduction in blindness attributed to congenital and hereditary anomalies, and the figure for these had risen from 37 to 68 percent of the total blindness load. These results illuminate a number of urgent biosocial problems — the need for genetic advisory services, the need for knowledge on which these are to be based, the need for early diagnosis for treatment and early antenatal diagnosis for avoidance by selective termination. Work in this area has tended to concentrate on the first two categories (monogenic and chromosomal) listed above.

Today for the population at large there is no reason why any child should develop phenylketonuria, because screening of all young infants can be achieved, economically and effectively, and dietary control initiated for those affected; nearly 50,000 per year are so screened in the Newcastle hospital region. Success means that bad genes are being passed on. Retinoblastoma can be detected in families at risk by regular screening of infants, so with adequate treatment survival to reproduce is today well over 90 percent. Again the genes are being passed on. A mother at high risk of producing a child with some inborn error of metabolism can be reassured, by the assay of relevant enzymes in amniotic fluid or cultured cells, that by selective termination, if she so requires, only normal children will be born; this procedure is now possible for some forty metabolic disorders. But it is mainly the recessive homozygotes, which would in any case fail to pass on their genes, that are detected and eliminated, and the heterozygotes which appear normal are retained.

For the sex-linked disorders, antenatal fetal sexing, again with the offer of selective termination, means that normal sons can be guaranteed where the father is affected. But women who are known carriers of serious sex-linked disorders opt for termination of male pregnancies and for retention of the female fetuses, half of whom are carriers. There has been considerable argument as to whether the effects of antenatal studies are dysgenic or eugenic. The answer lies in the extent of reproductive compensation for the terminated pregnancies, and about this crucial topic little is yet known. But all these advances relate to the numerically least important end of the spectrum, as shown by the mortality survey. The conspicuous finding was the high proportion of mortality in which the disorders of complex genetic etiology are involved. It is these about which least is known and about which least can so far be done in the antenatal situation. For the moment then, success in treatment and diagnosis has diminished the selection pressure against deleterious genes, which are in consequence increasing in frequency, and this has not yet been counterbalanced by the very real advances in antenatal and early diagnosis possible in a limited number of conditions.

SOCIAL IMPLICATIONS OF GENETIC DISEASE

The burden of genetic disease is not merely of concern at the population level. Evolutionary discussion is primarily in terms of population, into which the individual *per se* enters infrequently. But the impact of genetic disease on society can perhaps be illustrated most effectively by considering individuals, or rather a subpopulation of individuals.

Among the many babies with serious genetic defects who in former days would have died young, there are now, thanks to modern knowledge and treatment, a large proportion who survive the early years of life. Their defects impose varying degrees of disability on them. Besides the medical problems, which make an increasing demand on the health services, the disablements to which these conditions give rise produce a number of personal problems, emotional, social, and economic in nature. They can be well illustrated by the social impact of hemophilia. This discussion is based on a study of the quality of life in the population of hemophiliacs in the north of England (Boon and Roberts 1970).

A survey was made of the difficulties of hemophiliacs in the north of England, to answer the question, "What does it mean to be a hemophiliac?". On 1st September, 1968, 137 hemophiliacs were traced in our hospital area. Most cases were diagnosed at ages between six months and two years, during the exploratory phase of infant development when knocks are frequent. Some of the milder cases were not diagnosed until six to eight years, when deciduous teeth gave trouble, and there were a few patients diagnosed in adulthood. The age at diagnosis (see Figure 1) allows interpretation of the age distribution

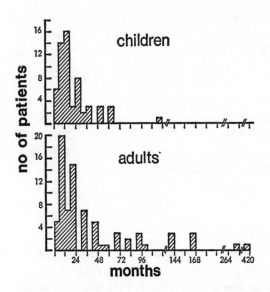

Figure 1. Hemophiliacs' age at diagnosis

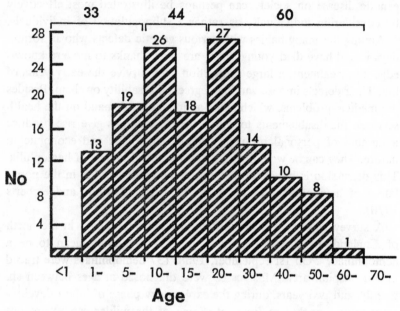

Figure 2.   Age distribution of surviving hemophiliacs

of the surviving hemophiliacs (see Figure 2). The apparent diminution in numbers in the youngest age groups does not indicate a diminishing number of patients, but rather that there are several in the region at these ages still to be diagnosed. In these patients the disease is of varying grades of severity, but they are all liable at any time to succumb to a bleeding episode, which may be severe and cause permanent damage or death. The types of hemorrhage are many and varied, joint involvement is particularly common, often leading to residual disability. These bleeding episodes can only be disruptive of normal living for the patient and his family. To cope with the episode, to heal the physical damage that may ensue, interferes with whatever the patient would normally be doing at the time, at school or at work. This, then, is the background of difficulty and disability.

Domestic

Of the seventy-eight adult patients, forty-three were married, all but one before they reached the age of thirty-two years (Table 2). Three of these were divorced or separated. Thirty-four of the married couples had produced sixty-nine children, thirty-four boys and thirty-five girls,

Table 2. Adult hemophiliacs: marital status and composition of the family

Age Group	Number	Married	Single	Divorced or separated	Children Male	Female
16–21	18	1	17			
22–31	27	14	12	1	3	9
32–41	14	11	2	1	16	10
42–51	12	11		1	8	12
52–61	6	6			7	4
62–71	1		1			
Total	78	43	32	3	34	35
					69	

the latter all carriers of the hemophilia gene. Eight of these couples had only one child, and in most cases had waited several years before producing it. Three couples did not intend to have any children, five others were recently married. It seems that hemophiliacs today do not have large families; their mothers, however, who are carriers of the gene, apparently do, but the means in Table 3 may be overestimates, for this table was compiled from family pedigrees, and so may be biased in favor of high fertility. The apparent excess of hemophiliacs over normal boys and the apparent excess of boys over girls is due to the sampling bias, to which Haldane and Philip (1939) drew attention, and when this is allowed for neither is significant.

Table 3. Number of children produced by proven female carriers

Age Group	Number of Mothers	Hemo-philiacs	Normal children Male	Female	Total	Average
40–49	11	15	12	24	51	4.6
50–59	12	18	10	17	45	3.8
60–69	8	17	9	12	38	4.8
70–79	8	16	9	24	49	6.1
80+	6	11	8	13	32	5.3
Total	45	77	48	90	215	4.8

As regards family life, the reaction to the diagnosis was always one of horror, dismay, and grave anxiety. The mother, after the initial shock, came to accept the situation and in most cases adapted her life accordingly. In many families the father reacted similarly but was never so intimately involved with the child, and three fathers appeared to be quite unconcerned. In those families where the appearance of a hemophilic boy was an isolated case, the impact was more severe.

One mother wrote "I should never wish another child to come into the world to suffer in childhood the way K has. There is nothing his father and I would not do to help K enjoy life as much as a normal child."

In the face of this reaction, it is not surprising that modern mothers tend to limit their families and in this, and in the contraceptive methods employed the two generations are clearly different (Table 4).

Table 4.   Contraceptive practices — comparison of two generations

Mothers	Numbers sterilized	Contraceptive		Dia-phragm	Rhythm or no Pre-cautions	Widows or Meno-pause
		Pill	Condom			
Of adults	0	2	3	2	1	15
Of children	16	13	4	0	9	5

The effect on the other children of the birth of a hemophiliac depended on his position in the family. If he was the eldest, the others grew up with his disability and realized that they must be careful. When there were older normal sibs, they were encouraged by the mother to care for the disabled child and to make sure he was not involved in rough play. In the larger families there seemed to be a strong bond of affection between the children and the hemophiliac, and his disability was accepted, but in two families the boy was difficult and caused family friction. Five hemophiliacs without sibs had had little or no child companionship in their early life. In two cases the activities of sibs had been restricted because of the hemophilic brother, but the sibs generally made friends outside the family without any difficulty.

For most adult patients housing was satisfactory. Of the eighteen married hemophiliacs who owned their own homes, no difficulty had been experienced in obtaining a mortgage.

Most of the children, too, were reasonably well housed, but this was partly due to the intervention of the hospital authorities. For hemophilic children, upstairs flats with steep stone stairways are unsuitable, and so are houses whose doors open directly to the street, both characteristic of northern England. One very severely affected boy as a toddler with his three sibs lived in a basement flat consisting of two rooms, and the backyard where they played was full of rubble and broken bricks — a most unsuitable environment for a hemophilic boy. The family was first moved to an upstairs council flat whose steep narrow staircase created enormous difficulties for a boy with calipers, crutches, and a wheelchair, and subsequently the family was moved to a council house with a ramp over the front doorstep, allowing chair access. Altogether, six families of the fifty-nine child hemophiliacs had been rehoused through hospital intervention.

As an index of social classification, the Registrar General's categories were used. The distribution of occupation of the adult patient as compared with that of his father was remarkably similar. However, the distribution of occupations of the fathers of affected children is significantly better than both these; the acquisition of technical skills now required for socioeconomic advancement is open to normal adults but not to hemophiliacs, for whom opportunity is as restricted as it was a generation ago.

Thirty-eight of the families with an affected child never went on holiday, either because they could not afford to go or because they were too uncertain about the health of the hemophilic boy to risk traveling any distance. Twenty-four mothers said they were unable to take part in activities or jobs outside the home because they did not wish to leave their sons, but the majority were able to go out for leisure persuits, the husbands taking turns to stay at home to look after the child. Thirteen of the fifty-nine mothers worked after marriage before the hemophiliac was born, but only seven, where the grandmother was able to care for the family during the mother's absence, worked parttime after the child's arrival. Fourteen mothers said it was a full-time job looking after a hemophilic boy, and they could not delegate the responsibility to others.

Education

The nature of the disease prevents the hemophiliac from undertaking many forms of manual labor; a good education is, therefore, essential so that he can subsequently obtain suitable work and lead a positive life. In the past professional opportunity through higher education was denied many hemophiliacs, for a severely affected boy could only look forward to a succession of interruptions of school life as a result of bleeding episodes. As regards the adults, five out of seventy-eight had not attended a primary school of any form. Many had succeeded in completing their education at normal school, most of these being only mildly affected and managing to avoid competitive games and rough play. Some had been allowed to arrive at school five minutes late and leave early, in order to avoid the scramble in cloakrooms and corridors. Six adults had attained grammar school standard. Of the forty-five child patients of school age, it is noteworthy that of the fourteen who were of age to progress to grammar school none had managed to do so. One of the boys at a village school at the age of twelve years had missed so much time that he can hardly read or write. Time lost from school (Table 5) shows a distinct improvement over the two generations, which can be attributed to the improved medical treatment available today. Whereas only a quarter of adults had achieved normal attendance, approximately half of the children have done so.

Table 5.   Time lost from school — comparison of two generations

Category	Normal attendance	Less than one-fourth	More than one-fourth	Total
Adults	19	23	36	78
Children	20	10	9	39

Employment

It is against this background of incomplete and interrupted education that employment problems are to be placed. Of the seventy-eight adults, sixty-four had passed no examinations of any kind, two had G.C.E. A-level attainments, seven some 0-level qualifications, and five had a trade or commerce certificate. The average age on starting work was fifteen and one-half years. Forty-six of the seventy-eight adults had received no special training, the types of their first employment clearly indicated the unskilled nature of their situations (Table 6). As regards present occupation, 20 percent are in sedentary occu-

Table 6.   Types of first employment

Employed	
Laboring (farm, colliery, shipyard)	16
Apprentice	20
Shop assistant	11
Clerk (junior office boy)	8
Errand boy	8
Remploy factory	4
Factory	2
Lift man	1
Window cleaner	1
Further education and training	
Government training center	3
University	1
Lord Mayor Treloar College	1
Unemployed	2
Total	**78**

pations. A surprising number (17 percent) are engaged on manual work of some kind, e.g. a blacksmith, two laborers, three sheet metal workers. There were two who had attained professional status, an accountant and a teacher. Most of the older men had kept their jobs for many years, but the younger ones had had many changes of employment. Repeated absences from work were a major factor in their dismissal, 50 percent deliberately changed jobs because of ill health, others for improvement of occupation or to seek more congenial surroundings. Altogether, only a quarter had had steady occupations throughout their working period, with no unemployment. Four men had never worked, one man aged thirty-nine was ineducable and unemployable. Fifty percent of the men were quite happy and satisfied with what they were doing, though they realized that the scope of work open to them was limited. Security was an important factor, and if they knew that the job would be kept open for them when they were absent sick, this was a great help in reducing anxiety.

Forty-six employers knew at the time of hiring that the man was a hemophiliac but twenty-five did not know because the employee did not wish to jeopardize his chances of obtaining the job by disclosing his disability. Some employers do not like to employ a man with this condition, for it is obviously a nuisance if he is repeatedly away from work; but our survey shows that the older men have fewer acute episodes necessitating long absence as they get older, they appreciate a good job, and they do not stay away without good reason. As regards transport to work, thirty-two go by car, some being taken by a friend or relative. Most of the remainder travel by bus. But the seriously affected are not able to wait for buses because of the strain on their knees; they find walking difficult and are not agile enough to get on and off vehicles easily, and they fear the trauma caused by jostling crowds at rush hours.

Sixteen men had never made any monetary claim from the state for unemployment benefit or supplementary benefit. The remaining sixty-two (79 percent) had received these aids or sickness benefit. One man, who applied for national assistance during a long illness, had been refused because he had managed to save a little money. Of the fourteen men who were unemployed, three were retired (two prematurely because of ill health). Four youths had been unable to get suitable employment. Though the average weekly income is better than that for all disabled persons, the hemophiliacs are considerably worse off than men in normal families, averaging in 1968 a weekly income of 14 pounds as compared with 19 pounds (see Figure 3).

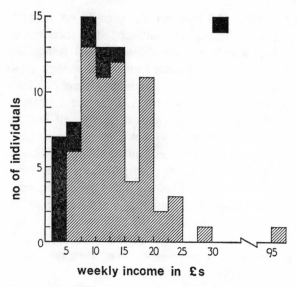

Figure 3.   Hemophiliacs — distribution of weekly income*
*   Solid black squares represent the income of part-time and unemployed workers.

What a hemophiliac does with his leisure time can be used as an indicator to show how well he is integrated into society. Formal religion played no part in these men's lives, apart from two. Television and radio formed the basis of practically all the home entertainment. Outside the home the cinema was at the top of the list of entertainment. As regards physical exercise, the majority could walk reasonable distances when fit, but took little advantage of physical exercise to strengthen muscles and joints.

Implications of the Hemophilia Findings

In summary, hemophilia does not appear to influence the domestic life of the patient seriously, insofar as marriage is concerned, or the decision to produce a family, but it does affect family size. The birth of a hemophilic child markedly affects the immediate family, particularly the mother who undoubtedly has the greatest burden to bear. The demonstration of educational inadequacy due mainly to time lost from school through hospitalization is one of the most serious results of the survey, for education is of vital importance to those most severely affected, and to a lesser extent to those with milder tendencies. Comparison of the child and the adult samples shows the effect of improved modern treatment, which entails much shorter stays in hospital, but time lost from school is still appreciable. With care and cooperation, most hemophilic boys can be taught in normal schools, except where there is an exceptionally poor family background or the child has a low IQ requiring special training.

The employment findings are equally important. The choice of employment was severely restricted by the limited education. Stability of employment was affected by the episodes of ill health during adulthood. Due to a lack of education a surprising number of patients are in work that is unsuitable for them. The more intelligent men have learned to live with their disability and to avoid accidents, but the less intelligent are forced repeatedly to take time out from work. A high proportion have been obliged to change their jobs because of ill health, and the highest incidence of insecurity was among the young age groups. In recreational activities these men could do more to help themselves, for most of them engaged in little or no physical exercise, but the manual workers all look physically fit. Hemophiliacs, then, are not contributing to society to the full extent of their potential, and society is doing little to allow them to do so. The changing pattern of treatment promises to cause less interruption of normal activity and hence less social undercontribution, but this is not applicable to all.

Hemophilia itself is but one of the many genetic disorders, some more and some less severe, to each of which a similar argument may be applied. As a result of treatment, selection pressure against the gene has declined. Haldane (1946) accepted a fitness of the hemophilia phenotype of .286. Employing the same procedure, comparing the fertility of hemophiliacs with their normal brothers, the nineteen hemophiliacs with completed families had thirty-one children by comparison with the twenty normal brothers, who had forty-eight children; the hemophiliac comparative fertility is .68, a distinct advance on Haldane's figure. The increase over Haldane's figure is probably greater still, on account of the improved survival today over that of the patients included in his calculation. If, however, we accept the figure of .68 as an estimate of fitness, then assuming constant mutation rate, the new equilibrium birth frequency to which we can look forward is one in 3,200. The figure generally quoted for Britain for the birth frequency of hemophiliacs is one in 11,000. A distinct increase is to be expected. Our survey shows there to be seventy-eight adult hemophiliacs in a regional population of 1,150,532 men of the same age, and fifty-nine boys in a regional population of 410,539 boys of the same age, and, as noted initially, this may be an underestimate. The frequency of adult hemophiliacs, then, is one in 14,750 (perhaps partly due to loss by mortality), the frequency of child hemophiliacs is one in 6,956. It appears that the increase toward the new equilibrium figure is already under way.

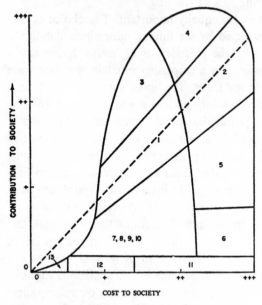

Figure 4.   Social fitness of human genotypes

DISCUSSION

The social fitness of human genotypes is very difficult to evaluate. A first attempt was made by Wright (1960) thirteen years ago, who treated the problem in terms of the balance between the contributions to society by individuals of different genotypes and what they cost society. He distinguishes the following categories (see Figure 4) of individuals:

1.   Those who contribute to society approximately what they cost at relatively modest levels. This category includes the bulk of the population — the ordinary orderly, stalwart, law-abiding man and woman.

2.   Those in whom there is a balance between contribution and cost at relatively high levels, namely professional men and women, technicians, experts, specialists into whose education society invests

heavily and who receive, as a result of their labor, a standard of living above the average of the population.

3. and 4.   These are the intellectual and technological elite — first-class artists or experts, creative and seminal minds, persons of genius, who make extraordinary contributions at either low or high cost to the society.

5.   Persons whose capacities are those of the first or second category, but who repay society much less than the cost of their maintenance. These for example include the possessors of unearned wealth, whose social contribution consists chiefly of high life, conspicuous consumption, but who play an important part in the economy by setting fashions and so stimulating the average person's consumption. Perhaps some of our hemophiliacs fit into this category.

6.   Criminal and antisocial persons of otherwise normal mental capacity.

7.   Those of subnormal physical constitution and health.

8.   Those of low intelligence but sufficient to take care of themselves under existing social conditions.

9. and 10.   Those normal in childhood but experiencing early physical or mental breakdown; it is in these categories that many of the more severe hereditary diseases come, in which the ages of onset and incapacitation fall in youth or young adulthood and so interfere with productive life.

11.   Those of physical or mental incapacitation throughout a life of normal duration.

12.   Those who die before maturity, too early for any appreciable contribution to society.

13.   Those who die at or before birth.

Each of these categories of course embraces a great multitude of genotypes. Categories 1 to 5 are the normal, those who keep society going. The remainder, numbers 6 to 13, in whom the social costs outweigh the returns, are the ones who are a burden on society and in some of these the genetic component of that burden is heavy. The burden that they impose on the remainder of society is tolerable if it is not too heavy, for despite it society can continue its efforts in getting a living, improving material rewards, improving standards and developing more efficient yet satisfying sets of ideas which will allow it to maintain its position *vis à vis* other societies. But if the burden gets too great, then too much of society's efforts will have to be devoted to carrying the burden, and society itself will suffer.

To decide into which of these categories an individual fits is difficult. It is a combination of the effects of his genetic endowment and effects of social transmission. The social endowment that a child receives is controllable, but its genetic heritage is much less so. The need is to adjust the first to the second. For example, it is a misuse of effort to give the education for a learned profession to an individual genetically unable to absorb it, and it may well prevent his receiving an alternative education through which he would have made a greater contribution to society utilizing his own special talents. Similarly, it is a clear waste of resources to society if the genetically gifted individual is not educated up to his ability. There is obviously need for much more detailed analysis along the lines of this first attempt at sociological genetics.

It has not been the intention of the present study to identify each individual in our survey with one or other of these categories. Rather, this scheme of Wright's has been introduced essentially to put into perspective the findings of our studies. In recapitulation, we showed first that an appreciable proportion of the burden of child mortality in Newcastle hospitals was genetic in origin. Hence an appreciable proportion of the services of hospitals caring for children are preempted by society's deleterious genes. Second, it has been shown that, using the example of hemophilia, individuals suffering from serious genetic disease are not contributing fully to society, partly because of the nature of the disease, and partly because society itself is not organized to allow them to do so, to recognize their special needs and to make allowances for them. Here much more can be done by social measures to diminish the gap between the patient's potential and his actual contribution. The third main point to emerge is that deleterious genes are increasing in frequency and will continue to do so until their new equilibrium levels are attained, which will depend on the changed fitness of the individuals concerned. It is here that hope for the resolution of the biological part of this problem lies. For if those to whom modern medicine has given their own lives, or those of their children, can be educated to reproduce responsibly, that is to say restrict their reproduction to a level below that of the population as a whole, then the maintenance of their genetic fitness at a lower level will prevent the new equilibrium gene frequency from rising to too high a point, and the total burden that society will have to face will be correspondingly reduced.

REFERENCES

BOON, R. A., D. F. ROBERTS
   1970   The social impact of haemophilia. *Journal of Biosocial Sciences* 2:237–264.

CARTER, C. O.
   1956   Changing patterns in the causes of death at the Hospital for Sick Children. *Great Ormond Street Journal* 11:65.

HALDANE, J. B. S.
   1946   The mutation rate of the gene for hemophilia, and its segregation ratios in males and females. *Annals of Eugenics* 13:262–271.

HALDANE, J. B. S., U. PHILIP
   1939   The daughters and sisters of hemophiliacs. *Journal of Genetics* 38:193.

ROBERTS, D. F., J. B. CHAVEZ, S. D. M. COURT
   1970   The genetic component in child mortality. *Archives of the Diseases of Childhood* 45:33–38.

STEVENSON, A. C.
   1959   The load of hereditary defects in human populations. *Radiation Research* (supplement) 1:306.

WRIGHT, S.
   1960   "On the appraisal of genetic effects of radiation in man," in *The biological effects of atomic radiation*. Washington, D.C.: National Academy of Sciences, National Research Council.

Genetic Adaptation and Sexual Selection in Sub-Saharan Africa

JEAN HIERNAUX

In his famous book on the descent of man, Charles Darwin (1871) stressed the role that sexual selection may have played in the differentiation of human populations. Selection, and heterosis as well, are based on the different rates of reproduction of genotypes. At a given locus, the two processes tend toward an equilibrium: monoallelic in the case of selection, polyallelic in the case of heterosis (or heterozygous advantage). Both will be discussed here under the term 'selection.' Selection may result from differential fertility of the genotypes, or from differential mortality of the latter before reproductive age, or from a combination of both. Rephrasing Darwin's view sexual selection takes place in a population when some individuals have hereditary traits which attract the opposite sex to a greater degree than other individuals and consequently beget more children (Hulse 1972). Such differential fertility will, however, result in selection only if it is not counterbalanced by a higher mortality of the genotypes favored by sexual selection.

To ascertain the balance of forces which act on the frequency of the genotypes from one generation to the next is a formidable task which has rarely been satisfactorily worked out except for a few loci like the one which controls the hemoglobin variants. In the case of polygenic characters such an undertaking would entail further assumptions. Yet some of these characters appear so important in regard to diversifying selection in man that a discussion of the possible selective forces that act on them seems valuable, however speculative it may be at present. A case in which sexual selection and selection by climate are seemingly at work will be discussed here: that of nose width in Ful Bororo communities. This variable is known to be partly controlled by heredity. In a sample of 132 Belgian families, Susanne (1971) estimates the genetical part of the between-sib variability of nose width to be 55 percent.

The Ful (or Fulani) are an ethnic group scattered over a wide area in western Sudan. Some are now sedentary, but many Ful communities (those called Bororo) keep their ancestral mode of life, transhumant pastoralism. There are firm reasons to believe that they descend from the neolithic pastoralists of the Sahara. As a whole, the Ful closely resemble the non-Ful of West Africa in their allele frequencies for blood trait systems and in their fingerprints. Their main quantifiable difference from the surrounding populations is in their narrower head, face, and nose. The difference in nose width is especially large (Hiernaux 1974).

In sub-Saharan Africa, nose width is correlated with climate: in a set of 179 populations, this measurement has a coefficient of correlation of $r = +.49$ with annual rainfall, and of $r = -.33$ with the mean maximum daily temperature of the hottest month. These correlations apparently reflect genetic adaptation of nose morphology to climate. The nose tends to be the narrowest in the dry climate with seasonal peaks of extreme heat, that of the Sahara and the Sahel, and the broadest in the damp climate without marked seasons which characterizes the equatorial forest (Hiernaux 1968). According to Weiner (1954), who discusses the correlation between the nasal index and climate in the entire human species, the selective forces underlying this correlation concern the main function of the nasal passage, to humidify inspired air and bring it to body temperature.

There are, therefore, reasons for explaining the narrower nose of the Ful as an ancestral adaptation to a drier environment. However, selection by climate would necessarily tend to put an end to the difference in nose width between the Ful and non-Ful populations who live in the same climatic zone. The Ful are known to have been settled for a long time in the Fouta Toro area of Senegal. Their language, which belongs to the West Atlantic class of the Niger-Congo family, is closely akin to that of the Wolof and Serer of the same area (Greenberg 1963). Their very wide present scattering appears to have originated from there about the eleventh century. How many generations they lived in contact with the broader-nosed, predominantly agriculturalist populations of Senegal is unknown. Archaeology tells us only that by the end of the second millenium B.C., climatic deterioration in the Sahara had become so severe that a large portion of the population had been forced to move to the south.

Along with selection by climate, whose strength has not yet been quantified, a second mechanism tends to put an end to the difference in nose width between Ful and non-Ful of the same areas, that of inter-breeding. This is known to occur. In a study of the Ful Bororo of northern Nigeria, Stenning (1965) mentions the union between a Ful man and a non-Ful woman as an accepted, although rare, type of marriage.

Despite these two mechanisms working to reduce the difference, the pastoral Ful retain a narrower nose. Of course, it is quite possible that this is a transient state and that the difference is actually in the process of disappearing. One may, however, suspect that there are intervening factors maintaining the differentiation. In the present case, we have no indication that differences in diet or in physical activity might act as differentiating factors (either by influencing the development of the nose or through selection). On the contrary, there is strong evidence of sexual selection in favor of a narrower nose in the Bororo.

The pastoral Ful attach much importance to physique. Their esthetic ideal is a gracile body build, long legs, a long and narrow nose. Nose shape is particularly important. A Ful proverb runs, "See the nose, understand the character" (Stenning 1965). Among the Wodaabe Bororo of Niger, young men prefer to court the girls of the Jijiru lineage, who are reputed to have a narrower nose than girls of other lineages. There is much sexual freedom before marriage, resulting in premarital reproduction.

Conforming more to the esthetic ideal of the community increase the probability of finding a temporary sexual partner, and hence the opportunity to reproduce. From time to time the *gereol* dance is held. It has similarities with the sexual display of many animal species: young men, watched by the girls and married women, try to display their beauty, grace, and sexual attractiveness. The dance temporarily brings together people from far and wide and leads to casual intercourse, adultery, and marriages (Dupire 1962). Although it has not been quan-tified, sexual selection seems powerful in such Ful communities.

It may be stated that the interaction of sexual selection and selection by climate on nose width in Ful populations has varied with time and place. They were synergetic where, and as long as, the adaptive optimum was a narrower nose, and antagonistic in the opposite case, which certainly occurs today in the relatively moist areas reached by the most southern expansion of the Ful, for example in the Adamawa highlands of Cameroon.

Sexual selection interacts with interbreeding also. Genetic admixture from surrounding populations tends to make the Ful communities more similar to the latter at all loci. Sexual selection in favor of a narrower nose and other distinctive features tends to maintain the dissimilarity of the Ful at the loci which control these features. This may explain why the Ful as a group are not distinctive in blood traits or in fingerprints; the action of interbreeding (and possibly of common selective forces also) was not counterbalanced by sexual selection for such traits.

REFERENCES

DARWIN, CHARLES
  1871   *The descent of man and selection in relation to sex.* London: John Murray.
DUPIRE, M.
  1962   *Peuls nomades. Etude descriptive des Wodaabe du Sahel Nigérien.* Paris: Institut d'Ethnologie.
GREENBERG, J. H.
  1963   *Languages of Africa.* The Hague: Mouton.
HIERNAUX, J.
  1968   *La diversité humaine en Afrique subsaharienne.* Bruxelles: Institut de Sociologie de l'Université Libre de Bruxelles.
  1974   *The people of Africa.* London: Weidenfeld and Nicolson.
HULSE, F. S.
  1972   Natural selection and differential population growth on human races. *Social Biology* 19:171–179.
STENNING, D. J.
  1965   "The pastoral Fulani of northern Nigeria," in *Peoples of Africa.* Edited by J. L. Gibbs, Jr., 361–402. New York: Holt, Rinehart and Winston.
SUSANNE, C.
  1971   *Recherche sur la transmission des caractères mesurables de l'homme.* Bruxelles: Institut Royal des Sciences Naturelles de Belgique, Mémoire 167.
WEINER, J. S.
  1954   Nose shape and climate. *American Journal of Physical Anthropology* 12:1–4.

Degree of Heterozygosity and Population Structure of South American Indians

FRANCISCO M. SALZANO

PROBLEMS IN THE STUDY OF NATURAL SELECTION

One of the basic questions in population genetics today is how the many polymorphisms that have been identified are being maintained. Several approaches to the investigation of this question in humans have been suggested (Morton, Krieger, and Mi 1966; Neel and Schull 1968). Some of them are clearly more promising than others, but for even the former the methodological problems are such that no unequivocal answers can be expected in the near future.

Two of the most ambitious investigations which tried to detect selection for polymorphisms by evaluating distortions in genetic ratios within families were those of Morton, Krieger, and Mi (1966) and Sing, et al. (1971). In the first study a sample of 1,068 families from northeastern Brazil comprising 6,864 tested persons and an additional 4,090 pregnancies was examined in an effort to find indications of selection in sixteen polymorphic systems. Only in relation to ABO were the results positive. Sing, et al. (1971) analyzed 2,507 Caucasian families in the United States, a total of 9,182 individuals, seeking this kind of evidence in eleven genetic systems. Significant deviations in the genetic ratios occurred two to three times more often than expected by chance alone. But the effects were distributed among six of the eleven systems, and in those showing a significant deviation the

The support of the Câmara Especial de Pós-graduação e Pesquisa da Universidade Federal do Rio Grande do Sul, Conselho Nacional de Pesquisas, Coordenação do Aperfeiçoamento de Pessoal de Nível Superior, Fundação de Amparo à Pesquisa do Estado do Rio Grande do Sul, and the Wenner-Gren Foundation for Anthropological Research is gratefully acknowledged.

departure from expectation was not present for all mating types.

These results were therefore inconclusive, and in the discussion of their data Sing, et al. (1971) rightly emphasized that larger samples and different approaches should be tried in studies whose aim is the solution of these questions.

DEGREE OF HETEROZYGOSITY, POLYMORPHIC INDEX, AND POPULATION STRUCTURE OF SOUTH AMERICAN INDIANS

Elsewhere (Salzano 1975) I have indicated some of the advantages of using tribal societies for the study of many biological problems in humans. Studies over the past fifteen years have accumulated a series of genetic and ecological data from several South American Indian tribes. In what follows, I will try to relate the degree of heterozygosity observed in different populations of these Indians with their population structure and will also compare the level observed among the Cayapo with the one found in a Caucasian, technologically more developed community (Tecumseh, Michigan). Many factors can influence the degree of heterozygosity of a group. It is hoped, however, that with studies such as these we may gain some insight into the nature of the selective processes that possibly operate to maintain the observed polymorphisms.

Spuhler (1963) has proposed an index, D, to measure the departure from the maximum degree of heterozygosity in a population for a locus with k alleles where x_i is the frequency of the i-th allele:

$$D = \left(\sum_{i=1}^{k} x_i^2 - \frac{1}{k} \right) \left(\frac{k}{k-1} \right)$$

D will be zero when there is no departure from the maximum degree of heterozygosity and will be unity when this departure is the largest (fixation of one allele and elimination of all others, known to be present in other populations).

Table 1 presents the results of the application of this index to populations of five South American Indian tribes. Four of them still have a subsistence based mainly on hunting and gathering with incipient agriculture, while the Caingang are basically agriculturalists. There are distinct differences in the degree of heterozygosity both among loci and among tribes. The loci showing the largest departures from the maximum level are those related to the secretion of ABH and the Diego blood group. On the other hand, with Kidd and Inv the

Table 1. Departure from the maximum degree of heterozygosity considering twelve loci in five South American Indian tribes

Loci	Tribes				
	Cayapo (N = 526)	Xavante (N = 539)	Caingang (N = 228)	Yanomamö (N = 2,516)	Makiritare (N = 539)
MNSs	0.177	0.101	0.181	0.168	0.068
Rh	0.219	0.277	0.208	0.588	0.281
P	0.020	0.076	0.308	0.024	0.016
Fy	0.164	0.008	0.008	0.024	0.212
Jk	0.012	0.024	–	0.004	0.128
Di^a	0.324	0.448	0.100	1.000	0.384
Secretion of ABH	0.172	0.072	0.296	1.000	1.000
Secretion of Le	0.000	0.068	0.246	0.002	0.010
Hp	0.024	0.004	0.284	0.448	0.024
Gc	0.080	0.140	0.044	0.588	0.408
Gm	0.332	0.332	0.232	–	–
Inv	0.028	0.010	0.032	–	–
Average	0.129	0.130	0.176	0.385	0.253

The gene frequencies are presented in Arends, et al. (1970); Gershowitz, et al. (1970, 1972); Salzano, et al. (1972a, 1972b); Salzano, Steinberg, and Tepfenhart (1973); Weitkamp, et al. (1972). W, the coefficient of concordance in ranking the degree of heterozygosity for these tribes and loci, is 0.133; F = 1.2 (nonsignificant). The number of individuals studied is not the same for all loci.

corresponding results are very near the attainable maximum. Considering the five averages, we see that the Cayapo, Xavante, and Caingang values are very similar (0.13 - 0.18). The Yanomamö, however, show about twice the departure (0.38) from the maximum degree of heterozygosity, while the Makiritare present an intermediate result (0.25). Following Spuhler (1963) we may use the coefficient W to measure the concordance in ranking the degree of heterozygosity in the five tribes by the twelve loci (see also Kendall 1970). The value obtained, 0.13, yields an F of 1.2, which is nonsignificant. This indicates variability in this ranking, a result different from the one obtained by Spuhler among Central American Indians.

Marshall and Jain (1969) proposed another measure to quantify results from different populations, the polymorphic index, defined simply as

$$PI = \frac{\Sigma q_i(1-q_i)}{n}$$

where q_i and $1 - q_i$ are the morph frequencies averaged over n characters. Its application to data from the same loci and the populations discussed above yields the results given in Table 2. They substantiate what was presented in Table 1: the indices are practically equal for the Cayapo, Xavante, and Caingang (0.18-0.19), lower for the Yanomamö (0.13), and intermediate for the Makiritare (0.17). These values do not correlate well with the indices of potential selection (Crow 1958) obtained for these populations, nor with the amount of genetic differentation BETWEEN villages of these tribes, as estimated by mean genetic distances (method of Cavalli-Sforza and Edwards 1967) or F-statistics (Neel and Ward 1972).

Table 2.   Estimation of several genetic parameters in five South American Indian tribes

Genetic parameter	Tribes				
	Cayapo	Xavante	Caingang	Yanomamö	Makiritare
Polymorphic index	0.190	0.190	0.181	0.135	0.168
Im	0.34	0.49	0.69	0.22	–
If	0.38	–	0.35	–	–
I	0.71	0.90	1.28	0.88	–
Mean genetic distance among villages	0.248	0.178	–	0.330	0.356
Mean F_{ST}	–	0.007	–	0.063	0.036

I = Index of potential selection; Im = fraction of this index due to mortality; If = fraction due to fertility differences (Crow 1958). Sources of the data for other parameters besides the polymorphic index: Salzano, Neel, and Maybury-Lewis (1967); Neel and Chagnon (1968); Salzano (1971); Salzano, et al. (1972b); Neel and Ward (1972).

How different is the degree of heterozygosity of a "primitive" population of hunters and gatherers from that of a technologically more advanced human community? In Table 3 we compared the data obtained among the Cayapo Indians with those reported by Shreffler, et al. (1971) for the community of Tecumseh, Michigan, United States. The list of loci considered is slightly different from that shown in Table 1. As can be seen, there exists some difference in the departure from the maximum degree of heterozygosity, which occurs in the expected direction (Cayapo: 0.27; Tecumseh: 0.18). The coefficient of concordance in the ranking of heterozygosity (0.19) furnishes an F of 2.3, which is again nonsignificant. The polymorphic indices obtained for the two, however, are not very different (0.12 and 0.15 respectively). It should be mentioned that Stewart, et al. (1970) found

Table 3. Departure from the maximum degree of heterozygosity considering eleven loci and the polymorphic index in the Cayapo Indians compared with similar data from the Caucasian population of Tecumseh, Michigan, United States

Loci and polymorphic index	Cayapo Indians (N = 526)	Tecumseh, Michigan (N = 8,965)
ABO	1.000	0.316
MNSs	0.177	0.075
Rh	0.316	0.244
P	0.020	0.000
Fy	0.164	0.020
Jk	0.012	0.000
K	1.000	0.860
Secretion of ABH	0.172	0.000
Secretion of Le	0.000	0.254
Hp	0.024	0.028
Gc	0.080	0.188
Average	0.270	0.180
PI	0.123	0.153

The gene frequencies are given in Shreffler, et al. (1971); Salzano, et al. (1972a, 1972b). W (coefficient of concordance in the ranking of heterozygosity) = 0.190; $F = 2.3$ (nonsignificant). The number of individuals studied is not the same for all loci.

exactly the same PI value (0.21) comparing data from twenty-one loci in southern Alaska Eskimos and Oregon Caucasians.

SUMMARY AND CONCLUSIONS

The main points that emerge from this analysis are that there are differences in the degree of heterozygosity (as ascertained especially by D and W) not only between the Caucasian and South American Indian populations which were compared and which are living under very diverse sociocultural conditions, but also among the five tribes considered here. This heterogeneity, however, does not correlate well with the degree of acculturation of these groups, estimates of potential selection, or the amount of genetic differentiation between villages, as assessed by two methods. Further comprehensive genetic studies of communities with different population structures, intensive searches for functional differences between the proteins determined by the polymorphic alleles, and simulation analyses using models derived from these investigations may help us to unravel the network of causes responsible for these human polymorphisms.

REFERENCES

ARENDS, T., L. R. WEITKAMP, M. L. GALLANGO, J. V. NEEL, J. SCHULTZ
1970   Gene frequencies and microdifferentiation among the Makiritare Indians, II: Seven serum protein systems. *American Journal of Human Genetics* 22:526–532.

CAVALLI-SFORZA, L. L., A. W. F. EDWARDS
1967   Phylogenetic analysis. Models and estimation procedures. *American Journal of Human Genetics* 19:233–257.

CROW, J. F.
1958   Some possibilities for measuring selection intensities in man. *Human Biology* 30:1–13.

GERSHOWITZ, H., M. LAYRISSE, Z. LAYRISSE, J. V. NEEL, C. BREWER, N. CHAGNON, M. AYRES
1970   Gene frequencies and microdifferentiation among the Makiritare Indians, I: Eleven blood group systems and the ABH-Le secretor traits: a note on Rh gene frequency determinations. *American Journal of Human Genetics* 22:515–525.

GERSHOWITZ, H., M. LAYRISSE, Z. LAYRISSE, J. V. NEEL, N. CHAGNON, M. AYRES
1972   The genetic structure of a tribal population, the Yanomamö Indians, II: Eleven blood-group systems and the ABH-Le secretor traits. *Annals of Human Genetics* 35:261–269.

KENDALL, M. G.
1970   *Rank correlation methods* (fourth edition). London: Griffin.

MARSHALL, D. R., S. K. JAIN
1969   Genetic polymorphism in natural populations of *Avena fatua* and *A. barbata. Nature* 221:276–278.

MORTON, N. E., H. KRIEGER, M. P. MI
1966   Natural selection of polymorphisms in northeastern Brazil. *American Journal of Human Genetics* 18:153–171.

NEEL, J. V., N.A. CHAGNON
1968   The demography of two tribes of primitive, relatively unacculturated American Indians. *Proceedings of the National Academy of Sciences, United States of America* 59:680–689.

NEEL, J. V., W. J. SCHULL
1968   On some trends in understanding the genetics of man. *Perspectives in Biology and Medicine* 11:565–602.

NEEL, J. V., R. H. WARD
1972   The genetic structure of a tribal population, the Yanomamö Indians, VI: Analysis by F-statistics (including a comparison with the Makiritare and Xavante). *Genetics* 72:639–666.

SALZANO, F. M.
1971   Demographic and genetic interrelationships among the Cayapo Indians of Brazil. *Social Biology* 18:148–157.

1975   "Multidisciplinary studies in tribal societies and man's evolution," in *Genetic factors in human differentiation.* Edited by C. Otten, R. Meier, and F. Abdel-Hameed. World Anthropology. The Hague: Mouton.

SALZANO, F. M., H. GERSHOWITZ, P. C. JUNQUEIRA, J. P. WOODALL, F. L. BLACK, W. HIERHOLZER

1972a Blood groups and H-Le^a salivary secretion of Brazilian Cayapo Indians. *American Journal of Physical Anthropology* 36:417–426.

SALZANO, F. M., J. V. NEEL, D. MAYBURY-LEWIS

1967 Further studies on the Xavante Indians, I: Demographic data on two additional villages: genetic structure of the tribe. *American Journal of Human Genetics* 19:463–489.

SALZANO, F. M., J. V. NEEL, L. R. WEITKAMP, J. P. WOODALL

1972b Serum proteins, hemoglobins, and erythocyte enzymes of Brazilian Cayapo Indians. *Human Biology* 44(3):443–458.

SALZANO, F. M., A. G. STEINBERG, M. A. TEPFENHART

1973 Gm and Inv allotypes of Brazilian Cayapo Indians. *American Journal of Human Genetics* 25:167–177.

SHREFFLER, D. C., C. F. SING, J. V. NEEL, H. GERSHOWITZ, J. A. NAPIER

1971 Studies on genetic selection in a completely ascertained Caucasian population, I: Frequencies, age and sex effects, and phenotype associations for 12 blood group systems. *American Journal of Human Genetics* 23:150–163.

SING, C. F., D. C. SHREFFLER, J. V. NEEL, J. A. NAPIER

1971 Studies on genetic selection in a completely ascertained Caucasian population, II: Family analyses of 11 blood group systems. *American Journal of Human Genetics* 23:164–198.

SPUHLER, J. N.

1963 "The scope for natural selection in man," in *Genetic selection in man*. Edited by W. J. Schull, 1–111. Ann Arbor: University of Michigan Press.

STEWART, R., E. LOVRIEN, S. ROWE, E. SCOTT

1970 Polymorphic index as an estimate of heterozygosity in Alaskan Eskimos. *American Journal of Human Genetics* 22:55a–56a.

WEITKAMP, L. R., T. ARENDS, M. L. GALLANGO, J. V. NEEL, J. SCHULTZ, D. C. SHREFFLER

1972 The genetic structure of a tribal population, the Yanomamö Indians, III: Seven serum protein systems. *Annals of Human Genetics* 35:271–279.

Marriages in Lewis and Harris, 1861 - 1966

E. J. CLEGG

The islands of Lewis and Harris lie some fifteen to twenty miles off the northwest coast of Scotland (Figure 1). Although described individually as islands, they are the two parts of a single land mass some sixty miles long which forms the northern end of the chain of islands known as the Outer Hebrides or "Long Island."

In both islands the terrain is hilly, and in Harris and the southwest portion of Lewis, Uig, it becomes mountainous. The center of the remaining portion of Lewis is equally inhospitable, being composed of blanket peat bog interspersed with numerous small lochs; it permits little human exploitation other than sheep grazing and forestry. Human settlements are almost invariably coastal, and in many areas, especially on the west coast, the presence of abundant sandy "machairs" enables some degree of arable farming and stock-rearing to be carried on.

Apart from this small-scale agriculture, the principal occupations are fishing and weaving, the three separate occupations forming the basis of the crofting way of life. The term CROFTING applies literally to the form of land tenure practiced, but it also implies a livelihood gained from one or more of the three occupations noted above. This form of economy has grown up in many parts of the Scottish Highlands over the last 150 years, during which the largely cattle-based economy of the glens was destroyed by the resettlement of communities on the coasts and the con-

I am grateful to the Registrar General for Scotland for permission to study birth and marriage registers, census reports, and census enumerations. In particular, I am indebted to the library staff of the General Register Office, Edinburgh, for their willing and cheerful cooperation.

I acknowledge with gratitude financial support from the University of Sheffield Research Fund.

Figure 1.   Map of the Outer Hebrides. Scale 1:2,000,000. Reproduced by permission of Messrs. George Philip and Son, London.

version of the interior to sheep walks. In Lewis and Harris these changes, never particularly severe, had ceased by the middle of the nineteenth century, and since then patterns of settlement have been fairly stable (see Geddes 1955; Caird 1959; Moisley 1962).

The commercial and administrative center for Lewis, and to a lesser extent for Harris, is the Burgh (town) of Stornoway. In 1861, at the beginning of the period covered by this survey, its population was 2,587. By 1966 it had risen to 5,190. Outside Stornoway the villages or townships of Lewis rarely exceed populations of 500. In Harris settlements are smaller, and Tarbert, the administrative center, had in 1961 a population of 416.

This investigation was undertaken as a result of a study of marriage distances in the two islands. Contrary to expectation, it was found that as the population of the two islands increased during the latter half of the nineteenth century, the number of marriages contracted in the islands decreased, both relatively and absolutely. The results to be described are an attempt to explain this phenomenon and to contrast marriage patterns in the "urban" metropolitan area, Stornoway, with those in the rural areas of Lewis and of Harris.

METHODS

Population Changes

Data were obtained from the decennial census reports for 1861–1961 and from the quinquennial sample census of 1966 (the sample in Lewis and Harris was 100 percent). The material extracted either from the reports or the enumerators' returns included total populations and age distributions of both sexes in the areas of Lewis Landward, Stornoway Burgh, Harris, Ross and Cromarty County (of which Lewis forms a part), Inverness County (of which Harris forms a part), and the whole of Scotland.

Marriages

In each census year the following information was obtained from copies of marriage certificates for the civil parishes of Lewis (Barvas, Stornoway, Lochs, and Uig) and of Harris:

1. date and place,
2. ages of spouses and whether first or later marriage,
3. residences of spouses (places and civil parishes), and
4. occupations of spouses and their parents.

From the data obtained, it was possible to construct curves showing changes in the numbers of marriages with time, and also changes in the frequency of marriage in the population as a whole and in particular age groups. It was immediately obvious that over the period of the study the numbers and frequencies of island-contracted marriages fell sharply. A possible explanation of this phenomenon could have been the inception and expansion of the practice, still present today, of solemnizing the marriage of two island spouses on the mainland. Clearly a search through all marriage registers, not only for Scotland but for many fishing ports of England as well, would have been out of the question, hence an indirect method of estimating the proportions of within- and without-island marriages was devised, using birth data.

Births

Again in census years the following information was obtained on births occurring within the islands:

1. date and place,
2. sex of child, and
3. date and place of marriage (illegitimate births excluded, but pre-marital conceptions included).

The following method was used to derive estimates of the proportion of marriages occurring outside the islands. For each census year (C), (1) the proportion (p) of marriages contracted outside the islands to total marriages represented by the births in that year and (2) the mean interval ($\bar{y}$) between marriage and birth were calculated. It was assumed that at year $C-\bar{y}$ a proportion p of marriages were solemnized outside the islands and that therefore $1-p$ were solemnized in the islands. Because $C-\bar{y}$ seldom fell on a census year, the number (m) of within-island marriages was derived by linear interpolation within the ten-year interval between censuses, hence the estimate of total numbers of marriages in year $C-\bar{y}$ is given by $M = \dfrac{m}{1-p}$.

Obviously, the distribution of y is highly skewed (Figure 2), because a high proportion of marriages produce children within one or two years, with smaller proportions after much longer periods, and values of y are never negative (at least in the context of this study) with marriage occurring after the birth of the child. Consequently, setting confidence limits to estimates is difficult. The arbitrary assumption was made that a proportion of the variability sufficiently high to indicate any existing trend would be included if the range of y were from 0 to $\bar{y}$. These values

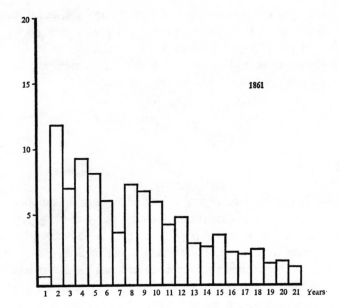

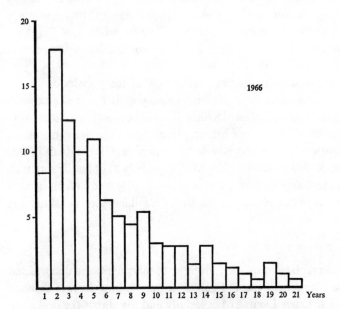

Figure 2. Distribution of marriage-birth intervals for Lewis (Stornoway Burgh and Landward) in 1861 and 1966. At both times the distribution was highly skewed, with the mode during the second year of marriage, but in 1966 more births occurred during the first year and the fall-off after the second year was more marked.

were used at each value of C to calculate numbers of marriages, and from population numbers at years C and from linear interpolations of population numbers for years C—ȳ, for marriage frequencies.

To avoid unnecessary complication and repetition, data are presented (except in the case of age at marriage) for women only.

RESULTS

Population Changes

These are shown in Figures 3–5. Figure 3 shows changes in the numbers of individuals as a whole and in the fifteen- to forty-four-year-old group. The patterns of changes in the island populations (Figure 3a) show some important differences from those of the counties and of Scotland as a whole (Figure 3b). There were rapid increases in Lewis Landward and in Harris with maxima at the 1911 census. Thereafter there were sharp falls until the end of the period under review. Only Stornoway Burgh underwent consistent expansion. Ross and Cromarty suffered severe and continuous population decline and the population of Inverness-shire showed similar, if less marked, changes. The population of Scotland continued to expand except during the first two decades of the present century.

Figure 4 shows changes in the proportions of the population in the fifteen to forty-four age group. In all the island populations and especially in Harris there were marked declines in this proportion. Stornoway Burgh at almost all times had higher percentages than the rural areas, possibly because of the comparatively large number of individuals in this age group employed in service industries, especially as domestic servants. The counties and Scotland as a whole showed fairly small changes until the third decade of this century; since then the fall has been considerable.

Marriage Rates

Table 1a shows female population, number of marriages, and uncorrected marriage rates for census years. In all three populations the rate declined after 1861. For Lewis Landward especially and for Harris the decline in numbers of marriages and in marriage rate was severe and the increase in rates in the last two census years was comparatively small. The changes for Stornoway were less marked.

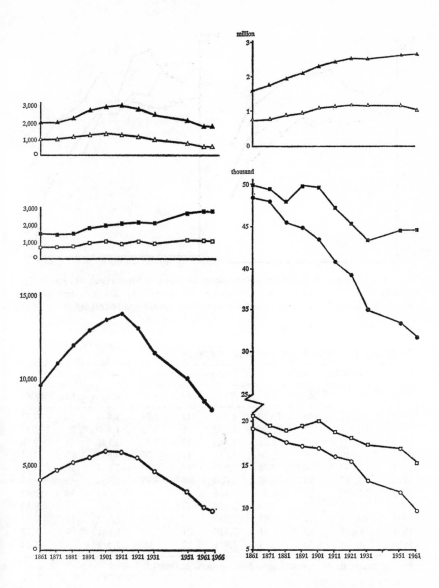

Figure 3a.   Female population changes.
    Lewis Landward, ●;
    Stornoway Burgh, ▧;
    Harris, ▲.
Solid points indicate total populations, open points populations in the fifteen to forty-four range.

Figure 3b.   Female population changes.
    Ross and Cromarty, ●;
    Inverness-shire, ▧;
    Scotland, ▲.
Solid points indicate total populations, open points populations in the fifteen to forty-four range.

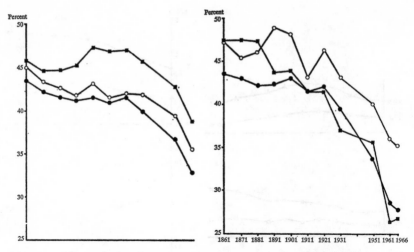

Figure 4. Women in the fifteen to forty-four age group as proportions of total female population.   Left figure: Lewis Landward, ●; Stornoway Burgh,○; and Harris, ■. Right figure: Ross and Cromarty,●; Inverness-shire,○; and Scotland,■.

Table 1a.   Females, all ages, all marital states

Year	Lewis Landward			Stornoway Burgh			Harris		
	P	M	MR	P	M	MR	P	M	MR
1861	9,605	146	15.20	1,484	11	7.41	1,949	19	9.75
1871	10,921	135	12.36	1,392	8	5.75	1,860	25	13.44
1881	11,994	102	8.50	1,477	11	7.45	2,152	21	9.76
1891	12,819	109	8.50	1,815	11	6.06	2,655	20	7.53
1901	13,459	98	7.28	1,949	15	7.70	2,834	26	9.17
1911	13,817	94	6.80	2,054	8	3.89	2,904	22	7.58
1921	12,980	88	6,78	2,166	17	7.85	2,744	30	10.93
1931	11,554	53	4.59	2,038	7	3.43	2,386	21	8.30
1951	10,044	41	4.08	2,847	10	3.78	2,072	13	6.27
1961	8,694	34	3.91	2,770	21	7.58	1,661	9	5.42
1966	8,140	50	6.14	2,751	22	8.00	1,514	9	5.94

P = population, M = marriages, MR = mariage rate/1,000

Table 1b shows uncorrected marriage rates for single, widowed, or divorced women of all ages. The most pronounced changes in rates were in Lewis Landward, where rates declined markedly until 1951; since then they have shown a slight increase. Stornoway shows the same trends, although there is a good deal more variation, possibly because of the much smaller population sizes. Marriage rates for Harris show little indication of any trend.

Table 1b.   Single, widowed, and divorced females, all ages.

	Lewis Landward			Stornoway Burgh			Harris		
			Marriage			Marriage			Marriage
	Number	Percent	rate	Number	Percent	rate	Number	Percent	rate
Year	Single	Total	/1,000	Single	Total	/1,000	Single	Total	/1,000
1861	6,302	61.42	23.17	828	55.79	13.29	1,251	64.18	15.19
1871	7,193	62.41	18.77	787	56.54	10.17	1,188	63.87	21.04
1881	7,667	63.91	13.30	942	63.85	11.68	1,423	59.27	14.76
1891	8,209	64.03	13.28	1,167	64.32	9.43	1,806	65.43	11.07
1901	8,436	62.68	11.50	1,266	64.96	9.48	1,854	65.42	14.02
1911	8,847	64.03	10.40	1,339	65.19	5.23	1,884	64.88	11.68
1921	8,082	62.27	10.76	1,337	61.73	10.47	1,752	63.85	17.12
1931	7,023	60.78	7.55	1,211	59.42	6.61	1,412	60.44	14.87
1951	5,455	54.31	7.15	1,399	52.85	7.15	1,148	55.41	11.32
1961	4,438	51.05	7.44	1,423	51.73	14.76	818	49.25	11.00
1966	4,031	49.52	12.40	1,345	48.89	16.36	703	46.43	12.80

Table 1c.   Women in the fifteen to forty-four age group, single, widowed, or divorced.

	Lewis Landward			Stornoway Burgh			Harris		
		Percent			Percent			Percent	
		of	Marriage		of	Marriage		of	Marriage
		age	rate		age	rate		age	rate
Year	Number	group	/1,000	Number	group	/1,000	Number	group	/1,000
1861	2,670	63.96	54.68	432	61.58	20.83	619	66.94	30.69
1871	3,049	64.89	44.28	377	59.73	23.87	586	66.48	42.66
1881	3,229	62.47	32.21	461	67.85	19.52	639	62.71	32.86
1891	3.501	64.67	31.13	597	67.16	16.75	784	67.59	26.79
1901	3,653	63.08	27.37	604	66.08	21.52	837	67.18	31.06
1911	3,827	66.92	24.30	623	69.22	12.84	799	66.31	27.53
1921	3,849	70.19	21.30	711	70.81	22.50	817	71.29	37.94
1931	3,320	72.84	15.36	595	68.00	11.76	580	65.83	36.21
1951	1,978	58.26	20.73	655	56.42	15.27	454	61.85	24.23
1961	1,203	48.78	28.26	466	47.26	45.06	236	53.64	42.37
1966	1,021	45.43	47.99	389	40.02	56.96	191	47.28	47.12

Table 1c shows data for single, widowed, or divorced women in the fifteen to forty-four age group. The trends are similar to those shown in Table 1b, although because of the smaller number of women in this group, marriage rates are increased overall.

Table 2a shows the proportion of within-island marriages derived from birth data during census years and corrected marriage rates, assuming that these proportions apply to marriages solemnized during these census years. Table 2b shows marriage rates further corrected for mean marriage-

Table 2a.   Women in fifteen to forty-four age group, single, widowed, and divorced (marriage rates corrected for out-island marriages).

	Lewis Landward			Stornoway Burgh			Harris		
Year	P	C	CR	P	C	CR	P	C	CR
1861	97.63	150	56.17	81.01	14	32.40	98.17	19	30.69
1871	97.19	139	45.58	74.68	11	29.17	93.79	27	46.07
1881	95.63	107	33.13	84.06	13	28.19	92.97	23	35.99
1891	92.41	118	33.70	64.29	17	28.47	94.69	21	26.78
1901	87.62	112	30.65	57.95	26	43.04	90.83	29	34.64
1911	86.03	109	28.48	62.90	13	20.86	82.50	27	33.79
1921	89.86	98	25.46	52.63	32	45.00	74.42	40	48.95
1931	79.15	67	20.18	39.34	18	30.25	68.00	31	53.44
1951	58.96	70	35.38	52.38	19	29.00	78.00	17	37.44
1961	49.38	69	57.35	43.33	48	103.00	65.63	14	59.32
1966	54.45	92	90.10	49.09	45	115.68	58.62	15	78.53

P = percent of island marriages, C = corrected total marriages, CR = corrected marriage rate/1,000.

Table 2b.   Women in fifteen to forty-four age group, single, widowed, and divorced (values corrected for out-island marriages and for mean marriage-birth interval [ȳ]).

	Lewis Landward			Stornoway Burgh			Harris		
Year	Estimated population	Estimated marriages	Estimated marriage rate /1,000	Estimated population	Estimated marriages	Estimated marriage rate /1,000	Estimated population	Estimated marriages	Estimated marriage rate /1,000
1863	2,846	148	52.00	421	11	26.13	612	21	34.31
1873	3,085	133	43.11	394	12	30.46	597	25	41.88
1883	3,283	111	33.81	488	13	26.64	668	23	34.43
1893	3,531	117	33.14	598	17	28.43	795	24	30.19
1903	3,688	113	30.62	608	20	36.41	828	28	34.04
1915	3,835	102	26.61	654	18	31.14	804	30	37.68
1924	3,690	84	22.92	676	28	42.08	722	37	52.01
1946	2,334	68	29.07	639	30	45.73	492	20	39.97
1956	1,598	69	43.32	562	38	65.87	391	15	39.25
1961	1,203	69	57.29	466	63	135.72	237	15	64.16

birth interval (ȳ). The data from these two tables are summarized in Figure 5. It will be seen that for Lewis Landward and for Harris the correspondences between the two sets of corrected marriage rates are very close. For Stornoway the correspondence is less, but it is clear that in all three populations the last twenty or thirty years have seen a great increase in marriage rates among women within the fifteen to forty-four age group. Before the immediate postwar period, though, the changes in marriage rates show some differences between populations. Harris and

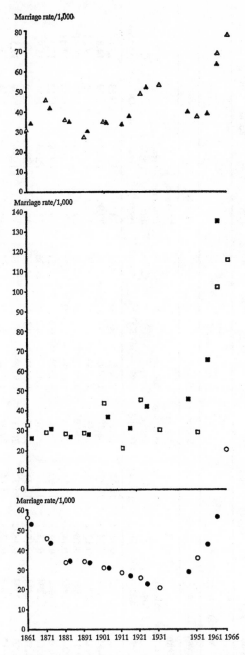

Figure 5. Corrected marriage rates for Lewis Landward, ⦿; Stornoway Burgh, ◼;
and Harris, ▲. Open points show rates corrected for out-island marriages, solid points
corrected for out-island marriage and mean marriage-birth interval (ȳ).

Table 3. Women older than fifty-five.

Year	Lewis Landward					Stornoway Burgh					Harris				
	Total	Single	Percent	Married	Percent	Total	Single	Percent	Married	Percent	Total	Single	Percent	Married	Percent
1861	1,244					186	46	24.73	52	27.96	238	52	21.85	90	37.82
1871	1,304					204	54	26.47	47	23.04	307	134	43.65	105	34.20
1881	1,543	199	12.90	753	48.80	250	65	26.00	63	25.20	417	96	23.02	147	35.25
1891	1,901	278	14.62	968	50.92	257	60	23.35	61	23.74	521	138	26.49	166	31.86
1901	2,050	289	14.10	956	46.63	290	67	23.10	72	24.33	557	137	24.60	225	40.39
1911	2,266	404	17.83	1,013	44.70	318	73	22.96	103	32.39	575			234	40.70
1921	2,527	503	19.91	1,102	43.61	415	116	27.95	137	33.01	580			225	38.79
1931	2,785			1,171	39.35	493			166	33.67					
1951	2,976			1,120	37.63	639			211	34.12					
1961	3,004	937	31.19	1,114	37.08	743	227	30.55	275	37.01	612	168	27.45	249	40.69
1966	3,066	980	31.96	1,184	38.61	837	253	30.23	304	36.32	628	166	26.43	267	42.52

Table 4a. Marriage ages of men.

Year	Lewis Landward				Stornoway Burgh				Harris			
	Mean marriage age (years)	Mean $\log_{10}$ (age − 16)	S.D.	C.V. percent	Mean marriage age (years)	Mean $\log_{10}$ (age − 16)	S.D.	C.V. percent	Mean marriage age (years)	Mean $\log_{10}$ (age − 16)	S.D.	C.V. percent
1861	27.18	1.0292	0.1304	12.67	25.75	0.9842	0.0762	7.74	28.81	1.0781	0.1628	15.10
1871	28.85	1.0596	0.1470	13.87	28.78	1.0798	0.1755	16.25	29.96	1.0516	0.1559	14.82
1881	28.62	1.0792	0.1382	12.81	27.13	1.0390	0.0892	8.39	31.89	1.1874	0.1102	9.28
1891	29.03	1.0841	0.1691	15.60	28.09	1.0372	0.2025	19.52	29.74	1.1191	0.1277	11.41
1901	30.80	1.1482	0.1404	12.23	29.64	1.0995	0.2002	18.21	32.54	1.1947	0.1443	12.08
1911	30.65	1.1422	0.1439	12.60	33.50	1.1324	0.3536	31.23	30.58	1.1386	0.1512	13.28
1921	34.13	1.2294	0.1591	12.94	32.50	1.1577	0.2345	20.36	32.58	1.1866	0.1651	13.91
1931	34.52	1.2414	0.1606	12.94	25.71	0.9671	0.1456	15.06	35.00	1.2611	0.1219	9.67
1951	33.60	1.2034	0.1892	15.72	26.00	0.9799	0.1425	14.54	36.93	1.2463	0.2439	19.57
1961	32.32	1.1743	0.1778	15.14	29.81	1.0728	0.2773	28.85	29.40	1.0664	0.2454	23.01
1966	31.26	1.1316	0.2218	19.60	25.82	0.9613	0.1715	17.84	30.10	1.0921	0.2154	19.72

Table 4b. Marriage ages of women.

Years	Lewis Landward				Stornoway Burgh				Harris			
	Mean marriage age (years)	Mean $\log_{10}$ (age — 16)	S.D.	C.V. percent	Mean marriage age (years)	Mean $\log_{10}$ (age — 16)	S.D.	C.V. percent	Mean marriage age (years)	Mean $\log_{10}$ (age — 16)	S.D.	C.V. percent
1861	24.49	0.8875	0.2209	24.89	25.00	0.8452	0.3330	39.40	25.72	0.9413	0.2012	21.33
1871	24.57	0.9004	0.1744	19.37	24.67	0.8803	0.2585	29.36	24.76	0.9008	0.1829	20.30
1881	25.13	0.9450	0.1393	14.60	24.27	0.9095	0.1005	11.05	26.33	0.9917	0.1684	16.98
1891	26.82	0.9960	0.1849	18.56	27.90	1.0378	0.2107	20.96	27.85	1.0571	0.1246	11.78
1901	27.57	1.0288	0.1814	11.63	28.09	1.0437	0.2175	20.19	26.88	0.9938	0.2012	20.24
1911	27.14	1.0256	0.1371	13.37	30.17	1.0582	0.3197	30.21	27.77	1.0132	0.2420	23.88
1921	30.54	1.1201	0.1957	17.47	27.92	0.9876	0.2915	29.52	28.07	1.0315	0.2159	20.93
1931	30.79	1.1305	0.1942	17.18	29.17	1.0917	0.1661	15.21	29.62	1.0235	0.2806	27.42
1951	27.92	1.0146	0.2387	23.53	27.50	1.0044	0.2291	22.81	30.42	1.0836	0.2613	24.12
1961	26.89	0.9740	0.2417	24.82	27.05	0.9262	0.3451	37.26	26.67	0.9538	0.2596	27.22
1966	25.49	0.9263	0.2565	27.69	22.72	0.7792	0.2406	30.88	25.22	0.8752	0.2936	33.55

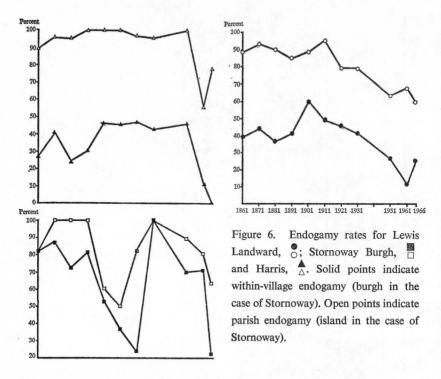

Figure 6.   Endogamy rates for Lewis Landward, ●; Stornoway Burgh, ▦ and Harris, ▲. Solid points indicate within-village endogamy (burgh in the case of Stornoway). Open points indicate parish endogamy (island in the case of Stornoway).

Stornoway seemed, during the period 1861–1951, to maintain fairly steady rates, with a certain amount of fluctuation. Lewis Landward, the largest of the three populations, underwent a consistent fall in rates over the whole of this period.

Changes in age-specific marriage rates are influenced principally by two factors — the proportion of people who marry and the age at which they marry. Information on the former was obtained from census reports and on the latter from marriage certificates. The results are shown in Tables 3 and 4a and 4b respectively. Table 3 is unfortunately incomplete, but it indicates that in Lewis Landward in particular the proportion of women remaining single at the age of fifty-five or more rose from 12.90 percent in 1881 to 31.96 percent in 1966. For Stornoway Burgh and for Harris the changes are less marked, but undoubtedly there is a tendency for proportions to be higher in the last two census years.

Tables 4a and 4b show mean ages at marriage of single men (4a) and single women (4b). Because the distribution of age at marriage is highly skewed, the mean of $\log_{10}$ (age — 16), an approximately normally distributed variable, is also given, together with its standard deviation and coefficient of variation. For both sexes there was a steep rise in marital age, maxima occurring for Lewis Landward in 1931, for Stornoway Burgh in 1911, and for Harris in 1951. In general, means for men are greater than for women, but for Stornoway in 1931 and 1951 the reverse was true, although differences are not statistically significant. There has been a tendency, most marked for Lewis Landward, for the coefficient of variation of $\log_{10}$ (age — 16) to increase during the last two census years. This reflects the widening of the range of marital age which was observed at these times.

A preliminary study of the degree of endogamy of the populations has been made and the results are presented in Figure 6. For Lewis Landward there has been a fairly steady decline in both village and parish endogamy during this century. In Harris high levels of endogamy were maintained until very recently, but the fall has been abrupt. In Stornoway the fall in burgh and island endogamy during the earlier years of this century was reversed during the 1920's and 1930's, but it has reappeared in the last few decades.

DISCUSSION

For Lewis Landward the causes of the fall in marriage rates over the 1861–1931 period were obviously an increasing tendency to remain single and, for those who did marry, a postponement of the event. The situation is different for Stornoway Burgh and Harris, where despite increasing marital ages, failure to marry at all did not become more common except in the period of the last two censuses, which in this context of course reflects trends present thirty or so years previously. The contrast between Lewis Landward, on the one hand, and Stornoway and Harris, on the other, suggests that changes in the proportions of individuals marrying are more important determinants of marriage rates than are changes in age at marriage, a suggestion that is supported by comparing the very considerable falls in the proportions of nonmarried women in the fifteen to forty-four age groups over the last three decades (Table 1c) with the still significant, but less marked, falls in marital ages (Table 4b).

The persistence until recent years of low marriage rates, high marital ages, and low proportions of ever-married puts Lewis and Harris well within the typical Western European marriage pattern of the past century (Hajnal 1965). Indeed the proportions of more than 30 percent of single women in the over fifty-five age group (Table 3) are extremely high, and even in 1901 the proportions single in Stornoway and Harris were greater than the proportions in the forty-five to forty-nine group given by Hajnal. Because proportions remaining single decline with increasing age, the extreme nature of the pattern of marriage in Lewis becomes obvious. The corrected values of Table 2b are generally comparable (except for Stornoway Burgh) with the 1961–1966 Irish county marriage rates given by Walsh (1970a). In addition, the historical changes in rates appear to be similar to those pertaining to Ireland. Walsh (1970b) gives county rates for 1871 and 1911 in the fifteen to forty-five age group, and the values found in this study fall within the range of Walsh's results. Marital age, too, seems to follow patterns similar to those seen in Ireland over the latter half of the nineteenth century (Connell 1950; Cousens 1964). However, within the fifteen to forty-four age group the proportions of those single, widowed, or divorced (Table 1c) seem much higher than the proportions of those single given for the different provinces of Ireland by Walsh (1970b) than could be accounted for by the addition, in Lewis and Harris, of widowed or divorced women to the totals in the numerators. Thus, it appears permissible to conclude that marriage rates in the islands of Lewis and Harris historically have perhaps even more extreme characteristics than those in Ireland. However, recent changes suggest that this pattern of low nuptiality is or has been breaking up, especially in Stornoway, and it might be expected that in the future, patterns of marriage will correspond more closely to United Kingdom norms.

In seeking explanations for these changes, both economic and cultural factors need to be considered. The fact that marital ages were in general highest between 1921 and 1931, coupled with the high proportion of single women over fifty-five in 1961, suggests that economic hardship, coupled with massive emigration during the 1920's, made marriage more unlikely for many women. This factor may also explain the high rates of burgh and island endogamy in Stornoway between 1921 and 1951, in that it resulted in a decreased mobility of marriageable individuals, so that where population density was high, marriage tended to be at short range. Where density was low and communities small, as in Lewis Landward, exogamy had to be the rule in any case, so that the effect was lessened.

The period since the end of World War II has been characterized by falling age at marriage, a rise in the proportion married in the fifteen to forty-four age group, and a decreased tendency to village or parish endogamy. These changes may be explained in part by improved economic circumstances (Geddes 1955), but in addition, the realization of the discrepancy between local patterns of marriage and those of other regions of the British Isles must have played a part. The discrepancy may have been actually experienced, through service in other areas or the migration to the islands of large numbers of "foreigners," or may have been at second hand, through improved channels of communication. Whatever the proximate cause, the result is not in doubt, and while fluctuations in rates will be observed from time to time, it appears unlikely that the low levels of nuptiality seen during the last century will ever return.

SUMMARY

Patterns of marriage of women in the islands of Lewis and Harris over the period 1861–1966 have been studied using census data and marriage certificates. When corrections are made for out-island marriages, there was, particularly for rural Lewis, a fall in marriage rates which persisted until 1951. Since then there has been a marked rise. Stornoway Burgh and Harris showed fairly stable rates until recent times, when there has also been a pronounced rise. In all three populations, marital ages rose considerably until 1921–1931, and since then they have fallen. The proportion of those over fifty-five who never married rose considerably in rural Lewis, but to a lesser extent in the other populations. In all of the aspects studied, patterns of marriage in Lewis and Harris appear similar to, and possibly more extreme than, those in Ireland.

REFERENCES

CAIRD, J. B.
  1959 *Park: a geographical study of a Lewis crofting district.* Nottingham: Geographical Field Group.
COLLIER, A.
  1953 *The crofting problem.* Cambridge: The University Press.
CONNELL, K. H.
  1950 *The population of Ireland, 1750–1845.* Oxford: The University Press.
COUSENS, S. H.
  1964 The regional variation in population changes in Ireland. *Economic History Review* 127:301–321.
GEDDES, A.
  1955 *The Isle of Lewis and Harris.* Edinburgh: The University Press.
HAJNAL, J.
  1965 "European marriage patterns in perspective," in *Population in history.* Edited by D. V. Glass and D. E. C. Eversley 101–143. London: E. Arnold.
MOISLEY, H. A.
  1962 *Uig, a Hebridean parish.* Nottingham: Geographical Field Group.
WALSH, B.
  1970a A study of Irish county marriage rates. *Population Studies* 24:205–216.
  1970b Marriage rates and population pressure: Ireland, 1871 and 1911. *Economic History Review* 23:148–162.

Culture Categories and High Life Expectancy in the Paros Community, Greece

JEFF BEAUBIER

Most epidemiological studies that attempt to determine the causal factors associated with long life deal with specific and separate variables such as genetic composition of the population, diet, psychological factors, or environmental influences. However, my study of interactive processes and models leads to the conclusion that the most fruitful investigation of longevity is an "open systems cultural analysis" that employs every possible input and uses human ecology as a frame of reference. With this in mind, the Greek islands are most suitable, since the problem of defining the boundary of a population and its resource base is greatly diminished by the boundaries imposed by the topography; the problem of defining the borders of areas smaller than countries has made many past analyses of doubtful significance.

Any epidemiological study is bound to present problems as the result of specific features of the population area surveyed, but the techniques used to gather the relevant materials are essentially those common to such field work. These techniques include:

1. direct observation of the population situation;
2. interviews with people of various ages, occupations, and economic classes; and
3. materials collected from the manuscript records of the community.

The materials for this paper were collected during the summers of 1970–1972 and the fall of 1972 from the Paros community on the island of Paros. Paros is the fourth largest island in the Cyclades. It consists of eight communities, one of which is the nearby island of Antiparos. Paros is 194.46 square kilometers and is only ninety nautical miles from

Piraeus. The climate is temperate with high temperatures in the summer and fairly low ones in the winter. In the fall and winter the island is windy with low humidity and hardly any rainfall from May to October. Paros is agriculturally more productive than the other Cyclades Islands but still suffers from an inadequate water supply.

The population of the island, including Antiparos, was 8,461, according to the 1961 census. With the exception of a handful of Catholics, the population is Greek Orthodox. The islanders live in small villages perched high on the sides of the mountains where the land is not arable, or by the seashore if they engage in fishing.

The islanders are sturdy and rugged-looking. They are very hospitable and courteous, and at the same time rather quiet and individualistic. They love the outdoors, and the evening promenade by the seashore is enjoyed by both young and old.

The town of Paroikia is the capital of the island with a population of 1,955, according to the 1971 census. Paroikia is in the Paros community, which has a total population of 2,703. The other seven communities are much smaller, numbering from 290 to 1,355 in population. Some of the villages consist of only a few families. The language of the island is Demotic with some local variations. Because the island depends on tourism for a fair portion of its livelihood, a number of people know some English, French, and, occasionally, German or Swedish.

The majority of the people engage in agriculture and fishing, while a large number of young men go to sea. The crops raised include grapes, olives, and vegetables such as tomatoes, beans, eggplant, and squash. They also raise some wheat, barley, and potatoes. Their protein diet consists of fish, beef, veal, lamb, chicken, rabbit, and, in the winter, some pork. They use a lot of cheese both in cooking and for snacks. Most of the cheese used is made on the island, but all sorts of imported cheeses are also available. Although they use potatoes and macaroni, the main starch is bread. Several vegetables, both cooked and raw, are served with every meal. The main meal is served at noon, followed by a siesta. Breakfast is usually the lightest meal and consists of hot milk with toast for the children, and milk and coffee or tea with toast or pastries for adults.

Cooking is an art and housewives spend a large portion of the day in the kitchen. Young girls are expected to know how to cook before they get married. The art of cooking is part of their dowry. It is only recently that some women have worked outside the home. Although by world standards the island is fairly poor, the nutrition is usually good to excellent. During World War II, the island was occupied by the Italians and the Germans. It was impossible to fish or engage in normal agricultural activities or, for that matter, in trade; thus, food became scarce and several people died of starvation.

Communication between the island and the rest of Greece is by sea. There are two large ferry boats that go from Piraeus to Paroikia every morning, and from Paroikia to Piraeus at eleven in the evening, in the summer. The rest of the year the ferries run only every other day. There are also several small ferries which connect Paros with the other Cyclades Islands. The interland traffic is fairly small. There are six buses which connect the capital with the rest of the island, and a very small number of cars. There is one main road around the coastal area that is mostly paved. In 1972, because of the increasing number of tourists, ten taxis were made available. There is a road from Paroikia to Lefkes and Marpissa that is also paved. However, donkeys and mules are still an important means of transportation.

The history of the island of Paros goes back to Neolithic times. However, the Cyclades civilization became very important during the Bronze Age, and Paros has played an important role ever since. Its marble quarries produced the marble from which Venus de Milo and several other important sculptures were made. In recent years, because of the cost of transportation, Paros marble was used only for local construction and low-grade road surfacing materials. The population of Lefkes community — where most of the marble quarries were — was 2,285 in 1920; in 1971 it had dropped to 744. Most of the marble workers moved to Penteli on mainland Greece to work in the quarries there. It is not surprising, then, that during the Periclean Age there were on Paros 150,000 people, most of them slaves, working the marble quarries.

The checkered history of Paros is part of the history of Greece. In recent times, Paros was under the Venetians, Turks, and Russians. It was also occupied during both World Wars. During the Civil War of 1946–1949, several of the young men of Paros were killed.

In the twenty-nine years prior to the 1971 census, there was a drop in population because many workers and young people had migrated to mainland Greece, especially Athens and Piraeus. The community leaders are trying to improve the economic conditions of the island and thus make it possible for young people to stay. Tourism is one way of developing Paros. In 1972, an annual wine and fish festival was initiated. Also, every summer an art school attracts students from all over Europe and the United States.

Modern records of the island's population go back more than one hundred years. Some population characteristics, however, are known as far back as classical times. In recent years, a census has been taken every

ten years. In the meantime, each community keeps a complete, ind
pendent record of its population. The community records office keeps
records of birth and death certificates, marriage licenses, and statistics
concerning migration within the island, outside the island, and overseas.
In addition, there is a complete record of each household on the basis
of occupation, economic level, education, and amount of property owned.
A very careful record of housing is kept for tax purposes. For example,
no renovation of any sort is allowed without a building permit and, since
building permits, taxes, and population records are all handled by the
same office, crosslisting is very accurate. This office also handles utili-
ties; consequently, the head officer is a very valuable source of information. One man has been director for twenty-one years and, since the
position is very prestigious, by cooperating with him one gets the cooperation of the rest of the community.

Table 1 shows the population of the eight communities for various
years, and the age group and sex structure of the community of Paros.

Table 1.   Population of Paros Island by administrative regions (communities); census
years, 1920–1971

Year	Paros	Naousa	Lefkes	Marpissa	Archi-lochos	Anti-paros	An-gairia	Kostos	Total
1920	2,952	1,410	2,285	1,396		543		339	8,925
1928	3,422	1,655	2,158	1,003	659	612		472	9,981
1940	3,264	1,421	1,560	954	777	606	555	462	9,599
1951	3,174	1,610	1,262	944	814	680	768	450	9,701
1961	3,030	1,481	972	745	677	631	578	347	8,461
1971	2,703	1,355	744					290	

Source: Manuscripts of the Koinotis Records Office of Paros

The communities of Lefkes and Marpissa show large population decreases, while Paros and Naousa have fairly constant populations. The
reason is that both Lefkes and Marpissa cover the marble quarries area.
Since marble is no longer quarried on a large scale, the laborers and their
families have migrated to the mainland where the quarries are active. On
the other hand, since Paros and Naousa are seaports, both maritime and
fishing activities have continued normally. One might also note a sizeable
increase at Naousa and Paros for the 1928 census. Part of the reason
was the resettling of the Asia Minor refugees of 1924. They were seafaring people and, thus, it was natural for them to settle by the sea.

The age group and sex structure of the population of the Paros community are shown in Tables 2, 3, and 4. The population pyramid is very
unusual for several reasons. Whole families move from the rest of the

Table 2. Age structure of population, Paros community, 1970

Age Group	Males	Females	Total	Difference F over M	Percent difference F over M
0–4	72	68	140	−4	−5.9
5–9	85	81	166	−4	−4.9
10–14	75	78	153	3	3.8
15–19	87	93	180	6	6.3
20–24	91	98	189	7	7.1
25–29	99	104	203	5	4.8
30–34	67	84	151	17	20.2
35–39	97	111	208	14	9.0
40–44	108	114	222	6	5.2
45–49	85	93	128	8	8.9
50–54	72	79	151	7	10.0
55–59	62	69	131	7	4.1
60–64	70	73	143	3	10.1
65–69	61	69	130	8	20.0
70–74	53	67	120	14	31.5
75–79	31	43	74	12	38.5
80–84	27	38	65	11	21.4
85–89	16	26	42	10	22.6
90–94	11	14	25	3	28.0
95–99	5	8	13	3	37.5
100+	1	2	3	1	50.0
Totals	1,275	1,412	2,687	137	9.7

Source: Manuscripts of the Koinotis Records Office of Paros

island to this community for better economic opportunities. These opportunities are realized in the meantime, the lower age bands are receding because of a rapid decline in the birth rate, coupled with migration from the island of people of higher fertility. Another factor that contributes to the general thickness of the pyramid is the natural longevity of the people.

The island of Paros, along with Antiparos, makes up one part of the larger unit, the Cyclades Islands. The island is made up of eight fairly independent units called communities. The Paros community is the largest and Paroikia is the capital of the whole island.

The residence pattern after marriage is variable but tends to be neolocal. The determining factor is often the economic self-sufficiency of the families concerned. Usually the girl has a dowry which consists of furniture, linens, property, if the parents have any, and a house. If the parents are poor they may be forced to share their own house with the newlyweds. In cases where the family has money but not land, the girl receives a sum of money plus the house and furniture.

Table 3.   Age structure by percentage, Paros community, 1970

Age group	Percent males	Percent females	Percent both sexes	Cumulative percent
0–4	5.6	4.8	5.2	5.2
5–9	6.7	5.7	6.2	11.4
10–14	5.9	5.5	5.7	13.9
15–19	6.8	6.6	6.7	20.6
20–24	7.1	7.0	7.0	27.2
25–29	7.8	7.4	7.6	31.8
30–34	5.2	6.0	5.6	35.2
35–39	7.6	7.9	7.7	40.8
40–44	8.5	8.1	8.3	48.5
45–49	6.7	6.6	6.6	56.8
50–54	5.6	5.6	5.6	63.4
55–59	4.9	4.9	4.9	69.0
60–64	5.4	5.2	5.3	79.2
65–69	4.8	4.9	4.8	84.0
70–74	4.2	4.7	4.5	91.3
75–79	2.4	3.0	2.8	94.1
80–84	2.1	2.7	2.4	96.5
85–89	1.3	1.8	1.6	98.1
90–94	0.9	1.0	1.0	99.1
95–99	0.4	0.6	0.5	99.6
100+	0.1	0.1	0.4	100.0

Source: Manuscripts of the Koinotis Records Office of Paros

With the exception of two or three women who had been elementary school teachers, and one or two laborers, most married women were house-wives until the early 1960's. Since then it has become possible for a woman to have a job outside the house. There are now a few married women who hold jobs as teachers, office clerks, and shopkeepers. Most of the women shopkeepers usually have small handicraft shops for tourists. There is also one woman dentist. As housewives, women play a very important role in the family. Because children are under their control and protec-tion, they exercise greater influence over them than men do. Grandparents also make an important contribution to the child's development, so much so that a young child without grandparents is considered unfortunate.

Although illegitimacy is fairly rare, it is not a stigma on the child. Usually the mother of an illegitimate child continues to live with her parents, and her father takes upon himself the role of father to the child.

Cooperation is the norm in all social patterns while, at the same time, individualism is considered a virtue. Respect is accorded to educated people, but social distance does not exhibit itself in the community. Be-cause of this social awareness and responsibility, even the poorest of people eat well. Adults will literally go hungry in order for children to

Table 4.   Live births, Paros community, 1935–1969

Year	Males	Females	Total	Five-year total
1969	17	19	36	
1968	26	25	51	
1967	19	20	39	
1966	18	19	37	
1965	20	19	39	202
1964	27	20	47	
1963	25	25	50	
1962	25	22	47	
1961	19	23	42	
1960	23	18	41	227
1959	28	35	63	
1958	27	20	47	
1957	22	24	46	
1956	23	31	54	
1955	27	30	57	267
1954	33	26	59	
1953	25	19	44	
1952	28	30	58	
1951	25	32	57	
1950	43	29	72	290
1949	40	29	69	
1948	34	39	73	
1947	42	39	81	
1946	39	41	80	
1945	50	40	90	393
1944	43	40	83	
1943	36	40	76	
1942	39	40	79	
1941	33	40	73	
1940	51	31	82	393
1939	59	46	105	
1938	43	41	84	
1937	40	51	91	
1936	54	43	97	
1935	52	47	99	476
Total	1,155	1,093	2,248	2,248

Source: Manuscripts of the Koinotis Records Office of Paros

be well fed. In the 1940's, however, when the community was first under the Germans and Italians — and later on when devastated by civil war — a large number of people died of hunger. For example, out of twenty-seven deaths in 1942, twelve were caused by hunger; three were war casualties.

The present economy of the island is based almost entirely on fishing and seafaring activities, farming, and tourism. In the last decade tourism has been the main reason for keeping some of the young in the community. Farming productivity is low because of inadequate water supplies. The cost of acquiring new water supplies is very high and, at present, the prospects are not very promising.

The Cyclades Islands make up one medical unit, with the island of Syros as the center. Although Syros is smaller than at least three of the other Cyclades Islands, it is centrally located and, therefore, easily accessible to everyone. For example, a small ferry boat takes only two hours to go from Paros to Syros. There is a large hospital with 155 beds. The only disease not treated there is cancer. Cancer cases are sent to Athens where special facilities exist.

In the whole of the Cyclades there are eighty doctors, twenty dentists, and fourteen pharmacies. Of the eighty doctors, fifty-five are non-specialists and the rest fall under the following categories: five pathologists, one obstetrician, six surgeons, two cardiologists, three pediatricians, two dermato-veneriologists, one anesthesiologist, three bacteriologists-hematologists, and two opthalmologists. Trained midwives are not included among the doctors.

There are seven public hospitals with 214 beds for all the Cyclades Islands. Charges at these hospitals are minimal. The doctors who work in the hospitals often have their own private practices.

In 1968, 2,992 patients were admitted to the seven public hospitals and 2,990 were discharged. That is, there was a 53 percent coverage of beds.[1]

Paros itself has seven doctors, two of them surgeons. The Paros community has two doctors, one of them a surgeon, and one midwife. There are two pharmacies in the community and a seven-bed hospital. Both the surgeon from the Paros community and the doctor from the Naousa community spend several hours a day at the hospital treating charity patients. These two doctors are appointed to the hospital by the Public Health Department. They both have private practices on the side. The hospital has a trained nurse around the clock. The distribution of medical services available for the whole island is as shown in Table 5.

Although the entire population both accepts and uses modern methods of treatment, there are still instances of folk medicine. Some of the customary folkways are herb tea treatment and belief in miracles. If a person is seriously ill he will be taken to a doctor or hospital; should a speedy recovery occur, an offering to a particular saint is promised. If the person recovers, the gift is taken to the particular church. However, if the patient

[1] *Statistical yearbook of Greece.* 1969:59–73. Athens: National Statistical Service of Greece.

Table 5.   Distribution of medical services on Paros Island and in Paros community

Population	Public health hospital	Doctors in private practice	Trained midwives
Paros Island 8,461	1	7	3
Paros community 3,030	1	2	1

does not recover, modern medicine is blamed, not the saint. Several churches in the community are very wealthy because of such gifts.

These islanders place a high value on personal hygiene and cleanliness in their homes and places of work. Every Friday they whitewash the cobblestones of the narrow streets in front of their houses, in preparation for the weekend. Households that are not very regular in this ritual are not respected. People whose personal hygiene does not conform to the high standards the community places upon them are often ridiculed and avoided.

At least since 1950 the three leading causes of death are heart disease, cancer, and stroke. Over 62 percent of the deaths are caused by these diseases. The actual figures in the individual years are given in Tables 6, 7, and 8.

Table 6.   Leading causes of death, male and female, as percent of total deaths; Paros community, 1950 – 1 July, 1970

Disease	Male	Percent Male	Female	Percent Female	Total	Percent total
Heart	65	25.2	57	24.7	122	24.9
Cancer	54	21.3	40	17.3	94	19.2
Stroke	37	14.3	53	22.9	90	18.4
Old age	27	10.5	34	14.3	61	12.5
Bronchial pnuemonia	17	6.6	7	3.5	24	4.9
Colitis	8	3.1	4	1.7	12	2.5
Uremia	6	2.3	6	2.6	12	2.5
Tuberculosis	4	1.6	5	2.2	9	1.8
Accidents	7	2.7	2	0.9	9	1.8
Tumor	4	1.6	3	1.3	7	1.4
Malformations	6	2.3	1	0.4	7	1.4
Diabetes	3	1.2	2	0.9	5	1.0
Other	20	7.8	17	7.4	37	7.6
Total	258	± 100.0	231	± 100.0	489	± 100.0

Source: Manuscripts of the Koinotis Records Office of Paros

Table 7.   Leading causes of death at age X in crude rates per 100,000 population; Paros community, 1950 – 1 July, 1970

Age X	HEART			CANCER			STROKE			OLD AGE			TOTAL ALL CAUSES		
	Male	Female	Total	Male	Female	Total	Male	Female	Total	Male	Female	Total	Male	Female	Total
0-9													671.6	239.3	439.5
10-19													84.5		39.1
20-29						10.5							42.7	20.8	31.6
30-39	38.2	00.0	17.4	21.3	16.0	8.7							114.6	47.9	78.3
40-49	100.1	18.4	57.5	80.1	55.2	67.1	20.0	18.4	19.2				300.3	110.5	201.4
50-59	209.9	26.9	119.6	105.0	134.7	119.6	26.2	53.9	39.9				472.3	269.3	372.1
60-64	209.0	100.3	153.4	156.8	200.5	179.1	52.3	50.1	51.2				836.1	501.3	665.4
65-69	566.4	117.5	334.2	503.5	117.5	303.8	314.7	352.4	334.2				1573.3	881.0	1215.3
70-74	1111.8	997.3	1051.8	1111.8	362.7	717.1	707.5	1088.0	908.4	101.1	90.7	95.6	3436.5	2901.4	3155.4
75-79	1028.0	1480.1	1258.7	899.5	1356.8	1132.8	771.0	1356.8	1069.9	385.5	493.4	440.5	3854.9	5057.0	4468.2
80-84	2464.8	3427.9	2964.5	1725.3	1371.2	1541.6	2464.8	2285.2	2371.7	1232.4	1371.2	1304.4	9119.8	10512.3	9842.4
85+	1591.5	2506.8	2056.3	1790.5	771.3	1273.0	1193.7	1928.3	1566.7	3581.0	4435.1	4014.7	9947.2	11184.1	10575.3
Total	204.8	164.5	183.7	170.2	115.4	141.6	116.6	153.0	135.5	85.1	98.1	91.9	813.0	666.6	736.4

Source: Manuscripts of the Koinotis Records Office of Paros

Table 8. Leading causes of death at age X in age-adjusted rates per 100,000 population; Paros community, 1950–1 July, 1970*

Age X	HEART			CANCER			STROKE			OLD AGE			TOTAL ALL CAUSES		
	Male	Female	Total	Male	Female	Total	Male	Female	Total	Male	Female	Total	Male	Female	Total
0–9													1464.8	521.9	958.6
10–19													141.3		65.4
20–29			23.7	25.7	21.18	12.7							51.6	25.1	38.1
30–29	52.0					11.9							156.1	65.3	106.7
40–49	125.5	23.5	72.1	100.4	69.2	84.1	23.1	23.1	24.1				376.4	138.5	252.5
50–59	211.1	27.1	120.3	105.6	135.5	120.3	26.4	54.2	40.1				475.0	270.9	374.2
60–64	83.2	39.9	61.1	62.5	79.9	71.3	20.7	20.0	20.4				333.0	199.7	265.0
65–69	197.7	41.0	116.6	175.7	41.0	106.0	109.8	123.0	116.6				549.0	307.4	424.1
70–74	293.8	263.6	277.7	293.8	95.9	189.5	187.0	287.5	240.1	26.7	24.0	25.3	908.2	766.8	833.9
75–79	175.0	252.0	214.3	153.2	231.0	192.9	131.2	231.0	182.2	65.6	84.0	75.0	656.4	861.1	760.8
80–84	217.2	302.0	261.2	152.0	120.8	135.8	217.2	201.3	209.0	108.6	120.8	114.9	803.5	926.2	867.2
85+	82.5	129.9	106.6	92.8	40.0	66.0	61.9	99.9	81.2	185.6	230.0	208.0	515.5	579.6	548.0

Source: Manuscripts of the Koinotis Records Office of Paros
* Derived using the Direct Method with a 1960 U.S. Standard Million.

Although the Paros community would not be considered a developed area on the basis of its economic structure, the overall health picture compares favorably with any country. Infectious diseases, including tuberculosis, have been brought under control. In the last ten years there has been only one tuberculosis death, and this was a seventy-nine year old woman. There are, at present, four active cases but, according to the doctor under whose care they are, treatment has been successful. All four cases are older people. The two main drugs used in the chemotherapy are streptomycin and PAS.

Although heart disease, cancer, and stroke are the leading causes of death, they occur for the most part late in life. Most of the people live beyond the age of sixty. If a child survives the first year, the likelihood of a long life is very high. At present there is an amazing number of people in their eighties and nineties. One man is 104 years old.

While in the United States accidents constitute the fourth leading cause of death, in Paros accidents are very rare. Records show that there has never been a death due to a motor vehicle accident. Also, even though they are a seafaring people, drowning accidents are rare. One fisherman drowned while fishing when he was eighty-five years old, and a young man of twenty-eight drowned while swimming. These are the only two such accidents within a twenty-year period.

It is possible that the high influx of tourism will impinge on their healthy, integrated, and relaxed way of life. For example, venereal diseases are epidemic, but have so far been confined mostly to the tourists; it is difficult to say how long this will be the case.

This study would not be complete without a life table. The crude rates per 100,000 population represent males, females, and the total from ages 0–85+ divided into ten-year intervals up to age sixty, and into five-year intervals from ages sixty to eighty-five.

The uses of the life table are many, and vary from investigator to investigator. In the study of population characteristics, it provides the following information: it formalizes death data in a consistent probability pattern; it organizes the mortality experience of a population; and it compares the life expectancy of a population at different times. Also, it permits estimates of case loads for the future by mapping survival patterns for a set of patients — cancer patients, for example. If selected causes of mortality can be eliminated or reduced, one may estimate age distribution. Table 9 shows the crude rates per 100,000 in the various age categories of the population over a twenty-year period. By applying these rates to a cohort of 100,000 persons, and applying the rates to each

Table 9.   Total deaths from all causes at age X in crude rates per 100,000 population;
Paros community, 1950 – 1 July, 1970

Age X	Male	Female	Total
0–9	671.6	239.3	439.5
10–19	84.0	0.0	39.1
20–29	42.7	20.8	31.6
30–39	114.6	47.9	78.3
40–49	300.3	110.5	201.4
50–59	472.3	269.3	372.1
60–64	836.1	501.3	665.4
65–69	1573.3	881.0	1215.3
70–74	3436.5	2901.4	3155.4
75–79	3854.9	5057.0	4468.2
80–84	9119.8	10512.3	9842.4
85+	9947.2	11184.1	10575.3

Source: Beaubier, Jeff, The descriptive epidemiology of Paros community, unpublished thesis, University of North Carolina, 1970.

age category, a life table was computed for both males and females, for
males alone, and for females alone (Tables 10, 11, and 12).

Column X represents the age categories. I use the upper limit as 125.00
so that I may satisfy the internal mathematical logic of the program.
Usually the age categories are specified by five-year intervals; in my data
in the lower range, however, it would have been cumbersome and not
very meaningful, because of the very low death rate.

P(X) is the probability of survival from birth to exact age X. For
example, in Table 10 a live male infant at birth has a probability of
.9350 of reaching age ten and has a remarkably high probability (.8103)

Table 10.   Life table, males; Paros community

X	P(X)	N(X)	T(X)	E(X)
0.00	1.0000	9.6716	74.8018	74.80
10.00	.9350	9.3111	65.1302	69.65
20.00	.9272	9.2520	55.8192	60.20
30.00	.9232	9.1796	46.5672	50.44
40.00	.9127	8.9914	37.3876	40.96
50.00	.8857	8.6512	28.3962	32.06
60.00	.8448	4.1372	19.7450	23.37
65.00	.8103	3.8960	15.6079	19.26
70.00	.7490	3.4407	11.7119	15.64
75.00	.6307	2.8683	8.2711	13.11
80.00	.5201	2.0885	5.4028	10.39
85.00	.3297	3.3143	3.3143	10.05
125.00	0.0000			

Source: Generated from Table 9 using University of North Carolina BIOS Library
Program; LIFTA written in FORTRAN by Nader Fergany and Dana Quade

Table 11.   Life table, females; Paros community

X	P(X)	N(X)	T(X)	E(X)
0.00	1.0000	9.8813	80.0395	80.04
10.00	.9764	9.7635	70.1582	71.86
20.00	.9764	9.7534	60.3917	61.86
30.00	.9743	9.7200	50.6413	51.98
40.00	.9697	9.6433	40.9214	42.20
50.00	.9590	9.4622	31.2780	32.61
60.00	.9335	4.6096	21.8159	23.37
65.00	.9104	4.4533	17.2062	18.90
70.00	.8712	4.0547	12.7529	14.64
75.00	.7535	3.3291	8.6982	11.54
80.00	.5852	2.2757	5.3691	9.17
85.00	.3460	3.0933	3.0933	8.94
125.00	0.0000			

Source: Generated from Table 9 using University of North Carolina BIOS Library Program; LIFTA written in FORTRAN by Nader Fergany and Dana Quade

Table 12.   Life table, total population; Paros community

X	P(X)	N(X)	T(X)	E(X)
0.00	1.0000	9.7834	77.5141	77.51
10.00	.9570	9.5513	67.7307	70.77
20.00	.9533	9.5176	58.1794	61.03
30.00	.9503	9.4655	48.6618	51.21
40.00	.9428	9.3342	39.1963	41.57
50.00	.9240	9.0707	29.8621	32.32
60.00	.8903	4.3782	20.7914	23.35
65.00	.8612	4.1776	16.4132	19.06
70.00	.8104	3.7485	12.2355	15.10
75.00	.6921	3.1013	8.4870	12.26
80.00	.5535	2.1859	5.3858	9.73
85.00	.3384	3.1999	3.1999	9.46
125.00	0.0000			

Source: Generated from Table 9 using University of North Carolina BIOS Library Program; LIFTA written in FORTRAN by Nader Fergany and Dana Quade

of reaching age sixty-five; namely eighty-one percent of all males at age zero will reach age sixty-five.

N(X) is the average number of years an individual lives in the age interval. T(X) is the total number of years lived by the hypothetical cohort of 100,000 persons from time 0. In Table 10, 100,000 males will live a total of 748,018 years. The survivors at age ten will live a total of 651,302 years beyond the total number of years they have already accumulated as a category. E(X) is the average expected years of life remaining for the survivors of the cohort beginning with each age interval. For example, in Table 10, the survivors, beginning at age ten, will have a life expectancy of 69.65 more years. The reason why the dip is so low in this particular category is that up to the age of fifty-five the greatest number of deaths are due to infant mortality. Thus, once a child lives beyond the first year, his chances of survival are very high.

Life expectancy for both males and females is 77.51 years; for males, 74.80 and for females, 80.04. Life expectancy in the Paros community is unusually high. It compares with Sweden's life expectancy of seventy-seven years. The social and economic organization of the community, coupled with the medical services available, undoubtedly contribute much to such a high life expectancy.

The significance of the life expectancy is especially revealed in comparison with rates from other countries, e.g. the United States:[2]

Total U.S. population	69.89 years
U.S. white male	67.55 years
U.S. white female	74.19 years
U.S. non-white male	61.48 years
U.S. non-white female	64.76 years

There is a rather high discrepancy between the life expectancy of the white population and that of the non-white.

Europe as a whole has a very high life expectancy, as shown by these figures: Sweden 74; Netherlands 74; Norway and Iceland 73; Denmark 72; France, the two Germanies, and Switzerland 71; U.S.S.R., Spain, Bulgaria, England, Italy, Ireland, and Hungary 70; Finland 69; and Portugal — with the lowest rate of life expectancy in Europe — 64. Asia, on the other hand, with the exception of Japan which has a life expectancy of 71, ranks much lower than Europe. Indonesia 44; India 50; Laos 50–54; Nepal 25–40; Pakistan 51; Philippines 50–60; and Thailand 53–58 years. Some African countries have very low life expectancy, as seen in the following examples: Lesotho 40–50; Kenya 43; Ethiopia 35; Guinea 33; Gabon 32; and Nigeria 50.[3]

Given these figures, we can surely appreciate the unusually high life expectancy in the Paros community.

---

[2] United States Department of Health, Education, and Welfare. Public Health Survey 1677:308. *Vital statistics rates in the U.S.* Table 50, Expectation of Life (ex) at five-year age intervals, by color and sex. United States, 1939–1941, and 1959–1961.
[3] *The New York Times encyclopedic almanac 1970*, 737–899 (under separate country listing).

REFERENCES

BEAUBIER, JEFF
   1970   "The descriptive epidemiology of Paros community." Unpublished thesis, University of North Carolina.
KOINOTIS RECORDS OFFICE OF PAROS
   1920–1971   Censuses 1920–1971.
New York Times
   1970   *New York Times encyclopedic almanac*, 737–899.
Statistical yearbook of Greece
   1969   Statistical yearbook of Greece. Athens: National Statistical Service of Greece.
UNITED STATES DEPARTMENT OF HEALTH, EDUCATION, AND WELFARE,
   n.d.   *Vital statistics rates in the United States.* Public Health survey 1677: 308. Washington D.C.: United States Government Printing Office.

PART THREE

Nutrition, Health, and Disease

Biobehavioral Adaptation in the Arctic

EDWARD F. FOULKS and SOLOMON H. KATZ

In an attempt to demonstrate the interactions of nutritional and be-havioral adaptations in Arctic Eskimos, it has been suggested (Wallace and Ackerman 1960; Katz and Foulks 1970) that piblokto, a form of acute hysterical psychosis occurring among the Thule Eskimo of Green-land, and other arctic hysterias occurring in Eskimo groups in Canada and Alaska (see Dall 1870; Freuchen 1935; Gussow 1960; Parker 1962) may be based on hypocalcemia that stems from an inability to adapt physiologically to low intake of calcium in the diet. This mental dis-order is precipitated by stress and is characterized by a prodomal period of tiredness, uncommunicativeness, and social withdrawal lasting several days. This period is followed by an acute, dissociative state, in which the afflicted individual may run around, tear off his clothing, perform repetitive behaviors such as beating sticks or a drum, make various attempts to defy gravity, and imitate the sounds of animals. The attack may last several hours, finally resulting in the individual's falling into an epileptiform state, with generalized tremors and carpopedal spasms. Following this attack he may either sleep in a comatose state or arise completely recovered and resume his normal everyday duties. There are no social stigmata attached to such attacks unless they occur with great frequency. Eskimos explain that the afflicted person lost his soul temporarily to the spirit world. The attacks can occur in males and females at any time of the year. However, it is most frequently reported as occurring in early spring in women.

Special gratitude is extended to Dr. Peter Morrison and William Galster from the Institute of Arctic Biology, University of Alaska College for their contributions in support and in the analysis of serum calcium in our subjects.

Katz and Foulks (1970) proposed that piblokto hysteria was precipitated by acute anxiety accompanied by hyperventilation which produced decreased serum calcium ion concentration and resulted in the classic symptoms of hypocalcemia tetany, i.e. carpopedal spasms, in those individuals whose total serum calcium concentration was already lowered. Furthermore, it was· suggested the low calcium influenced the functioning of the central nervous system and resulted in the characteristic behavioral changes. The Eskimo diet is low in calcium. In addition, synthesis of vitamin D, which is involved in intestinal absorption of calcium, is retarded during the dark arctic winter months. Further data regarding deficiencies of calcium in the arctic Eskimo diet were reported by Hoygaard (1941). He discovered severe deficiencies in dietary intake of calcium among Eskimos of Greenland. Steffansson (1945:286–288) also noted that the exclusively carnivorous diet of the Eskimo was very low in calcium. More recently, a nutritional survey was conducted in Alaska by Heller and Scott (1961). They collected a total of 4,840 dietary records for seven days' duration on a seasonal basis for both sexes and all age levels from nine Eskimo and two Athabascan villages. The data from these records were converted by machine calculation into mean daily intakes of eleven major nutrients (calories, proteins, fats, carbohydrates, calcium, iron, vitamin A, thiamin, riboflavin, niacin, and ascorbic acid) and were compared with the United States National Research Council (1958) recommendations.

The mean daily calcium intake levels among Eskimos for all ages and both sexes were considerably below those recommended (0.8 to 1 gram) by the National Research Council. Three-fourths or more of the diets for each age and sex were deficient in calcium. It should be noted, however, that there may be physiological readjustments which produce more efficient absorption of calcium in cases where dietary intake of calcium is low. Heller and Scott (1961) estimated the probable intake level in aboriginal times by comparing the calcium content of adult female diets of Hooper Bay (southwestern Eskimo) and Point Hope (northern Eskimo). The southwestern Eskimos obtained from whole blackfish and needlefish more than three times as much calcium as did northern Eskimos. However, the fish sources of even the southern Eskimos are not continuously available throughout the year, nor are they so abundant that significant supplies can be dried or otherwise preserved for off-season use. Levels of mean daily intake and availability of calcium from local foods and imported foods are consistently low for northwestern Alaskan Innuit villages.

With regard to the relationship between chronic hypocalcemia and behavioral disorders, Denko and Kaebling (1962) collected 268 case histories of individuals in the medical literature who suffered hypoparathyroidism, a condition resulting in hypocalcemia. They pointed out that hypocalcemia was seldom considered in the differential diagnosis of psychiatric disorders, and they enumerated symptoms that they found to be commonly associated with this condition. Acute episodes of hysterical behavior often characterized their reported cases. The behavior, as described, shares many features in common with the arctic hysterias. Symptoms particularly important were moodiness, hyperventilation, and short-lived hysterical attacks followed by tiredness and amnesia.

Accordingly, in 1969–1970 a field study was undertaken among the Eskimo population of north Alaska, where arctic hysteria had been frequently reported. During the year's study, ten individuals were found to have manifested such attacks. Each was investigated according to many psychiatric and medical parameters (see Foulks 1973; Foulks and Katz 1973). This paper will report our findings regarding the status of serum calcium, phosphate, and magnesium in these subjects.

METHODS

Ten cubic centimeters of blood was collected without venous stasis in Vacutainer tubes (Becton-Dickenson, Rutherford, New Jersey) from ten north Alaskan Eskimos who had manifested arctic-hysteria-like behavior. All were volunteers and subjects had been fasting over eight hours prior to the venipuncture. After sitting for fifteen minutes at room temperature, the blood was centrifuged at 2,000 revolutions per minute. Five cubic centimeters of serum were then transferred to a small polyethylene container and frozen immediately. Specimens were analyzed for total calcium by fluorometry using the method of Kepner and Hercules (1963) modified for the Techicon Autoanalyzer. Serum magnesium was determined by Perkin Elmer atomic absorption spectrophotometry (Model 3B) and phosphoruous by the methods of Fiske and Subarow.

Calcium exists in human serum in three fractions. Total calcium determinations reflect the summation of the three fractions (Table 1). The biologically active portion of serum calcium is ionized. It is only this fraction that is available for direct effect on synaptic transmission and axonal conduction within the nervous system. Methods of directly assaying ionized calcium were not established until recently. Farese,

Table 1. Total calcium, phosphate, and calcium-phosphate products in Innuits with arctic hysteria

	Subject Number	Total Calcium (milligram percent)		Phosphate (milligram percent)		Calcium-Phosphate Products*	
		July 1969	July 1970	July 1969	July 1970	July 1969	July 1970
Children	1	10.0	9.4	4.4	4.7	40.4	34.1
	2	9.3	—	5.8	—	53.9	—
	3	8.8	—	5.3	—	46.6	—
Adults	1	9.3	—	4.3	—	40.0	—
	2	9.2	8.9	3.6	3.5	33.1	31.2
	3	9.8	9.5	4.0	3.0	39.2	28.5

* Normal Adult (Ca) (PO_4) values range from 30–46
  Normal Children (Ca) PO_4) values range from 40–55

Mayer, and Blatt (1970) discussed a method which separates protein-bound calcium from calcium bound to inorganic molecules. Because the particular focus of our study is the effect of calcium ion on the central nervous system, we utilized a procedure for measuring the ultra-filterable portion of calcium. Blood was collected by the methods outlined for total calcium. Serum was diluted in phosphate buffer (pH 7.40), and ionized calcium was separated with the Centriflo (Amicon Corporation) high flux ultrafiltration membrane. This fraction of calcium was then analyzed by fluorometry. Normal values of ionized calcium determined by ultrafiltration methods range from 45 to 57 percent of total calcium (Henry 1964:374).

RESULTS

We were able to follow several individuals seasonally throughout the year and thus study the possible effects of low sunlight level during the winter months. The results are presented in Figure 1. Case 5 was hypocalcemic in November, 1969, but normocalcemic in July, 1968. The remaining subjects maintained low normal levels of total serum calcium throughout the change of seasons. There were decreases in levels as one would expect during the dark winter months if there were significant decreases in vitamin stores. However, Bohlen (1970) and Foulks (1973) have previously demonstrated that urinary calcium was the only chrono-biological variable of a whole series to show random fluctuations in excretion. The mean levels for this group did not differ significantly from the levels generally established for the north Alaskan Eskimo population. While within the normal physiological range, the serum

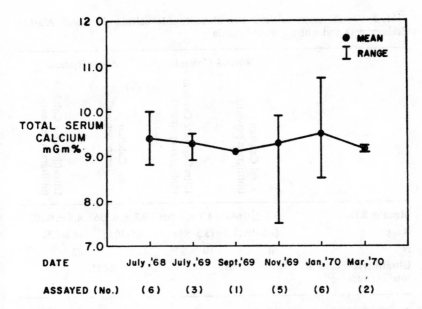

Figure 1. Seasonal variations in total serum calcium of subjects with arctic hysteria

calcium levels of subjects 3, 4, 5, 6, and 7 were on the low side, and it is not inconceivable that under conditions producing hyperventilation they could have precipitated low ionized states in these individuals. Unfortunately, we were not able to collect serum from any of our subjects just prior to or during an attack. These levels represented the basal state of our subjects from samples taken one to fourteen days following an episode of arctic-hysteria-like behavior, as well as from samples drawn periodically through the year. However, there were no differences between samples taken after an attack and the other samples drawn.

Serum inorganic phosphate was determined at the same time as total calcium for several of our subjects. Phosphate and calcium-phosphate product did not deviate from the range of normal.

Our subjects and the matched group of twenty-one normal Eskimos residing in the same population showed no significant differences in total calcium or ultrafilterable calcium levels (Table 2). However, more recent data developed by Katz using an Orion Company calcium ion electrode indicate that the serum calcium ion has a much narrower physiological range than that obtained by the method of Farese, Mayer, and Blatt (1970) used in this paper. Mean total calcium was within the range of normal for both groups; percent of the ultrafilterable portion was also normal.

Table 2. Total serum calcium and ultrafilterable calcium in North Alaskan Eskimos with and without arctic hysteria

	Normal Controls		Arctic Hysteria	
	Total Calcium (milligram percent)	Ultrafilterable Calcium (milligram percent)	Total Calcium (milligram percent)	Ultrafilterable Calcium (milligram percent)
Mean ± S.D.	9.3 ± 0.683	4.7 ± 0.506	9.2 ± 0.736	4.8 ± 0.297
Range	(7.6–10.2)	(3.3–5.6)	(7.5–10.0)	(4.4–5.5)
N	10	10	22	22
Ultrafilterable calcium/ total calcium	0.505		0.521	

MAGNESIUM

Magnesium was another important divalent cation measured whose action is related to that of calcium. Its physiological role in the body and more particularly the central nervous system is only now being understood. Deficiencies of magnesium can produce neuromuscular irritability similar to that produced by hypocalcemia, including psychosis, tetany, seizures, and positive Chvostek's and Trousseau's signs (Davidson 1963; Wintrobe, et al. 1970). Similarly, magnesium deficiencies may result from the diet (i.e. lack of vegetables) and from states of intestinal malabsorption, or from severe alcoholism (Mendelson, Ogata, and Mello 1969).

Because vegetables are relatively infrequent items in Eskimo diet, because enteric infections are relatively common, and because alcoholism is not unknown, it was decided to examine serum magnesium levels in several of the individuals who manifested arctic-hysteria-like behavior. This is especially important because magnesium deficiency so closely mimics the symptoms of hypocalcemia. For this determination seven of the subjects were matched with twenty normals from the same villages and for time of venipuncture.

The physiological range for serum magnesium is normally 1.6 to 2.6 milligrams percent (2.1 mean). Mean levels for both subjects and normals were within these limits (Table 3) and did not differ from each other significantly. One individual with arctic-hysteria-like behavior did demonstrate an exceptionally low serum magnesium level (Case 7 — 0.75 milligram percent). This individual is presently being investigated in more detail.

Table 3. Total serum magnesium concentration

	Normal Controls (milligram percent)	Arctic Hysteria (milligram percent)
Mean ± S.D.	2.16 ± 1.03	2.26 ± 0.730
Range	0.75–3.10	1.7–3.8
N	22	7

DISCUSSION

Several articles have suggested that the arctic hysterias may represent behaviors associated with hypocalcemia (Wallace and Ackerman 1960; Katz and Foulks 1970). Lack of adequate dietary calcium and low levels of vitamin D synthesis during the arctic winter were proposed as chronic causes for this condition. Total serum calcium determination from ten Innuit who manifested arctic-hysteria-like behaviors revealed normocalcemic levels during all seasons of the year. However, several subjects did demonstrate calcium levels that were decidedly on the low side of normal. Levels of the ultrafilterable fraction of serum calcium were also determined. These levels were again within normal limits and did not differ significantly from a group of matched controls. Subjects also maintained serum inorganic phosphate levels within the normal range.

Our studies, therefore, indicate that the behaviors seen in the arctic hysterias in the north Alaskan Eskimo populations are not accompanied by states of CHRONIC hypocalcemia. This finding does not exclude the possibility, however, that hyperventilation with anxiety or alterations in diurnal calcium rhythms could play a role in precipitating the attacks, especially in view of low levels in several subjects.

The ability of the Eskimo to generally maintain normal levels of calcium in spite of dietary deficiencies needs further explanation, however. It has recently been demonstrated that there is increased calcium absorption with increases in protein intake because of the formation of a soluble complex with amino acids (Mountcastle 1968). Thus, the high protein diet of the Eskimo may allow for more efficient utilization of the low levels of calcium normally ingested by these people.

Serum magnesium was also measured in our subjects, because the action of this cation partially resembles that of calcium in the central nervous system. The mean level of our subjects was normal and did not differ significantly from a group of covillagers who were free of hysterical symptoms. However, one individual, assessed within forty-eight hours of an episode of arctic hysteria, demonstrated hypomagnesemia. Mendelson, Ogata, and Mello (1969) recently reported correlations between depressed serum magnesium levels and the appearance of alcohol withdrawal signs and symptoms. Poor dietary intake during prolonged drinking plus enhanced urinary excretion of magnesium when blood ethanol levels are rising combine to produce magnesium deficiency and may account for the low levels found in one of our subjects.

Carrying the physiological perspective further, we have also investigated the parameters of medical and genetic history and have examined the functioning of our subjects' central nervous systems through the electroencephalograph. Our preliminary findings suggest that temporal lobe epilepsy, which is manifested in acute, psychomotor seizures, also may be implicated in the behaviors seen in the arctic hysterias. This is especially important because this seizure pattern is found in Eskimo populations with some frequency (see Foulks 1973). Furthermore, factors in the environment of the Eskimo may contribute to this temporal lobe epilepsy; these factors include a high incidence of fevers, middle ear infections, and meningitis in early childhood, which are related to dry, drafty, overcrowded housing, as well as the daily round of visiting of infection-carrying adults that is typical of Eskimo society. Thus, it is entirely possible that under the conditions of low serum calcium levels, low serum magnesium levels, and/or the history and potential of temporal lobe seizures, various social or physical environmental events could induce sufficient anxiety, crises, ventilation, and generalized stress to trigger an episode of arctic hysteria. In summary, it is also clear that each case has sufficient variation to indicate that no single explanation such as hypocalcemia can explain all the data on the occurrence of the arctic hysterias. Instead, the data suggest that a multifactoral approach may in the future provide the most comprehensive explanation of this behavioral phenomenon.

ADAPTIVE AND EVOLUTIONARY IMPLICATIONS

In a broader sense, this paper demonstrates the complexity of carrying out multifaceted investigations involving nutritional adaptability and behavioral disorders. Nevertheless, it does suggest that significant interrelations are possible and in fact do occur, as in the case of abnormally low serum magnesium. Futhermore, we suggest that nutritional adaptations may be expressed as maladaptations not only at metabolic levels but also at behavioral levels. Abnormalities of the latter mean that other adaptations must occur at familial and sociocultural levels. In other words, when biological adaptations influence the function of the central nervous system, the behavioral manifestations can require adjustments in the social group in which they occur. The approach we have developed in the attempt to unravel the complexity of these interrelationships involves analyses of the neurology, psychology, physiology, and biochemistry of individuals, as well as of the nutritional intake and social context of the population adapting to a particular ecosystem.

While all problems of human adaptability are not as complex as those involving behavioral disorders, the ubiquitous occurrence (Kiev 1972) of such disorders makes them an important factor to be considered in various models of human adaptation and evolution (Katz 1973). This is especially pertinent under any conditions where rapid social change and concomitant changes in nutrition and other health factors are occurring. Finally, these kinds of studies imply that our current evolutionary models involving ecologically adaptive variations in morphology, physiology, and biochemistry must be expanded to include the interaction of these variations directly and indirectly upon the behavioral functions of the central nervous system in adapting to the sociocultural dimensions present in all human populations.

REFERENCES

BOHLEN, J.
   1970   "Circadian and circannual rhythms in Eskimos." Unpublished Ph.D. dissertation, University of Wisconsin, Madison.
DALL, W.
   1870   *Alaska and its resources.* Boston: Lee and Shepherd.
DAVIDSON, C.
   1963   *Cecil-Loeb Textbook of medicine* (eleventh edition). Edited by P. Beeson and W. McDermott. Philadelphia: W. B. Saunders.
DENKO, F., R. KAEBLING
   1962   The psychiatric aspects of hypoparathyroidism. *Acta Psychiatrica* 164(38):1–70.
FARESE, G., M. MAYER, W. BLATT
   1970   A membrane ultrafiltration procedure for determining diffusible calcium. *Clinical Chemistry* 16(3):226–228.

FOULKS, E.
1973   "The arctic hysterias of the north Alaskan Eskimos." Anthropological Studies, no. 10. American Anthropological Association Press, Washington D.C.

FOULKS, E., S. KATZ
1973   The mental health of the Native Alaskan. *Acta Psychiatrica Scandinavica* 49:91–96.

FREUCHEN, P.
1935   *Arctic adventure.* New York: Farrar and Rinehart.

GUSSOW, Z.
1960   Piblokto (hysteria) among the polar Eskimo: an ethnopsychiatric study. *The Psychoanalytic Study of Society* 1:218–236. Edited by Meunsterberger, Axelrod.

HELLER, C., E. SCOTT
1961   *The Alaska dietary survey 1956–1961.* Public Health Service Publication 999–AH–2. Washington, D.C.

HENRY, R.
1964   *Clinical chemistry: principles and techniques.* New York: Hoeber.

HOYGAARD, A.
1941   Studies on the nutrition and physiopathology of Eskimos. *Skrifter Utgitt Av Det Norske Videnskaps — Adademi I Oslo Mat — Naturv Klasse 9.*

KATZ, S.
1973   "Genetic adaptation in twentieth-century man," in *Genetics and human evolution.* Edited by Crawford, Workman, and Spuhler. Albequerque: University of New Mexico Press.

KATZ, S., E. FOULKS
1970   Mineral metabolism and behavior: abnormalities of calcium homeostasis. *American Journal of Physical Anthropology* 32:229–304.

KEPNER, B., D. HERCULES
1963   Fluorometric determination of calcium in blood serum. *Analytic Chemistry* 35:1238–1240.

KIEV, ARI
1972   *Transcultural psychiatry.* New York: Free Press.

MENDELSON, J., M. OGATA, N. MELLO
1969   Effects of alcohol ingestion and withdrawal on magnesium states of alcoholics: clinical and experimental findings. *Annals of the New York Academy of Sciences* 162(2):918–933.

MOUNTCASTLE, V., editor
1968   *Medical physiology.* St. Louis; C. V. Mosby.

PARKER, S.
1962   Eskimo psychopathology. *American Anthropologist* 64:74–76.

PAULS, F., W. THOMPSON, R. LAESSIG
1969   Serological and clinical chemistry patterns of Wainwright Eskimos. Paper delivered at the 134th Annual Meeting of the American Association for the Advancement of Science, Boston, Massachusetts, 1969.

STEFFANSON, S. P.
  1945   *My life with the Eskimo.* New York: Collier.
UNITED STATES NATIONAL RESEARCH COUNCIL, FOOD AND NUTRITION BOARD
  1958   *Recommended dietary allowances.* Publication 589. Washington,
         D.C.; Government Printing Office.
WALLACE, A. F. C., R. ACKERMAN
  1960   An interdisciplinary approach to mental disorder among the polar
         Eskimos of northwest Greenland. *Anthropologica* 11(2):11–12.
WINTROBE, M., G. THORN, R. ADAMS, *et al., editors*
  1970   *Harrison's Principles of internal medicine* (sixth edition). New
         York: McGraw-Hill.

The Anthropological and Nutritional Significance of Traditional Maize Processing Techniques in the New World

SOLOMON H. KATZ, MARY L. HEDIGER, and
LINDA A. VALLEROY

Three major agricultural revolutions, closely associated with the origins of the great civilizations, have occurred within the last ten thousand years. These changes in subsistence base have had a profound effect on the evolutionary course of modern man. They have allowed, among others, for considerable shifts in diet, rapid increases in population size, major changes in the social and cultural organization of various populations, and the laying of the foundations for the development of modern technology. Each of these revolutions was associated with particular cultigens. Wheat and other cereal grains were first domesticated in the Middle East, rice appeared next in western Asia, and finally maize (Indian corn) in the western Hemisphere.

The earliest reported archaeological evidence of maize dates back to the wild precursors that existed some 7,000 years ago in central Mexico (MacNeish in Byers 1967:3–33, 114–131, 290–310). By 1,500 to 2,000 years later maize was already likely to have been under cultivation and was very much involved in the subsequent rise of the great Mesoamerican civilization. In South America, maize[1] was also involved, along with other major cultigens, in the rise of the Andean civilizations.

We would like to acknowledge the excellent advice and suggestions of Dr. Robert Sharer, Department of Anthropology, University of Pennsylvania and Dr. Vernon Young, Department of Nutrition, Massachusetts Institute of Technology. Also, we would like to acknowledge the excellent assistance of Ms. Kathy Silverman and Mr. Don Miller in assembling this manuscript.

[1] There is a long-standing controversy as to whether domesticated Andean maizes were a result of diffusion from Mesoamerica, or whether there was an independent focus of domestication in this area.

It did not play as important a role, however, as in Mesoamerica.

Over this period of time maize has become an obligatory cultigen which in modern times has been hybridized to produce strains of corn capable of yielding a variety of nutritional and agricultural characteristics. Corn is still the largest single harvest in the United States, and maize still provides the largest source of food and protein for many of the peoples of Central America (Wilkes 1972).

Each of the plants domesticated in the various geographical areas has its nutritional limitations, and maize is no exception, especially in terms of the quantity and quality of its essential amino acids and niacin. In fact, unless corn is appropriately prepared by specific techniques, its nutritional value as a dietary source for human consumption is at best marginal, and dietary dependency would lead to significant malnutrition in any population relying on it as a major staple.

The central theme of this paper is to demonstrate the precise role that the appropriate cooking technique plays in the freeing of otherwise unavailable nutrients in corn and to demonstrate its significance for various anthropological data, concepts, and theories. Throughout the paper, the term "corn" will be used to refer collectively to both the current hybrid and aboriginal races of *Zea mays,* while "maize" will refer specifically to the aboriginal races.

In order to carry out this analysis, we have organized this paper into sections dealing with the biology and biochemistry of corn including the effects of alkali treatment upon indigestible protein fractions in corn; hypotheses concerning cooking and alkali treatment; cultural data from fifty-one societies coded in the Human Relations Area Files to test these hypotheses; and a discussion emphasizing the biocultural, evolutionary, and other anthropological implications of the data.

THE BIOLOGY AND BIOCHEMISTRY OF CORN

The tremendous importance of corn in the Western Hemisphere and elsewhere around the world has led to thorough studies of the nutritional value of this plant food, especially its implications in Mexico and Central America, where it predominates as a chief source of nutrition. In general, studies in Mexico and Central America have paid particular attention to the extensive use of tortillas, an alkali-treated cooked corn food, as the major dietary staple of the people (Cravioto, et al. 1945; Bressani et al. 1958). A number of animal experiments with rats and pigs[2] have demonstrated that diets consisting of tortillas yield better animal growth patterns than diets of raw corn (Laguna and Carpenter 1951; Kodicek; et al. 1956; Bressani and Scrimshaw 1958). Nevertheless, it has been demonstrated by chemical analyses that, in the process of preparing tortillas, a certain amount of the nutritional value of the corn is lost (Bressani, et al. 1958). This has led investigators to question how the preparation of tortillas enhances the biologically effective nutritional value of corn while simultaneously reducing its total nutritional content.

In order to discuss this question more adequately, it is necessary to introduce some background information on the biology and bio-chemistry of corn. Because the chief nutritional limitation of corn is the quality and quantity of its proteins, this discussion will basically center on the identification, composition, and nutritional characteristics of corn protein. Corn consists of several anatomical parts. Included are the outer covering of the kernel consisting of the pericarp and aleurone, the endosperm comprising the largest fraction of the kernel, and the germ consisting of the embryo and scutellum (see Figure 1).

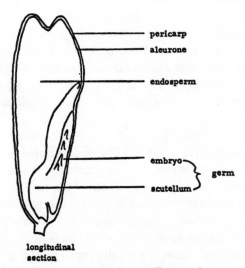

longitudinal
section

Figure 1.   Longitudinal section of corn kernel (*Zea mays*)

[2] It should be noted that experiments with rats have not been as definitive as those with pigs. For example, Pearson (1957) reported that rats fed boiled corn thrived almost as well as rats fed alkali treated corn. Furthermore, two other reports indicate that rats eating raw corn had the same growth rate as those on an alkali treated corn diet (McDaniel and Hundley 1958; Krehl, et al. 1946). This discrepancy is probably due to the fact that rats are more efficient in the conversion of tryptophan to niacin than humans (Kodicek, et al. 1956).

Of these anatomical divisions of the corn kernel, protein comprises approximately 6.8 to 12.0 percent of the kernel by weight. The remainder is starch at 7.45 percent, water at 12.0 percent, fats at 3.4 percent, and approximately 1.0 percent of ash and crude fibers (Heinz Company 1963). There are several classes of proteins categorized on the basis of solubility which have been identified principally in the endosperm and germ portions of the kernel. The latter two portions together comprise 90 to 95 percent of the protein in corn (Mertz, et al. 1966). Within these two portions, there are four classes of proteins: (1) albumins and globulins, extractable in dilute saline solution; (2) zein, a heterogeneous protein with a molecular weight of 20,000 to 50,000, which is classed as a prolamine and is extractable in ethanol solution; and (3) glutelin, a heterogeneous protein varying in molecular weight from 20,000 to 1,000,000 and extractable in alkali solution (Mertz, et al. 1966) (see Table 1). This wide range of molecular weight of glutelin is due to the extensive disulfide linkages between cysteine residues which accounts for the protein's tertiary structure and its particular sensitivity to denaturation in dilute alkali (Paulis, et al. 1969).

In general, corn is deficient in lysine, tryptophan, and niacin. With regard to lysine, approximately two-thirds of this essential amino acid is within the glutelin fractions in the endosperm and germ which is normally indigestible *in vivo*. Even under ideal laboratory conditions the quantity of lysine that can be extracted is only minimally adequate for dietary consumption. Thus, any way of enhancing its nutritional qualities for *in vivo* consumption would have significant nutritional benefit.

In the case of tryptophan, another essential amino acid and precursor to niacin Aguirre, et al. (1953), demonstrated in some twenty-three varieties of Guatemalan corn that the average was 88 percent of the minimum daily requirements (M.D.R.) of tryptophan, when the corn was analyzed under laboratory conditions. On the other hand, the niacin content of the same corn varieties averaged only 59 percent of the M.D.R. Because the metabolism of tryptophan is associated with endogenous production of niacin, it is significant to point out that if there is high consumption of maize, then it is likely that pellagra could develop from niacin deficiencies when other dietary constituents are not present on a seasonal basis to supplement the tryptophan and/or niacin (Hawkes, et al. 1971)[3] Indeed, pellagra was rampant in the southern

---

[3] Another important nutritional supplement to the marginally deficient status of tryptophan in maize is the rather plentiful supply which occurs in beans. Thus a reciprocal relationship frequently exists with respect to beans or squash with the

Table 1. Amount of various nitrogenous components of the endosperm and germ of normal varieties of *Zea mays*

	Total Nitrogen Endosperm[e]	Total Nitrogen Germ[f]	Lysine Endosperm	Lysine Germ	Tryptophan Endosperm	Tryptophan Germ	Niacin Endosperm	Niacin Germ	Leucine Endosperm	Leucine Germ	Isoleucine Endosperm	Isoleucine Germ
Saline Soluble Portion (similar but not exactly the same as albumins and globulins)	16—[a] / 26%	30—[a] / 40%	2.9%[a] / 1.8 g/100 g[a] protein	6.4%[a]						10.1 g/100 g[a] protein		3.0 g/100 g[a] protein
Zein	41—[a] / 60%	5—[a] / 10%	0.3%[a] / 0.3 g/100 g[a] protein		0.8%[a]	defi-[a]cient			19.5 m. mol./100 m. mol. protein[d]	20.3 g/100 g[a] protein	4.2 m. mol./100 m. mol. protein[d]	4.2 g/100 g[a] protein
Glutelin	17—[a] / 31%	49—[a] / 54%	2.2%[a] / 3.6 g/100 g protein		5.8%[a]				9.1 m. mol./100 m. mol. protein[d]	8.6 g/100 g[a] protein	4.2 m. mol./100 m. mol. protein[d]	3.4 g/100 g[a] protein
Total	98% (residue = 2%)	98% (residue = 2%)	180 g/[a] 100 g corn	549 g/[a] 100 g corn	2.68 ×[b] 10^{-6} g/100 g corn (MDR = 0.80 g adult/day)	0.44 g/100 g[c] (MDR = .250 g adult/day)	2.78 × 10^{-7} g/100 g corn	.0018 g/100 g[e] (MDR = .0150 g/adult/day)	1.29 g/100 g[a] corn (MDR = 1.10 g adult/day)		0.59 g/100 g[a] corn (MDR = 0.70 g adult/day)	

[a] Mertz, et al. (1966). [b] Teas and Newton (1951). [c] Aguirre, et al. (1953). [d] Sodek and Wilson (1971). [e] The endosperm comprises 54.1% of the corn kernel. [f] The germ comprises 19.7% of the corn kernel.

United States during the Depression[4] and is still a major disease in South Africa and India. The disease has a very low rate of occurrence in Mesoamerica (May and McClellan 1972).[5]

Finally, there is evidence to suggest that pellagra can be induced by an unfavorable isoleucine-to-leucine ratio, where there is excessive leucine in the diet. Such is the case in a diet heavily dependent on corn (Gopalan 1968; Hawkes, et al. 1971). The leucine in 500 grams of corn is approximately twice the recommended adult intake and four times the M.D.R. (Bressani, et al. 1958). Because the antagonistic effects of leucine on the conversion of tryptophan to niacin are ameliorated by increases in isoleucine, then any rise in the ratio of isoleucine to leucine as a result of cooking with alkali would help to minimize the effects of niacin deficiency.

Two important experiments (Bressani, et al. 1958; Bressani and Scrimshaw 1958) demonstrated the effect of the cooking processes on corn with particular reference to these problems of low levels of lysine, tryptophan, and niacin, as well as the high levels of leucine. In the first experiment, Bressani, et al. (1958) documented overall losses of significant quantities of thiamin, riboflavin, niacin, nitrogen, fat, and crude fiber resulting from the preparation of tortillas from raw corn.[6]

Briefly, the process of making Central American tortillas consists of heating dried corn to almost boiling in a 5 percent lime-water solution for 30 to 50 minutes, cooling, discarding the supernatant, washing the corn thoroughly, finely grinding the remaining corn into a dough called *masa,* and then forming this dough into a pancake shape and cooking it on a hot clay griddle for approximately two minutes on each side. The effect of the lime is to yield a dilute calcium hydroxide solution which is basic or alkaline. While this cooking process, and particularly

---

effective utilization of corn. However, it should be pointed out that corn tends to be more stable with respect to production and stability. On this basis there could have been more seasonal variation in the availability of these important supplements. In this context it is interesting to note that beans became cultigens considerably after maize.

[4]   This was probably associated with the extensive use of corn grits which were not alkali-treated.

[5]   Elsewhere in Latin America the high consumption of coffee, which is rich in niacin, and the consumption of beans, which have a high tryptophan content, probably explain the apparent absence of pellagra in various modern countries such as Guatemala.

[6]   While it is not the intent of this paper to discuss the benefits of cooking with lime as opposed to other alkali yielding salts, it is important to point out that Bressani and Scrimshaw (1958) reported a very significant increase in the calcium content of maize occurring as a result of the lime treatment. See Katz and Foulks (1970) for a brief synopsis of calcium metabolism.

the lime treatment, clearly decreases the overall nutrient content of the corn, Bressani and Scrimshaw (1958) have demonstrated that lime-cooking selectively enhances the nutritional QUALITY of corn.

This qualitative change results from a relative decrease in the solubility of the zein portion of the corn proteins, which is very deficient in lysine and tryptophan, as compared to the glutelin fraction which is rich in high quality protein. Because chemical extraction procedures which do not approximate *in vivo* digestion demonstrated no significant differences between cooked (with alkali) and uncooked corn in milligrams amino acid per gram nitrogen with the exception of lowering the leucine, Bressani and Scrimshaw (1958) attempted an *in vitro* enzymatic digestion to determine if the outcome of this process differed from the chemical extraction procedure.

Table 2. Ratios of essential amino acids in cooked (tortilla) and uncooked (raw) corn from chemical hydrolysis and following twelve hours of *in vitro* digestion with pepsin (computed from data of Bressani and Scrimshaw 1958)

Amino acid	Chemical hydrolysis ratio tortilla/corn	*In vitro* enzyme digestion ratio tortilla/corn
Histidine	0.857	2.333
Isoleucine	0.790	2.135
Leucine	0.425	1.158
Lysine	1.038	2.800
Methionine	0.714	2.090
Phenylalanine	0.418	1.135
Threonine	0.964	2.627
Tryptophan	0.500	1.285
Valine	0.379	1.020

While chemical hydrolysis yields the absolute quantities of essential amino acids for purposes of constructing these ratios, it is perhaps more significant to point out that the *in vitro* enzymatic digestion more closely parallels the ratios which would be obtained following *in vivo* digestion.

The evidence for this effect can be seen on Table 2, which represents the results of an *in vitro* enzymatic digestion of raw corn versus lime-cooked tortillas with pepsin for twelve hours. This experiment was carried out to determine if the cooking processes produced significant effects on the differential susceptibility of cooked (alkali-treated) and uncooked corn to *in vitro* enzymatic digestion. The results on the table are calculated from the data of Bressani and Scrimshaw (1958) and indicate the ratio of amino acid content in the tortilla to the raw corn.

The results demonstrate on a gram-per-100-grams of corn basis an absolute lowering of most essential amino acids in the lime-cooked corn, with the exception of lysine. However, this is not unexpected because there are considerable losses of total nitrogen during the cooking process. What is most interesting is the relative enhancement of the values when calculated on the basis of milligrams amino acid per gram of nitrogen. Any increase in the ratio for this calculation would indicate that cooking selectively enhances the quality of the corn protein available for enzymatic digestion.

Under these conditions, the relative amount of lysine is increased 2.8 times, tryptophan is increased slightly, and both the relative and absolute ratios of isoleucine to leucine are increased 1.8 times. Also, other essential amino acids such as histidine, methionine, and threonine are relatively doubled in concentration. Not only is the relative essential amino acid composition significantly improved by this process, but also the *in vivo* availability of both the precursors to niacin and niacin itself appear to be enhanced (cf. McDaniel and Hundley 1958). Thus, as long as maize is plentiful, then cooking techniques which use alkali and heat clearly enhance the balance of essential amino acids and free the otherwise almost unavailable niacin, which is a necessary vitamin.

HYPOTHESIS CONCERNING THE SIGNIFICANCE OF ALKALI COOKING TECHNIQUES

In effect, without the alkali-processing of corn, there would have to be considerable nutritional supplementation with foods rich in these amino acids and vitamin constituents. While it is conceivable that increases in the quantity of corn consumed may overcome some of these malnutrition problems in adults,[7] it is unlikely that children during phases of rapid growth and development could adapt to nutritional deficiencies without serious problems of malnutrition. Based on this nutritional evidence, we would hypothesize that all societies principally dependent on maize as a dietary staple and a cultigen practice alkali-cooking techniques in order to maximize its nutritional quality. Any society principally dependent on maize and not practicing this technique would either be decimated by malnutrition, especially among its population of children, or adopt a pattern of nutrition and diet supplementing the maize which would decrease its agricultural effectiveness.

In order to test the hypothesis, we have made a study of a large

---

[7] It is important to point out, however, that the leucine-to-isoleucine ratio would continue to rise in uncooked corn (Bressani and Scrimshaw 1958) and, therefore, tend to nullify the effects of the increased quantity of tryptophan consumed.

group of extant or only recently extinct societies for which there is extensive ethnographic data in order to determine the extent of maize cultivation, consumption, and whether or not some form of alkali treatment is used. These societies were chosen from only those ecological areas that would allow for the cultivation of maize. The alkali treatments can include lime yielding calcium hydroxide in solution, wood ashes yielding potassium hydroxide, or lye yielding sodium hydroxide.

CULTURAL DATA

Our sample comprises fifty-one societies as represented in the Human Relations Area Files (HRAF). It is restricted to include only those New World societies located within defined cultural and geographical areas (Driver 1969; Kroeber 1939; Murdock 1951) where the cultivation of

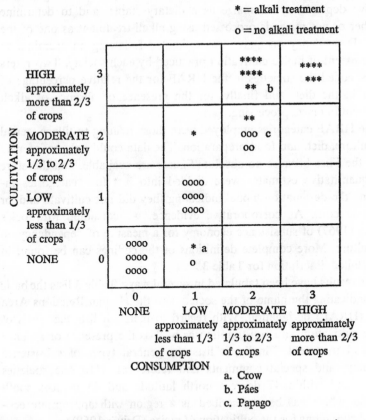

Figure 2. Alkali and nonalkali use in corn cultivation and consumption

corn is an ecological possibility (see Figure 2). The restriction is based on the assumption that maize cannot have been utilized as a dietary staple independent of either purposeful tillage or direct contact with peoples who cultivated it.

The areas are, for North and Central America, Kroeber's (1) East and North, (2) Intermediate and Intermountain, (3) Southwest, and (4) Mexico and Central America (Kroeber 1939). Excluded from the North and Central American sample are those societies in the Arctic Coast and Northwest Coast areas. For South America, the areas surveyed fall into Murdock's larger areas (1951) that he terms the (1) Andean encompassing the Isthmus, Colombian, Peruvian, and Chilean coasts and highlands, as well as the Caribbean, and (2) central western portion of the Tropical Forest area, excluding the Amazon basin. The Steppe-Hunting areas, and smaller peripheral hunting or fishing areas were not surveyed because little or virtually no maize was aboriginally cultivated.

The purpose of our coding was to rate the societies according to their relative dependency on maize as a dietary staple, and to determine whether or not maize is processed using alkali treatment as one of the steps. Dependency on maize was estimated following an examination of the extent of maize cultivation practiced by each society. Two raters jointly coded the societies in the HRAF for the relative percentage of maize in the diet, and finally, for the presence or absence of alkali treatment in maize processing.

The HRAF categories employed were those relating to tillage, cereal agriculture, diet, and food preparation. The data could only be inferred from the Files because no absolute figures are available, and therefore our quantitative estimates were divided into just four categories including the designation 'none' indicating they did not cultivate and/or consume corn. As corroborative evidence, we consulted Murdock's coding (1967) of subsistence economy for a measure of dependency on agriculture. More complete definitions of the codings can be found in the detailed description for Table 3.

The results have been tabulated in several ways. Table 3 lists the basic data indicating the name of the society and the Human Relations Area Files (HRAF) designation. With regard to maize, it lists the levels of maize cultivation and consumption as well as the presence or absence of alkali treatment. Finally, it lists the general types of subsistence economy, and special comments and references. Fifty-one societies were found within 47 degrees north latitude and 43 degrees south latitude, which has been described as a region with appropriate ecological conditions for the cultivation of maize (Driver 1969).

There is also a seasonal dimension to the processing and preparing of maize for consumption, which our results in Table 3 do not indicate but bears mentioning in conjunction with cultural explanations of alkali processing. With few exceptions, both the alkali-using and nonalkali-using societies roast maize. It is principally when the maize is green or not fully ripened that it is roasted in the husk under ashes. While there are important effects that may ensue from this process, they have yet to be developed fully in the nutritional literature and hence will not be elaborated upon in his paper.[8]

The roasting is only done in those seasons when crops of all sorts are being harvested, wild flora is abundant, and a variety of foods are available for consumption. It is the fully ripened or stored maize that is generally processed using the alkali technique which is usually described as a way of softening the tough outer kernel (see Note 3 above).

Table 3. Summary of cultural information

The resulting data are summarized in tabular form, arranged according to area. The columns bear the following explanations:

Column 1: *Society*. The column indicates the given name of the society (coded) with parenthetical reference to the particular coded subgroup when appropriate.

Column 2: *Human Relations Area Files Designation*. The alphabetical and numerical designations are those of the HRAF as indicated in Outline of World Cultures (Murdock 1972).

Column 3: *Percentage Maize Cultivation*. The codings represent the estimated relative percentage of maize cultivation practiced by each society in relation to the total crop production obtained by means of cultivation. The digits are defined as follows:

(0) — none.

(1) — less than 33 percent of the total crop production — defined as when there are other major cultigens whose products contribute to diet, and maize plays an insignificant role in the agricultural effort.

(2) — 33 to 66 percent of the total crop produce — defined as when maize is cultivated fairly intensively but there is also substantial or comparable cultivation of other crops.

(3) — over 66 percent of the total crop production — defined as when maize is

---

[8] See Notes 2, 3, and 6 above.

cultivated intensively as the major subsistence item with little or no cultivation of other crops.

Column 4: *Percentage Maize Consumption*. The codings represent the estimated relative percentage of maize in each society's total diet. It does not account for seasonal variation but only dietary intake within a yearly span. The digits are defined as follows:

(0) — none.

(1) — less than 33 percent of diet defined in conjunction with (1) above when maize is only sporadically cultivated, or where maize is not cultivated but obtained as a trade item from peoples of other societies.

(2) — 33 to 66 percent of total diet defined as when maize may be the major agricultural crop but there is also a dietary dependency on other forms of subsistence, such as hunting or gathering.

(3) — over 66 percent of total diet defined as when maize, being the major cultigen, is also the major staple food with only very minor supplementation by other cultigens, wild plants, or animal produce.

Column 5: *Alkali Treatment*. Column 5 indicates the presence (+) or absence (—) of alkali treatment during the processing of corn. This can include both the use of lime, wood ash, or lye in soaking or boiling. It does not include the process of exclusively roasting or baking under ashes as its value for alkali hydrolysis would be questionable. Baking bread or roasting cobs under ashes is practiced throughout South America and in North America among the Papago.

Column 6a: *Subsistence Economy*. The set of five digits is that of Murdock (1967: 46–47) in which each digit represents the relative dependency of the society on the five major types of subsistence economy.

1st digit — the gathering of wild plants and small land fauna

2nd digit — hunting, including trapping and fowling

3rd digit — fishing, including shellfishing and the pursuit of large aquatic animals

4th digit — animal husbandry

5th digit — agriculture

The digits in each column are defined as follows (in percent):

(0) — 0 to 5 dependence	(5) — 46 to 55 dependence
(1) — 6 to 15 dependence	(6) — 56 to 65 dependence
(2) — 16 to 25 dependence	(7) — 66 to 75 dependence
(3) — 26 to 35 dependence	(8) — 76 to 85 dependence
(4) — 36 to 45 dependence	(9) — 86 to 100 dependence

Columns 6b: *Comments*. The comments are brief notes as to the major subsistence staple of each society, especially for those which practice intensive agriculture but only secondarily cultivate corn. There may also be reference to how corn is obtained by those societies which utilize it in their diets but do not cultivate corn.

Column 7: *References*. The references are the name and date of publication for the ethnographic sources consulted in the Human Relations Area Files.

Table 3. Summary of cultural information (cont.)

East and North — North America

1 Name	2 HRAF designation	3 Maize cultivation	4 Maize consumption	5 Alkali	6a Murdock subsistence economy	6b Comments	7 References
1 Ojibwa (Chippewa)	NG 6	2	1	+ soda, lye	22402	gather wild rice, equally cultivate beans, squash, pumpkins	Densmore (1929)
2 Micmac	NJ 5	0	0	—	15400	hunting, gathering, fishing	Parsons (1928), Speck and Dexter (1951), Wallis and Wallis (1955)
3 Delaware (Munsee)	NM 7	3	2	+ hardwood ashes	22204	hunting, fishing, gathering	Heckewelder (1819), Tantaquidgeon (1942), Kinietz (1946), Newcomb (1956)
4 Iroquois (Seneca)	NM 9	3	2	+ lye, ashes	13204	hunting, fishing, gathering	Morgan (1901 [1850]), Waugh (1916), Quain (1937), Lyford (1945), Speck (1945)
5 Comanche	NO 6	0	1	—	19000	buffalo hunters, maize obtained as trade item from Kiowas, Witchitas, and some eastern tribes	Wallace and Hoebel (1934), Hoebel (1940)
6 Natchez	3	NO 8	2	+ ashes	03205	hunting, fishing	Swanton (1911)
7 Winnebago	NP 12	3	2	+ ashes	23203	hunting, fishing, gathering	Radin (1915–1916), Lurie (1961)

Table 3. Summary of cultural information (cont.)

1 Name	2 HRAF designation	3 Maize cultivation	4 Maize consumption	5 Alkali	6a Murdock subsistence economy	6b Comments	7 References
8 Crow	NQ 10	0	1	+ ashes	28000	maize obtained as trade item from the Hidatsa; buffalo hunters	Lowie (1935) Morgan (1959)
9 Dhegiha (Omaha)	NQ 12	3	2	+ ashes	14104	hunting, fishing, gathering	Dorsey (1881–1882) Fletcher and La Flesche (1905–1906)
10 Gros Ventre	NQ 13	0	0	—	28000	buffalo hunters	Kroeber (1908) Flannery (1953)
11 Mandan	NQ 17	3	2	+ ashes	03205	hunting, fishing	Will and Spinden (1906) Will and Hyde (1917)
12 Pawnee	NQ 18	3	2	+ ashes	14005	gathering, buffalo hunting	Lesser (1933), Wedel (1936), Weltfish (1965)
Intermediate and Intermountain — N.A.							
13 Northern Paiute (Paviotso)	NR 13	0	0	—	52300	acorn gatherers	Lowie (1924)
14 S.E. Salish (Coeur d'Alene)	NR 19	0	0	—	34300	acorn gatherers	Teit (1927–1928)
15 Pomo (Eastern Pomo)	NS 18	0	0	—	43300	acorn gatherers	Loeb (1926)
16 Tübatulabal	NS 22	0	0	—	53200	acorn gatherers	Wheeler-Voegelin (1938)
17 Yokuts	NS 29	0	0	—	43300	acorn gatherers	Gayton (1948)
18 Yurok	NS 31	0	0	—	41500	acorn gatherers	Heizer and Mills (1952)
19 Washo	NT 20	0	0	—	43300	acorn gatherers	Barrett (1925) d'Azevedo, et al. (1963)

Southwest — N.A.

20	E. Apache (Chiricahua)	NT 8	0	0	—	hunting, gathering	64000	Opler (1941)
21	Navaho	NT 13	3	2	+ ashes	pastoralists	21034	Hill (1938), Leighton and Leighton (1944), Kluckhohn and Leighton (1946), Reichard (1950)
22	Plateau Yumans (Havasupai)	NT 14	3	2	+ ashes	maize is major crop	32005	Curtis (1908), Spier (1928), Smithson (1959)
23	River Yumans	NT 15	2	2	+ lye, ashes	shifting to wheat cultivation	41203	Spier (1933)
24	Tewa	NT 18	3	3	+ ashes, lime	maize is major crop	01018	Robbins, et al. (1916), Whitman (1940), Laski (1958)
25	Zuñi	NT 23	3	3	+ ashes, lime	maize is major crop	11008	Stevenson (1901–1902), Cushing (1920), Bunzel (1929–1930)
26	Papago	NU 28	2	2	—	shifting to wheat cultivation	32005	Castetter and Underhill (1935), Castetter and Bell (1942), Pijoan, et al. (1943)[a]
27	Seri	NU 31	0	0	—	hunting, gathering, fishing	22600	McGee (1895–1896)

Mexico and Central America

28	Aztec	NU 7	3	3	+ ashes, lime	maize is major crop	01207	Bandelier (1876–1879), Vaillant (1941), de Sahagun (1957)

[a] As a result of their diet, Pijoan, et al. (1943) have noticed subclinical signs of avitaminosis.

Table 3. Summary of cultural information (cont.)

1 Name	2 HRAF designation	3 Maize cultivation	4 Maize consumption	5 Alkali	6a Murdock subsistence economy	6b Comments	7 References
29 Tarahumara	NU 33	3	3	+ ashes, lime	01207	maize is major crop	Bennett and Zingg (1935) Fried (1953) Pennington (1963) Champion (1963)
30 Tarasco	NU 34	3	3	+ ashes, lime, soda	01207	maize is major crop	Beals and Hatcher (1943) Beals (1946) West (1948)
31 Tzeltal	NV 9	3	3	+ lime	not coded	maize is major crop	Brom and LaFarge (1927) Villa Rojas (1969) Nash (1970)
32 Yucatec Maya	NV 10	3	3	+ lime	01207	maize is major crop	Gann (1918) Redfield and Villa Rojas (1934)
33 Mosquito	SA 15	1	1	—	32212	plantain is major crop	Villa Rojas (1945) Conzemius (1932)
Andean and Tropical Forest							
34 Talamanca	SA 19	1	1	—	11215	tubers mainly cultivated	Gabb (1876) Stone (1962)
35 Cuna	SB 5	1	1	—	01306	plantain is major crop	Densmore (1926) Wafer (1934) McKim (1947)
36 Cagaba	SC 7	2	2	—	00028	also cultivate beans and yucca extensively	Bolinder (1925) Reichel-Dolmatoff (1949–1950)

									References
37	Goajiro	SC	13	1	1	—	pastoralists	01171	Armstrong and Métraux (1948)
38	Páez	SC	15	2	3	+ ashes	maize is major crop	11026	Santa Cruz (1960); Bernal Villa (1954)
39	Cayaba	SD	6	2	2	—	also cultivate potatoes extensively	11215	Barrett (1925); Murra (1948); Altschuler (1965)
40	Jivaro	SD	9	1	1	—	maize is major crop	12106	Karsten (1935); Sterling (1938)
41	Inca	SE	13	2	2	—	also cultivate potatoes and guinea	01027	Rowe (1946)
42	Aymara	SF	5	1	1	—	cultivate potatoes and guinea	00136	Tschopik (1946); La Barre (1948)
43	Chiriguano	SF	10	2	2	—	cultivate variety of crops as well	11215	Schmidt (1938); Métraux (1948)
44	Ura (Chipaya)	SF	24	0	0	—	cultivate potatoes and guinea	not coded	Métraux (1935); Métraux (1935–1936); La Barre (1946)
45	Araucanians (Mapuche)	SG	4	1	1	—	wheat is major crop	10126	Titiev (1951); Hilger (1957)
46	Mataco	S	17	1	1	—	cultivate pumpkins and watermelons	22411	Pelleschi (1896)
47	Choroti	SK	6	1	1	— —	principally hunters	43201	von Rosen (1924)
48	Callinago	ST	13	1	1	— —	cultivate bitter and sweat manioc	01504	Rouse (1948)
49	Puerto Rico	SU	1	1	1	—	variety of crops	not coded	Hodge and Taylor (1957); Steward, et al. (1956)
50	Haiti	SV	3	1	1	—	cultivate yams	not coded	Courlander (1960)
51	Jamaica	SY	1	2	2	+ ashes	corn is major crop along with cassava	not coded	Beckwith (1929)

Of the fifty-one societies, seven were classified as both high consumers and high cultivators and all seven used alkali treatments in the preparation of their maize. Conversely, none of the twelve societies classified as both low cultivators and consumers used alkali treatments. Table 4 indicates the overall mean difference between users and non-users of alkali treatment levels of both cultivation and consumption. The table uses only those societies which either consume or cultivate some maize. Those societies where maize is a potential cultigen but is neither cultivated nor consumed (rated O, consumption; and O, cultivation) were excluded from the statistical analyses.

On this basis, the mean difference between users and nonusers was highly significant at $P<.001$ and .005 for both consumption and cultivation. Figure 4 represents a plot for all fifty-one societies of the degree of cultivation versus consumption. On this figure, a "plus" (+) indicates alkali treatment, and a "zero" (0) indicates no alkali treatment. It indicates a striking, almost one-to-one, relationship between those societies having high consumption and cultivation of maize with those who use alkali treatment. On the other hand, those societies practicing lowered consumption and cultivation almost invariably do not practice alkali extraction.

Table 4.   Results of statistical analysis — student t-test

	Alkali	Nonalkali
Cultivation	N = 20	N = 17
Mean Rating	2.85	1.29
Standard Deviation	± 0.37	± 0.47
Student "t"	11.11	
p	« .001	
Consumption	N = 21	N = 18
Mean Rating	2.24	1.28
Standard Deviation	± 0.63	± 0.46
Student "t"	5.52	
p	« .001	

The student t-test was carried out only on those societies that scored one or greater for consumption. Of course, the zero consumers were eliminated from this statistical test because they have to consume corn in order to use alkali treatment.

Figures 3, 4, 5, and 6 indicate the geographic distribution of the societies studied, the type of alkali used, if any, and the degree to which maize was cultivated and consumed. From these it is important to note that not all societies either consumed or cultivated maize. For example, the seven Indian populations around California predominantly gathered acorns, and this seemed to impede the need for a staple like corn.

Figure 3.   Location of cultures studied (numbering is the same as in Table 3)

Also we should note that lime use is restricted to Mesoamerica and the Southwestern United States. While lime is an important source of alkali, it is also an excellent source of calcium (Bressani and Scrimshaw 1958). This is unlike the high level of potassium in wood ashes or sodium in lye. Finally, the overall lack of alkali treatments in most Andean populations may have implications for the history of maize cultivation.

Figure 4.   Map of cultures displaying the ratings given to maize cultivation (cultures utilizing alkali processing have circled rating numbers)

DISCUSSION

This paper attempts to explain the use of alkali treatment as a necessary concomitant of intensive maize agriculture and consumption. In this way, the clarification of the real import of this simple processing technique can have wide-ranging ramifications for anthropological theory. Basically, in this portion of the paper we expect to demonstrate that

Figure 5. Map of cultures displaying the ratings given for maize consumption (cultures utilizing alkali processing have circled rating numbers)

knowledge of this previously uninterpreted, but important, variable can modify and/or help to substantiate a number of our interpretations about the origins, development, and spread of maize cultivation in the New World, and its associated sociocultural systems.

The data in Figure 2 and Table 4 strongly suggest a clustering of high degrees of maize cultivation and consumption with alkali treat-

The symbols designate type of alkali.

    commercial lye, soda   △

    ashes   ○

    lime   •

Figure 6.   Map of cultures utilizing alkali processing techniques

ment. In the case of low cultivation or consumption alkali is not used
with one exception. This highly significant relationship strongly supports
the associated concepts that alkali is necessary for high consumption
and, by correlation, for high production of maize (see Figure 4 and
Table 4). On this basis, we can begin to question whether or not the
lower production and consumption of maize in South America is
directly due to the lack of the discovery of this technique.

It is possible to hypothesize that because alkali treatment is not and apparently was not used in these populations, it was necessary for them to develop other crops which may not have been as successful in terms of production as the reported 12 to 1 nonagricultural worker-to-agricultural worker ratio (Coe 1966; Marcus 1973) for the high maize cultivation and consumption in the Yucatán. However, at this time testing such hypotheses would involve complicated assumptions about ecological variables, the timing of the discovery and use of other cultigens, agricultural-to-nonagricultural production ratio estimates and other economic factors for both areas which are not currently available.

While the statistical evidence is overwhelmingly in favor of significant differences between consumption and production of alkali and non-alkali users, this study provides an example in which the statistical approach can also be strongly supported by analysis of descriptive historical data. The historical dimension adds further evidence to the already strong statistical evidence by explaining and accounting for several important exceptions to the almost universal relationship between the production, consumption and use of alkali among the Papago, the Crow and the Páez (see Table 3).

The Papago of the Southwestern United States were classified as moderate producers and consumers of maize aboriginally, but unlike the remaining societies of the Southwest, no evidence could be found that they processed corn using alkali. The Crow do use alkali but cultivate no corn and only sporadically consume it, obtaining it as a trade item from the neighboring Hidatsa, who are agriculturalists. The Páez, on the other hand, deviate from the apparent South American pattern by cultivating maize as their major subsistence item and processing it using alkali. In each of these cases, ecological, historical, and ethnographic evidence provides the necessary insights to the exceptions. In the case of the Papago, the explanation is chiefly ecological.

According to Castetter and Bell (1942), the Papago are seminomadic, living in an arid environment which prohibits year-round cultivation and sedentism. The land is also not fertile enough to allow for large crop yields. Due to the scarcity of food during most seasons, and nomadism during the dry seasons, the Papago do not store their maize nor do they allow it to fully ripen. They eat the majority of it in the roasting-ear stage, gorging themselves when other food is abundant.

The case of the Crow bears an even simpler historical explanation. The Crow once formed a single people with the Hidatsa (Lowie 1935), splitting off from that society to take up existence as nomadic buffalo hunters on the plains. This is supported both ethnohistorically and linguistically. Like the other sedentary village farmers of the Upper Missouri River, the Mandan and the Arikara, the Hidatsa do process maize using alkali (Will and Hyde 1917). The Crow continued to have contact with the Hidatsa, trading their buffalo meat for maize, and it follows that they merely persisted in their tradition carried on from sedentary days of processing maize with alkali.

In order to explain the exception of the Páez, it is necessary to make use of archaeological data. The Páez are Chibchan speakers, living in the highland basins of Colombia. The archaeological evidence supports the theory (Reichel-Dolmatoff 1965) that there was late introduction of maize in Colombia, and it was not from the Andes, but from Mesoamerica. It arrived as a fully developed complex along with other Mesoamerican cultigens probably coming in with an actual influx of peoples from Mesoamerica. The alkali processing technique most probably came into Colombia in conjunction with the cultigens.

Evidence for the utilization of alkali treatment may provide us with further insight into the questions surrounding the independent invention versus the diffusion of maize cultivation in the Americas. It is interesting to note that the Páez are the only South American society in our sample practicing alkali treatment and they use wood ashes. In their case, the evidence points to a late introduction of maize, probably from Mesoamerica (Reichel-Dolmatoff 1965). Thus it is likely that the treatment technique diffused in conjunction with a cultigen complex. This is further evidenced by the fact that all the North American producers and consumers of maize utilize wood-ashes alkali treatment, whereas none, except the Páez, do in South America (see Figure 6).

While this is not proof of independent domestication and invention of maize agriculture in the Andean areas, or elsewhere in South America, it does seem to stand in support of this theory. Along these lines, the evidence from North America favors diffusion since all moderate (and heavy) cultivators and consumers use the process. Lime, as a source of alkali, is predominantly found in Mesoamerica and sporadically in the Southwest. Ashes and lye as sources of alkali are used elsewhere. This fact may have ecological significance regarding the presence and availability of limestone.

From evidence in this paper, it would seem likely that as soon as maize became an extensive part of the diet, alkali treatment had to have been used. This means that forthcoming archaeological evidence should support this hypothesis. There is evidence (Charles Kolb, personal communication) that lime-soaking pots were already in use by 100 B.C. at Teotihuacan, the first urban center in Mesoamerica. The economic implications of the early utilization of lime suggest important questions as to its production, distribution, sale,[9] and trade throughout Meso-america.

While most societies analyzed in our survey used either lime, lye, or wood ashes as a source of alkali, Katz has recently observed that the Lacandon Maya of Chiapas, Mexico, after eating fresh water mussels, cremate the shells as a source of alkali. This practice may have important achaeological implications in other lowland jungle areas of the Yucatán and Guatemala, where the natural sources of limestone are scarce, or even if available, may not be preferred to alkali made from shells.

In this regard it is interesting to juxtapose the reports of plentiful supplies of fresh water shells from snails during the Pre-Classic period, ending in A.D. 250 in Copan (Longyear 1952) and in the Mayan Belize River valley (Willey, et al. 1965:528). However by the Classic period Longyear (1952) has also noted a steady and sharp decline in the abundance of shells and small animal bones in Copan.

Elsewhere in the Mayan region, Haviland (1967) has documented from human skeletal remains at Tikal both a reduction in stature from Pre-Classic through Late Classic times (A.D. 550–900) and an increasing problem of malnutrition as evidenced by radiological analyses of long bones. He attributed these findings to malnutrition stemming from increasing population density which is also present in the Belize River Valley (Marcus 1973) and decreasing sources of high quality protein from wild game. As a whole the evidence suggests a parallel decline in protein resources from both small animal bones and small shells that was probably due to overconsumption in the regions where the population density was rising beyond the carrying capacity of their ecosystem.

If this decrease in snails was also associated with a decrease in the availability of sufficient shells for alkali production in those areas where other alkali resources such as limestone were unused or scarce, then such developments could have had serious nutritional implications for maize processing in addition to those already suggested. Of course, these suggested implications await further testing, because to our knowledge there are no published reports of the use of shells in the preparation of alkali or treatment of maize during these times.

[9]   That there were specific agents who sold lime in urban centers is well documented (de Sahagun 1957) for Aztec times.

PREVIOUS EXPLANATIONS

Because this paper appears to represent the first published report[10] relating the evidence for the nutritional efficacy of alkali processing of corn to the cross-cultural and anthropological literature, it is important to discuss the nature of previous explanations of its use as indicated both by the native populations practicing it and by ethnographers studying their culture. In general, the processing of maize with alkali has been described extensively in the ethnographic literature.

The explanation that most anthropologists have offered for the significance of this treatment in each society is that alkali softens and "hulls" the tough pericarp of the maize. At one level, this explanation is accurate and has closure and may underlie the reason why only a few ethnographers have extended the explanation further, postulating, for example, the benefits that alkali treatment may offer in the general digestive process.

According to Beals (1946), the Tarascans grind maize on the metate with bicarbonate of soda in order to prevent constipation. Tantaquidgeon (1942) notes that the Delaware utilize hominy as the appropriate food for the sick. In describing the practices of the same society, Lindestrom (1925) states that the ashes in which bread is baked function, as sand does for birds, "to clean their stomachs." However, among the Yucatec Maya the maize which is offered to the gods during various ceremonies is never treated with alkali, varying in this respect from the usual preparation of maize for human consumption (Redfield and Villa Rojas 1934). Bennett and Zingg (1935) are among the few anthropologists who mention the cross-cultural significance of alkali treatment. They comment that boiling with alkali "is an essential corn preparation technique" which has migrated northward with the diffusion of maize.

What rather strongly emerges in this brief review of the various anthropological explanations of alkali processing of corn is the lack of a significant biological dimension in the conceptual paradigm of the ethnographic anthropologist.[11] By juxtaposing the biological dimension with the cross-cultural literature, alkali processing techniques assume highly significant proportions by apparently setting a type of critical

[10]   The first report of this finding was actually made by Katz in a paper presented in Paris in 1972, which represented the first detailed study of the phenomenon.
[11]   This concept has been extensively reviewed and synthesized in Katz (1972). Winton (1970) has also explicitly reviewed this problem for ethnographic literature on the Colombian Indians.

limit on the consumption of maize. This concept of a critical limit can be used to enhance, in a significant manner, our understanding of the past and present distribution of maize agriculture and suggest new testable hypotheses to interpret basic anthropological theories such as those concerned with independent invention and diffusion.

ADAPTIVE AND EVOLUTIONARY IMPLICATIONS

The theoretical ramifications of this type of investigation are also very significant for investigations of human adaptability and evolution. These strongly imply that evolutionary anthropologists must take increasing account of the interacting relationships of human biology and culture in adapting to various problems in particular ecosystems. This has been borne out well at genetic levels in studies of diseases like sickle cell anemia (Katz 1973). The concept must be expanded to include other alterations in this basic biological, ecological, and social paradigm.

It is increasingly difficult to accept evolutionary concepts where biological and cultural evolution are separate. In this case, there are tremendous social advantages to maize agriculture, such as reliability of subsistence, residential stability, and so forth. Yet, without the appropriate alkali cooking techniques, a high degree of dependence on corn produces serious malnutrition. The evidence favors strongly the hypothesis that it is not possible to have one without the other.

When we consider the bioevolutionary implications of these nutritional limitations in raw maize, it is unlikely that we would find biological evidence of specific genetic adaptations to nonalkali-processed maize diets because any genetic change would have to involve many essential nutritional pathways. Instead, we find evidence that one of the chief adaptations which allowed for the intensification of maize agriculture and associated changes in sociocultural complexity and organization, occurs at a cultural-technical level with the discovery of the effectiveness of alkali treatment upon what became their major source of nutrition. This adaptation, which stems from a cultural adaptation, probably allows for sufficient adaptations at a variety of other demographic, ecological, and social levels to influence ultimately the genetic composition of the population. On the other hand, the cultural universality among high cultivators and consumers of corn of what in previous ethnographic terms is an apparently innocuous cooking technique used principally for softening the outer kernel, would if looked at in the cultural context alone, be rather insignificant without knowledge of its adaptive advantages at a biological level. Finally, this case suggests that it would be productive for the sciences of humanity to alter previous concepts which separate biological and cultural evolution and to develop concepts which combine both in the study of biocultural evolution.

REFERENCES

AGUIRRE, F., R. BRESSANI, N. S. SCRIMSHAW
  1953   The nutritive value of Central American corns, III: Tryptophan, niacin, thiamin and riboflavin content of 23 varieties in Guatemala. *Food Research* 18:273.

ALTSCHULER, M.
  1965   The Cayapa: a study in legal behavior. Ann Arbor: University Microfilms.

ARMSTRONG, J. M., A. MÉTRAUX
  1948   "The Goajiro," in *Handbook of South American Indians*, volume four. Edited by J. Steward, 369–383. Washington, D.C.: Government Printing Office.

BANDELIER, A. F.
  1876–   On the art of war and mode of warfare of the ancient Mexicans.
  1879   Peabody Museum of American Archaeology and Ethnology Reports, 95–161. Cambridge, Massachusetts: Harvard University Press.

BARRETT, S. A.
  1925   *The Cayapa Indians of Ecuador.* New York: Museum of the American Indian, Heye Foundation.

BEALS, R. L.
  1946   *Cheran: a Sierra Tarascan village.* Washington, D.C.: Smithsonian Institution.

BEALS, R. L., E. HATCHER
  1943   The diet of a Tarascan village. *America Indigena* 3:295–304.

BECKWITH, M. W.
  1929   *Black roadways: a study of Jamaican folk life.* Chapel Hill: University of North Carolina Press.

BENNETT, W. C., R. M. ZINGG
  1935   *The Tarahumara: an Indian tribe of northern Mexico.* Chicago: University of Chicago Press.

BERNAL VILLA, S.
  1954   Economia de los Páez. *Revista Colombiana de Antropologia* 3: 291–367.

BLOM, F., O. LA FARGE
  1927   *Tribes and temples: a record of the expedition to Middle America conducted by the Tulane University of Louisiana in 1925,* volume 2. New Orleans: Tulane University.

BOLINDER, G.
1925 *Die Indianer der Tropischen Schneegebirge: Forschungen im Nördlichsten Südamerika.* Stuttgart: Strecker und Schroder.

BRESSANI, R., R. PAZ, Y. PAZ, N. S. SCRIMSHAW
1958 Chemical changes in corn during preparation of tortillas. *Journal of Agricultural and Food Chemistry* 6(10):770–774.

BRESSANI, R., N. S. SCRIMSHAW
1958 Effect of lime teatment on *in vitro* availability of essential amino acids and solubility of protein fractions in corn. *Journal of Agricultural and Food Chemistry* 6(10):774–8.

BUNZEL, R. L.
1929– *Introduction to Zuñi Ceremonialism.* Bureau of American Ethno-
1930 logy Annual Report 47:467–544.

BYERS, D., *editor*
1967 *The prehistory of the Tehuacan Valley,* volume one: *Environment and subsistence.* Austin: The University of Texas Press.

CASTETTER, E. F., W. H. BELL
1942 *Pima and Papago Indian agriculture.* Albuquerque: University of New Mexico Press.

CASTETTER, E. F., R. M. UNDERHILL
1935 *Ethnobiological studies in the American Southwest,* volume two: *The ethnobiology of the Papago Indians.* Albuquerque: University of New Mexico Press.

CHAMPION, J. R.
1963 "A study of cultural persistence: the Tarahumaras of northwestern Mexico." Ann Arbor: University Microfilms.

COE, M. D.
1966 *The Maya.* New York: Praeger.

CONZEMIUS, E.
1932 *Ethnographical survey of the Miskito and Sumu Indians of Honduras and Nicaragua.* Washington, D.C.: Smithsonian Institution.

COURLANDER, H.
1960 *The drum and the hoe: life and lore of the Haitian people.* Berkeley: University of California Press.

CRAVIOTO, R. O., *et al.*
1945 Nutritive value of the Mexican tortilla. *Science* 102:91–93.

CURTIS, E. S.
1908 "The Havasupai", in *The northern American Indians,* volume two, 97–102. Cambridge.

CUSHING, F. H.
1920 *Zuñi breadstuff.* New York: Museum of the American Indian, Heye Foundation.

D'AZEVEDO, W. L., *et al.*
1963 *The Washo Indians of California and Nevada.* Salt Lake City: University of Utah Press.

DENSMORE, F.
1926 *Music of Tule Indians of Panama.* Washington, D.C.: Smithsonian Institution.

1929   *Chippewa customs.* Washington, D.C.: Government Printing Office.

DE SAHAGUN, B.
1957   *Florentine codex,* books four and five. Translated by C. E. Dibble and A. J. O. Anderson. Santa Fe: School of American Research and the University of Utah.

DORSEY, J. O.
1881–   *Omaha sociology.* Bureau of American Ethnology Annual Report 3.
1882

DRIVER, H.
1969   *Indians of North America* (second edition). Chicago: University of Chicago Press.

FLANNERY, R.
1953   *The Gros Ventres of Montana,* part one: *Social life.* Washington, D.C.: Catholic University of America.

FLETCHER, A. C., F. LA FLESCHE
1905–   *The Omaha tribe.* Bureau of American Ethnology Annual Report
1906   27.

FRIED, J.
1953   The relation of ideal norms to actual behavior in Tarahumara society. *Southwestern Journal of Anthropology* 9:286–295.

GABB, W. H.
1876   On the Indian tribes and languages of Costa Rica. *American Philosophical Proceedings* 14:483–602.

GANN, T. W. F.
1918   *The Maya Indians of southern Yucatan and northern British Honduras.* Washington D.C.: Government Printing Office.

GAYTON, A. H.
1948   *Yokuts and Western Mono ethnography.* Berkeley: University of California Press.

GOPALAN, C.
1968   Leucine and pellagra. *Nutrition Reviews* 26(11):323.

HAVILAND, W. A.
1967   Stature at Tikal, Guatemala: implications for ancient Maya demography and social organization. *American Antiquity* 32:316–326.

HAWKES, L. V., *et al.*
1971   Tryptophan metabolism in patients with pellagra: problem of vitamin B_6 enzyme activity and feedback control of tryptophan pyrrolase enzyme. *The American Journal of Clinical Nutrition* 24:730–739.

HECKEWELDER, J. G. E.
1819   *An account of the history, manners, and customs of the Indian nations, who once inhabited Pennsylvania and the neighboring states.* Philadelphia: Abraham Small for the American Philosophical Society.

HEINZ COMPANY
1963   *Nutritional Data.* Pittsburgh: H. J. Heinz Company.

HEIZER, R. F., J. E. MILLS
1952   *The fair ages of Tsurai: a documentary history of the Indian village on Trinidad Bay.* Translation of Spanish documents by D. C. Cutter. Berkeley: University of California Press.

HILGER, M. I.
1957   *Araucanian child life and its cultural background.* Washington, D.C.: Government Printing Office.

HILL, W. W.
1938   *The agricultural and hunting methods of the Navaho Indians.* New Haven: Yale University Press.

HODGE, W. H., D. M. TAYLOR
1957   The ethnobotany of the Island Caribs of Dominica. *Webbia* 12: 513–644.

HOEBEL E. A.
1940   *The political organization and law-ways of the Comanche Indians.* Menasha, Wisconsin: American Anthropological Association.

JACOBS, M. B., *editor*
1951   *The chemistry and technology of food and food products.* New York: Interscience.

KARSTEN, R.
1935   *The head-hunters of western Amazonas: the life and culture of the Jibaro Indians of eastern Ecuador and Peru.* Helsingfors: Centraltrycheriet.

KATZ, S. H.
1972   "The unity and diversity of man from the point of view of social and cultural anthropology." Unpublished manuscript.
1973   "Genetic adaption in 20th century man," in *Methods and theories of Anthropological genetics.* Edited by M. H. Crawford, and P. L. Workman, 403–422. University of New Mexico Press.

KATZ, S. H., E. F. FOULKS
1970   Mineral metabolism and behavior: abnormalities of calcium homeostasis. *American Journal of Physical Anthropology* 32:299–304.

KINIETZ, W. V.
1946   *Delaware culture chronology.* Indianapolis: Indiana Historical Society.

KLUCKHOHN, C., D. C. LEIGHTON
1946   *Delaware Culture chronology.* Indianapolis: Indiana Historical So-

KODICEK, E., R. BRAUDE, S. K. KORN, K. G. MITCHELL
1956   The effect of alkaline hydrolysis on the availability of its nicotinic acid to the pig. *British Journal of Nutrition* 10:51.

KREHL, W. A., *et al.*
1946   Factors affecting the dietary niacin and tryptophan requirement of the growing rat. *Journal of Nutrition* 31:85.

KROEBER, A. L.
1908   *Ethnology of the Gros Ventre.* New York: American Museum of Natural History.
1939   *Cultural and natural areas of native North America.* University of California Publications in American Archaeology and Ethnology 48.

LA BARRE, W.
1946   "The Uru-Chipaya," in *Handbook of South American Indians,*
        volume two. Edited by J. Steward, 575–585. Washington, D.C.:
        Government Printing Office.
1948   *The Aymara Indians of the Lake Titicaca Plateau, Bolivia.* Me-
        nasha: American Anthropological Association.

LAGUNA, J., K. J. CARPENTER
1951   Raw versus processed corn in niacin deficient diets. *Journal of
        Nutrition* 45:21.

LASKI, V.
1958   *Seeking life.* Philadelphia: American Folklore Society.

LEIGHTON, A. H., D. C. CROSS LEIGHTON
1944   *The Navaho door: an introduction to Navaho life.* Cambridge:
        Harvard University Press.

LESSER, A.
1933   *The Pawnee Ghost Dance hand game.* New York: Columbia Uni-
        versity Press.

LINDESTROM, P.
1925   *Geographia Americae with an account of the Delaware Indians.*
        Philadelphia: The Swedish Colonial Society.

LOEB, E. M.
1926   *Pomo folkways.* Berkeley: University of California Press.

LONGYEAR, J. M.
1952   *Copan ceramics: a study of southeastern Maya pottery.* C.I.W.
        Publication 597. Washington, D.C.

LOWIE, R. H.
1924   *Notes on Shoshonean ethnography.* Anthropological Papers of the
        American Museum of Natural History 20:187–314. New York.
1935   *The Crow Indians.* New York: Farrar and Rinehart.

LURIE, N., *editor*
1961   *Mountain Wolf Woman, sister of Crashing Thunder; the auto-
        biography of a Winnebago Indian.* Ann Arbor: University of
        Michigan Press.

LYFORD, C. A.
1945   *Iroquois crafts.* Lawrence, Kansas: Haskell Institute.

MARCUS, J.
1973   Territorial organization of the lowland classic Maya. *Science* 180:
        911–916.

MAY, J. M., D. L. MC CLELLAN
1972   *The ecology of malnutrition in Mexico and Central America.* New
        York: Hafner.

MC DANIEL, E. G., J. M. HUNDLEY
1958   Alkali-treated corn and niacin deficiency. *Federation Proceedings*
        17:484.

MC GEE, W. J.
1895–   *The Seri Indians.* U.S. Bureau of American Ethnology Annual
1896   Report 17(1).

MCKIM, F.
1947 *San Blas: an account of the Cuna Indians of Panama. The forbidden land: reconnaissance of upper Bayano River, R.P., in 1936.* Edited by Henry Wassen. Goteborg: Etnografiska Museet.

MERTZ, E. T., O. E. NELSON, L. S. BATES, O. A. VERON
1966 *Better protein quality in maize in world protein resources.* American Chemical Society, Advances in Chemistry Series 57.

MÉTRAUX, A.
1935 Contribution à l'ethnographie et à la linguistique des Indiens Uro d'Ancoaqui (Bolivie). *Société des Americanistes de Paris, Journal,* n.s. 27:75–110.
1935– Les indiens Uro'Cipaya de Carangas. *Société des Americanistes*
1936 *de Paris, Journal,* n.s. 27:111–128, 325–415; 28:155–207, 337–394.
1948 "Tribes of the eastern slopes of the Bolivian Andes," in *Handbook of South American Indians,* volume three. Edited by J. Steward, 465–485. Washington, D.C.: Government Printing Office.

MORGAN, L. H.
1901 *League of the Ho-de-no'-sau-nee or Iroquois,* volume one. Revised edition, edited and annotated by H.M. Lloyd. New York: Dodd, Mead. (Originally published 1850.)
1959 *The Indian journals 1859–1862.* Ann Arbor: University of Michigan Press.

MURDOCK, G. P.
1951 South American culture areas. *Southwestern Journal of Anthropology* 7:415–436.
1967 *Ethnographic atlas.* Pittsburgh, Pennsylvania: University of Pittsburgh Press.
1972 *Outline of world cultures* (fourth edition). New Haven: Human Relations Area Files.

MURRA, J.
1948 "The Cayapa and Colorado," in *Handbook of South American Indians,* volume four. Edited by J. Steward, 277–291. Washington, D.C.: Government Printing Office.

NASH, J. C.
1970 *In the eyes of the ancestors: belief and behavior in a Maya community.* New Haven: Yale University Press.

NEWCOMB, W. W., JR.
1956 *The culture and acculturation of the Delaware Indians.* Ann Arbor: University of Michigan.

OPLER, M. E.
1941 *An Apache life-way: the economic, social and religious institutions of the Chiricahua Indians.* Chicago: University of Chicago Press.

PARSONS, E. C.
1928 Micmac notes. *Journal of American Folklore* 39:460–485.

PAULIS, J. W., C. JAMES, J. S. WALL
1969   Comparison of glutelin proteins in normal and high-lysine corn endosperms. *Journal of Agricultural and Food Chemistry* 17(6): 1301–1305.

PEARSON, W. N.
1957   The influence of cooked versus raw maize on the growth of rats receiving a 9% casein ration. *Journal of Nutrition* 62:445.

PELLESCHI, JUAN
1896   Los Indios Matacos y su lingua. *Instituto Geográfico Argentino, Boletin* 17:559–623; 18:173–350.

PENNINGTON, C. W.
1963   *The Tarahumara of Mexico; the environment and material culture.* Salt Lake City: University of Utah Press.

PIJOAN, M., C. A. ELKIN, C. O. ESLINGER
1943   Ascorbic acid deficiency among Papago Indians. *Journal of Nutrition* 25:491–496.

QUAIN, B. H.
1937   "The Iroquois," in *Cooperation and competition among primitive peoples.* Edited by Margaret Mead, 240–281. New York: McGraw-Hill.

RADIN, P.
1915– *The Winnebago tribe.* Bureau of American Ethnology Annual
1916   Report 37.

REDFIELD, R., A. VILLA ROJAS
1934   *Chan Rom: a Maya village.* Chicago: University of Chicago Press.

REICHARD, G. A.
1950   *Navaho religion: a study of symbolism.* New York: Bollingen Foundation.

REICHEL-DOLMATOFF, G.
1949– *Los Kogi: una tribu de la Sierra Nevada de Santa Marta, Colom-*
1950   *bia*, volume one. Instituto Etnológico Nacional, Revista 4.
1965   *Excavaciónes Arquelogias en Puerto Hormiga.* Bogotá: Ediciones de la Universidad de los Andes.

ROBBINS, W. W., J. P. HARRINGTON, B. FREIRE-MARRECO
1916   *Ethnobotany of the Tewa Indians.* Washington, D. C.: Smithsonian Institution.

ROUSE, I.
1948   "The Carib," in *Handbook of South American Indians,* volume four. Edited by J. Steward, 547–565. Washington, D.C: Government Printing Office.

ROWE, J. H.
1946   "Inca culture at the time of the Spanish conquest," in *Handbook of South American Indians,* volume two. Edited by J. Steward, 183–330. Washington, D.C.: Government Printing Office.

SANTA CRUZ, A.
1960   Acquiring status in Goajiro society. *Anthropology Quarterly* 33: 115–127.

SCHMIDT, M.
1938   *Los Chiriguaros e Izozos.* Sociedád Cientifica del Paraguay, Revista 4(3).

SMITHSON, C. L.
1959   *The Havasupai woman.* Salt Lake City: University of Utah Press.

SODEK, L., C. M. WILSON
1971   Amino acid composition of proteins isolated from normal, opaque-2, and floury-2 corn endosperms by a modified Osborne procedure. *Journal of Agricultural and Food Chemistry* 19(6):1144–1150.

SPECK, F. G.
1945   *The Iroquois, a study in cultural evolution.* Bloomfield Hills, Michigan: Cranbrook Institute of Science.

SPECK, F. G., R. W. DEXTER
1951   Utilization of animals and plants by the Micmac Indians of New Brunswick. *Washington Academy of Sciences, Journal* 41:250–259.

SPIER, L.
1928   *Havasupai ethnography.* New York: American Museum of Natural History.
1933   *Yuman Tribes of the Gila River.* Chicago: University of Chicago Press.

SQUIBB R. L., J. E. BRAHAM, G. ARROGAVE, N. S. SCRIMSHAW
1959   A comparison of the effect of raw corn and tortillas (lime-treated corn) with niacin, tryptophan or beans on the growth and muscle niacin of rats. *Journal of Nutrition* 67:351–361.

STERLING, M. W.
1938   *Historical and ethnographical material on the Jivaro Indians.* Washington, D.C.: Government Printing Office.

STEVENSON, M. C.
1901–   *The Zuñi Indians: their mythology, esoteric fraternities, and cere-*
1902   *monies.* Bureau of American Ethnology Annual Report 23.

STEWARD J. H., *et al.*
1956   *The people of Puerto Rico: a study in social anthropology.* Urbana: University of Illinois Press.

STONE, D. Z.
1962   *The Talamancan tribes of Costa Rica.* Cambridge: Peabody Museum.

SWANTON, J. R.
1911   *Indian tribes of the Lower Mississippi Valley and adjacent gulf coast of Mexico.* Bureau of American Ethnology Bulletin 43.

TANTAQUIDGEON, G.
1942   *A study of Delaware Indian medicine practice and folk belief.* Harrisburg: Pennsylvania Historical Commission.

TEAS, H. J., A. C. NEWTON
1951   Tryptophan, niacin, and indoleacetic acid in several endosperm mutants and standard lines of maize. *Plant Physiology* 26:494.

TEIT, J. A.
1927– The Salishan tribes of the western plaeau, the Coeur d'Alêne.
1928   Edited by Franz Boas. *Bureau of American Ethnology, Annual Report* 45:23–197.

TITIEV, M.
1951   *Araucanian culture in transition*. Ann Arbor: University of Michigan Press.

TSCHOPIK, H., JR.
1946   "The Aymara," in *Handbook of South American Indians*, volume two. Edited by J. Steward, 501–573. Washington, D.C.: Government Printing Office.

VAILLANT, G. C.
1941   *Aztecs of Mexico: origin, rise and fall of the Aztec nation*. Garden City: Doubleday, Doran.

VILLA ROJAS, A.
1945   *The Maya of east central Quintana Roo*. Translated by B. Lifschultz, W. McSurely, I. Shlow, and R. Redfield. Washington, D.C.: Carnegie Institute of Washington.
1969   "The Tzeltal," in *Handbook of Middle American Indians*, volume seven. Edited by Robert Wauchope, 195–225. Austin: University of Texas Press.

VON ROSEN
1924   *Ethnographical research work during the Swedish Chaco-Cordillera Expedition 1901–1902*. Stockholm: C. E. Fritze.

WAFER, L.
1934   *A new voyage and description of the Isthmus of America*. Oxford: Hakluyt Society.

WALLACE, E., E. A. HOEBEL
1934   *The Comanches: lords of the south plains*. Norman: University of Oklahoma Press.

WALLIS, W. D., R. S. WALLIS
1955   *The Micmac Indians of Eastern Canada*. Minneapolis: University of Minnesota Press.

WAUGH, F. W.
1916   *Iroquois foods and food preparation*. Ottawa: Government Printing Bureau.

WEDEL, W. R.
1936   *An introduction to Pawnee archeology*. Washington, D.C.: Government Printing Office.

WELTFISH, G.
1965   *The lost universe*. New York: Basic Books.

WEST, R. C.
1948   *Cultural geography of the modern Tarascan area*. Washington, D.C.: Smithsonian Institution .

WHEELER-VOEGELIN, E.
1938   *Tübatulabal ethnography*. Berkeley: University of California Press.

WHITMAN, W.
   1940   "The San Ildefonso of New Mexico," in *Acculturation in seven American Indian tribes.* Edited by R. Linton, 390–460. New York: D. Appleton-Century.
WILKES, H. G.
   1972   Maize and its wild relatives. *Science* 177:1071–1077.
WILL, G. F., G. E. HYDE
   1917   *Corn among the Indians of the upper Missouri.* Lincoln: University of Nebraska Press.
WILL, G. F., H. J. SPINDEN
   1906   *The Mandans: a study of their culture, archaeology, and language.* Cambridge, Massachusetts: Harvard University Press.
WILLEY, G. R., W. R. BULLARD, J. B. GLASS, J. C. GIFFORD
   1965   *Prehistoric Maya settlements in the Belize valley.* Peabody Museum Series 54. Cambridge, Massachusetts: Harvard University Press.
WINTON, M.
   1970   Nutritional adaptation of some Colombian Indians; in the Symposium on Human Adaptation. *American Journal of Physical Anthropology* 32(2):293–297.

Interaction of Social and Ecological Factors in the Epidemiology of Helminth Parasites

HUGUES PICOT and JEAN BENOIST

Relationships between man and parasites make up one of the essential types of adjustment our species must make to the rigors of the environment. This adaptation involves mechanisms pertinent to all fields of anthropobiology, from immunology and adaptive phenotypic transformation to genotypic selection. Many studies have been carried out in this area, and, in the interest of brevity, we have chosen not to repeat them here. However, they have provided significant theoretical contributions, particularly in the case of the interaction between the abnormal hemoglobins and malarial disease.

Numerous investigations have dealt with the effects of ecological changes due to human activities which have lead to the redistribution of pathogenic agents. Moreover, studies have also been carried out on the frequency and geographical distribution of infectious or parasitic diseases such as malaria, bilharzia, or schistosomiasis.

There is, however, another aspect of the relationship between man and parasite that has received less attention from anthropologists and epidemiologists. This is the case where, within a given society, through the cultural rules governing their daily lives, men establish relationships with the parasitic environment. At this level, it is culture and its functioning that appear to be the intermediaries necessary between the biological organism — man — and the natural environment. In what manner is this relationship formed? Of what particular cultural elements does it consist? Shouldn't one take into account both the nature of cultural elements and their patterns? And what, then, are the biological effects of social and cultural change, when we consider past relationships between man and his environment as well as new ones?

The problem is immense. It involves demonstrating the biological consequences of culture and social organization, through their influence on parasitic infestation. Sociocultural rules thus interfere with the challenge posed by the environment, and the net result to be observed is a mixture of the components of the relationships which are thoroughly indistinguishable. Here we will attempt to provide, through preliminary results of ongoing research, a specific bit of clarification to the immense problem of "biosocial adaptation."

The first question to present itself is methodological. In order to unravel such a knotty issue, one should start with the best understood facts and, by relying upon them, proceed to the heart of the problem. For this reason we began with a systematic study of the prevalence of intestinal parasitic infection within a particular area, so that we might then proceed to examine the causes of variation in the prevalence of such infections.

The prevalence of parisitism within a particular society depends upon a great many factors; the natural environment influences the survival and dispersal of the pathogenic agent, while human behavior also affects the survival of the parasite and the probability that certain individuals will be infected. Work done by hygienists deals with both of these areas simultaneously. Change in the risk of infection due to the natural environment leads to fairly clear directives, for the specific features of this environment are relatively easy to analyze and are directly accessible to preventative measures. But the same is not true of the human environment. Therapeutic and preventive medicine are faced with unknowns that can cause apparently well-planned and well-executed projects to fail.

The researcher himself is also confronted by these residual elements, grouped under the rubric of "economic, social, and cultural factors," whenever natural conditions alone do not explain the observed data. Thus, the different behaviors of man respond to the biological demands of the parasite, fixing the conditions of accessibility of the parasite to its host. Health education and hygiene can work to change these behaviors, setting up barriers against infestation even where the natural conditions of the environment favor it. But, independently of any intervention on the part of hygienists, there exist in all cultures certain rules relevant to the cycle of man-parasite relationships. Eating customs, traditional therapeutic measures, organization of the habitat, organization of spatial surroundings and way of life all affect this cycle and many classic examples can be found to demonstrate their effects.

In addition, we must also ask whether or not a point-by-point analysis will neglect the fundamental datum in any social or cultural life-style: variability of behavior, the unequal application of the rules from one subunit to another within the same human group.

The problem is not only one of identifying the role of a particular cultural practice in the occurrence of parasitism, but also of assessing the possible inequality of different human communities in the face of such infestations, as well as the inequality among individuals or sub-groups within these communities. Beyond the variations directly associated with the natural environment (temperature, humidity, sunlight, etc.), all variations appear to be strongly related to the cultural choices of a community in a particular environment. Within a community, these variations have to do with the unequal participation of individuals or other subunits in the setting-up of norms and behaviors for the group. It is really the total participation of the individual, or the social sub-unit, in the group activities of the community rather than a particular cultural trait that determines the relationship between man and parasite.

It is obvious that such a model is all the more likely to be valuable when entry of the parasite into the system of the human host requires the active participation of the latter, as is generally the case with the helminth parasites. But we must not fail to consider circumstances in which the part played by culture and social organization in the relationship between man and pathogenic agents is apparently less clear-cut. In an interesting study, Sangree (1970) shows how the differential incidence of trypanosomiasis among the various "sections" of a Nigerian tribe relates to the differentiation of religious activities. Only the "sections" entrusted with religious power have access to the sacred wood, where the tse-tse fly swarms, and for this reason they have a high mortality rate which the tribe attributes to the danger associated with their contact with the supernatural.

The action of various sociocultural intermediaries is, therefore, not only one of the major factors to consider in parasite epidemiology, but it is also one of the ways in which human groups adapt to their environment. From the latter point there derives a field of considerable theoretical importance. We shall present here a preliminary report of a study that was conducted within this framework, both for theoretical purposes and with the practical aim of setting up a health education program.

Our studies were carried out in 1972 and 1973 in several communities on the island of Réunion. These communities were chosen because of the ecological and cultural contrasts they presented. Réunion is an island located within the southern inter-tropical zone in the Indian

Ocean. Because of its rugged relief, it offers great ecological variety superimposed upon the general base of a humid tropical climate (see Table 1). The altitude and orientation of the island in relation to the prevailing winds produces considerable variation in temperature and humidity in different regions. The communities studied showed appreciable contrasts in this respect.

Table 1.   Altitude, temperature, and rainfall in the four areas studied

	Altitude (meters)	Mean annual rainfall (mm)	Mean rainfall of the driest month (mm)	Mean annual temperature (°C)	Mean temperature of the coldest month (°C)
Bois-Blanc	120	4365.0	377.0 (September)	18.8	16.3 (September)
Dos-d'Ane	930	1471.0	19.0 (October)	17.3	14.7 (September)
Grègues Plains area	600	1834.0	81.3 (September)	19.5	16.5 (September)
Saint-Gilles-les-Hauts	350	847.0	10.5 (August)	21.8	19.9 (September)

Moreover, Réunion society was formed by successive waves of migration (European settlers, Malagasy and African slaves, South Indian indentured workers, Chinese and North Indian shopkeepers, workers from the Comoros). Some of these groups have remained relatively faithful to their native cultures, while at the same time interacting in a mixed creole society. The communities examined here were chosen to represent the principal ethnic components of the island: areas with a majority of creoles, an area where Indians were numerous, and one area with a preponderance of people of European origin.

Nevertheless, these communities have a certain number of features in common. They are all populated by rural people who have been far removed from schools and modern medicine for a long time and whose economic and sanitation levels are, therefore, quite low. Within each community we have tried to define possible ecological and social subunits (neighborhoods, groups of households), as well as cultural (ethnic) and economic ones (occupations, standard of living), and to investigate the living conditions.

COPROLOGICAL METHODS USED; EPIDEMIOLOGICAL RELATIONSHIPS

We present here the results from four small geographical zones; for each one nearly all of the total population was examined. The coprological techniques included direct examination and physico-chemical concentration of eggs or cysts. The numbering of eggs eliminated per gram of stool was used to determine the egg-count. The methods of detection were almost certainly deficient and repeated tests would have probably allowed us to increase our figures somewhat. The parasites discovered were protozoans, as well as helminths, both quite often occurring in the same individuals.

Table 2 shows the overall results from all four areas. We have listed only the parasites that were obviously endemic on the island, i.e.:

1. protozoans (*Entamoeba coli, Entamoeba hystolitica,* and *Giardia intestinalis*);
2. nematodes, (*Trichiuris trichiura, Ascaris lumbricoides, Ancylostoma duodenale, Necator americanus,* and *Strongyloides stercoralis*); and
3. one cestode (*Hymenolepis nana*) which is limited to a particular ethnic group and presents a special epidemiological problem.

All of these intestinal parasites can be disseminated in the environment via human excrement when there are no sanitary installations capable of neutralizing them.

Table 2. Frequency of parasitic infection in the four areas studied

	Subjects examined	Number of households	Tricocephalus	Ascaris	Ancylostoma	Anguillulina	Hymenolepis	Giardia	E. coli	E. hystolitica
ois-Blanc	238	41	230 97%	177 74%	162 68%	120 50.4%	0	56 23%	55 23%	1 0.4%
os-d'Ane	384	72	338 93%	223 58%	29 7.5%	38 9.9%	1	98 25%	120 30.5%	18 4.5%
règues Plains area	138	36	110 80%	32 23.1%	37 26.8%	26 18.8%	0	29 21%	32 23%	3 2.1%
aint-Gilles-les-Hauts	375	66	228 60%	125 33%	10 2.6%	12 3%	33 8%	79 21%	88 23%	6 1.6%

COMPARISON OF RESULTS FROM THE DIFFERENT COMMUNITIES EXAMINED

In looking at Table 2 it can be seen that the frequency of protozoans is relatively uniform in all the areas studied. Investigation of other areas, which are not discussed here but which include urban populations, has confirmed this fact. In contrast to this, the prevalence of helminth infestation is quite different from one area to another.

The Village of Bois-Blanc

This village shows the highest incidence of parasites. If we judge these figures according to the "survey count" the number of parasites harbored is quite high. All of the ecological conditions favorable to these parasites can be found: the temperature is high and the rainfall (which is abundant) occurs evenly throughout the year. The ground is shaded by large trees which keeps it moist. The village is surrounded by forest, and the houses are built quite close together; defecation areas are found close to areas of domestic activities; vegetables are not grown locally and come from unsanitary areas. Fecal contamination is, therefore, quite likely and the risk of infection is high for every inhabitant.

Under these endemic conditions, individuals who have remained unaffected are rare. Most such individuals belong to a single small group of households, clearly less affected than the others (see Table 3).

Table 3.   Parasitic infection in Bois-Blanc

Total households in area: 41	Trichocephalus	Ascaris	Ancylostoma	Anguillulina
Households with no cases	0	1	2	5
Slightly affected households (less than ¼ of the people infected)	0	5	7	15
Greatly affected households (more than ¼ of the peopple infected)	41	22	25	16

The Hamlet of Dos-d'Ane

This settlement is located at an altitude of between 930 and 1100 meters on the leeward side of the island. The temperature is thus rather cold in winter (without, however, going below 9° C.) and there is a rather long dry season. The relative sparseness of the tree cover means that the soil surface is usually warmed and dried by the sun. The population is more dispersed than at Bois-Blanc. Fields and lands lying fallow separate the houses from one another and defecation can take place at a distance from the dwellings. Latrines and modern vermifuge techniques are as rare here as they are in Bois-Blanc. Water is obtained from springs and rivers that are just as poorly protected.

Carriers of trichocephalus are as numerous here as they were in Bois-Blanc, but there are proportionately fewer carriers of ascaris (58%). The average parasite load per individual is lower than at Bois-Blanc. The occurrence of cases of ascaris infestation is, however, not uniform and some households are clearly less affected.

Ancylostoma and anguillulina are rare and this is probably due to the occurrence of seasonal dryness. Nevertheless, the life cycle of these parasites can be completed at Dos-d'Ane since there are individuals who have never left the area who have been infected there, either during the warm and humid season or in favorable microhabitats.

The fact that the incidence of these parasites is concentrated in certain households would seem to argue in favor of the second possibility (see Table 4). Twenty of the 38 cases of anguillulina infection are found in three families, totalling 24 people; 14 of the 29 cases of

Table 4. Parasitic infection in Dos-d'Ane

	Trichoce-phalus	Ascaris	Ancylostoma	Anguillulina
Household unaffected	0	9	58	54
Slightly affected	0	12	12	12
Greatly affected	71	21	1	3

ancylostoma are found in three famiiles, totalling 27 people. Moreover, these last three families, who were the carriers of ancylostoma, were also infected with anguillulina. It is likely, therefore, that the larvae which infected these people were present in the domestic habitat. However, because of biotopes favorable to the larvae in families that have only one carrier, it is difficult to explain why the infection has not spread to the other members of these families. Study of interfamilial relationships and movement of individuals from one home to another in the affected families would be most useful. This would aid in analyzing the possibilities of interfamilial infection and determining whether or not these isolated cases have been infested in other areas.

The Grègues Plains Area

This farming village is located at an altitude of 500 meters in the rainy area of the island. The climate is almost as favorable to parasites as is that of Bois-Blanc. The drinking water here, like that of Dos-d'Ane, is derived from springs near the dwellings. The prevalence of parasitism here is, however, much less significant than at Bois-Blanc and Dos-d'Ane: 13 percent of the population, found in family groups, are free from any sort of helminth infection, and trichocephalus is more rare (see Table 5).

Table 5.   Parasitic infection in the Grègues Plains area

	Trichoce-phalus	Ascaris	Ancylostoma	Anguillulina
Households with no cases of parasitism	0	16	7	13
Households slightly affected	3	6	11	11
Households greatly affected	23	3	2	3

Table 6.   Households most affected in the Grègues Plains area

Number of the household	Population in each house	Number of carriers of ascaris	Number of carriers of ancylostoma	Number of carriers of anguillulina	Total
8	10	3	4	1	8
21	5	1	2	4	5
22	8	7	0	1	8
23	7	6	2	4	12
31	6	6	4	4	20
Total	36	23	12	14	
Frequency in these households		64%	33%	40%	

FAMILIES AFFECTED BY PARASITES   The positive cases here as well are most often found within a few families (see Table 6). These five families (out of thirty-six) include: 23 of the 32 cases of ascaris infection in the entire area (66 percent); 12 of the 37 cases of ancylostoma (33 percent); and 14 of the 26 cases of anguillulina (54 percent). It should be added that the egg-count among the positive subjects, and especially in Families 22, 23, and 31, is quite elevated (6708 eggs, on the average, per individual), indicating that positive individuals have been subject to frequent or massive infestation.

These families are sociologically heterogeneous compared to the rest of the community. They are mainly composed of individuals born outside the community, who have become members of it following marriage. While the community is largely made up of small farmers tilling their own lands, these families are composed of hired farm workers, who work irregularly. Analysis of the physical conditions of the habitat indicates that these factors are not directly relevant. The nature of the soil around the home-sites, the water provisions, etc. are no different from those of their neighbors. The essential differences seem to lie in the behavior of the family and the functioning of the various households.

FAMILIES UNAFFECTED BY PARASITES   Conversely, other families seem to have entirely escaped infection. These families, all linked by multiple kinship ties, are descended from the first settlers of the highlands who came in the nineteenth century, and who were well-to-do landowners. Subdivision of the land by inheritance has impoverished their descendants.

Their income has been modest but regular, and, since it has tended to increase over the past few years, many changes have occurred. The houses themselves have been improved by the use of "solid" construction, the installation of latrines and sometimes even the addition of bathrooms. Defecation now takes place in the garden, and muddy areas are cemented or covered with stones.

In the course of our research we noted a good traditional knowledge of rules of hygiene relative to toilet activities and to the purity of springs and fountains. Perception of a state of good health is keener, while in Bois-Blanc and Dos-d'Ane the problems caused by parasites were felt to be unavoidable evils that could be alleviated by a "collar of corks" and a "garlic clove." In the Grègues Plains area these same troubles prompted people to go to the town and consult the doctor.

Saint-Gilles-les-Hauts

This group of households, in the neighborhood of the village of Saint-Gilles-les-Hauts, is located at an elevation of 350 meters, on the dry side of the island in the middle of an area of sugar cane plantations. The temperature never drops as low as that of Dos-d'Ane or the Grègues Plains area. Rainfall is slight and quite concentrated in the four-month period from January to April. Dwellings made of sheet metal are separated from one another by fields covered with high grass. Some courtyards that are quite isolated are enclosed by fences, but others are adjacent to one another and there is nothing to prevent rainwater from trickling from one yard to another. The floors of the huts are rarely cemented. There is no sewer system and most of the inhabitants of this neighborhood relieve themselves in the surrounding grassy areas. Water is furnished by a communal system and is untreated. It is transported, stored, and handled in receptacles of dubious cleanliness. In some yards, as in Dos-d'Ane, there are permanent cakes of mud near where the water enters which might provide refuge for larvae.

With such an environment, one might expect the prevalence of parasitism to be analogous to that of Dos-d'Ane, where natural conditions are unfavorable to parasites whose larvae must remain in the soil, while conditions of habitat and health are favorable to the transmission of other intestinal parasites. But in fact, the results are quite different; parasites are rather rare. Even trichocephalus is less frequent and 23 percent of the inhabitants show no effects of ANY of the usual nematodes.

1.   Parasites whose larvae must survive in the soil are even more sporadic here than at Dos-d'Ane. The 10 cases of hookworm found are widely dispersed throughout the population. These carriers have not infected their entire families. It is not known whether they were infected locally themselves. On the other hand 8 of the 12 cases of anguillulina belong to two families, otherwise heavily infested with parasites.

2.   The climate alone is not responsible for the low frequencies of trichocephalus and ascaris. Only the habits of the population in general explain this decrease in fecal parasites. In fact, entire family groups are only slightly or not at all affected by one or another of the various species of nematodes.

More precisely, considering the distribution of parasites, it can be observed that: two households have no carriers of either trichocephalus or ascaris; nine households have no carriers of ascaris and a few rare cases of trichocephalus; one household has no carriers of trichocephalus and a few cases of ascaris; and six households, only slightly affected by parasites, have a few cases of both.

3.   In the community of Saint-Gilles-les-Hauts we discovered the presence of a cestode (*Hymenolepis nana*) which is rarely encountered in other areas of the island. In Saint-Gilles-les-Hauts this parasite was found in 8 percent of the inhabitants while it was found only 4 times

in about 3,000 individuals examined on the rest of the island. The larvae of this cestode can gain access to the host organism through the digestive tract in two different ways, either in the form of unhatched eggs in the earth, through the water or the soil which clings to raw vegetables, or in the form of larvae present in the digestive tracts of predatory arthropods found in grain and flour which are then ingested with bread, cakes, or badly cooked porridge.

If the first manner of entry were the most common it is difficult to understand why this parasite would not be disseminated in the same manner as ascaris or trichocephalus. The fact that we found it most frequently in a predominantly Indian community suggests that its access to the organism is related to ingestion of a traditional cake during religious feasts in this community. It appears more frequently among children than among adults and seems to have no correlation with the occurrence of ascaris or trichocephalus.

DETERMINANTS OF VARIATION

We shall present the precise statistical analysis of all our results in a more detailed report at a later time and limit ourselves here to remarks on their bearing upon the questions posed at the beginning of this paper.

The Household, Social Unit of Parasite Infestation

Our positive results are significantly concentrated in a few households, i.e. among individuals, related or not, who share the same houses. The situation is the same for the negative results. This tendency occurs not only where dispersal of dwellings provides a sort of barrier to infestation among nearby residents, but also obtains when lands owned by different families are adjacent and when the population density is quite high. In several cases, the contrast between neighboring households is significant, all the members of a particular home being healthy, while those of a neighboring one are infected with numerous different parasites.

An important fact is that the contrast is all the more marked when the general frequency of parasite infestation is reduced. In other words, in the communities where, as in Bois-Blanc, the general level of infestation is quite high, the difference between the most affected and least affected households is less marked than where, as in Saint-Gilles-les-Hauts, infestation remains at a moderate level. However, even at Bois-Blanc the contrast is clear.

Differences among Communities and Differences among Households

We briefly mentioned in passing ecological differences among the communities. The potential consequences of these differences upon the total incidence of parasites are well known, and we shall not repeat them here. It is certain that the warm and humid environment of Bois-Blanc is most favorable to parasites whose larvae must live in the soil, while that of Dos-d'Ane or of Saint-Gilles-les-Hauts is much less favorable to them.

But several questions remain unanswered after these basic assertions have been made. Detailed examination of the ecological conditions, or of the physical features of the habitat, is not sufficient to explain certain very important contrasts, such as that between Dos-d'Ane and the Grègues Plains area or Saint-Gilles-les-Hauts.

It would seem that analysis of the contrasts among households of a single community might provide a new system of explanation that would be relevant to some aspects of the contrasts that obtain among communities. We shall summarize the conclusions to be drawn from the detailed examination of our research. This analysis focuses on the relationship of various social and cultural features of the households concerned to the incidence of parasitism in these households.

Economic status, at least in terms of the very slight variations apparent in these communities, seems to play only an indirect role. In fact, the most marked contrasts in household and environmental management do not depend on economic status but rather on the choices and attitudes of the household regarding concern or neglect of their surroundings. Components of the economic life of the household, other than just income, correlate with the incidence of parasitism. Landowners, and in a general sense all the people who have been settled for several generations in the same area, tend to be least affected by parasites, no matter what their status. However, Bois-Blanc does not entirely conform to this generalization.

Moreover, while the current income level does not seem to correlate with the degree of parasitic infestation, the economic dynamics of the household reveal a clear relationship. It is not just a question of access to outside sources of revenue, but also of the tendency of the members of households to invest rather than to buy, both in terms of their actual purchases and in their activities (making household improvements, etc.). This point seems to be particularly important and merits a detailed analysis. At this level one sees the entire behavior of the household *vis-à-vis* the surrounding world, and the threat of parasitic infestation can be viewed as only one of the components of this environment.

Another variable shown to be of primary importance is the ethnic group of the subjects. Saint-Gilles-les-Hauts provides a good deal of contrast in this respect, between households that are basically Indian, which are only slightly or not at all affected by parasites, and creole households of various origins, in which the incidence of parasitism in quite high. Despite extensive research it has not been possible for us to relate these differences to the use of traditional therapeutic methods. Such practices are widely used, but even when they succeed in eliminating some parasites they never result in complete destruction of parasites in the individuals treated. While these practices may perhaps explain some of the differences in egg-counts among different communities, they do not account for the variation among ethnic groups within a single community.

We must search elsewhere for the causes of differences in the incidence of parasitism. The Indians of Réunion, despite a good deal of acculturation to creole society in activities which connect them to this society, have maintained in their domestic life a large number of Indian rules and behaviors. The latter, because of their foreignness, have even acquired a certain sacred value, being transmitted to children along with religious values and beliefs. This tends to give them a rather emphatic strictness, further sanctioned by the power of parental authority, which is stronger than among most creole groups.

In this manner a separation of the pure from the impure, of the clean from the dirty, is made explicit. There are certain activities to be performed with the right hand or the left, depending upon the nature of the task and whether it is pure or impure. There is ritual washing of the hands, frequent bathing, and shoes are considered unclean. All of these practices and others, such as the partitioning of the living space, work together to set up a barrier between man and the environment, even where the economic level is low. On the other hand, among the creole people, even when they have been instructed in methods of good hygiene, this barrier has neither the same strength nor the same systematic nature.

As counter-evidence to these data, the occurrence of *Hymenolepis nana*, found almost exclusively in Saint-Gilles-les-Hauts, demonstrates that behavioral factors can either prevent or promote the diffusion of a parasite. It would be erroneous to interpret these behaviors as solely hygienic. They are in reality social rules which have been elaborated for completely different purposes. By their existence they contribute to the modification of an ecosystem which, according to physical circumstances, will be either favorable or unfavorable to parasites.

Other aspects of social organization must also be taken into account. The lack of infestation of children who live close to a household in which everyone has been severely affected by parasites is due to interdictions upon visiting between household. Thus, individual enmity and ethnic compartmentalization play their roles as well. Detailed analysis of systems of kinship and visitation in the area of Saint-Gilles-les-Hauts has thus permitted us to uncover the cryptic side effects of certain interpersonal conflicts which have created real sanitary barriers between certain groups of households.

At our current state of knowledge it is still difficult to generalize about these few facts and even more difficult to state their overall importance to the epidemiology of helminth parasites on Réunion. However, approaching the problem within a single community, from household to household, we may make possible an intercommunity comparison that would be based on the nature of households within these communities and on relative frequencies within each of them. The conclusions that it might be possible to make would be of the greatest theoretical and practical interest. By relating parasite epidemiogy to the total social environment, which determines in the final analysis the whole network of social life of each community, we should be able to appreciate, and eventually to control, the effects of social change upon parasitic infection.

CONCLUSION

The nature and intensity of parasitic disease suffered by members of a human community do not depend solely upon the well-known effects of the natural environment. Social organization and cultural traditions also operate in this relationship. In the case of the helminth parasites, each household unit resists or surrenders to parasitism as a whole, and this result is linked to a network of rules and behaviors that we have only begun to analyze.

However, the contrast between "households with parasites" and "households without parasites" is all the more clear when the risk of infection due to the natural environment is less significant. In such cases, everything transpires as if each single family unit had a different threshold of defense against parasitism. This threshold depends upon a large number of social and cultural factors which work together to either raise or lower it. If the risk of infection is too high, this barrier gives way. If the risk is moderate, clear differences in the defense system will appear among different households, or among the more important social subunits. Below a certain level, the risk no longer produces this sort of differential effect.

Analysis of our data demonstrates that the level of the threshold is more closely linked to the social and cultural cohesiveness of a co-residential group than to its economic level, and that where a break in this cohesiveness appears, resistance to helminth infection is weakest. Resistance to parasitic disease thus appear to be closely related to a whole set of sociocultural adaptations to the environment.

REFERENCES

SANGREE, W. H.
   1970   Tribal ritual, leadership, and the mortality rate in Irigwe, Northern Nigeria. *Southwestern Journal of Anthropology* 26:32–39.

Effects of Behavioral and Ecological Variations upon the Incidence of Parasitic Disease among La Gente of Concepción, Peru

JOHN M. McDANIEL, H. WILLIAM HARRIS, JR., and
SOLOMON H. KATZ

In recent years medicine and physical anthropology have become increasingly concerned with the investigation of disease using a "population" as the unit of analysis. In addition, one can no longer ignore the culture or subculture of the population undergoing analysis. Many previous studies should now be considered incomplete for although an epidemiological approach was used, numerous cultural groups were inappropriately lumped together as a single entity. Clearly such examples as those of Alland's (1969) description of parasitic susceptibility in Africa or Gajdusek's (1964) ingenious explanation of the disease Kuru present a more complete picture of disease phenomena.

Human parasitism is a particularly good example of a class of diseases that can only be fully understood and described at a population level. These parasitic diseases include the viruses, bacteria, fungi, protozoa, helminths, and arthropods. The study reported here is an examination of the incidence of helminth parasites among the people living in the settlement of Concepción, Peru. The purpose of this paper is to describe and integrate the cultural, environmental, and biological factors influencing parasitic populations. It was undertaken with the recognition that these factors cannot be treated separately, but are intimately associated with the complexity of the helminth parasites. With an understanding of these intricate relationships, one can begin to deal with the selective factors involved in the pathogenesis of human parasitic disease as well as potentially develop more effective measures to reduce its frequency.

THE POPULATION AND ITS ENVIRONMENT

Concepción is a recently founded, small (total population of 212), and isolated settlement. Located southeast of the town of Puerto Maldanado, Concepción is situated on the banks of the Madre de Dios river within that eastern section of Peru known as la Montaña. This geographic zone is a tropical forest environment that is unique to South America. Its proximity to the Andes is attested to by the many surrounding hills and fast flowing streams.

The mean annual rainfall in Concepción ranges from fifty-nine to seventy-eight inches. Mean daily temperature varies from sixty-five to eighty degrees Fahrenheit. The soil is either a loose loam or clay. In those areas in which trees and low growth have been removed, small pools of water are regularly encountered. The combination of these climatic and environmental conditions produces an environment that is conducive to the proliferation of helminth parasites.

The settlement was established in 1956 by a secular Roman Catholic missionary. The population consists of three clearly defined cultural groups: the administrators, la Gente and los Serranos. The administrative element is composed of Spanish individuals who have come to the montaña to provide leadership to settlements such as Concepción. Los Serranos are individuals native to the Sierra (highlands) of Peru who travel to the montaña settlements in search of economic opportunities. La Gente are natives of la Montaña.

La Gente are the largest of the three groups living in Concepción. All members of this group are born in la Montaña, have at least one parent who is a native of la Montaña, and are fluent in Spanish. Living in isolated nuclear family units, la Gente clear and maintain small farms known as *chacras*. All families engage in slash-and-burn agriculture, and the agricultural harvest is supplemented by hunting and fishing. Within the settlement and in surrounding villages la Gente are beginning to augment their traditional economic pursuits by acquiring part-time jobs providing a cash income. The exposure to wage earning and the concomitant interaction with members of other cultural groups have resulted in increased acculturation of la Gente.

La Gente maintain a spirit of freedom and resourcefulness. Males, in particular, are quick to boast that no deep ties bind them to their families and present locations. They consider themselves highly adaptable and capable of adjusting easily to new environments and economic opportunities.

Members of la Gente display an impressive lack of concern for most

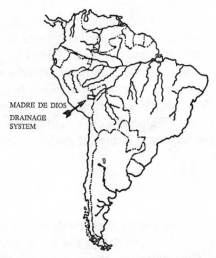

Map 1. South America

health problems endemic to the area. In this context, children are taught to endure discomfort and pain with stoicism and courage. Adults tolerate problems that are culturally defined as being of "minor significance" despite the frequent and severe discomforts these ailments may cause. Included within the category of "minor health problems" are those symptoms produced by helminth parasites. La Gente display little concern for sanitation. Only one family has built a latrine, others rely exclusively on open air locations near their homes. Shoes are seldom worn by most members of the group. Food is stored, prepared and eaten with little concern for possible disease transmission. Little care is displayed with respect to the purity of drinking water.

Despite the fact that la Gente of Concepción share many basic values and beliefs and engage in similar ways of life, there are significant variations in their behaviors and attitudes toward health problems. These differences are apparent between ages, sexes, and specific families.

In order to carry out this investigation, McDaniel spent thirteen months in Concepción collecting relevant cultural data. Traditional ethnographic field techniques of participant observation were employed in this endeavor. Collection of ten gram stool samples was carried out during the last two weeks of field study. Samples were obtained for 136 or 91 percent of the 154 members over six months of age of la Gente in Concepción. We were unable to collect samples from infants under six months old. Each subject was provided with necessary materials and instructed as to their use. Immediately after collection, the samples were transferred to a prepared container filled with formalin. These were then prepared for transportation to the Pennsylvania State Parasitology Laboratories, Landis Hospital, Philadelphia, Pennsylvania. The samples were analyzed using the Faust Concentration Technique. Six helminths were studied: *Ascaris lumbricoides, Necator americanus, Trichurus trichuria, Enterobius vermicularis, Hymenolepis nana,* and *Strongyloides stercoralis.* Samples were scored on the basis of the presence or absence of any stage in the life cycle of the above parasites.

RESULTS

The la Gente possess extremely high incidence levels of Ascaris l., Necator a. and Trichurus t. (Table 1). The parasites *Strongyloides s., Enterobius v.* and *Hymenolepis n.* however, are present at much lower frequency (Table 2). Similar frequencies of all six parasites have been documented in other southeastern sections of Peru (Cornejo 1959, del Rio 1960). Lumbreras (1963) suggests that frequencies documented for *Strongyloides s.* result from the implementation of an invalid technique; moreover he supports the use of the 'Baermann Modified Cup Technique' which he claims provides accurate results. Table 3 demonstrates the differences found, by the use of the Faust and Baermann techniques, in the prevalence of *S. stercoralis* infections of a given sample. From these data it may be inferred that the frequency of *Strongyloides*

Table 1. Infection with *A. lumbricoides, N. americanus,* or *T. trichuria* among 136 la Gente subjects

Intestinal nematode	Number of subjects	Number positive	Number negative	Percent positive
A. lumbricoides	136	108	28	79
N. americanus	136	105	31	76
T. trichuria	136	113	23	83

Table 2. Infection with *S. stercoralis, E. vermicularis,* or *H. nana* among 136 la Gente subjects

Intestinal nematode	Number of subjects	Number positive	Number negative	Percent positive
S. stercoralis	136	17	119	13
E. vermicularis	136	4	132	3
H. nana	136	2	134	1.5

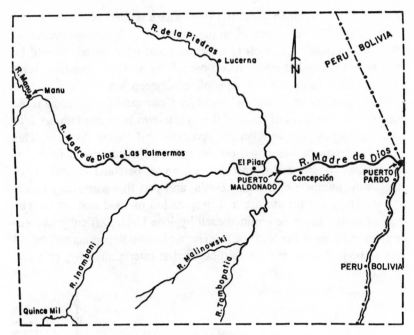

Map 2.   Madre de Dios drainage, southeastern Peru

among la Gente may be much higher than recorded. The low frequency of *Enterobius v.* may be attributed to the method of stool collection. *Enterobius* deposits its eggs in the perianal region of the human host,

Table 3.   Comparison of the Baermann technique and Faust technique of analyzing stools of 114 hospital patients infected with *S. stercoralis*; $X^a = 45.113$, p 0.009 (after Lumbreras 1963)

Stool technique	Number of subjects	Number positive	Number negative	Percent positive
Faust	114	22	92	19
Baermann	114	73	41	64

consequently fecal examination results in a distortion of the sample data (Smyth 1962). The scarcity of *Hymenolepis nana* within la Gente remains inexplicable. *Hymenolepis* is characterized as a "weak" parasite and is known to elicit a particularly strong host immune response (Heyneman 1962), yet this does not explain its particularly low frequency in this community.

Good sanitation and hygiene practices are most often cited as effective methods of preventing the spread or maintenance of parasitic disease. Interruption of a parasite's life cycle is the most effective way to prevent its proliferation (Brown 1969). There is however, only partial understanding of how much of an improvement in hygiene is needed to effectively reduce high levels of parasitism and what criteria should be used to judge family hygiene on an overall basis. These questions were investigated in reference to the people of Concepción.

After termination of the fieldwork in Concepción, McDaniel rated the hygienic practices of each of the twenty-two la Gente families into three categories: Above Average, Average, and Below Average. This overall assessment was based on the following criteria: cleanliness of the kitchen, dining areas, and sleeping areas, personal cleanliness of the family, numbers of insects, vermin, and pets that gain ready access to the home, and the storage and preparation of food and water. The sum of these ratings determined each hygiene level. Difficulty was encountered because the level of hygiene and sanitation practiced by all was so poor that at first it was thought that interfamilial hygienic dif-

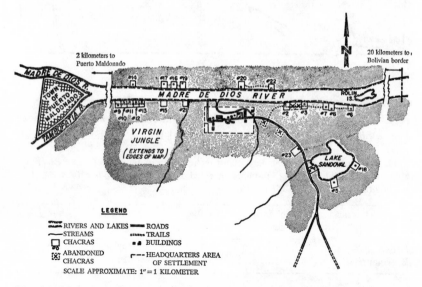

Map 3.   Settlement of Concepción

ferences would be of little consequence. None of the listed categories could be described as having adequate hygiene as judged by Western standards. Even the Above Average hygiene group was continually exposed to risk of parasitic infection. However, Tables 4 and 5 demonstrate that there are differences in parasitic incidence as a result of these hygienic practices. When the frequency, as measured on a percent positive basis for each of the three parasites, is calculated, there is an

Table 4.   The frequency of infection by *Ascaris l., Necator a.,* and *Trichurus t.* among 133 la Gente subjects according to hygienic practices

Hygienic practices

Intestinal nematodes	Above average number of subjects				Average number of subjects				Below average number of subjects			
	Total	Negative	Positive	Percent positive	Total	Negative	Positive	Percent positive	Total	Negative	Positive	Percent positive
Ascaris l.	18	9	9	50	65	19	46	71	50	6	44	83
Necator a.	18	8	10	53	65	21	44	68	50	11	39	78
Trichurus t.	18	7	11	61	65	16	49	76	50	10	40	80

Table 5.   Statistical comparison of the number of infected individuals among 133 la Gente subjects according to hygienic practices (see Table 4 for the numbers of infected individuals)

Intestinal nematodes

	Ascaris l.		*Necator a.*		*Trichurus t.*	
Hygiene comparison	X^2	P value	X^2	P value	X^2	P value
Above average versus average number of infected individuals	1.870	0.172	0.458	0.499	0.810	0.368
Average versus below average number of infected individuals	3.971	0.046	1.025	0.311	0.130	0.717
Above average versus below average number of infected individuals	9.016	0.0026	2.29	0.130	1.612	0.204

increase in infestation as the estimated level of family hygiene decreases. The values are statistically significant for only some of these comparisons. *Ascaris* is significant for the comparisons between: Above Average versus Below Average and Average versus Below Average, while approaching significance in the third category. *Necator* and *Trichurus* approach significance only when one compares the extremes of hygiene practices.

The best explanation of these data can be found in the different modes of transmission of the particular parasites. *Ascaris* is contracted through ingestion of unclean food and water, *Necator* enters the host by boring through the individual's feet, and *Trichurus* is spread through both of these vectors. Therefore, the frequency of *Ascaris* is affected by changes in food preparation and household cleanliness, while *Necator* depends on the soil conditions and the disposal of human waste. Since no la Gente families possess adequate waste disposal facili-

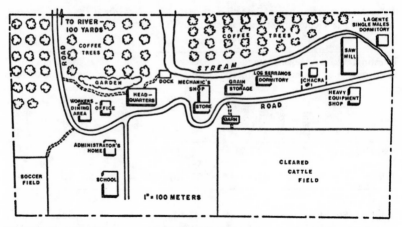

Map 4.   Headquarters area of settlement: enlargement

ties, all are at high risk of contracting *Necator* and *Trichurus*. There do exist, however, variations in the soil conditions around la Gente *chacras*. Some families have cleared the land around their *chacras*, others allow the jungle growth to extend to the very edge of the dwellings. The comparison between the Above Average and Below Average hygiene groups does approach significance because the members of the Below Average group tend not to clear their living areas and are subject to greater *Necator* risk. The factors involved in this increased risk will be discussed in the next section. *Trichurus*, utilizing both oral and cutaneous entrances into the host, is only influenced by the combination of discussed hygiene differences and soil conditions. It therefore shows a negligible correlation.

Differences in the parasitic frequencies of these assigned hygiene groups is further demonstrated by scoring the number of individuals within a given hygiene rated family that are infected by one, two, or all three of the tested parasites (Table 6). The percentage of the family members with "high" infestation — all three parasites — was then ranked into three categories: Greatest, Moderate, and Least degree of parasitism. The Least category is somewhat misleading, for families ranked least averaged 40 percent of their members harboring "high" infestations. These assigned degrees of family parasitism were then compared to the formulated hygiene ratings. As Tables 6 and 7 demonstrate, one can judge the degree of parasitism of a family by its hygienic practices. This is indeed a crude estimating device, for many families gave partial agreement, but one can conclude that small differences in

Table 6. Nematodal infections by *Ascaris l.*, *Necator a.*, and *Trichurus t.* among the members of 22 la Gente families and the influence of hygienic practices upon the multiplicity of infections

	Family number																					
	1	2	3	4	5	6	7	8	9	10	11	12	13	14	15	16	17	18	19	20	21	22
Low infection (Number without parasites or single species)	1	1	1	4	0	2	0	0	4	1	3	1	2	5	2	2	2	0	0	0	1	2
High infection (Number with two or three parasitic species)	8	5	11	2	5	6	3	8	4	2	3	3	4	3	5	1	4	3	5	4	5	3
Number of family members	9	6	12	6	5	8	3	8	8	3	6	4	6	8	7	3	6	3	5	4	6	5
Percent of family members with high infestation	90	85	95	30	100	75	100	100	50	66	50	75	66	40	70	33	66	100	100	100	85	60
Assigned degree of family parasitism	G	G	G	L	G	M	G	G	L	M	L	M	M	L	M	L	M	G	G	G	G	M
Family Hygiene Practices:	A	A	A	A	A	A	BA	BA	AA	AA	AA	A	A	A	BA	A	A	BA	BA	BA	BA	BA
AGREEMENT:	±	±	±	±	±	±	+	+	+	±	+	±	+	±	+	±	+	+	+	+	+	±

G = greatest (80 percent)
M = moderate (60-80 percent)
L = least (60 percent)

AA = Above Average
A = Average
BA = Below Average

+ = agreement
± = partial
− = no agreement

Table 7.   The influence of family hygiene practices on the occurrence of nematodal infections in 133 members of 22 la Gente families

Hygienic practices

Number of infections in family members	Below average	Average	Above average
Greatest	7	4	0
Moderate	2	3	1
Least	0	3	2

the hygiene levels of families produce significant differences in the prevalence of parasites whose life cycles are affected by these hygienic distinctions, e.g. *Ascaris*.

The la Gente families are scattered in a more or less random fashion throughout the area of Concepción. The composition of the soil does not vary significantly over the settlement's expanse, but its condition varies markedly depending on each family's preference and economic status. All grow much the same crops: dry rice, yucca, bananas, beans, and some leafy vegetables using the standard methods of slash-and-burn agriculture. Families do differ in the amount of cleared area around their dwellings. Families with "cleared" *chacras* possess areas surrounding their living quarters where the soil is well drained, dry, and cleared of encroaching jungle growth. "Uncleared" *chacras* are characterized by the encroachment of jungle vegetation which results in the poor

Table 8.   The frequency of parasitic infections in the members of families with cleared *chacras* compared with that in families with uncleared *chacras*

Intestinal nematodes

		Ascaris l.	*Necator a.*	*Trichurus t.*
Cleared chacra family members $n = 10$	Number positive	7	4	7
	Number negative	3	6	3
	Percent positive	70	40	70
Uncleared chacra family members $n = 55$	Number positive	39	40	42
	Number negative	16	15	13
	Percent positive	71	73	84
Cleared v. uncleared parasitic infections	X^2	0.102	2.782	0.0009
	P value	0.749	0.095	0.976

drainage of the area immediately surrounding the home. As a rule, families have defecation areas that are a short distance from the house, usually slightly beyond the immediate premises. Table 8 reveals that the families with "cleared" *chacras* have a much lower frequency of *Necator*, while *Ascaris* and *Trichurus* show no correlation. These data are compiled from only families rated Average; all tested practiced much the same household sanitation. The infective larvae of *Necator* are known to migrate long distances through the soil whereupon they climb to the highest part of the moist ground and await their host (Chandler 1922). The physical appearance of the "cleared" soil indicates that the *Necator* larvae would be more restricted in their migratory movements and present less of an infective threat to the people nearby.

Six la Gente families (numbers 14, 16, 17, 19, 20, 22) live on the north bank of the Madre de Dios river. None of the six *chacras* are contiguous, and the few trails through the thick jungle provide for limited personal communication among the families. These families are then relatively isolated from each other and the community at large. In contrast, nine la Gente families (numbers 1, 2, 3, 4, 5, 6, 7, 8, 18) are located relatively close together within the busiest area of the settlement. A road and many trails make for frequent day to day contact between the members of all these families. These nine are termed "mobile" families. All fifteen families were selected with regard to hygiene practices, and an effort was made to randomize these selections. The "isolated" category numbers two average hygiene families and three below average, while the "mobile" has five average and four below average families. Table 9 presents data of the mobile-isolated comparison. None of the respective comparisons produce significant results, the parasites must therefore be effectively exploiting the vectors that are available to them in each case and the relative isolation of some families of Concepción confers no protection from these helminth parasites.

Originally compiled as part of the cultural data, the age and sex of each la Gente individual were then used in this investigation, and the prevalence of *Ascaris*, *Necator*, and *Trichurus* was tested accordingly. In Concepción, the females and males have very different social, economic, and household roles. The machismo concept is practiced among la Gente and the males are by far the more mobile and domineering sex. The females are sedentary, living on the *chacra*, engaged in childcare and domestic chores. La Gente women rarely go to the main settlement or to the larger town, Puerto Maldonado, ten kilometers away. The greater number of males (83) than that of females (53) is not a result

Table 9.   Comparative frequency of parasitic infection among isolated and mobile la Gente families

| Family characteristic | | Intestinal nematode | | |
		Ascaris l.	Necator a.	Trichurus t.
Isolated total = 29	Number positive	20	21	23
	Number negative	9	8	6
	Percent positive	69	73	79
Mobile total = 61	Number positive	52	49	43
	Number negative	9	12	18
	Percent positive	85	80	71
Isolated versus mobile	X²	2.318	0.328	0.396
	P value	0.128	0.567	0.529

of differential survival, but is due to the wishes of some of the members of la Gente who leave all or part of their families in other towns. However, the parasitic data do show differences in the frequencies of infected males and females (Tables 10, 11). When individually tested,

Table 10.   The frequency of parasitic infections among la Gente males as compared with la Gente females

| | | Intestinal nematodes | | |
		Ascaris l.	Necator a.	Trichurus t.
Males total = 83	Number positive	63	64	70
	Number negative	20	19	13
	Percent positive	75	76	83
Females total = 53	Number positive	39	33	38
	Number negative	14	20	15
	Percent positive	75	64	73
Infected males versus	X²	0.010	2.797	2.435
infected females	P value	0.919	0.095	0.119

each parasite shows no significance; however when grouped together and tested as a block for their presence or absence the results are significant. It is impossible to discern the specific causation(s) of the above difference, but both biological factors (Blumberg, personal communication, July 1972) and cultural practices (Alland 1969) have been

Table 11. The proportion of infected and uninfected la Gente males as compared with la Gente females

Ascaris, Necator, and *Trichurus*		Number of subjects	
		Males (83)	Females (53)
	Present	79	43
	Absent	4	10
	Percent infected	95	83
Infected males versus infected females	X² = 5.475 P value 0.0193		

shown to play a role in the type and severity of diseases that are experienced by both sexes. It is presumed in the case of Concepción that the reason for this frequency difference is a combination of culture and biology. Parasitic prevalence can also be found to be a function of the age of the individual (Tables 12, 13, 14). The presence of parasites is scanty in the category of ages one and two years, after which their presence rises rapidly and reaches a constant value of about 70 percent. *Ascaris* shows a slight decline starting at ages eleven to fifteen (Figure

Table 12. Infection by *Ascaris l., Necator a.,* and *Trichurus t.* according to the age of the subjects

Age groups (in years)	Total	*Ascaris l.*	*Necator a.*	*Trichurus t.*	Not infected
1– 2	15	7	2	8	5
3– 5	15	14	10	12	1
6–10	34	26	26	24	4
11–15	22	19	17	17	0
16–25	20	16	12	17	2
26–39	17	11	14	14	1
40	13	6	10	10	1

Table 13. Concomitant infections by *Ascaris l., Necator a.,* and *Trichurus t.* in la Gente subjects according to age

Age groups (in years)	Total	Number of individuals with:			
		Triple infections	Double infections	Single infections	No infection
1– 2	15	2	3	5	5
3– 5	15	10	2	2	1
6–10	34	20	6	4	4
11–15	22	12	7	3	0
16–25	20	12	5	1	2
26–39	17	8	7	1	1
40	13	4	6	2	1

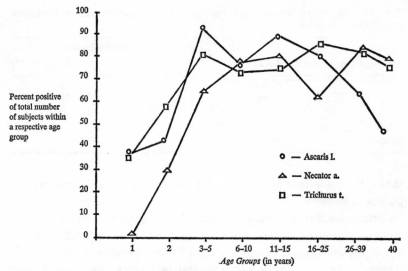

Figure 1.   Percent positive infections by *Ascaris l., Necator a.,* and *Trichurus t.* in respective age groups of la Gente subjects

1). This difference, like other smaller variations in the graph, is not statistically significant and may be biased as a result of sample size. The immune response of the host (Jackson, et al. 1970), improved hygiene upon reaching adulthood, and other host resistance factors (Larsh 1951) may contribute to this decline; however to our knowledge no-where has it been documented that *Ascaris* is more susceptible to bio-

Table 14.   Comparative frequency of parasitic infections of one-to-two-year and three-to-five year-old la Gente subjects

		Intestinal nematode			
Age groups (in years)	Total	Subjects	*Ascaris l.*	*Necator a.*	*Trichurus t.*
1–2	15	Number positive	7	2	8
		Number negative	8	13	7
		Percent positive	47	13	53
3–5	15	Number positive	14	10	12
		Number negative	1	5	3
		Percent positive	93	68	80
Age (1–2) versus age (3–5)		X^2	5.714	6.805	1.350
		P value	0.017	0.009	0.245

logical host resistance mechanisms than is *Trichurus* or *Necator*. Improved personal hygiene should certainly affect *Ascaris* frequencies, but no continuing improvement after the attainment of adulthood was observed.

The marked frequency difference between age groups one to two and three to five years is directly attributable to cultural practices. The child under two years of age benefits from the attention of its mother or older siblings; moreover, the mobility of the infant is restricted, he is kept off the ground and is breast fed or ingests small quantities of food prepared separately from the main fare. Consequently he is afforded a degree of protection from the vectors of the helminth parasites. *Ascaris* and *Trichurus* spread by vectors such as contaminated food or play objects are present at a frequency of approximately 35 percent. *Necator*, contracted only by bare foot exposure, is not a danger at this age. The child between the ages of three and fourteen years is, in contrast, free to play anywhere in the *chacra*. His freedom and the relative neglect displayed by his parents subject him to an extremely high risk of infection. This immediate increase in parasitism in young children after their infancy has also been documented by De Rivas (1935). The subsequent frequency of infestation does not vary markedly after this initial rise, but remains a relatively constant 70 percent with the exception of *Ascaris* as aforementioned. This is in spite of field observation indicating a marked improvement in personal hygiene upon initiation into adulthood, about age fourteen. It is unfortunate that no longitudinal data are available to test whether the same individuals retain parasitic infections throughout their lifetimes or whether a dynamic equilibrium is established between infected and uninfected individuals.

DISCUSSION AND CONCLUSION

From a review of the data, it is apparent that host-parasite interactions are complicated and the investigation of these mechanisms is perhaps best carried out in a laboratory. However, laboratory results provide no information on the natural complexity of living human communities where a multiplicity of interrelationships are involved. These relationships are best investigated on a local level. For example, large random sampling over a wide area of the jungle will result only in the discovery of the frequency of a particular parasite, which alone is of little value since helminth parasites are already well known in this ecosystem. However, study of parasitism on a local level yields parasitic frequency data, possible modes of transmission that exist in that specific community, and insight into the nature of the people who are infected. The latter is especially important in parasitic disease for the existing culture propagates and maintains the people of Concepción and results in significant differences in the observed parasitic infestation of the community. A major concern at the inception of this investigation was the failure of all studied hygiene groups to practice adequate sanitation as judged by Western standards. The data strongly suggest that to achieve a large reduction in the frequency of helminth parasites, small changes such as cleared, dry areas around an individual's dwelling do make a significant difference.

In a community such as Concepción, parasitism must represent a strong selective force. *Necator* and *Trichurus*, which ingest large quantities of blood, can produce anemia and are particularly dangerous to growing children. *Ascaris* can produce intestinal obstruction and pneumonia (Phills, et al. 1972). During the period of field study a death of a juvenile was directly attributable to parasitic infection, while many more children suffer from chronic diarrhea, stomach pain, and loss of vitality. The parasitism of these children must also have harmful effects on their growth and development (Robbins and Stanley 1967).

Much of the recent work concerning culture and disease has been oriented to a consideration of the way in which "the culture" of a group influences the health problems of its members. However, it has been the attempt of this study to clarify the way in which the cultures of subgroups within a community can influence the disease susceptibility of their membership. The concept of subcultures within a group which may exhibit significant variations in values and practices is pursued in detail by Goodenough (1963). The data from Concepción demonstrate that the members of subcultures within this small la Gente community are exposed to varying risks of parasitic infection. It appears that variations in the behavior of members of this cultural group are, in part, responsible for the documented variations in parasitic incidence.

From the perspective of human evolution, these variations in behavior among subcultures suggest that they are capable of imposing unique selective pressure upon the membership. While the biological anthropologist has pursued the effects of physical environmental variations upon the biology of human populations, these data suggest that examination of small variations in cultural behavior are also essential in understanding biological adaptation and evolution of human populations. Investigation of disease within a cultural group by an interdisciplinary team of specialists should provide detailed data relevant to the problem and, one would hope, improve the life and public health of the residents of communities such as Concepción.

REFERENCES

ALLAND, A.
1969   "Ecology and adaptation to parasitic diseases," in *Environment and cultural behavior*. Edited by A. P. Vayda, 80. New York: Natural History Press.

BROWN, H. W.
1969   *Basic clinical parasitology*. New York: Saunders.

CHANDLER, A. C.
1922   *Animal parasites and human disease*. London: John Wiley and Sons.

CORNEJO, D.
1959   Incidencia de parasitismo intestinal por helmintos y protozoos en el Departamento de Madre de Dios. *Anales Facultad de Medicina* 42:281. Lima.

DEL RIO, GONZALEZ
1960   "Cinco Anos de Medico en el Madre de Dios." Instituto de Estudios Tropicales, Pio Aza.

DE RIVAS, D.
1935   *Clinical parasitology and tropical medicine*. Philadelphia: Lea and Febiger.

GAJDUSEK, C.
1964   Factors governing the genetics of primitive human populations. *Cold Spring Harbor Symposium on Quantitative Biology* 29:121–136.

GOODENOUGH, W. H.
1963   *Cooperation in change*. New York: Russell Sage Foundation.

HEYNEMAN, D.
1962   Studies on helminth immunity: comparison between lumenal and tissue phases of infection in the white mouse by *H. nana*. *American Journal of Tropical Medicine* 11:46–63.

JACKSON, G. L., R. HERMAN, I. SINGER
1970   *Immunity to parasitic animals*, volume two. New York: Meredith Corporation.

LARSH, J. E.
1951   Host-parasite relationships in cestode infections with emphasis on host resistance. *Journal of Parasitology* 37:343–346.

LUMBRERAS, H.
1963   Strongyloidosis: I. Evaluación de la "técnica de Baermann modificada en copa" en el estudio de la Strongyloidosis. *Revista Medica Peruana* 32(334).

PHILLS, J. A., A. J. HAROLD, G. V. WHITEMAN, TARELMUTTER
1972   Pulmonary abnormalities and esosinophila due to *Ascaris suum*
       New England Journal of Medicine 282:18–23.
ROBBINS, S., B. STANLEY
1967   *Pathology*. Boston: W. B. Saunders.
SMYTH, J. D.
1962   *Introduction to animal parasitology*. London: English University
       Press.

The Focus of Hyperendemic Goiter, Cretinism, and Associated Deaf-Mutism in Western New Guinea

D. C. GAJDUSEK and R. M. GARRUTO

Hyperendemic goiter and cretinism present a serious problem in many inland mountainous regions of New Guinea. Taken together with the usual but not invariable association of a high level of congenital deaf-mutism, the conditions present a crippling load of defect on many populations. Endemic goiter and the associated neurological defects appear in higher incidence in the Central Highlands of Western New Guinea than in other populations in Oceania or Australasia and this extends through a population of about 100,000, which represents almost half of the highland population of Western New Guinea.

The original descriptions of the Mulia focus dealt exclusively with the problem in the valley of the Upper Ruffaer River, around the Mulia Mission Station in the Western Dani linguistic group (Gajdusek 1959, 1960a, 1960b, 1961a, 1961b, 1962; Kidson and Gajdusek 1962; van Rhijn 1960). Subsequently, extensive thyroid function studies were carried out in the population (Adams, et al. 1968; Choufoer, et al. 1963; Choufoer, van Rhijn, and Querido 1965), and irregular unsustained efforts at providing iodine to the population around the mission stations were started.

In recent years it has been possible to delineate further the extent of this focus. We now know that goiter, cretinism, and deaf-mutism have attained astonishingly high incidence in the Mulia region and that further westward in the Western Dani and Moni and Uhunduni populations yet higher incidences prevail (Gajdusek 1969; Garruto, Gajdusek, and ten Brink 1974; Gunawan 1971; Kawengian 1968; ten Brink 1961, 1962a; van Rhijn 1969). The area of severe endemic goitrous cretinism is now known to extend from just east of the Ekari (Kapauku) populations

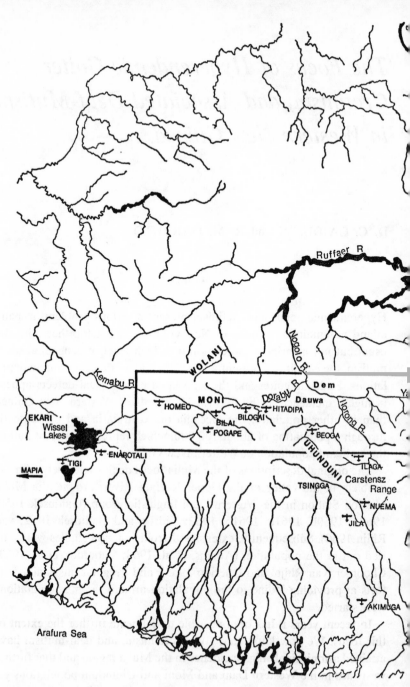

Map 1. Map of the Central Highlands of Western New Guinea showing the belt of high incidence goitrous cretinism and other sites of lower goiter incidence. Small plane airstrips in and around the goiter belt are indicated. Sites of lower goiter incidence (< 40 percent) are in the Swart River valley and at Bokondini, Mapia, Tsingga, Jila, Nuema and Kiwirok. Interestingly, Ilaga and Ilu, on the

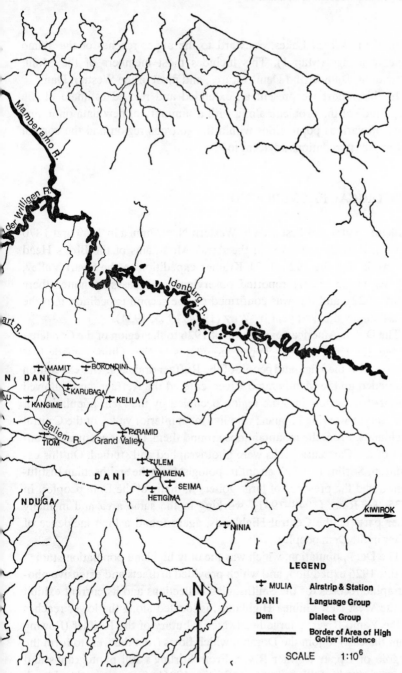

LEGEND

✛ MULIA   **Airstrip & Station**

DANI   **Language Group**

Dem   **Dialect Group**

————   **Border of Area of High Goiter Incidence**

SCALE   1:10⁶

upper reaches of valleys where goiter occurs in high incidence in populations living downstream, are goiter free. The additional region of high goiter incidence in the northeast quadrant of the Bird's Head Peninsula is not shown; it lies to the west of the area shown on this map around the Wissel Lakes, eastward to the upper reaches of the Yamo River drainage (Map 1). This includes most members of the Moni, Uhunduni, Dauwa, and Dem cultures, and most of the Western Dani.

In this report we present an extended and revised estimate of the magnitude of the problem, along with a summary of new data on iodine levels in various populations within the goitrous region and the control goiter-free populations adjacent to it.

HISTORICAL BACKGROUND

Endemic goiter was first seen in Western New Guinea in 1869 and 1870 by Von Rosenberg (1875) in the Arfak Mountains of the Bird's Head Peninsula. On the 1920–1921 Kramer expedition to the Swart Valley, Bijlmer (1923, 1927) reported observing some cases of goiter there (Wirz 1922), and this was confirmed on the second expedition into the Swart Valley the next year by Wirz (1924, 1925, 1934).

The Dutch-American expedition of 1926 to the region of the Carstensz Range, the highest snow-capped mountains in New Guinea, made first contact with the Highland people of the Ruffaer drainage. This expedition proceeded up the Memberamo River, entered the Ruffaer, and followed it to its headwaters into the region occupied by the Dem population of phallocrypt-wearing Papuans who live in an interior valley of the Central Highlands. From the mountaintops around them, the snow-covered summits of the Carstensz peaks were photographed and studied. On this expedition, Stirling (1926a), an anthropologist from the Smithsonian Institution, noted the presence of large goiters in many of the Dem peoples. In 1935, Le Roux (1948–1951), working in the same area and in many other parts of the Central Highlands, again found a high incidence of goiter in the Dem peoples.

The Dem population, which was the only highland population studied on this 1926 expedition, and which provided artifacts and extensive photographic records for the Smithsonian collections and its current exhibit on the West New Guinea Highlands, is located along the lower reaches of the Yamo River, a large headwater tributary of the Ruffaer (flowing from the east) to join the Dorabu, which flows from the west to form the Nogolo or Upper Ruffaer River. From Stirling's still photographs and cinema records of this expedition (Stirling 1926b; Sorenson and Gajdusek 1966), it is evident that the first outsiders to enter the region encountered the same type of goiter and cretinism that was rediscovered when the missionaries entered the Mulia region on the Yamo drainage from the

Swart Valley in 1958, and when the valleys of the Dorabu and Beabu were restudied by Le Roux in 1935. It is thus clear that the appearance of this syndrome in these regions cannot be attributed to known earlier contacts with European or Asian peoples. (Of considerable interest to the study of verbal tradition and verbal history in New Guinea is the finding that, by the time of their rediscovery in 1970, the people had failed to transmit any information about Europeans and these earlier contacts with civilization to their own succeeding generations. The Dem had lost all knowledge of the 1926 expedition, whose members had lived with them and photographed them extensively. In fact, even Le Roux's later contact with them in 1935, only thirty-five years before, was no longer recalled.

In 1935 Bijlmer (1939) also noted goiter some distance west of the Wissel Lakes at Mapia and south of the lakes in the Tapiro Mountains. In 1938, Roushdy found a high incidence of goiter (24 percent) in the Kemabu Valley and his observations were confirmed by Boelen (1953), Bliek (1955), Couvée (1958, 1960), and Jiskoot (1962). Romeijn (1958) recorded an even higher incidence of goiter in the Dugi and Beoga valleys than in the Kemabu Valley. In 1959, the Unevangelized Field Missionaries, who had entered the Mulia region in 1958, reported to one of us the very high incidence of goiter in that region, and in 1959 we started our studies there (Curtain, et al. 1974; Gajdusek 1962; Gajdusek, Garruto, and Dedecker 1974; Garruto, Gajdusek, and ten Brink 1974).

GEOGRAPHIC DISTRIBUTION OF GOITER IN WEST NEW GUINEA

The goiter belt in West New Guinea starts in the Bird's Head (Vogelkopf), with many scattered foci in the northeast quadrant of this enormous peninsula (Tamrau, Rawarra, Meijos) and with particular concentration in the valleys of the Arfak Range north (Prafi, Wariori) and south (Ransiki, Momi) of the Anggi Lakes. West of the Wissel Lakes there is a moderate focus of goiter in the Mapia Valley. The main goiter belt, however, starts just east of these lakes and extends continuously through the Central Highlands to the upper reaches of the Yamo River drainage beyond the valley of the Guderi River tributary of the Yamo.

Beyond the Guderi River tributary to the Yamo, goiter incidence drops markedly within a distance of a few miles. At Ilu, in the uppermost Yamo Valley, goiter is very rare. Eastward across the divide which separates the Upper Ruffaer drainage from the Swart (Toli) River drainage, the populations of the Swart Valley have a low incidence of goiter, below 5 percent, and the same is true eastward at Bokondini. Further east, at Jalimo, no goiter is found, and sporadic cases again appear in low incidence in the Ok language family near the Papua New Guinea border at Kiwirok and in valleys to the west.

The Ilaga region, directly north and under the snow-capped Carstensz peaks, is free of goiter and forms a notable gap in the belt of high incidence. South of the Swart and Bokondini valleys, the large Dani populations of the Baliem Valley are goiter free; however, as one passes to the valleys south of the Central ranges, many additional goiter foci are found. In the sparse populations of highlanders in the south of the Central ranges, in the Tapiro population south of the Wissel Lakes, in the Tsingga population south of the Carstensz peaks, and in the lower Baliem drainage populations at Hetigima, Kiniageima, and Ninia (ten Brink 1962b), one again encounters goiter.

Van Rhijn (1969) has made a strong point of the fact that the goiter regions in the Central Highlands and in the Vogelkopf are areas of mesozoic geological stratification adjacent to highland areas of tertiary strata in which goiter-free populations are found. He points out that the mesozoic soft sedimentary rocks, which include sandstone, slate, and schists, have been deeply eroded by heavy rainfall, producing narrow V-shaped valleys wherein populations suffer from a high incidence of endemic goitrous cretinism. The populations living in wider valleys of much harder tertiary limestone are uniformly goiter-free. Van Rhijn believes that geographic factors alone determine the goiter incidence and that diet, rainfall, and elevation are not critical, nor is the genetic constitution of the people or their isolation.

Within a single cultural and linguistic group, goiter may attain a very high incidence in one region and a very low incidence in an adjacent region, without any change in diet, other cultural factors, language, or genetic origin. Thus, the Western Dani in three different neighboring locations show three very different patterns of goiter incidence. In the Yembi-Mulia-Guderi valleys goiter incidence is high (greater than 50 percent); in the Mamit and Karubaga areas of the Swart Valley it is low (less than 5 percent); and in the Ilu region goiter is absent, except when introduced in a rare immigrant. Similarly, the Uhunduni people of Ilaga, Nuema, and Beoga suffer from goiter at rare, low, and high incidences, respectively. Because the populations of the regions with low incidence of goiter apparently have no higher serum protein bound iodine levels than do the severely affected populations (see below), serum iodine determinations do not serve to indicate the severity of the goiter problem in a given region.

The young of goats, sheep, and cows, introduced into West New Guinea in the Ransiki region in the 1950's, were born with goiters. In areas of most severe iodine deficiency, most young were stillborn (Zwart 1959); iodine deficiency has been demonstrated to be the cause of goiter and stillbirths. The same happened in the 1960's in Mulia, when goats were introduced.

SERUM PROTEIN BOUND IODINE LEVELS

In Table 1 we have summarized the serum protein bound iodine (PBI) determinations which we and other investigators have done on blood specimens from New Guinea populations of high, moderate, and low goiter incidence and on those which are goiter-free. Our own data, which are included, come from 233 Central Highlands subjects who fall into all four of these categories. Mulia Western Dani (32) and the Bilogai Moni (60) peoples are communities of hyperendemic goitrous cretinism, with goiter incidence above 50 percent. The Nuema Uhunduni (21) and the Swart Valley Western Dani (35) are communities with a low incidence, below 5 percent, of goiter. The Ilaga (Uhunduni) are a community remarkable for the absence of goiter, although their enclave is surrounded by hyperendemic goitrous areas. We have also included the Baira area of Tairora-speaking highlanders of the Eastern Highlands of Papua New Guinea, where endemic goiter occurs in moderate incidence (about 10 percent). Table 1 also includes serum PBI data from two other groups of workers who have also reported on New Guinea goitrous and goiter-free communities.

It is remarkable that the PBI levels are as low in the area of rare, sporadic goiter as in the areas of hyperendemic goitrous cretinism. In the goiter-free enclave, PBIs are in the high normal range. The goitrous subjects had slightly lower PBIs than nongoitrous subjects in the same area, but the differences are not great.

Cretins with goiter had slightly lower PBIs than those without goiter and also slightly lower than goitrous noncretins. Cretins without goiter had lower PBIs than normal nongoiter subjects, but not quite as low as goitrous noncretin subjects (Butterfield and Hetzel 1971).

Table 1.   Serum protein bound iodine (PBI) levels in Melanesian populations with various incidences of goiter and cretinism

Area	Goiter status	Protein Bound Iodine (PBI) μg/100 ml (mean ± S.E.)	Number of subjects	Year of study	Author (see note)
High goiter incidence (hyperendemic) (> 50 percent)					
Mulia, West New Guinea	Goitrous	2.9 ± 0.2	14	1961	1
	Nongoitrous	3.4 ± 0.3	18	1961	1
	Total	3.2 ± 0.2	32	1961	1
Bilogai, West New Guinea	Nongoitrous	3.9 ± 0.2	60	1969	1
Mulia, West New Guinea	Goitrous	1.5 ± 0.2	30	1962	2
	Nongoitrous	1.9 ± 0.3	17	1962	2
Wain and Naba areas, Huon Peninsula, Papua New Guinea	Goitrous	2.9	85	1964	3
	Nongoitrous	4.9	119	1964	3
	Total	4.1	204	1964	3
Moderate goiter incidence (10–50 percent)					
Baira, Papua New Guinea	Goitrous	2.3 ± 0.3	26	1961–62	1
	Nongoitrous	3.8 ± 0.2	35	1961–62	1
	Total	3.1 ± 0.2	61	1961–62	1
Low goiter incidence (< 5 percent)					
Swart, West New Guinea	Nongoitrous	3.5 ± 0.4	35	1963	1
Nuema, West New Guinea	Nongoitrous	3.8 ± 0.4	21	1962	1
Goiter-free					
Ilaga, West New Guinea	Nongoitrous	7.5 ± 0.3	24	1962	1
Tiom, West New Guinea	Nongoitrous	6.0 ± 0.2	15	1962	2
Lae, Papua New Guinea	Nongoitrous	6.0 ± 0.9	19	1964	3

1   Garruto, Gajdusek, and ten Brink (1974).
2   Choufoer, et al. (1963).
3   Butterfield, et al. (1965).

ENDEMIC GOITER AND CRETINISM IN EASTERN NEW GUINEA AND ITS PROPHYLAXIS WITH INJECTIONS OF IODIZED OIL

In Eastern New Guinea the intense focus of endemic goitrous cretinism in the Huon Peninsula has attracted more attention than any other goiter area since the original work there by McCullagh in the late 1950's (McCullagh 1959, 1963a,b,c,d). It is the most severe focus of goiter on the eastern side of the island and resembles the situation in the Mulia region and in the Bird's Head Peninsula in the western part of the island in incidence of goiter and the severity of the problem of endemic goitrous cretinism and associated deaf-mutism and other central nervous system defects. By 1957 McCullagh had already started the first program of injections of iodized oil for the prevention of goitrous cretinism (Clarke, McCullagh, and Winikoff 1960; McCullagh 1959). Studies of thyroid function, iodine metabolism, and growth and the continued use and evaluation of the efficacy of the iodized oil injections have continued mostly in this region since then (Butterfield, et al. 1965, 1966; Butterfield and Hetzel 1967, 1969; Hennessy 1964).

Further search for goiter foci elsewhere in Eastern New Guinea has revealed that goiter occurs in a wide belt throughout the highlands, but nowhere in as high an incidence and over as large a population as on the Huon Peninsula. Endemic cretinism is regularly associated with goiter wherever it reaches high incidence, and the congenital central nervous system defects of this syndrome have a major effect on mortality and morbidity in the areas of severe iodine deficiency. Our studies in the Baira villages of Tairora-speaking Eastern Highlanders in the Upper Lamari River region (see Table 1) were in one such highland goiter focus. Another focus of goitrous cretinism in the valley of the Jimi River has also been intensively studied (Butterfield and Hetzel 1971; Pharoah 1971).

A single injection of iodized oil produces persistently elevated PBI levels for a period of over four and one-half years after injection. The efficacy of these injections in preventing the congenital defects of endemic cretinism and in preventing the appearance of congenital and postnatal goiter has been demonstrated (Hennessy 1964).

THE SPECTRUM OF CONGENITAL DEFECT USUALLY REFERRED TO AS ENDEMIC CRETINISM

The Mulia population, with over 50 percent of the female adults in most villages suffering from goiters, many of which are of very large size, also has a high incidence of deaf-mutism and obvious cretinism. However, we noted in our original study at Mulia (Gajdusek 1962) that the various neurological and skeletal defects usually associated with classical cretinous dwarfism were often dissociated and that severe dwarfism occurred only in a few of the cretinoid subjects and occasionally in those who were neither deaf-mutes nor severely mentally defective. In contrast, some deaf-mutes with motor and mental defects were not of dwarf stature. Ataxia and hyperlordotic stance with bent hips and knees, hypertonic musculature, and cretinoid vacant facies with large tongue, narrowed palpebral fissure, and often with strabismus were common, sometimes associated with, and at times not associated with severe mental defects, deaf-mutism, or dwarfism. Many of the severe deaf-mutes appeared to be as intelligent as other normal Mulia Dani.

We have now confirmed these observations of a wide and continuous spectrum of cretinoid defects in varying combinations in the Bilai and Bilogai areas of the Kemabu Valley. This endemic cretinism in the New Guinea Highlands is not associated with hypothyroidism, whether or not a goiter is present in the cretinoid individual. Much confusion has resulted from failure to distinguish this form of fetal damage *in utero* (and, perhaps, also in neonatal life), which probably is caused by severe iodine deficiency in the mother during her pregnancy, from the sporadic hypothyroid cretinism which is usually associated with severe dwarfism.

We have the impression that a very high proportion of the population of Mulia may have suffered from some degree of neuromuscular retardation in infancy. Among older children and adults the so-called endemic cretinism may be very mild in many, shading imperceptibly into mild skeletal, facial, and motor defects, with or without minimal mental subnormality. Choufoer, van Rhijn, and Querido (1965) consider this a hazardous claim; yet, our reassessment of the problem leads us to reaffirm that few people in the areas of highest goiter incidence and severe cretinism are as bright and alert and well-coordinated as the majority of the people in surrounding goiter-free populations.

We know that the evaluation of intelligence and subtle motor skills across cultural boundaries is a very imprecise endeavor. It is extremely difficult to establish criteria by which to assess, or even to define, intelligence in non-Western, preliterate cultures. No nonverbal tests prove

Plate 1. Five women and three men with large goiters at Mulia. The photograph was taken a few minutes after blood specimens were collected for antithyroid antibody levels, PBIs, and other biochemical determinations. The women are holding cotton wads in their left antecubital fossae. These studies were undertaken before European trade goods or trade salt had been widely distributed in the area. One of the goitrous men is squatting on the left, the other two are standing behind the women, between the first and second and between the fourth and fifth women from the left. (June 1959)

Plate 2. Three male Mulia residents with goiters. The youth on the left is in his twenties; the boy in the center in his mid-teens; and the man on the right over thirty years of age. In the Mulia Valley itself, with a population of about 1,000, some 60 percent of the women have visible or palpable goiters. The incidence in adult males is only about 25 percent. (June 1959)

a   b

c

Plate 3 (a, b, c).   A rather intelligent male adult cretin, who shows the dwarfism which is not always present in Mulia region cretins, even in some with severe mental retardation, deaf-mutism, ataxia, hyperlordosis with bent hips and knees. In the picture c he stands beside a man with a large goiter. He understood gestures very well and cooperated with our examiner. Dr. J. ten Brink (in picture a). (Guderi Valley, November 1961)

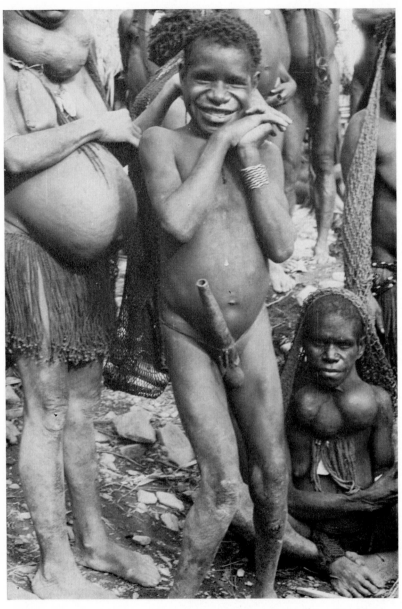

Plate 4. A feebleminded cretinoid adolescent boy of Mulia in hyperlordotic stance with bent hips and knees, between two women with huge goiters. The boy walked with marked ataxia, but without support, and he took an active part in the social life and work of the community although he was a deaf-mute and tended to giggle a great deal. The woman on the left is in her third trimester of pregnancy. (June 1959)

Plate 5. A mother carrying her severely defective cretinoid deaf-mute child, who, although already over five years of age, cannot yet walk or stand unassisted. The child shows the blank facies, squinting, and hyperflexibility common among juvenile cretins of the Mulia region. (Mulia 1961)

Plate 6. A mother with large nodular goiter, with her slightly retarded child of over two years of age. The child cannot yet sit unsupported, has flabby musculature, with head usually falling back on an extended neck. (Upper Yamo Valley, June 1961)

Plate 7. Another mother, with moderate size goiter, whose very retarded infant shows limpness, drooling, poor sucking, a lack of attentiveness, and squinting, with poor control of the head, which usually falls back on a hyperextended neck when he is carried. His older sister, on the lower right, also has a large goiter. (Mulia, June 1959)

Plate 8. Two defective Mulia children: the older boy is not able to talk and requires support even to stand. His knees show calluses from crawling; he has a gaping mouth and often drools, and has a somewhat spastic musculature. The infant, already over a year old, sits with rounded back and cannot yet pull himself erect or walk. His musculature is floppy and there is no sign that he understands speech or is ready to talk. (June 1959)

adequate for all cultures. However, culturally similar Western Dani natives from adjacent goiter-free areas, such as at Ilu, themselves refer to the Mulia goiter region people as subnormal, unintelligent, and generally defective people. They find all the inhabitants not quite up to par, not only the obvious cretins and deaf-mutes. This has also been the impression of the missionaries who have worked with the Western Dani in goiter-free areas as well as in Mulia.

The learning speed for new tasks, or the speed with which the Mulia people transmit ideas to each other, i.e. "get their point across," appears to be distributed about a lower mean than elsewhere in the highlands. The number of obvious deaf-mutes and feebleminded subjects and those whose intelligence can be quickly assessed as inferior by numerous nonverbal procedures, as well as by the comment of their fellow villagers and kinsmen, is extraordinarily high. It becomes difficult here to speak categorically of cretinism, deaf-mutism, or feeblemindedness, for one has a spectrum of all degrees of these syndromes from barely detectable abnormality to gross, easily recognizable defects.

During prolonged contact with the Mulia people, one becomes accustomed to encountering a wide range of personality and intellectual endowment, as elsewhere in New Guinea. One may easily assume that the general slow speed of learning, slow and repetitive manner of speech, delayed grasp of instructions, and general appearance of intellectual shallowness are rather the result of the linguistic barrier and the cultural distance of this exotic ethnic setting from our own culture. However, the sudden trip by plane from Mulia to other Western Dani communities, neighboring people of the same linguistic and cultural stock whose pattern of life is quite the same as at Mulia, affords a most surprising contrast. The inability of the Mulia native to comprehend complex instructions, coupled with his slow learning speed, which one has learned to accept in Mulia, are suddenly seen as woeful deficiencies in contrast with the other Western Dani-speaking people outside the region of high endemic cretinism. This subjective and unquantified impression is sufficiently marked to be clearly apparent to Western and Melanesian observers. Furthermore, deaf-mutism and cases of obvious severe feeblemindedness are not as frequent in these goiter-free communities as they are throughout the Mulia, Yembi, and Guderi valleys.

The incidence of children of all ages with severe mental or neuromotor defects or deaf-mutism is over 12 percent, and reaches 20 percent in some villages. Severe congenitally defective infants, recognized as such by their parents, who attribute the defect to their knees and ears, are markedly hypotonic, with drooling, poor sucking, and lack of attentiveness. These characteristics may lead to malnutrition and early death (Gajdusek, Garruto, and Dedecker 1974). Furthermore, these infants often support their heads poorly, letting them fall back with the neck in hyperextension, and they show generalized limpness, sitting hunched over, with rounded back even when supported. The palpebral fissures often appear to be narrowed and the forehead furrowed, as though the child were squinting from photophobia, and there is in some subjects an alternating strabismus, often with difficulty in upward gaze.

Less severe congenital defects, expressed only as retarded neuro-muscular development and retarded mental development, are seen in many infants. There are many children over two years of age who cannot talk, cannot walk well, and who do not sit well unsupported at one year of age. The hearing defect may be of differing severity (Hornabrook 1971) and may lead to markedly or slightly retarded speech development rather than full mutism. There is even a suggestion that hearing may improve with age (Paine 1971). When children with such early defects reach later childhood, it may be difficult to demonstrate residual motor, sensory, speech, or mental defects.

The incidence of significant developmental retardation among infants in different villages varies greatly, even within the areas of highest goiter incidence. It may exceed one-third of the children between the ages of one and five years. This is a very different situation from that encountered in the neighboring goiter-free populations of the Western Dani and Uhunduni peoples, where such a high incidence of floppy babies with retarded motor and speech development is not seen.

SOCIAL FACTORS WHICH MAY INFLUENCE THE OCCURRENCE OF ENDEMIC GOITER AND CRETINISM IN AREAS OF LOW OR MARGINAL IODINE AVAILABILITY

Iodine deficiency is probably the cause of all endemic goiter and cretinism in New Guinea which we have reviewed here, and we have good reason to believe that these diseases will disappear when adequate iodine is supplied either as injections of iodized oil or in the diet. We have found no evidence for genetically determined metabolic block as the cause of these goiters in inland population enclaves. Although it has been well demonstrated that goitrogenic substances can produce high levels of goiter in a population which resides in an area of normal iodine intake in the diet and drinking water (Clements 1960; Clements and Wishart 1956), we have found no such goitrogens in the areas of our studies.

However, our urinary iodine excretion data indicate that water and dietary iodine intake may be much the same in areas of low and high goiter incidence. It thus seems appropriate to enquire what additional factors may determine the appearance of goiter in populations on low or marginally adequate iodine intake.

Goiter has newly appeared in populations that remained sedentary and has slowly disappeared in others, without noticeable alteration in the diet. Observers have made numerous hypotheses to explain these variations. Greenwald (1950, 1960a, 1960b, 1963) has suggested over the years that an infection which interferes with thyroid function may be a critical factor in the appearance, disappearance, and reappearance of goiter in the same area. We have suggested (Gajdusek 1962) in analogy to goitrogenic action of cabbage in man and experimental animals, that the quantity of iodine-binding sweet potato leaves in the diet might be critical in goitrogenesis in areas of marginal iodine deficiency, through bulk loss of iodine in the stool. In order to further investigate this possibility, quantitative observations to determine the extent of iodine-binding by sweet potato leaves are needed and a quantitative demonstration of greater use of the leaf in the diet of high goiter than in the low goiter or goiter-free areas would be necessary. However, it may well be, as van Rhijn (1969) claims, that the degree of iodine deficiency in different geological regions is important above all else in determining the incidence of endemic goiter and cretinism in New Guinea.

In the Jimi River region, there are a moderate number of youthful cretins, yet very few adult cretins. The people claim that the syndrome is new among them, often attributing its appearance to the arrival of the white man. The higher mortality of cretins from malnutrition and accident does not appear to account for this situation (Pharoah 1971). Infanticide is practiced in many areas where endemic cretinism occurs, as elsewhere in New Guinea, but always at the time of birth. Because even a severe cretin could not then be recognized, it is unlikely that this practice influenced the incidence of cretinism greatly. In the Jimi River area introduction of uniodinized salt for barter rapidly replaced use of traditional mineral springs as a source of salt and some iodine in the already iodine deficient "pre-goitrous" population. This precipitated the new appearance of goiter and cretinism.

In the Mulia, Yembi, and Guderi regions, much of the population wandered into the region from areas of the southeast, which are goiter-free. Those who were born there and have immigrated into the goiter region do not demonstrate cretinoid syndromes. Those who have immigrated only in recent years are not goitrous; some of those who immigrated to Mulia many years ago have developed goiter. Mulia people know that goiter was not present in their population when they dwelt in the region from which they came. However, much of the immigration occurred several generations ago and goiter and cretinism were major problems with them in the Yamo Valley long before their first contact with Europeans.

SUMMARY

The focus of hyperendemic goiter, cretinism and associated deaf-mutism extends through a population of over 100,000 people in the Central Highlands of Western New Guinea. Geographically, the area of severe endemic goiter and cretinism extends from just east of the Wissel Lakes and the Ekari (Kapauku) populations, eastward to the upper reaches of the Yamo River drainage, and includes most of the Moni, Uhunduni, Dauwa and Dem cultures and most of the Western Dani.

Historically, the first reports of this focus were recorded in the late nineteenth century and later confirmed by the early expeditions of the 1920's and 1930's. We started our original description of this goiter focus in 1959, just one year after the Unevangelized Field Missionaries had entered the Mulia region and established the Mulia mission station. Subsequent to this time, extensive studies were carried out and it has been possible to further delineate the extent of this focus.

Serum protein bound iodine (PBI) levels have been determined by ourselves and other investigators on blood specimens from New Guinea populations of high (>50 percent), moderate (10–50 percent) and low (<5 percent) goiter incidence and on those which are goiter-free. A summary of these results indicates that PBI levels are as low in the area of rare or sporadic goiter as in the areas of hyperendemic goiter and cretinism. In addition, goitrous subjects had only slightly lower mean PBI levels than non-goitrous subjects of the same area. These results were determined at a time when only irregular unsustained efforts at providing iodine to the population around the mission station were started. Furthermore, our early observations of a wide and continuous spectrum of various neurological and skeletal defects associated with endemic cretinism in the Mulia population has been confirmed by later observations in the Bilai and Bilogai area of the Kemabu valley. This endemic cretinism in the New Guinea highlands is not associated with hypothyroidism, but is a result of fetal damage *in utero* due to iodine deficiency in the mother during pregnancy; this is distinguished from the sporadic hypothyroid cretinism that is usually associated with severe dwarfism.

Explanation for the severe focus of hyperendemic goiter and cretinism has been offered and reviewed, but it appears that iodine deficiency is probably the cause of all endemic goiter and cretinism in New Guinea which we have reviewed, and we believe that these conditions will disappear when adequate iodine is supplied either as injections of iodized oil or in the diet.

REFERENCES

ADAMS, D. D., T. H. KENNEDY, J. C. CHOUFOER, A. QUERIDO
  1968   Endemic goiter in Western New Guinea, III: Thyroid stimulation activity of serum from severely iodine-deficient people. *Journal of Clinical Endocrinology and Metabolism* 28:685–692.
BIJLMER, H. J. T.
  1923   Anthropological results of the Dutch scientific central New Guinea expedition 1920. *Nova Guinea* 7:355–448.
  1927   Les Papous pygmées de la Nouvelle Guinée. *Revue Anthropologique* 37:156–158.
  1939   Tapiro-pygmies and Paniai mountain Papuans. Results of the anthropological Mimika expedition in New Guinea. *Nova Guinea* 3:113–184.
BLIEK, D. C.
  1955   "Verslag van een tournee naar Wandai in de Kema-vallei." Unpublished manuscript.
BOELEN, K. W. J.
  1953   "Verslag over een tournee naar Uwagimoma in de Kemavallei." Unpublished manuscript.
BUTTERFIELD, I. H., M. L. BLACK, M. J. HOFFMAN, E. K. MASON, B. S. HETZEL
  1965   Correction of iodine deficiency in New Guinea natives by iodized oil injection. *Lancet* 2:767–769.
BUTTERFIELD, I. H., M. L. BLACK, M. J. HOFFMAN, E. K. MASON, M. L. WELLBY, B. F. GOOD, B. S. HETZEL
  1966   Studies of the control of thyroid function in endemic goiter in Eastern New Guinea. *Journal of Clinical Endocrinology and Metabolism* 26:1201–1207.
BUTTERFIELD, I. H., B. S. HETZEL
  1967   Endemic goitre in Eastern New Guinea with special reference to the use of iodized oil in prophylaxis and treatment. *Bulletin World Health Organization* 36:243–262.
  1969   Endemic cretinism in Eastern New Guinea. *Australasian Annals of Medicine* 18:217.
  1971   "Endemic cretinism in Eastern New Guinea: its relation to goitre and iodine deficiency," in *Endemic cretinism*. Edited by B. S. Hetzel and P. O. D. Pharoah, 55–69. Papua New Guinea: Institute of Human Biology.

CHOUFOER, J. C., M. VAN RHIJN, A. A. H. KASSENAAR, A. QUERIDO
   1963   Endemic goiter in Western New Guinea: iodine metabolism in
          goitrous and non-goitrous subjects. *Journal of Clinical Endocrino-
          logy and Metabolism* 23:1203–1217.

CHOUFOER, J. C., M. VAN RHIJN, A. QUERIDO
   1965   Endemic goiter in Western New Guinea, II: Clinical picture, in-
          cidence and pathogenesis of endemic cretinism. *Journal of Clinical
          Endocrinology and Metabolism* 25:385–402.

CLARKE, K. H., S. F. MC CULLAGH, D. WINIKOFF
   1960   The use of an intramuscular depot of iodized oil as a long-lasting
          source of iodine. *The Medical Journal of Australia* 1:89–92.

CLEMENTS, F. W.
   1960   Naturally occurring goitrogens. *British Medical Journal* 16:133.

CLEMENTS, F. W., J. W. WISHART
   1956   A thyroid-blocking agent in the etiology of endemic goiter. *Meta-
          bolism* 6:623–629.

COUVÉE, L. M. J.
   1958   "Verslag over het tournee naar Homejo (Kemavallei)." Unpublish-
          ed manuscript.
   1960   "Verslag over het tournee naar het Degewogebied (Kemavallei)."
          Unpublished manuscript.

CURTAIN, C. C., D. C. GAJDUSEK, D. O'BRIEN, R. M. GARRUTO
   1974   Congenital defects of the central nervous system associated with
          hyperendemic goiter in a neolithic highland society of Western
          New Guinea, IV: Serum proteins and haptoglobins, transferrins
          and hemoglobin types in goitrous and adjacent non-goitrous West-
          ern Dani. *Human Biology* 46:331–338.

GAJDUSEK, D. C.
   1959   *New Guinea Journal,* June 10, 1959 to August 15, 1959. National
          Institute of Neurological Diseases and Stroke, Bethesda, Mary-
          land.
   1960a *West New Guinea Journal,* May 6, 1960 to July 10, 1960. Na-
          tional Institute of Neurological Diseases and Stroke, Bethesda,
          Maryland
   1960b *Mulia: A Ndani Speaking Highland Population Suffering from
          Hyperendemic Goitrous Cretinism, Netherlands New Guinea.* May
          8–13, 1960. Research Cinema Film 60–7, Archive of Child
          Growth and Development and Disease Patterns in Primitive Cul-
          tures. National Institute of Neurological Diseases and Stroke,
          Bethesda, Maryland.
   1961a *Western Dani: Central Nervous System Disease in a Region of
          Hyperendemic Goitrous Cretinism, Central Highlands, West New
          Guinea.* October 23–November 6, 1961. (Part 1, Oct. 23–26; Part
          II, Oct. 26–Nov. 6). Research Cinema Films 61–4A and 61–4B,
          Archive of Child Growth and Development and Disease Patterns
          in Primitive Cultures, National Institute of Neurological Diseases
          and Stroke, Bethesda, Maryland.

1961b *New Guinea Journal*, October 21, 1961 to August 4, 1962. Part I. National Institute of Neurological Diseases and Stroke, Bethesda, Maryland.

1962   Congenital defects of the central nervous system associated with hyperendemic goiter in a neolithic highland society of Netherlands New Guinea, I: Epidemiology. *Pediatrics* 29:345–363.

1969   *Journal of expeditions to the Soviet Union, Africa, the islands of Madagascar, la Réunion and Mauritius, Indonesia and to East and West New Guinea, Australia and Guam to study kuru and other neurological diseases, epidemic influenza, endemic goitrous cretinism and child growth and development, with explorations on the Great Papuan Plateau and on the Lakes Plain and Inland Southern Lowlands of West New Guinea*, June 1, 1969 to March 3, 1970. National Institute of Neurological Diseases and Stroke, Bethesda, Maryland.

GAJDUSEK, D. C., R. M. GARRUTO, R. DEDECKER
1974   Congenital defects of the central nervous system associated with hyperendemic goiter in a neolithic highland society of Western New Guinea, V: A note on birth weights and infantile growth rates in the Mulia population. *Human Biology* 46:339–344.

GARRUTO, R. M., D. C. GAJDUSEK, J. TEN BRINK
1974   Congenital defects of the central nervous system associated with hyperendemic goiter in a neolithic highland society of Western New Guinea, III: Serum and urinary iodine levels in goitrous and adjacent non-goitrous populations. *Human Biology* 46:311–329.

GREENWALD, I.
1950   Endemic goiter: deficiency, intoxication or infection? *Transactions American Goiter Association*, 369–377.

1960a The significance of the history of goiter for the etiology and prevention of the disease. *American Journal of Clinical Nutrition* 8:801–807.

1960b "Heredity, deficiency, intoxication or infection?" in *Clinical endocrinology*, volume one. Edited by E. B. Astwood, 123–132. New York: Grune and Stratton.

1963   Possible reconciliation of the "iodine-lack" and "infection" hypothesis. *American Journal of Clinical Nutrition* 13:393–394.

GUNAWAN, S.
1971   "Struma dan cretinisme endemik di Irian Jaya." Paper presented at the First Indonesian Congress of Internal Medicine, Jakarta, September 1971.

HENNESSY, W. B.
1964   Goitre prophylaxis in New Guinea with intramuscular injections of iodized oil. *The Medical Journal of Australia* 1:505–512.

HORNABROOK, R. A.
1971   "Neurological aspects of endemic cretinism in Eastern New Guinea," in *Endemic cretinism*. Edited by B. S. Hetzel and P. O. D. Pharoah, 105–107. Papua New Guinea: Institute of Human Biology.

JISKOOT, K.
  1962   "Verslag van een tournee naar Homejo en Zanepa (Kemavallei)."
         Unpublished manuscript.

KAWENGIAN, B.
  1968   Report of a survey of endemic goiter and cretinism in the Central
         Highlands of West Irian, Indonesia. Public Health Department,
         Djayapura, West Irian.

KIDSON, C., D. C. GAJDUSEK
  1962   Congenital defects of the central nervous system associated with
         hyperendemic goiter in a neolithic highland society of Nether-
         lands New Guinea, II: Glucose-6-phosphate dehydrogenase in the
         Mulia population. Pediatrics 29:364–368.

LE ROUX, C. C. F. M.
  1948– De Bergpapoea's van Nieuw-Guinea en hun Woongebied, three
  1951   volumes. Leiden: E. J. Brill.

MC CULLAGH, S. F.
  1959   Goiter control project. Papua and New Guinea Medical Journal
         3:43–47.
  1963a The Huon Peninsula endemic, I: The effectiveness of an intra-
         muscular depot of iodized oil in the control of endemic goiter. The
         Medical Journal of Australia 1:769–777.
  1963b The Huon Peninsula endemic, II: The effect in the female of
         endemic goitre on reproductive function. The Medical Journal of
         Australia 1:806–808.
  1963c The Huon Peninsula endemic, III: The effect in the female of
         endemic goitre on reproductive function. The Medical Journal of
         Australia 1:844–849.
  1963d The Huon Peninsula endemic, IV: Endemic goitre and congenital
         defect. The Medical Journal of Australia 1:884–890.

PAINE, BRENDA G.
  1971   "Pediatric manifestations of endemic cretinism in Eastern New
         Guinea," in Endemic cretinism. Edited by B. S. Hetzel and P. O.
         D. Pharoah, 89–103. Papua New Guinea: Institute of Human
         Biology.

PHAROAH, P. O. D.
  1971   "Epidemiological studies of endemic cretinism in the Jimi River
         Valley in New Guinea," in Endemic cretinism. Edited by B. S.
         Hetzel and P.O.D. Pharoah, 109–116. Papua New Guinea: In-
         stitute of Human Biology.

ROMEIJN, T.
  1958   "Verslag van een tournee door het westelijk Centraal Bergland van
         Enarotali naar Ilaga." Unpublished manuscript.

ROUSHDY, A.
  1940   De penetratie van de Djonggoenoe's in het Wisselmeren gebied.
         Tijdschrift Koninklijk Nederlandsch Aardrijkskundig Genootschap
         57:56. Amsterdam.

SORENSON, E. R., D. C. GAJDUSEK

1966   The study of child behavior and development in primitive cultures. A research archive for enthnopediatric film investigations of styles in the patterning of the nervous system. *Pediatrics* 37: 149–243.

STIRLING, M. W.

1926a   "Journal of an expedition to Dutch New Guinea in the year 1926." Mimeographed manuscript. Washington, D.C.: Smithsonian Institution.

1926b   *The Dem: Indigenes along the Upper Roufaer (Yamo) River in the Nassau Mountains, Netherlands New Guinea, September- December 15, 1926. Part I, September; Part II, September to December 15.* Research Cinema Films 26-STIR-4A and 26-STIR-4B. Archive of Child Growth and Development and Disease Patterns in Primitive Cultures. National Institute of Neurological Diseases and Stroke, Bethesda, Maryland.

TEN BRINK, J.

1961   "Report of a goiter survey in the Central Highlands." Unpublished manuscript.

1962a   "Rapport over de gevolgen van een influenza epidemie in de Ilaga vallei." Unpublished manuscript.

1962b   "Verslag over een tournee naar Ninia." Unpublished manuscript.

VAN RHIJN, M.

1960   Verspreiding van het endemisch struma in Nederlands Nieuw-Guinea. *Mededelingen van de Dienst van Gezondheidszorg in Nederlands Nieuw-Guinea* 7:55ff.

1969   *Een endemiek van struma en cretinism in het centrale bergland van West Nieuw-Guinea.* Zaltbommel, The Netherlands: Avanti.

VON ROSENBERG, D. B. H.

1875   *Reistochten naar de Geelvinkbaai op Nieuw-Guinea in de jaren 1869 en 1870.* Den Haag.

WIRZ, P.

1922   "Anthropological and ethnological results of the Central New Guinea expedition 1921–1922." Unpublished manuscript, Basel.

1924   Scientific results of 1921 expedition to Swart Valley. *Nova Guinea* 8.

1925   "In the heart of New Guinea. A diary of an expedition into the interior of New Guinea." M.I.S., Southwest Pacific Unit.

1934   Ethnologische Ergebnisse der Zentrale Neu Guinea Expedition 1921–1922. *Nova Guinea* 16:1–148.

ZWART, D.

1959   Struma bij geiten in Nederlands Nieuw-Guinea. *Tijdschrift Diergeneeskunde* 84:550.

Anthropometry Among Disadvantaged Peoples: Studies in Southern Africa

P. V. TOBIAS

The last decade has witnessed a major change in emphasis in medical education: the concept of community health has arrived, to complement the established emphasis on the health of the individual patient. To human biologists, long used to studying populations, this is no surprising development — indeed it is overdue. What is important for the human biologist is that the rise of community medicine has brought a new emphasis on sick and healthy communities, on high-risk and low-risk communities, on communities which have and which have not. Each of these variant forms of community is likely to be found to possess its own peculiar spectrum of disease, its own potentialities and weaknesses. In this setting, it becomes critically important to be able to identify the community living below par and to define the nature and extent of its environmental inadequacy. Malnutrition is without doubt the commonest form of inadequacy of the "have-not" communities today, though there are many other manifestations of the disadvantaged condition of life.

I shall examine here the role that anthropometry can play in laying bare the state of environmental adequacy or insufficiency in any community. I shall pose the following questions and discuss each in the light of studies carried out in sub-Saharan Africa:

1. To what extent can the study of adult stature alone provide some kind of indicator of the degree of environmental adequacy?

2. To what extent is the secular trend toward increasing adult stature

I thank the Medical Research Council of South Africa, the S. L. Sive Memorial Travelling Fellowship Committee, the University of the Witwatersrand, Miss C. J. Orkin, Mr. P. Faugust and Miss J. Walker for their counsel and assistance in the preparation of this material.

a reflection of improving environmental circumstances?
3.   Is the secular trend evident in African populations?
4.   Can variations in the degree of sexual dimorphism of stature in various human populations be used as a gauge of environmental adequacy?

THE STATURE OF ADULTS IN SOUTHERN AFRICA

The raw data comprise a series of samples drawn from the negriform populations of ten territories. These territories are Angola, Botswana, Lesotho, Malawi, Moçambique, Rhodesia, South Africa, South-West Africa, Swaziland, and Zambia. Their total population is just over fifty million or about 22 percent of the estimated 240 million people of sub-Saharan Africa. Of the fifty million, about 85 percent are classified linguistically as belonging to one or other of the family of Bantu language groups. The remaining eight million people in southern Africa comprise whites, Cape Coloreds, Asians and non-Negro African groups such as San (Bushman), Khoikhoi (Hottentots), Griqua, and Twa.

To represent the statures of the negriform populations of these territories, there are available data for some 90 adult male series drawn from S. African Negro groups and 22 from Khoisan populations and pooled sets. Only samples of 20 individuals and over have been used in the compilation of these series.

Tables 1 and 2 show the distribution of the means from each territory, in the recognized categories of SHORT (1500 to 1600 millimeters),

Table 1.   Territorial distribution of samples of S. African Negro males in stature classes

	Short 1500–1600 millimeters	Medium 1600–1700 millimeters	Tall 1700–1800 millimeters
Malawi	–	28	–
Moçambique	1	9	2
Zambia	–	6	1
Angola	–	7	5
South-West Africa	–	1	1
Botswana	–	1	2
Rhodesia	–	1	–
South Africa	–	20	1
Swaziland	–	1	–
Lesotho	–	2	–
Mixed	–	1	–
Total	1	77	12

Table 2. The distribution of samples of San and Khoikhoi in stature classes*

	Short 1500–1600 millimeters	Medium 1600–1700 millimeters	Tall 1700–1800 millimeters
San	19	1	–
Khoikhoi	1	1	–
Total Khoisan	20	2	–

* Adult male samples of 20 or more individuals each

MEDIUM (1600 to 1700 millimeters) and TALL (1700 to 1800 millimeters).

Among the S. African Negro groups, the spread of population sample MEANS is from 1590 to 1719 millimeters, i.e. from the upper part of the SHORT category through the MEDIUM to the lower part of the TALL. None of the populations has a mean falling in the PYGMY category (<1500 millimeters) or in the VERY TALL category (>1800 millimeters). Of the 90 sample means, 77 fall in the medium class, only 1 in the short and 12 in the tall category (Table 1). Of the 77 samples with means in the range from 1600 to 1700, no fewer than 65 have means between 1650 and 1700. The median of the 90 sample means lies in the lowest part of the 1671 to 1680 category, while the mean stature for the mixed population of Morrison, et al. (1968: 275–279) is about 17 millimeters higher, namely 1687.5. Clearly, the southern African Negro peoples are of medium height, with moderately taller populations, especially in the northwestern and, to a lesser extent, in the northern territories. Thus, nine of the twelve populations with means in the tallness range are in Angola, Zambia, South-West Africa, and Botswana. A second apparent focus of moderate tallness is encountered especially among the Nguni-speaking peoples of the eastern Cape, Natal, Swaziland, and Moçambique.

The population means of the San and Khoikhoi groups range from 1539 to 1626 millimeters, i.e. from the lower half of the SHORT category to the lower part of the MEDIUM (Table 2). Actually, all of the San means fall in the SHORT category, save for De Castro e Almeida's Vasekele of Angola, whose mean falls just in the lowermost part of the MEDIUM category. The median lies in the upper part of the 1570–1580 decade, while no fewer than 15 out of 20 series have means lying between 1570 and 1595 millimeters. Of two Nama Khoikhoi series one has a mean of 1596 and the other of 1626 millimeters. No Khoisan groups have means in the PYGMY or in the TALL categories.

Clearly, the height distribution of San peoples is shunted to the left compared with that of S. African Negroes. At first blush, one may be tempted to attribute this difference to the fact that most of the San groups are predominantly hunter-gatherers and therefore living with very low energy and nutrient intakes, whereas the southern African Negro groups are at worst simple hoe-agriculturalists and at best urban dwellers. However, there is much evidence for genetic differentiation between the San and the southern African Negroes (Tobias 1966, 1972a; Jenkins 1972) and the probability must be countenanced that their genetic differentiation includes genetic determinants of stature.

Hence, on their own, stature data for adult male samples are insufficient to tell us anything about the nutritional status of the populations. When, however, we compare adult male statures taken at various times, or in diverse environments, indications of environmental effects clearly emerge.

THE SECULAR TREND TOWARD INCREASED ADULT STATURE

The secular trend toward a speedup of growth and maturative processes and toward increased adult stature has generally been attributed to "better nutrition and generally improved environmental circumstances" (Tanner 1962: 148). The possibility, however, has been raised of a genetic effect entering the picture, not through natural selection for genetically determined tallness, but through an increase of outbreeding (heterosis). Indeed, Broman, et al. (1942) suggested that the acceleration of the growth process represents a response to environmental improvements, whereas the increase in adult stature is genetical in origin and consequential upon the breaking down of genetical isolates. This heterotic effect in man has been supported, inter alia, by the data of Hulse (1957) and Lasker (1960). However, the occurrence of a secular trend toward increased adult stature without overt evidence of the breaking down of genetic isolates would support the idea that the increase in stature, too, could be laid at the door of environmental amelioration, at least in certain situations. It is suggested (Tobias 1962) that the secular trend demonstrated in the San (Bushmen) is of environmental rather than genetic determination, for there is little overt evidence of the breaking down of genetic isolates, whereas there is evidence of slight environmental improvement (boreholes, distribution of famine relief). It would seem fair, therefore, to consider the secular trend toward increased adult stature as being caused by both sets of factors, with environmental determinants playing the major role in marginal populations like the San and both environmental and variably operating genetical determinants being responsible in other situations. In both sets of circumstances, however, it would seem that the evidence justifies the attribution of the secular trend, in part or in toto, to environmental betterment.

A SEARCH FOR THE SECULAR TREND TOWARDS INCREASED ADULT STATURE IN AFRICANS

The marked paucity of early data, strictly comparable with recent data, has militated against the demonstration of a secular trend in Africa. The first and thus far the only reasonably convincing demonstration of the secular trend in Africa was provided by an analysis of San (Bushman) statures taken at various periods. There is evidence that the San manifest the secular trend towards increased adult mean stature (Tobias 1962). Measurements taken before World War I, between the Wars, and since World War II, showed a consistent rise, in both males and females, in northern and central San. In Figure 1, a simplified analysis (data before 1935 and after 1950) shows this trend for both sexes in three major subgroups of San, namely northern, central and southern (Tobias 1970, 1972b).

As far as is known, this was the first demonstration that the secular trend toward increased adult stature applied as well to Africans.

Subsequently, Walker, et al. (1965), in a preliminary communication, drew attention to the fact that their findings betrayed a secular growth trend. Their statement was based on studies of South African Negro schoolchildren, not on adult data.

In Moçambique, da C. Martins (1968) found evidence for a secular growth trend over the past thirty years in Lourenço Marques schoolchildren of four populations (white, Negro, mixed, and Asian), but she considered her results to be statistically valid only for the white population.

A careful scrutiny of our tabulated data for adult Africans provides no clear-cut indication of the secular trend.

The following are examples of data collected at earlier and later dates on broadly comparable populations:

Zambia
"Zambezia" (n = 319) x̄ = 1632.0 (Brodie cited by Turner 1910–1916)
Valley Tonga (n = 311) x̄ = 1657.0 (Tobias 1958a, 1958b)

COMMENT   There is no certainty who the people of "Zambezia" were

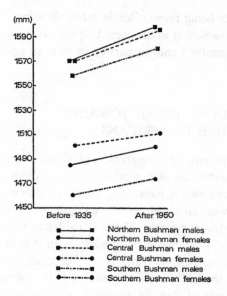

Figure 1.   Mean statures of Bushmen before 1935 and after 1950

nor where they came from: it MAY have been the north bank of the Zambezi where the Valley Tonga and some other chiefdoms are located. As Brodie's measurements were on mine recruits, his sample may well have included a proportion of adolescents.

Angola
Chokwe (n = 90) x̄ = 1695 (Correa 1918)
Northeastern Luanda (n = 10,586) x̄ = 1599.9 (Santos David 1972)

COMMENT   Although the northeastern Luanda sample includes Chokwe, it has also Luanda, Cacongo, Matabe and is "strongly influenced by pygmoid elements and most probably modified by the presence of other bushmanoid ones," both the latter of which might be expected to contribute to a lowering of mean stature.

South Africa
Venda (n = 168) x̄ = 1676.0 (Stayt 1931)
Venda Rural (n = 201) x̄ = 1664.7 (De Villiers 1969)
Venda Urban (n = 148) x̄ = 1668.9 (De Villiers 1969)

COMMENT   It is very likely that De Villiers' rural Venda are of a population comparable with Stayt's (1931) Venda. Yet the more recent populations — both urban and rural — have a lower mean stature than the 1931 sample. Is this a REVERSED SECULAR TREND?

Zulu Eshowe (n = 30) $\bar{x}$ = 1703.7 (Cipriani 1930–1931)
Zulu Polela (n = 696) $\bar{x}$ = 1663.0 (Kark 1954)
Zulu Natal in general (n = 72) $\bar{x}$ = 1682.8 (Laing 1964)
Zulu Durban-Urban (n = 106) $\bar{x}$ = 1660.5 (Slome, et al. 1960)

COMMENT The first three groups are predominantly rural and perhaps comparable. It looks like another instance of REVERSAL of the secular trend, but Cipriani's (1930–1931) sample is very small (30). Curiously enough, the usual rural-urban relationship is reversed — the urban Zulu in Durban have the smallest mean of the four series!

Xhosa (n = 26) $\bar{x}$ = 1650.3 (Turner 1910–1916)
Xhosa (n = 462) $\bar{x}$ = 1689.2 (Laing 1964)

COMMENT This looks like an example of the secular trend, but Turner's sample is too small for this to be convincing. Furthermore, Turner's series was of mine recruits and may have included nonmature subjects.

South Sotho (n = 79) $\bar{x}$ = 1688.4 (Brodie cited by Turner 1910–1916)
South Sotho (n = 689) $\bar{x}$ = 1677.0 (Laing 1964)

COMMENT Despite the fact that Brodie's series may have included some nonmature individuals, their mean value on a fair-sized sample is greater than the recent series of Laing (1964). Is this another instance of a REVERSAL of the secular trend?

South-West Africa
Nama Khoikhoi (n = 71) $\bar{x}$ = 1626.0 (Schultze 1928)
Nama Khoikhoi (n = 31) $\bar{x}$ = 1596.0 (Wells 1953)

COMMENT This comparison of Nama mean statures determined at an interval of twenty-five years looks like yet another suggestion of a REVERSED SECULAR TREND.

Moçambique
Maravi (n = 46) $\bar{x}$ = 1589.9 (Turner 1910–1916)
Maravi (n = 462) $\bar{x}$ = 1657.0 (Laing 1964)

COMMENT   Turner's sample probably includes some nonmature individuals. The sample size for the earlier group is much smaller than that for the later group. Nevertheless, the discrepancy is so great as to suggest that this may represent an example of the secular trend in operation.

East Coast (n = 1337) x̄ = 1689.1 (Brodie cited by Turner) 1910–1916)
Miscellaneous (n = 319) x̄ = 1691.7 (Laing 1964)

COMMENT   These two samples are ROUGHLY comparable, comprising mainly Shangana, Chopi, and Tsonga. If Brodie's figure has been slightly reduced by the inclusion of some juveniles, these figures suggest an absence of any stature increase over a period of fifty years. But the comparison could be completely vitiated if one sample includes more of the taller Chopi than the other.

The results of this search are highly unsatisfactory. No unequivocal indication — and indeed only two or three suggestions — of the secular trend toward increased adult stature have been unearthed; against that are three or four suggestive comparisons pointing to a possible reversal of the secular trend. The data pointing toward such a reversal are slightly more convincing than those pointing in the opposite direction. They raise a distinct possibility that under conditions of deteriorating environmental circumstances a secular trend toward decreased adult mean stature may become evident. It may well be that, under conditions of overcrowding, poor farming methods and soil erosion, subeconomic subsistence, gross susceptibility to "imported" diseases and other repressive circumstances, a REVERSED SECULAR TREND should be recognized.

Up to the present, therefore, the increase in adult mean stature of samples of San people over the last sixty and more years would seem to remain as the only fairly clear-cut example of the secular trend toward increased adult stature in Africa.

SEXUAL DIMORPHISM OF STATURE

In 1962, I showed that the secular trend among the San had affected the two sexes to different degrees. For each group of Bushmen, the absolute increase in mean stature was roughly twice as great in males as in females; as a result, "there is an increase in sexual dimorphism in stature" (Tobias 1962: 807). Figures 2 and 3 show the increase of

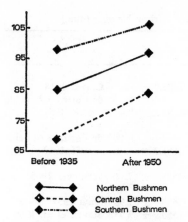

Figure 2. Absolute sexual dimorphism of Bushman stature before 1935 and after 1950
($\male\bar{x} - \female\bar{x}$ in mm)

absolute and percentual sexual dimorphism of stature for three groups of San.

Hiernaux (1968) reviewed the available data on sexual dimorphism of stature in European and sub-Saharan African populations. However, he included only two southern African Bantu Negro populations, the Nyungwe of Moçambique and the Venda of the Transvaal. Table 3 lists data for these and for eight other southern African Negro groups

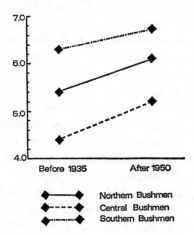

Figure 3. Relative sexual dimorphism of Bushman stature before 1935 and after 1950
$$\frac{(\male\bar{x} - \female\bar{x} \times 100)}{\male\bar{x}}$$

Table 3.   Stature in male and female southern African Negroes (mm.)

Population	Males		Females		References
	n	$\bar{x} \pm s\bar{x}$	n	$\bar{x} \pm s\bar{x}$	
Chokwe of Angola	90	1695.0 ± —	22	1603.0 ± —	Correa 1918
Kwangare of Angola	109	1708.4 ± 5.30	25	1593.2 ± 13.40	de Castro e Almeida 1956, 1957
Mbukushu (Mucusso) of Angola	100	1702.4 ± 5.70	25	1501.2 ± —	de Castro e Almeida 1956, 1957
Herero (Shimba) of Angola	54	1711.1 ± 8.58	30	1625.8 ± 7.76	Weninger 1965
Venda (Transvaal)	168	1676.0 ± 4.60	56	1540.0 ± 7.90	Stayt 1931
Zulu (Durban)	106	1660.5 ± 5.92	219	1558.9 ± 3.95	Slome, et al. 1960
Zulu (Polela)	696	1663.0 ± —	1,846	1564.0 ± —	Kark 1954
Nyungwe of Moçambique	120	1680.0 ± 5.00	46	1570.0 ± 8.10	Dos Santos 1944
Ambo (South-West Africa)	50	1702.0 ± —	20	1605.0 ± —	Galloway 1937
Northeastern Luanda (mainly Chokwe and Luanda) of Angola	10,586	1599.9 ± —	13,341	1514.9 ± —	Santos David 1972

(data for San, Khoikhoi, Griqua, Colored, and other groups are not included in the table).

Appreciable dimorphism is present in each instance (Table 4, Figures 4 and 5). In absolute dimensions, the preponderance of the male sample mean over the female varies from 85.0 millimeters (in Northeastern Luanda) to 201.2 millimeters (in Mbukushu). Expressed as percentages of the male sample means, these male-female differences range from 4.99 percent (Herero) to 11.82 percent (Mbukushu). That is, the mean statures of the 10 female samples range from 88.18 to 95.01 percent of the respective male mean statures. Thus, there is both appreciable sexual dimorphism of stature and considerable variation from one southern African population to another. How significant these differences in sexual dimorphism are depends, of course, on the representativeness of the samples: in this respect, it should be noted that 5 out of the 10 female samples number fewer than 40, namely the four Angolan samples of Correa (1918), de Castro e Almeida (1956, 1957) and Weninger (1965), and the South-West African Ambo sample of Galloway (1937).

In Table 4, the male-female differences for the 10 southern African

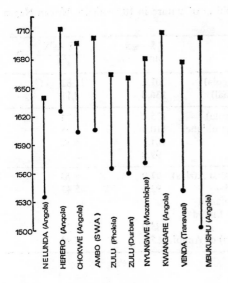

Figure 4. Sexual dimorphism of stature among Southern African Bantu-speaking Negroes
(male and female means in mm)

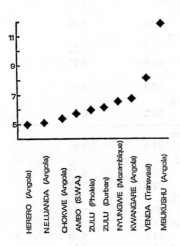

Figure 5. Relative sexual dimorphism of stature among Southern African Bantu-speaking Negroes
$$\left(\frac{\eth\bar{x} - \varphi\bar{x}}{\eth\bar{x}} \times 100 \right)$$

Table 4. Degree of sexual dimorphism of stature in 10 southern African Negro samples

	Population	$\eth\bar{x} - \female\bar{x}$ mm.	$\dfrac{\eth\bar{x} - \female\bar{x}}{\eth\bar{x}}$ %
High sexual dimorphism	Mbukushu (Angola)	201.2	11.82
	Venda (Transvaal)	136.0	8.11
Medium sexual dimorphism	Kwangare (Angola)	115.2	6.74
	Nyungwe (Moçambique)	110.0	6.55
	Zulu (Durban)	101.6	6.12
	Zulu (Polela)	99.0	5.95
Low sexual dimorphism	Ambo (South-West Africa)	97.0	5.70
	Chokwe (Angola)	93.0	5.43
	Northeastern Luanda (Chokwe and Luanda) of Angola	85.0	5.31
	Herero (Shimba) of Angola	85.3	4.99

Table 5. Degree of sexual dimorphism of stature in San populations

	Population	$\eth\bar{x} - \female\bar{x}$ mm.	$\dfrac{\eth\bar{x} - \female\bar{x}}{\eth\bar{x}}$ %
High sexual dimorphism	—	—	—
Medium sexual dimorphism	Magon (Tobias 1962)	105.0	6.65
	Kung (Bleek 1927-1929)	105.0	6.59
	Vasekele (De Castro e Almeida 1957)	102.4	6.38
	/?Auni – ‡Khomani (Dart 1937)	98.0	6.29
	Kung (Wells 1953)	97.0	6.13
	*Northern San (pooled later)	97.2	6.09
	Naron (Tobias 1955–1956, 1962)	96.2	6.04
Low sexual dimorphism	*N. + C. San (pooled after 1950)	93.8	5.89
	*N. + C. San (pooled 1925–1935)	91.4	5.78
	Kung (Lebzelter 1931)	91.0	5.77
	Auen (Tobias 1955–1956, 1962)	90.9	5.74
	*Northern San (pooled earlier)	84.7	5.40
	*Central San (pooled later)	83.6	5.24
	*N. + C. San (pooled before 1915)	77.5	4.97

* Data from various studies pooled

Negro groups are expressed in absolute terms and as a percentage of the respective male means. The data are grouped in categories of high, medium, and low sexual dimorphism. Similarly, data for San samples, as well as those based on pooled San series, are given in Table 5.

In his analysis of sexual dimorphism, Hiernaux (1968) used a graphical method based on distribution ellipses, such as those employed by E. Defrise-Gussenhoven. Noting the distribution of these ellipses about the straight line of Teissier, Hiernaux concluded that 3 of his African samples showed significantly greater, and 5 significantly lesser sexual dimorphism, than the average. The Venda were among the group with elevated dimorphism.

This author has reexamined the data amassed by Hiernaux and has computed the male-female differences, absolute and percentual, for all of his 35 sub-Saharan African populations and 41 European populations. The distribution of Hiernaux's samples together with the additional 8 southern African Negro samples and 6 San (unpooled) series added by the author is summarized in Table 6, along with the distribution of indices computed from the 41 sets of European data listed by Hiernaux.

The method used here, namely the percentual sex differences, suffices to confirm Hiernaux's conclusion that sexual dimorphism in sub-Saharan Africa is on the average less than it is in Europe. Thus, the mean of the percentual sex discrepancies for sub-Saharan Africans is 6.183 percent for Hiernaux's 35 African sample percentages or 6.212 for 49 African sample means (Hiernaux's 35 plus 14 additional sample means added by the present author); the corresponding mean of 41 European sample means is 6.784 percent.

There is a clear-cut shift to the left in the distribution of the sub-Saharan African populations as compared with that of the European populations (Figure 6). The southern African samples corroborate this trend, save for the unusually high dimorphism value for the Mbukushu of Angola (11.82 percent): the latter value is probably a sampling effect, the female sample size being only 25.

Table 6. Summary of distributions of percentual sex differences in stature for 49 sub-Saharan African and 41 European populations

	4–5%	5–6%	6–7%	7–8%	8–9%	>9%	Total
African populations	5	17	20	4	2	1	49
European populations	0	9	14	16	2	0	41

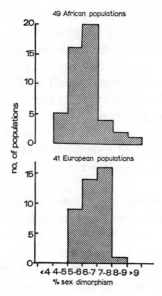

Figure 6

ENVIRONMENTAL ADVERSITY AND SEXUAL DIMORPHISM

The explanation for the different degrees of sexual dimorphism of stature in Africa and Europe, as Hiernaux (1968) points out, may be genetic, environmental or both. While no clear evidence is presently available for genetic differences being responsible, there is certainly a well-attested environmental factor which would seem to influence the degree of sexual dimorphism.

As long ago as 1947, Greulich (1951) studied Guamanian (Chamorro) children, following the Japanese occupation of Guam. He found that all children were retarded in stature, weight, and skeletal maturity relative to American whites, but that boys were in all respects relatively more retarded than girls. In this and subsequent studies (Greulich, Crismon, and Turner 1953; Greulich 1957), he found evidence to support the view that the human male is less successful than the female in withstanding the challenges of an unfavorable environment. Greulich's results were supported by those of Acheson and Hewitt (1954) in the Oxford Child Health Survey; Dreizen, Spirakis, and Stone (1964) on the effects of chronic undernutrition in Alabama children; Hiernaux (1965) on growth patterns in Rwanda; and Ashcroft, Heneage, and Lovell (1965) on Jamaican schoolchildren. If adverse nutritional circumstances affect growing males more than females, it would follow that populations exposed to such conditions should show a lesser degree of sexual dimorphism of stature. African populations, in general, are subject to less favorable environmental conditions, including nutritional, than European populations. Herein may lie the main cause of the lower sexual dimorphism of stature in sub-Saharan African populations.

An interesting corollary is that this fact may provide us with an index of environmental including dietary amelioration. As living conditions in Africa improve, we may expect the population to show not only an increase in mean stature (the secular trend), but an increase in the degree of sexual dimorphism. So far, this deduction is supported only by the Bushman data, which reveal the secular trend accompanied by an increase in sexual dimorphism. It would be interesting to analyze in this way the available data from all other populations, where results of earlier and later studies are on record.

Perhaps the harmless people, the San or Bushmen, may prove to have pointed the way to a concept of some heuristic value in further studies on the adaptability of human populations.

CONCLUSIONS AND SUMMARY

Studies of male adult stature in populations at a single point in time do not provide a useful pointer to the degree of environmental adequacy of those populations. However, when such data are compared with mean adult statures taken on comparable groups at an earlier period, useful data are obtained on the presence or absence of the secular trend toward increased adult mean stature. The presence of the secular trend may fairly be assumed to depend on environmental improvement, though in certain populations the environmental effect may be added to by a genetic effect based on the breakdown of genetic isolates and a consequential heterotic or outbreeding effect. Data for some 90 sub-Saharan African populations measured over the past ninety years are reviewed, and a careful search is made for indications of the secular trend. Apart from the trend toward increased adult stature already shown for San (Bushmen), no clear-cut illustration of the secular trend in black Africans of southern Africa could be found; on the contrary, several suggestions of a REVERSED secular trend came to light — pointing, perhaps, to an environmental (nutritional) deterioration over the period under review.

A second way in which adult mean statures may point up environmental inadequacies, it is suggested, is by the determination of the degree of sexual dimorphism in stature. Owing to the now well-known greater susceptibility of males to adverse conditions, sexual dimorphism of stature may be expected to be smaller among adults who had been reared under inadequate circumstances: this inference is corroborated by the smaller index of dimorphism first demonstrated in 1962 among the San and since shown to characterize most African populations studied, as compared with the degree of dimorphism in Caucasiform populations of Europe. As a corollary, it is of interest to note that the secular trend toward increased adult stature among San over the last ninety years has been paralleled by a SECULAR TREND TOWARD IN-CREASED SEXUAL DIMORPHISM.

It is well known that the study and comparison of growth rates among juveniles provides a useful yardstick of nutritional status of a community. Furthermore, the author has suggested earlier that some reliance may be placed upon sexual dimorphism of growth curves, in the assessment of environmental adequacy. More particularly, if we define the age period between female crossing over and male crossing back as "the period of female ascendancy," a poor environment might be expected to be accompanied by a LATER age at which the female stature curve crosses over and exceeds the stature curve of boys of the same age and by an increased duration of the phase of female ascendancy. Conversely, environmental betterment may be accompanied by a decrease in the age and duration of the phase of female ascendancy in juveniles (Tobias 1970, 1972b).

It is suggested that a simple and useful gauge of environmental betterment may be provided by: (1) a secular trend toward increased adult mean stature; and (2) a secular trend toward an absolute and relative increase in the degree of sexual dimorphism of mean adult stature in poorly nourished populations.

REFERENCES

ACHESON, R. M., D. HEWITT
   1954   Oxford Child Health Survey. Stature and skeletal maturation in the pre-school child. *British Journal of Preventive Medicine* 8:59–65.
ASHCROFT, M. T., P. HENEAGE, H. G. LOVELL
   1965   Heights and weights of Jamaican schoolchildren of various ethnic groups. *American Journal of Physical Anthropology* 24:35–44.
BLEEK, D. F.
   1927–1929   Bushmen of central Angola. *Bantu Studies* 3: 105–125.

BROMAN, B., G. DAHLBERG, A. LICHTENSTEIN
1942 Height and weight during growth. *Acta paediatrica* 30:1–66. Uppsala.

CIPRIANI, L.
1930– Osservazioni antropometriche su indigeni asiatici e africani, Part
1931 3: Zulu; Part 4: Batonga. *Archivio per l'antropologia e la etnologia* 60–61:189–286.

CORREA, A. A.
1918 Bi-N'bundo, Andulos e Ambuelas-Mambundas: Notes antropologicas sobre observaçoes de Fonseca Cardoso. *Archivio de anatomie e antropologia* 4:283–321. Lisbon.

DA C. MARTINS, D.
1968 "Dinamica do Crescimento e Desenvolvimento da Crianca em Moçambique." Unpublished doctoral dissertation, Coimbra Faculty of Medicine.

DART, R. A.
1937 The physical characteristics of the /?Auni- ≠ Khomani Bushmen. *Bantu Studies* 11:175–246.

DE CASTRO E ALMEIDA, M.
1956 Da estatura, peso e sua correlaçao em gentes nativas de Angola. *Gargia de Orta, Rev. da Junta das Missoes Geograf. e de Invest. do Ultramar* 4(3):349–358.
1957 Canones de Mulheres Indigenas de Angola. *Public. do XXIII Cong. Luso-Espanhol, 1956,* 5:5–16.

DE VILLIERS, H.
1969 "IBP: Human Adaptability Survey of Venda Males, July-September 1968." Johannesburg: University of the Witwatersrand, Department of Anatomy.

DOS SANTOS, J., JR.
1944 *Contribuiçao paro e estudo da anthropologia de Moçambique. Algumas tribos do distrito de Tete.* Ministerio das Colonias, Memorias, serie anthropol. ethnol. 2. Lisbon.

DREIZEN, S., C. N. SPIRAKIS, R. E. STONE
1964 Chronic undernutrition and post-natal ossification. *American Journal of Diseases of Children* 108:44–52.

GALLOWAY, A.
1937 A contribution to the physical anthropology of the Ovambo. *South African Journal of Science* 34:351–364.

GREULICH, W. W.
1951 The growth and development status of Guamanian schoolchildren in 1947. *American Journal of Physical Anthropology* 9:55–70.
1957 A comparison of the physical growth and development of American-born and native Japanese children. *American Journal of Physical Anthropology* 15:489–515.

GREULICH, W. W., C. S. CRISMON, M. L. TURNER
1953 The physical growth and development of children who survived the atomic bombing of Hiroshima and Nagasaki. *Journal of Pediatrics* 43:121–145.

HIERNAUX, J.
   1965   La croissance des écoliers rwandais. *Bruxelles: Académie Royale des Sciences d'Outre-Mer: Classe des Sciences Naturelles et Médicales* n.s. 16(2):3–204.
   1968   "Variabilité de dimorphisme sexuel de la stature en Afrique Subsaharienne et en Europe," in *Anthropologie und Humangenetik*, 42–50. Stuttgart: Gustav Fischer.

HULSE, F. S.
   1957   Exogamie et hétérosis. *Archives suisses d'anthropologie générale* 22:103–125.

KARK, S. L.
   1954   "Patterns of health and nutrition in Southern African Bantu." Unpublished M.D. thesis, University of the Witwatersrand, Johannesburg.

JENKINS, T.
   1972   "Genetic polymorphisms of man in southern Africa." Unpublished M.D. thesis, University of London.

LAING, J. G. D.
   1964   A height/weight table for African mine labourers. *Journal of the South African Institute of Mining and Metallurgy* (March) 406–417.

LASKER, G. W.
   1960   Variances of bodily measurements in the offspring of natives and of immigrants to three Peruvian towns. *American Journal of Physical Anthropology*, n.s. 18:257–261.

LEBZELTER, V.
   1931   Zur Anthropologie der Kung Buschleute. *Anzeiger der Akademie der Wissenschaften* 68:24.

MORRISON, J. F., C. H. WYNDHAM, N. B. STRYDOM, J. J. BETTENCOURT, J. H. VILJOEN
   1968   An anthropometrical survey of Bantu mine labourers. *Journal of the South African Institute of Mining and Metallurgy* (January): 275–278.

SANTOS DAVID, J. H.
   1972   Height growth of melanodermic natives in northeastern Luanda (Angola). *South African Journal of Medical Science* 37:49–60.

SCHULTZE, L.
   1928   Zur Kenntnis des Körpers der Hottentoten und Buschmänner. *Jenaische Denkschriften* 17:147–228.

SLOME, C., B. GAMPEL, J. H. ABRAMSON, N. SCOTCH
   1960   Weight, height and skinfold thickness of Zulu adults in Durban. *South African Medical Journal* 34:505–509.

STAYT, H. A.
   1931   *The Bavenda* London: Oxford University Press.

TANNER, J. M.
   1962   *Growth at adolescence* (second edition, third printing). Oxford: Blackwell Scientific Publications.

TOBIAS, P. V.

1955– Les Bochimans Auen et Naron de Ghanzi Contribution à l'étude
1956 des "Anciens jaunes" Sud-Africains. *L'Anthropologie* 59:235–252, 429–461; 60:22–52, 268–289.

1958a Tonga re-settlement and the Kariba Dam. *Man* 58:77–78.

1958b Kariba resettlement: an experiment in human ecology. *South African Journal of Science* 54:148–150.

1962 On the increasing stature of the Bushmen. *Anthropos* 57:801–810.

1966 "The peoples of Africa south of the Sahara," in *The biology of human adaptability*. Edited by Paul T. Baker and J. S. Weiner, 111–200. Oxford: Clarendon Press.

1970 Puberty, growth, malnutrition and the weaker sex — and two new measures of environmental betterment. *The Leech* 40(4): 101–107.

1972a Recent human biological studies in southern Africa, with special reference to Negroes and Khoisans. *Transactions of the Royal Society of South Africa* 40(3):109–133.

1972b "Growth and stature in southern African populations," in *Human biology of environmental change*. Edited by D. J. M. Vorster. Human Adaptability Section of IBP Conference held in Blantyre, Malawi, April 1971:96–104.

TURNER, G. A.

1910– "Some anthropological notes on the South African Coloured mine
1916 labourer." Unpublished manuscript, Johannesburg.

WALKER, A. R. P.

1963 The nutritional state of South African child population groups as reflected by height, weight, and nitrogen partition in the urine. *South African Medical Journal* 37:400–403.

WALKER, A. R. P., B. D. RICHARDSON, A. NURSE, B. F. WALKER

1965 The changing pattern of growth and other parameters in South African Bantu children. *South African Medical Journal* 39:103–104.

WELLS L. H.

1953 Physical measurements of a Hottentot-Bushman hybrid. *South African Journal of Science* 49:283–284.

WENINGER, M.

1965 Chimba und Vatwa, bantuide Viehzüchter und nicht-bantuide Wildbeuter. *Mitteilungen der Anthropologischen Gesellschaft in Wien* 95:180–190.

PART FOUR

Growth and Development

Late Adolescent Changes in Weight

ALEX F. ROCHE, GAIL H. DAVILA, and E. DAVID MELLITS

Within individuals, little is known about changes in weight, after the age of peak height velocity. There is, however, marked interest in related questions, such as whether children maintain similar centile levels for weight across age (Mossberg 1948; Asher 1966; Eid 1970). The present analysis has shown that the rates of growth in weight in individuals alter at about the ages when growth in stature ceases and that these ages differ markedly between individuals. The ages at which changes occur in the rates of growth in weight, together with the total increments in weight after particular growth and developmental landmarks, should interest not only research workers but all those responsible for the professional care of adolescents and young adults.

Boothby, et al. (1952) reported annual weight increments, with large sample sizes, to about 18 years in males and 21 years in females. At all ages with adequate sample sizes, the means for the males markedly exceeded those for the females. Mean annual increments exceeding one kilogram occurred to 20 years in the males and 17 years in the females. Von Verschauer (1954) reported the weights of twins measured at two ages separated by about eighteen years. The total increments in weight between the two measurements were calculated for the first listed of each pair of monozygous twins and for each dizygous twin. The mean increments, from about 19 to 37 years, were 8.7 kilograms (s.d., 7.91) in 11 males and 6.6 kilograms (s.d., 7.13) in 27 females. A national probability sample of the adult United States population was studied in the Health Examination Survey. These data were

This work was supported by Contract 72-2735 and Grants HD-03472 and HD-04629 from the National Institutes of Health, Bethesda, Maryland.

weighted to provide estimates for the total noninstitutionalized United States population (Stoudt, et al. 1965). Consequently these cross-sectional data allow estimates of median increments for males (21-30 years, 5.4 kilograms; 30-40 years, 0.9 kilograms) and females (21-30 years, 1.8 kilograms; 30-40 years, 3.2 kilograms).

MATERIAL AND METHODS

The present data were derived from southern Ohio white children (118 boys; 111 girls) in The Fels Longitudinal Sample. They were weighed serially from 1 month to at least 22 years, and, in some cases, to ages exceeding 40 years. The mean ages of the last weights were 30 years in each sex. These measurements were made at visits scheduled five times in the first year and then six-monthly, except after 18 years when they were scheduled at biennial intervals.

The weights were measured to the nearest 0.1 kilograms with the subjects wearing standard light indoor clothing. Data recorded during pregnancy were excluded. The statures of these children were used to obtain six-monthly increments (Roche and Davila 1972). The midpoint of the interval with the largest increment in stature was recorded as the age of peak height velocity (PHV). When two successive increments were equally the largest, the midpoint of the combined interval was recorded as PHV.

Consideration was given to combining successive six-monthly stature increments to annual increments, thus reducing seasonal effects. This was not done because PHV would be determined less reliably, and this was not justified by the small seasonal variations in increments in a subset of the children. Furthermore, PHV should be considered the midpoint of the largest increment regardless of the factors, seasonal or otherwise, that are responsible for the changes in the rates of growth.

Age at menarche was obtained by six-monthly inquiry at appropriate ages. The ages at which the distal end of the femur and the proximal end of the tibia became mature were recorded as those of the first radiographs in which the corresponding epiphyseal lines were completely obliterated. Children were excluded from this part of the study if the interval between this radiograph and the immediately preceding radiograph of the knee exceeded 1.7 years. The mean ages at which PHV and menarche occurred (Table 1) were similar to those in other healthy American children (Frisch and Revelle 1971; Maresh 1971). Hand-wrist skeletal age was recorded as the mean of bone-specific

Table 1. Centiles for ages (years) of achieving developmental landmarks

	N	10	50	90
PHV boys	115	12.7	13.7	15.2
PHV girls	101	10.2	11.7	13.2
Menarche	104	11.5	12.8	14.6

skeletal ages obtained using the Greulich-Pyle atlas (1959).

Applying the method of Mellits (1965, 1968), two polynomial lines were fitted to all available weight data for each individual, recorded after the age of PHV. This procedure was applied in 57 boys and 58 girls; in the remainder there were too few data points at later ages. This procedure assumes a discontinuity exists between data pertaining to earlier and later ages.

Piecewise regressions are calculated to locate the junction between these earlier and later data subsets for the individuals. The method fits the most precise estimates for the two polynomials considered together. A 2-degree polynomial was fitted to the earlier data and a 1-degree polynomial was fitted to the later data. This junction was accepted as an age at which the rate of growth in weight changed in each individual.

Statistical tests showed that these polynomials were more appropriate than higher order ones. The choice appears appropriate from a biological viewpoint also. During the earlier period, weight is decelerating; this reflects a nonlinear multiplication process rather like the second part of a sigmoid growth curve. In the later period, growth in stature has ceased and the changes in weight are approximately constant across time.

When two or fewer data points were later than the junction at which the goodness of fit was maximized, the junction with the second-best fit was chosen. This was done in 12 boys and 7 girls. In some individuals, the goodness of fit, for the two polynomial lines combined, varied only slightly between some junctions. In addition, after 18 years, the data points were at intervals of at least two years. Consequently, it was impossible to determine precisely the age at which the rate of growth in weight changed in each individual.

Due to the mathematical form of the equations when combined 2-degree and 1-degree polynomials are fitted to a set of data points, there may be two junctions between these polynomials within the age range covered by the data. When this occurred, the earlier junction was used in the analysis because the second has no biological meaning. Also, it is possible that the polynomials will not actually intersect. However, in these cases, the most precise estimates of the two lines will indicate points of discontinuity between the two junctions.

These discontinuities are essentially "intersections." In 11 of the children studied, this was in fact the case. For convenience, the junction between the early and late data subsets at which the fit was best will be referred to as the "intersection" although there were two intersections in some children and none in others. Essentially the same group of children were included in a corresponding analysis of stature (Roche and Davila 1972).

RESULTS

Completely longitudinal data from 118 boys and 111 girls were used to obtain six-monthly increments for weight from 12.5 to 18 years (Figure 1). The medians for the boys exceeded those for the girls at all ages and the patterns of change differed between the sexes in ways that reflected the timing of pubertal growth spurts. The median increments increased with age in the boys until 14-14.5 years but decreased later; in the girls they decreased fairly regularly throughout the whole period. The median increments in the girls were less than 1 kilogram for each interval after 14.5-15 years but only for the interval 17.5-18 years in the boys. The ranges from the tenth to the ninetieth centiles were larger in the boys than the girls for each interval.

The median ages of intersection of the polynomial lines fitted to the earlier and later data subsets were 21.1 years in the boys and 18.4 years in the girls. These ages varied markedly with ranges of more than 8 years from the tenth to the ninetieth centile in each sex (Table 2).

Table 2. Centiles for ages of intersection of polynomial lines for weight in 57 boys and 58 girls

	10	50	90
Chronological age (yr) — boys	16.9	21.2	25.1
Chronological age (yr) — girls	15.8	18.4	24.6
Years after PHV — boys	4.0	8.2	11.5
Years after PHV — girls	3.5	7.3	12.8
Years after menarche	2.5	5.6	11.8
Years after SA[a] 13 years — boys	3.9	8.4	12.3
Years after SA[a] 11 years — girls	4.3	7.3	14.0

[a]   SA = skeletal age.

The median ages at which the two lines intersected were 8.2 years after PHV in the boys and 7.3 years after PHV in the girls.

The median difference between age at menarche and age at the

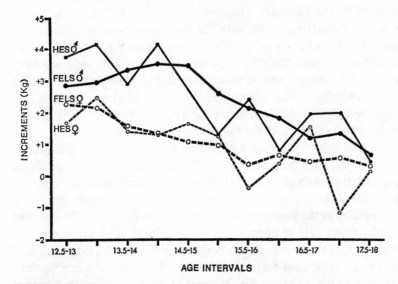

Figure 1.　Median six-monthly increments for weight in the present sample (Fels) and in the United States Health Examination Survey (HES). The latter data are from Hamill, et al. (1972)

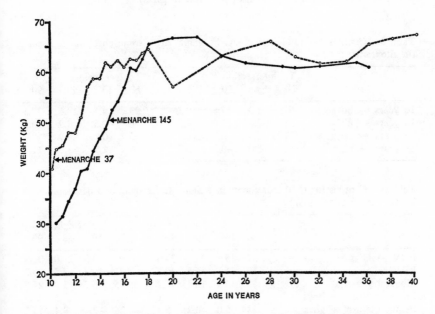

Figure 2.　Graphs of weight against age for two girls differing markedly in age at menarche. The girl with menarche at 10.2 years (No. 37) gained more weight after menarche than the girl with menarche at 14.8 years (No. 145)

intersection was 5.6 years. There was a tendency for age at menarche to be associated negatively with the total increment in weight after menarche (r = − 0.42, n = 75). Figure 2 shows serial weight data for an early (No. 37) and a late (No. 145) maturing girl. In the early maturing girl, the intersection was at 22.4 years and the increment in weight from menarche to the intersection was 18.5 kilograms. In the late maturing girl, the intersection was at 19 years and the increment in weight from menarche to the intersection was 15.5 kilograms.

The variability of the ages at intersections, as judged by the range from the tenth to the ninetieth centile, was similar for chronological age, and the intervals after PHV, menarche, and particular skeletal ages (Table 2). The ages at intersections were significantly correlated with weights at the intersections in boys (r = + 0.37, p < .01) but not in girls. These ages at intersections were influenced by the age ranges from the first to the last datum point in each individual. In each sex, there was a significant association between the ages at the intersections and the ages when the last weights were recorded, although the ages of the last weights were not associated significantly with the slopes of the 1-degree polynomials. In each sex, the ages at the intersections for weight were significantly correlated with the ages at PHV (r = + 0.38, p < .01 in boys, and r = + 0.26, p < .05 in girls).

Table 3. Centiles for total increments in weight after some chronological ages (in kilograms)

	To intersection				To last weight			
	N	10	50	90	N	10	50	90
16 years — boys	57	1.3	7.5	19.3	93	4.1	14.0	27.5
16 years — girls	58	−2.2	1.6	4.2	76	−2.6	3.9	13.8
18 years — boys	57	−2.4	3.2	12.5	93	−0.2	7.9	20.2
18 years — girls	58	−5.0	−0.3	2.7	76	−2.9	2.5	11.8

Table 4. Centiles for total increments in weight after growth and developmental landmarks (in kilograms)

	To level of intersection				To last weight			
	N	10	50	90	N	10	50	90
PHV — boys	57	15.7	24.2	34.0	90	14.8	28.0	39.3
PHV — girls	57	11.1	15.5	26.0	73	10.3	18.5	33.2
Menarche	58	3.5	10.4	16.7	75	5.7	11.2	25.2
Femur mature — boys	24	1.2	5.5	15.1	29	3.0	14.2	29.7
Femur mature — girls	24	−5.0	0.7	5.4	28	−2.4	3.4	13.3
Tibia mature — boys	26	0.1	6.1	13.8	31	3.1	13.2	26.1
Tibia mature — girls	25	−4.0	0.7	5.5	29	−1.7	5.2	11.7

The total weight increments after particular chronological ages were considerably larger in the boys than the girls whether the increments considered were to the levels of the intersections of the polynomials or to the last weights available (Table 3). For example, the median increments from 18 years to the last weight were 7.9 kilograms in the boys but only 2.5 kilograms in the girls. The corresponding values for increments to the levels of the intersections of the two polynomials were 3.2 kilograms for the boys and -0.3 kilograms for the girls. A sex difference remains, if the increments in girls after 16 years are compared with those in the boys after 18 years, although this comparison compensates for the two-year sex difference between the median ages for PHV (Table 1). The median increments after 16 years were markedly larger than those after 18 years, in both boys and girls.

The data in Table 4 show the total increments in weight after some phenomena of growth and development. These were markedly variable in each sex whether calculated to the ages of intersection of the polynomial lines or to the last weights recorded. The increments were markedly larger in boys than in girls after PHV, after the femur was mature, and after the tibia was mature. This sex dichotomy was relatively greater after the completion of maturation in long bones than after other chronological and developmental landmarks. It was reflected in the slopes of the 1-degree polynomials that were fitted to the late data subset (Table 5). The slopes were more commonly positive and tended to be steeper in the boys than the girls. As expected, from the generally positive slopes of the 1-degree polynomials, the median increments to the last recorded weights were consistently greater than those to the intersections.

Table 5. Centiles for the slopes of the 1-degree polynomials that were fitted to the later data (57 boys; 58 girls)

	Centiles		
	10	50	90
Boys	-0.40	0.48	1.14
Girls	-0.40	0.23	1.01

DISCUSSION

The median ages of intersection for weight are almost the same as those reported for stature in boys but are about one year later in girls (Roche and Davila 1972). As for stature, the variability of the ages at intersection for weight is similar whether considered in relation to chronological age, PHV, menarche, or skeletal age, indicating that these ages have little relationship to rates of maturation in individuals.

These ages of intersections are much more variable in timing than those for stature. Growth in stature is more regular than growth in weight and, at the intersections, the minimum variances tended to be higher for weight than for stature. Precise ages for individuals, at which the rates of growth in weight changed, could not be determined due to the nature of the available data. However, the ages obtained in this analysis were shown to be reasonable by checking against the original data.

There are few reported data with which the present findings can be compared. The six-monthly increments indicate considerably lesser rates of gain than those reported by Boothby, et al. (1952). They are, in general, similar to national estimates for the United States (Hamill, et al. 1972) but the present data show more regular trends. Presumably, this reflects the longitudinal nature of the present data.

The total increments after 18 years are similar to those reported by von Verschauer (1954) for males but they are markedly less than the values he reported for females. On the other hand, the present total increments from 18 to 30 years are slightly higher than recent national estimates for the United States for the age interval 21-30 years (Stoudt, et al. 1965). These differences are proportionately similar in each sex and probably are due, in large measure, to differences in the age ranges considered.

The present median values show sex-associated differences in the patterns of weight change during adolescence. The girls reached PHV about two years before the boys and were about two years younger than the boys when the median six-monthly increments became less than 1 kilogram. Nevertheless, the intersections of the polynomials occurred about three years earlier in the girls than the boys. The marked tendency for boys to exceed girls in total weight increments after the femur or the tibia became mature probably reflects sex differences in the growth of the length and circumference of the trunk during late adolescence (Anderson, et al. 1963; Hansman 1970).

The sex differences in increments are not due entirely to variations in rates of maturation. This can be seen in comparisons between increments for ages differing by two years and by comparisons between increments after PHV. Furthermore, the total weight increments after menarche were only moderately associated with age at menarche.

The intersections located with this statistical approach indicate that changes occur in the rates of growth in weight. However, these points of intersection are only moderately reliable guides to the ages at which these changes occurred. These ages were influenced by the age ranges of the available data and, necessarily, their reliability was limited by the infrequency of the examinations after the age of 18 years. The present data do, however, provide new knowledge of growth during the poorly documented period between late childhood and early adulthood. They should help define the nutritional needs of adolescents and assist the management of children in whom weight levels or the patterns of change in weight are unusual.

REFERENCES

ANDERSON, M., W. T. GREEN, M. B. MESSNER
  1963   Growth and predictions of growth in the lower extremities. *Journal of Bone and Joint Surgery* 45-A: 1–14.

ASHER, P.
  1966   Fat babies and fat children; the prognosis of obesity in the very young. *Archives for Diseases of Childhood* 41:672–677.

BOOTHBY, E. J., M. A. GUY, T. A. L. DAVIES
  1952   The growth of adolescents. *Monthly Bulletin, Great Britain Ministry of Health* 11:208–223.

EID, E. E.
  1970   Follow-up study of physical growth of children who had excessive weight gain in first six months of life. *British Medical Journal* 2: 74–76.

FRISCH, R. E., R. REVELLE
  1971   Height and weight at menarche and a hypothesis of menarche. *Archives for Diseases of Childhood* 46:695–701.

GREULICH, W. W., S. I. PYLE
  1959   *Radiographic atlas of skeletal development of the hand and wrist* (second edition). Stanford: Stanford University Press.

HAMILL, P. V. V., F. E. JOHNSTON, S. LEMESHOW
  1973   *Height and weight of youths, 12-17 years, United States.* National Health Survey, Vital and Health Statistics, Series 11, Number 124. Washington, D.C.: U. S. Government Printing Office.

HANSMAN, C.
  1970   "Anthropometry and related data, anthropometry skinfold thickness measurements," in *Human growth and development.* Edited by R. W. McCammon. Springfield, Illinois: Charles C. Thomas.

MARESH, M. M.
  1971   Single versus serial assessment of skeletal age: either, both or neither? *American Journal of Physical Anthropology* 35:387–392.

MELLITS, E. D.
  1965   "Estimation and design for intersecting regressions." Unpublished M. D. thesis, Johns Hopkins University School of Hygiene and Public Health.

1968   "Statistical methods," in *Human growth; body composition, cell growth, energy and intelligence*. Edited by D. B. Cheek. Philadelphia: Lea and Febiger.

MOSSBERG, H.-O.
1948   Obesity in children; clinical-prognostical investigation. *Acta Paediatrica Scandinavia* 35, supplement 2.

ROCHE, A. F., DAVILA, G. H.
1972   Late adolescent growth in stature. *Pediatrics* 50:874–880.

STOUDT, H. W., A. DAMON, R. MCFARLAND
1965   *Weight, height, and selected body dimensions of adults, United States — 1960–1962*. National Health Survey, Vital and Health Statistics, PHS Publication 1000, Series 11, Number 8. Washington, D.C.: U. S. Government Printing Office.

VON VERSCHAUER, O. F.
1954   *Wirksame Faktoren im Leben des Menschen; Beobachtungen an ein- und zweieiigen Zwillingen durch 25 Jahre*. Wiesbaden: Franz Steiner Verlag GMBH.

Critical Weights, A Critical Body Composition, Menarche, and the Maintenance of Menstrual Cycles

ROSE E. FRISCH

It is commonly observed that human beings, like other mammals (Bullough 1951), must first grow to maturity before they are capable of reproduction. It is rarely considered, however, on what scale maturity is to be measured, e.g. on a chronological, ponderal, or another bodily scale; how a synchronization is brought about (Kennedy and Mitra 1963), and what the significance is for successful bearing and nursing of young.

Analysis of each event of the adolescent growth spurt of girls and boys, using the new approach of determining the height and weight of each girl and each boy at the age of each adolescent event from longitudinal growth data, and studying the individual heights and weights as a function of the age of each of the events, showed that the ponderal scale, weight, is more closely associated with sexual maturation than is the chronological scale, age (Frisch 1972; Frisch and Revelle 1969b, 1970, 1971a, 1971b; Frisch, Revelle, and Cook 1971).

Analysis of the components of the "critical weight" at menarche and at initiation of the spurt in girls defined the association of weight and menarche more precisely as a particular body composition, a ratio of lean body weight to fat in the range of 3 : 1, or a proportion of fat in the body weight in the range of 20 percent (Frisch 1974a, 1974b; Frisch, Revelle, and Cook 1972, 1973). The maintenance of a minimum level of stored fat also seems to be necessary for the onset and maintenance of menstrual cycles (Frisch and McArthur 1974).

CRITICAL WEIGHTS

These findings were first indicated by an analysis of cross-sectional body

weight data of Asian and Latin American peoples in relation to calorie
supplies. When the age of fastest growth in weight of the adolescent
growth spurt (hereafter termed peak weight velocity) was studied in relation to calorie intake, it was found that undernutrition delayed the age of
peak weight velocity and high levels of nutrition advanced the age of this
event (Frisch and Revelle 1969a), as had already been observed for the
adolescent spurt in general (Tanner 1962). Unexpectedly, however, peak
weight velocity, which normally precedes menarche, seemed to take place
at the same mean weight for a particular racial group, regardless of
whether the age of the event was advanced or delayed, in accordance
with the calorie supplies (Frisch and Revelle 1969a).

To pursue this interesting finding, each event of the adolescent growth
spurt was analyzed using longitudinal growth data, as described above. A
velocity curve of height and weight growth from birth to age 18 years
(Figures 1, 2, and 3) was plotted for each of the 201 girls and 209 boys
of the three comparable, completed, longitudinal growth studies: the

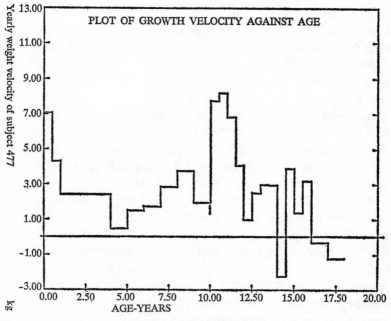

Figure 1.   Computer plotted yearly weight velocity (annual gain in weight) versus
age, of a CRC girl, a rapid grower, showing initiation of the adolescent weight
spurt at age 10 years. Age of menarche is 12.3 years. Note childhood acceleration
in weight gain at ages 5–8 years. Such a velocity curve was plotted for each of
201 girls. Reprinted from Frisch and Revelle (1971a) by the kind permission of the
editor of *Human Biology* and the Wayne State University Press.

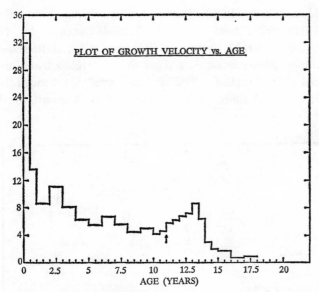

Figure 2.   Computer plotted yearly height velocity (annual gain in height) versus age of a CRC girl, slow growing, late maturer, showing initiation of the adolescent height spurt at 11.0 years. Age of menarche is 14.6 years. Reprinted from Frisch and Revelle (1971a) by the kind permission of the editor of *Human Biology* and the Wayne State University Press.

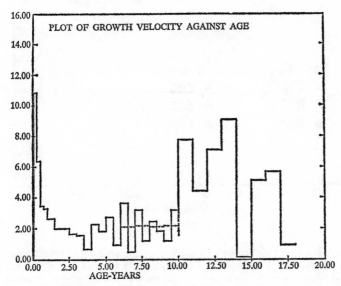

Figure 3.   Computer plotted yearly weight velocity (annual gain in weight) versus age of a HSPH boy showing the abrupt initiation of the adolescent weight spurt at age ten years. Note the seasonal difference in half-yearly increments in growth. Dotted line is yearly rate of gain in weight.

Berkeley Guidance Study (BGS) (Tuddenham and Snyder 1954), the
Denver Child Research Council Study (CRC), made available through
the kindness of Dr. Robert McCammon (1970) and Dr. Charlotte Hansman, and the longitudinal studies of child health and development of the
Harvard School of Public Health (HSPH), made available through the
kindness of Dr. Isabelle Valadian and Dr. Robert .W Reed (Stuart, Reed,
et al. 1959).

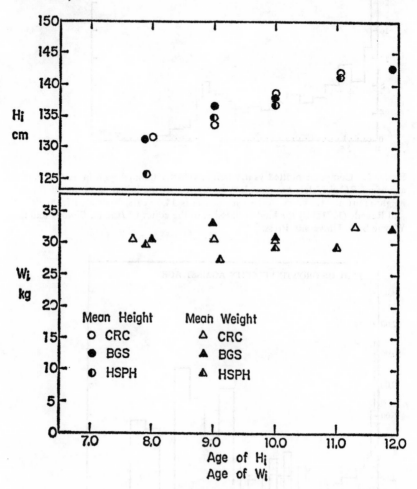

Figure 4. Mean height [H_i] at age of initiation of the adolescent height spurt
versus mean age (years) of initiation of the height spurt (Age of H_i); and mean
weight [W_i] at initiation of the adolescent weight spurt versus mean age (years) of
initiation of the weight spurt [Age of W_i] for girls of CRC, BGS, and HSPH growth
studies grouped by mean age of initiation of the height and weight spurt respectively.
Reprinted from Frisch and Revelle (1971a) by the kind permission of the editor
of *Human Biology* and the Wayne State University Press.

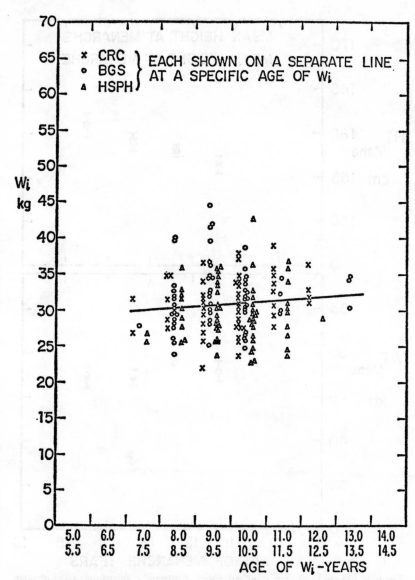

Figure 5. Weight [W_i] at initiation of the adolescent weight spurt versus age of initiation of the adolescent weight spurt [age of W_i] of girls of the CRC, BGS, and HSPH growth studies. Regression line of W_i on age of W_i does not differ significantly from zero. Reprinted from Frisch and Revelle (1971a) by the kind permission of the editor of *Human Biology* and the Wayne State University Press.

We found that the mean weight of girls at the time of initiation of the adolescent growth spurt (30 kg.) (Figures 4 and 5; Frisch and Revelle 1971a), at the time of maximum rate of weight gain (peak velocity) (39

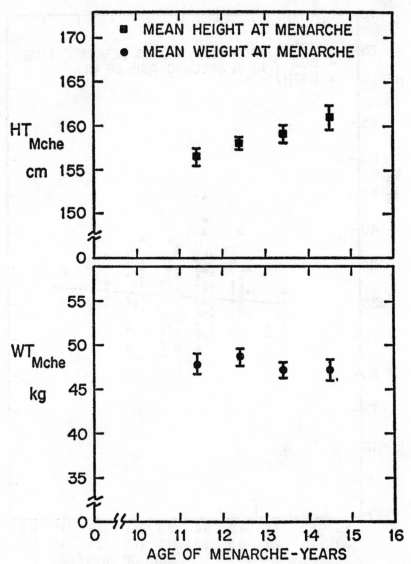

Figure 6. Mean height (± standard error) at menarche versus mean age of menarche, and mean weight (± standard error) at menarche versus mean age of menarche of CRC, BGS, and HSPH girls grouped by age of menarche.

kg.) (Frisch and Revelle 1969b), and at menarche 47 kg. (Figures 6 and 7; Frisch and Revelle 1970, 1971b; Frisch, Revelle, and Cook 1971) did not differ for early and late maturing girls, whereas their mean height at each of these events increased significantly with age of the event (Table 1; Figures 5, 6, and 8).

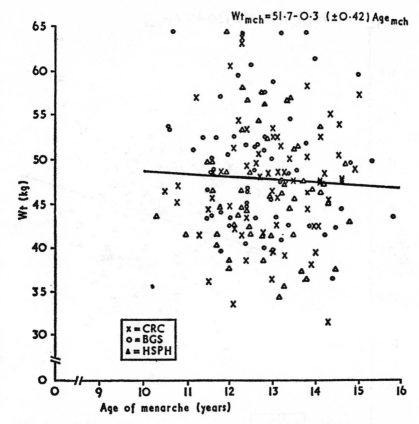

Figure 7. Weight at menarche [Wt_{mch}] versus age of menarche [Age_{mch}] of each CRC, BGS, and HSPH girl. Slope of regression line of Wt_{mch} on Age_{mch} does not differ significantly from zero. Reprinted from Frisch and Revelle (1971b) with kind permission of the editor and publisher of *Archives of Disease in Childhood.*

These results accounted for the many observations in the literature (Tanner 1962) that early maturers have more weight for height than late maturers at spurt initiation and throughout the adolescent spurt, including menarche. It was unexpected, however, that three of the major events of adolescence in human beings were each related to an unchanging mean weight.

Evidence from Animal Data

That puberty is more closely related to weight than to age is, however, well known for other mammals: data for rats (Widdowson and McCance

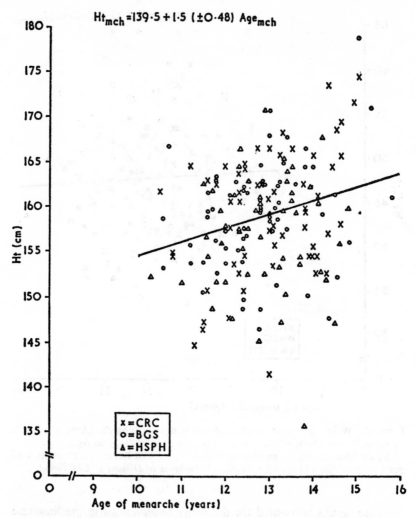

Figure 8. Height at menarche [Ht_{mch}] versus age of menarche of each CRC, BGS, and HSPH girl. Slope of regression line of Ht_{mch} on Age_{mch} differs significantly from zero ($P < 0.01$). Reprinted from Frisch and Revelle (1971b) with kind permission of the editor and publisher of *Archives of Disease in Childhood*.

1960; Widdowson, Mavor, and McCance 1964; McCance 1962; Kennedy 1969; Kennedy and Mitra 1963); mice (Barnett and Coleman 1959; Monteiro and Falconer 1966); pigs (Dickerson, Gresham and McCance 1964), and cattle (Crichton, Aitken and Boyne 1959; Joubert 1963) show that sexual maturity, defined by vaginal opening, or more precisely by first oestrus, is attained at the same mean weight for slow growing ani-

Table 1.　Mean age, height and weight of BGS, CRC and HSPH girls at initiation of the adolescent spurt, peak velocity, menarche, and age 18

Adolescent event	Number	Age of Ht. event	Age of Wt. event yr	Height (cm.)	Weight (kg.)
				Mean ± S.E.	
Initiation[d]	184	9.6 ± 0.1	9.5 ± 0.1	136.5 ± 0.84[a]	30.6 ± 0.30[b]
Peak velocity[e]	170	11.8 ± 0.1	12.1 ± 0.1	146.5 ± 0.50[a]	39.3 ± 0.45[b]
Menarche[f]	181		12.9 ± 0.1	158.5 ± 0.50[a]	47.8 ± 0.51[b]
at age 18[e]	181		—	165.6 ± 0.48[b]	57.1 ± 0.57[c]

a　Increases significantly (p <.01) with increasing age of event.
b　Does not change significantly with increasing age of event.
c　Decreases significantly (p <.02) with increasing age of event.
d　Frisch and Revelle (1971a).
e　Frisch and Revelle (1969b).
f　Frisch and Revelle (1970, 1971b).

mals as it is for fast growing animals, but at a significantly later age for those that grow slowly.

Dickerson, Gresham, and McCance (1964) specifically state that the female pigs did not ovulate until they were "approaching the body weight at which ovulation normally occurs." Widdowson and McCance (1960) state that "sexual development [of the rat] was determined primarily by size . . ."; Kennedy (1969) states: "Puberty is determined by weight rather than age."

There is also an example from primates: female rhesus monkeys treated with androgens gained weight rapidly and had menarche at age one year instead of the normal age of two years, but at the weight and length characteristic of two-year-old animals (van Wagenen 1949).

Thus, the relationship between a specific body weight and sexual maturation found by us in human beings is a common phenomenon among other mammals, including primates.

Heights and Weights of Boys at Adolescent Events

Our basic finding was also true for boys (Table 2), but their ages, weights, and heights differed from those of the girls, and the latest maturing boys were slightly but significantly heavier at both spurt initiation (Frisch and Revelle 1971a) and at peak weight velocity (Frisch and Revelle 1969b). Boys attained each event about two years later than the girls, at a mean weight about 6 kg. heavier and a mean height about 11 cm taller than that of the girls at the corresponding event (Table 2). This suggests that

Table 2. Mean age, height and weight of BGS, CRC, and HSPH boys at initiation of the adolescent spurt, peak velocity and age 18

Adolescent event	Number	Mean ± S.E.			
		Age of Ht. event yr.	Age of Wt. event	Height (cm.)	Weight (kg.)
Initiation[e]	179	11.7 ± 0.1	11.6 ± 0.1	147.3 ± 0.49[a]	36.9 ± 0.36[b]
Peak velocity[f]	189	14.0 ± 0.1	14.1 ± 0.1	158.3 ± 0.48[a]	47.3 ± 0.52[b]
at age 18[e]	179			178.1 ± 0.46[c]	68.2 ± 0.69[d]

a) Increases significantly (p <.01) with increasing age of event.
b) Latest maturers slightly but significantly (p <.01) heavier than earlier age groups.
c) Does not change with increasing age of event.
d) Decreases significantly with increasing age of event.
e) Frisch and Revelle, 1971a.
f) Frisch and Revelle, 1969b.

"genarche" in boys, the ability to reproduce, comparable to menarche in girls, may be attained at a mean age of 14.9 years, at a mean weight of 55 kg. (121 pounds), and a mean height of 169 cm. (66.5 inches).

Only the results for the girls will be discussed in detail in this paper.

THE CRITICAL WEIGHT HYPOTHESIS

Based on these findings of an invariant mean weight in girls, we proposed that there is a direct relation between a critical body weight, representing a critical metabolic rate, and menarche. The mechanism proposed, adapted from that of Kennedy and Mitra (1963), assumes that the attainment of the critical weight, which we now know represents a critical body composition (Frisch 1974a, 1974b; Frisch, Revelle, and Cook 1972, 1973), causes a change in metabolic rate per unit mass, which in turn affects the hypothalamus-ovarian feedback by decreasing the sensitivity of the hypothalamus to estrogen. The feedback is then reset at a level high enough to induce the maturation resulting in menarche (Frisch and Revelle 1970, 1971b).

Kulin, Grumbach, and Kaplan (1969, 1972) have found evidence for such a change of sensitivity of the hypothalamic "gonadostat" in girls and boys.

Whatever the mechanism, the assumption that a critical weight triggers menarche explains simply many unexplained observations associated with early or late age of menarche.

Observations of earlier menarche are associated with attaining the critical weight more quickly. The most important example is the secular trend to an earlier menarche of about three or four months per decade in Europe in the last one hundred years (Tanner 1966). Our explanation is that children now are bigger sooner (Tanner 1966), and therefore girls, on the average, reach 47 kg., the mean critical weight, more quickly. (The twenty-fifth percentile of weight at menarche is 43 kg.; the seventy-fifth percentile is 51.5 kg. [Frisch and Revelle 1971b]). According to our hypothesis also, the secular trend should end when the weight of children of successive cohorts remains the same because of the attainment of maximum nutrition and child care (Frisch and Revelle 1971b).

There is evidence for this explanation of the secular trend. The mean weight at menarche for Caucasian girls in this decade (Frisch 1972; Maresh 1972; Johnston, Malina, and Galbraith 1971; Van Wieringen, et al. 1971) is the same as the mean weight we found for girls of three decades ago (Frisch and Revelle 1970, 1971b; Figure 9).

Historically, Boas' weight data (1895) for California girls in 1895 show that 47 kg. would be attained at about 14 years, which is consistent with menarcheal ages recorded for about 1900 in the United States. And Quetelet's growth data of 1835 show that Belgian girls of average social class attained a weight of 46 kg. at about age 16 1/2 years, which is consistent with the existing data on age of menarche of a century and a half ago (Figure 9; Frisch 1972).

Another example of more rapid attainment of the critical weight is the earlier menarche of most obese girls (Donovan and van der Werff ten Bosch 1965; Zacharias, Wurtman, and Schatzoff 1970).

Conversely, a late menarche is associated with body weight growth that is slower prenatally, postnatally, or both, so that the critical weight is reached at a later age: malnutrition delays menarche (Dreizen, Spirakis, and Stone 1967; Frisch and Revelle 1969a); altitude delays menarche (Valšik, Študovský, and Bernátová 1963; Valšik 1965; although the estimate of three months per 100 meters must be an error; per 1,000 meters is reasonable); and twins have later menarche than singletons of the same population (Tisserand-Perrier 1953).

In the case of undernourishment, the mean weight at menarche of control girls and undernourished Alabama girls did not differ, although the mean age of menarche of the underfed girls was two years later, and the latter were significantly taller than the controls (Frisch 1972; Figure 10).

In the self-inflicted starvation of anorexia nervosa, anorexic girls, whose weight is restored to that normal for their height, resume menstrual cycles while those who remain critically underweight do not (Crisp

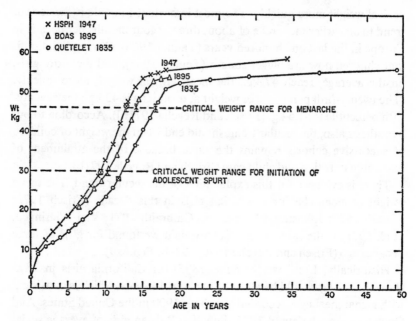

Figure 9.   Weight growth with age of Belgian girls in 1835 (drawn from data of
Quetelet 1869: 87); and United States girls in 1895 (drawn from data of Boas
1895: 402) and during 1930–1950, average year of menarche 1947 (drawn from data
of Reed and Stuart 1959: 904), showing age of attainment of the critical weight
range, ⨯̇, at menarche and at the initiation of the adolescent growth spurt,
⊗   computed mean ± standard error, from Frisch and Revelle (1971a, 1971b).
⊠   "Avant la puberté" (before puberty, which seems to mean the time of appearance of secondary sex characters and the initiation of the growth spurt
(Quetelet 1869: 90). Reprinted from Frisch (1972) with kind permission of the
editor of *Pediatrics* and the American Academy of Pediatrics.

and Stonehill 1971).

   Similarly, the effects of altitude caused the well-nourished, upper
middle-class girls of the CRC Denver (altitude 5,280 feet) study to attain
menarche at the same mean weight as the comparable California (BGS)
sea level subjects, but at a later age; the birth weights of the Denver girls
were significantly lighter than those of the California girls, and the
Denver girls grew more slowly up to the time of initiation of the adolescent spurt (Frisch and Revelle 1971a, 1971b).

   We have also proposed (Frisch and Revelle 1971a) that the initiation
of the adolescent growth spurt may be triggered by a critical weight,
which causes a change in metabolic rate, at which level the hypothalamus
stimulates the pituitary to increase output of adrenocorticotrophic hor-

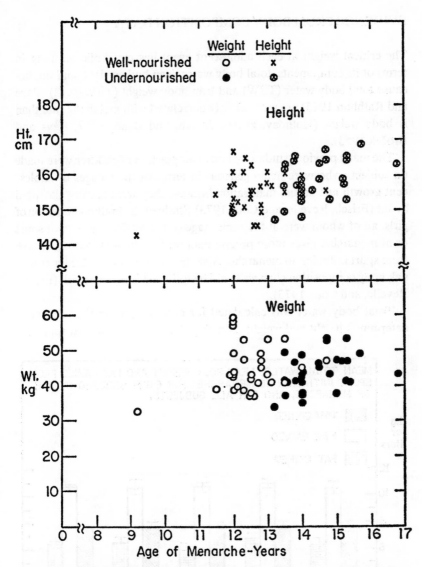

Figure 10. Heights and weights at menarche versus age of menarche of thirty well-nourished and thirty undernourished girls of the same ethnic stock. Reprinted from Frisch (1972) with kind permission of the editor of *Pediatrics* and the American Academy of Pediatrics.

mone (ACTH) and/or growth hormone. Or, the change to a new metabolic rate may remove an inhibition so that there is increased androgen production, which in turn stimulates the hypothalamus-pituitary axis to increased growth hormone output (Martin, Clark, and Connor 1968).

EVIDENCE FROM BODY COMPOSITION DATA

The critical weight at each adolescent event has metabolic meaning in terms of its components, total body water, lean body weight, and fat, because total body water (TBW) and lean body weight (TBW/0.72) (Pace and Rathbun 1945) are more closely correlated with metabolic rate than is body weight (Holliday, Potter, Jarrah, and Bearg 1967; Keys and Brožek 1953).

The many previous studies on body composition of children were made on subjects who were heterogeneous in terms of their stages of adolescent growth and sexual maturation because they were usually classified by age (Frisch, Revelle, and Cook 1973). Study of the body composition of girls, all of whom were at the same stage of the adolescent growth spurt or at menarche, gives more precise data on the changes that take place from spurt initiation to menarche. Also, because the data were longitudinal, body composition changes could be followed in the same girls (Frisch, Revelle, and Cook 1973).

Total body water was calculated for each girl, using the previously determined height and weight of each girl at menarche and at spurt ini-

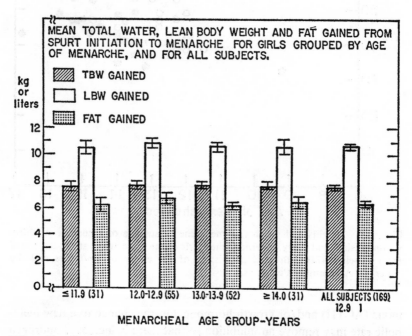

Figure 11. Comparison of mean (± standard error) total body water calculated by the equation of Mellits and Cheek (1970) and by that of Moore, et al. (1963) for CRC, BGS, and HSPH girls grouped by age of menarche, and for all subjects.

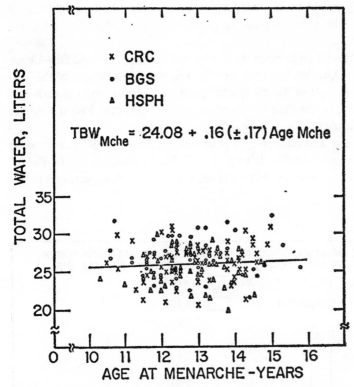

Figure 12. Total body water (TBW) versus age menarche on the same scale as Figure 7, and for the same CRC, BGS, and HSPH girls. Slope of the regression line of total body water on age of menarche does not differ significantly from zero. Reprinted with permission from Frisch, Revelle, and Cook (1973).

tiation (Frisch and Revelle 1970, 1971a, 1971b) in the regression equation of Mellits and Cheek (1970) from deuterium oxide measurements:

1. TBW = -10.313 + 0.252 (Wt.$_{kg}$) and 0.154 (Ht.$_{cm}$), when height ⩾110.8 cm.

and also, for comparison, at menarche, by the equation of Moore et al. (1963) from deuterium oxide measurements:

2. TBW = 11.63 + 0.318 (Body Wt.) (kg.)

The total body water at menarche for all subjects calculated by equations 1. and 2. were comparable, 26.2 ± 0.18 (S.D. 2.4) liters, and 26.8 ± 0.16 (S.D. 2.2) liters respectively (Figure 11).

Total body water calculated by either equation does not change significantly with increasing age of menarche (Figure 12), and the variability is 36 percent less than that of weight at menarche (Figure 12). Because lean body weight is calculated by TBW/0.72, lean body weight also is invariant with increasing age of menarche (Frisch, Revelle, and Cook 1972, 1973).

All further results given here were calculated by the Mellits-Cheek equation (1), which was preferred because the range of ages of the subjects covered all of the adolescent spurt and because the use of height and weight, rather than weight alone, usually gives the lowest variance (Friis-Hansen 1956).

The mean lean body weight at menarche, 36.3 ± 0.3 kg., and mean fat at menarche, 11.5 ± 0.3 kg., are similar to those plotted by Forbes (1972) and Forbes and Hursh (1963) at ages 12.5–13 years from K[40] counting.

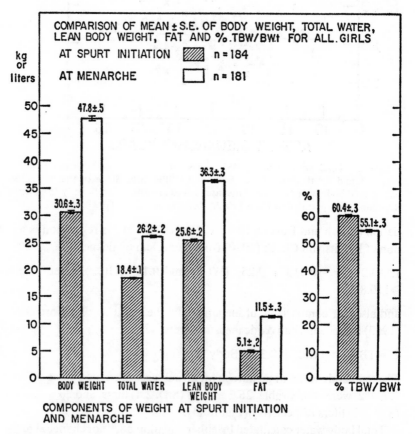

Figure 13.   Components of weight at initiation of the adolescent growth spurt and at menarche: mean (± standard error) of body weight, total body water, lean body weight, fat, and total body water as percent of body weight (TBW/BWt).

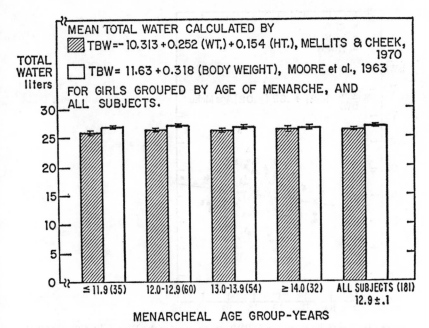

Figure 14. Mean total body water (TBW), lean body weight (LBW) and fat gained from initiation of the adolescent spurt to menarche for girls grouped by age of menarche, and for all subjects. Reprinted with permission from Frisch, Revelle, and Cook (1973).

Changes in Body Composition During the Adolescent Growth Spurt

Late maturing girls (those with menarche after the mean age of 12.9 ± 0.1 years) grow more slowly than early maturing girls (those with menarche before the mean age) during the adolescent growth spurt, including the year of menarche (Figures 1, 2; Frisch and Revelle 1970, 1971b). However, even though they grow at different rates, early and late maturers gain the same amount of weight, about 17 kg., from initiation of the spurt to menarche, and the components of this weight gain are also the same for early and late maturers: about 8 liters of body water, 11 kg. of lean body weight, and 6 kg. of fat (Figures 13, 14). Thus both groups increase lean body weight by 44 percent and fat by 120 percent from spurt initiation to menarche, resulting in a change of ratio of lean body weight to fat from 5 : 1 at spurt initiation to 3 : 1 at menarche (Frisch, Revelle, and Cook 1972, 1973).

A fall in metabolic rate/kg. body weight (BMR/kg.) would be expected from this change in body composition, particularly from the

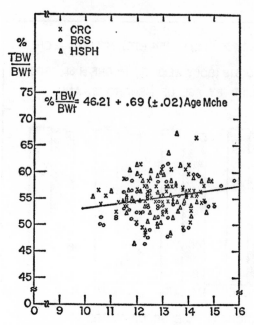

Figure 15. Total body water (TBW) as percent of body weight (BWt) (TBW/
BWt%) versus age of menarche for CRC, BGS, and HSPH girls. Reprinted with
permission from Frisch, Revelle, and Cook 1973.

change due to the large increase in fat, because the internal organs, which
contribute the most heat to the basal metabolism (Brožek and Grande
1955; Holliday 1971; Holliday, et al. 1967), make up a smaller proportion of the body weight (Holliday 1971; Holliday, et al. 1967). In fact,
the BMR/kg. by Talbot's standards (1938) is 35 cal./kg. per day at the
mean weight (30 kg.) of initiation of the adolescent spurt in girls (Frisch
and Revelle 1971a), and the BMR/kg. is 28 cal./kg. per day at the mean
weight (47 kg.) of menarche (Frisch and Revelle 1970, 1971b). This decrease of BMR/kg. as body weight and fat content increases "has the
biological advantage of diminishing heat production as the surface to
volume ratio decreases" (Holliday, et al. 1967).

An alternative explanation for the fall in metabolic rate/kg. is the
probability that adipose tissue is an important site of heat production
(Cahill 1962; Benedict 1938).

Total Body Water as Percent of Body Weight

Total body water as a percent of body weight is a more important index

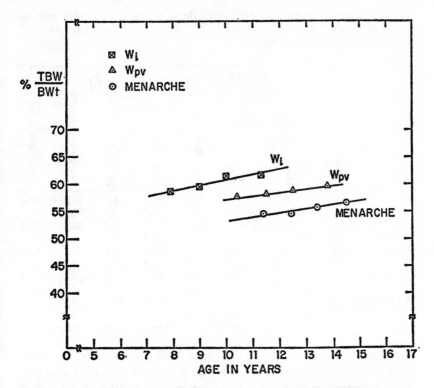

Figure 16. Total body water (TBW) as percent of body weight (BWt) versus age in years at each adolescent event, initiation of the spurt (W$_i$), peak velocity (W$_{pv}$) and menarche for CRC, BGS, and HSPH girls grouped by the age at which each girl attained each adolescent event. Early maturers are fatter, and thererefore have less total body water as percent of body weight, at each event.

than the absolute amount of total body water because it is an index of concentrations and body composition (Anderson 1963; Friis-Hansen 1956). Early maturers have a lower total body water/body weight percentage because they are fatter than late maturers (Friis-Hansen 1956; Frisch, Revelle, and Cook 1972, 1973); (Figures 15 and 16).

When girls are grouped by height at menarche (Table 3) rather than by age at menarche, the shortest, lightest girls and the tallest, heaviest girls differ in height by 20 cm. and in weight by 12 kg., but these two extreme groups have the same body composition; this is shown by the fact that their percentages of total body water/body weight are similar: 56.3 ± 0.5 percent and 55.3 ± 0.5 percent, respectively. Both these values are similar to the mean for all subjects, 55.1 ± 0.3 percent (Table 3).

Further, although the shortest, lightest girls at menarche have a smaller

Table 3.   Height, weight, total body water/body weight (TBW/BWT) percent, lean body weight (LBW), fat, fat/body weight percent, and ratio of LBW to fat of girls grouped by height at menarche

Height category (cm)	Number		Height (cm.)	Weight (kg.)	TBW/BWT %	LBW (kg.)	Fat (kg.)	Fat/body weight %	Ratio LBW to fat
					All ages of menarche				
≤152.0	25		147.8	40.2	56.3	31.4	8.9	21.8	3.5:1
		SD	3.6	3.5	2.4	1.7	2.0	3.3	
152.1–158.0	58		155.1	46.9	54.7	35.2	11.6	24.6	3.0:1
		SD	1.8	6.6	4.2	2.4	4.3	5.8	
158.1–164.0	64		161.0	49.5	54.8	37.5	12.1	23.8	3.1:1
		SD	1.5	6.0	3.7	2.2	3.8	4.6	
≥164.1	34		167.4	51.9	55.3	39.7	12.3	23.2	3.2:1
		SD	3.4	5.7	3.2	2.3	3.7	4.4	
All subjects	181		158.5	47.8	55.1	36.3	11.5	23.5	3.2:1
		SD	6.5	6.9	3.6	3.4	3.9	4.8	

absolute amount of fat, 8.9 ± 0.4 kg., compared to the tallest, heaviest girls, 12.3 ± 0.6 kg., (the mean for all subjects is 11.5 ± 0.3 kg.), in both extreme groups about 22 percent of their body weight is fat at menarche, as is true of all subjects (Table 3); and the ratio of lean body weight to fat in both groups is in the range of 3 : 1, as it is in all subjects (Table 3).

Thus, we found the variability of total body water as a percent of body weight at menarche is 55 percent less than that of weight at menarche (Figure 15).

PREDICTION OF MENARCHE

Quartiles of total body water/body weight percent are essentially quartiles of fatness. It is especially significant for our hypothesis — that a critical metabolic rate/kg.,associated with a critical body composition, is a signal for menarche — that 82 percent of the 169 girls who could be followed from spurt initiation to menarche, remained in the same quartiles of total body water/body weight percent from initiation to menarche; in comparison, only 47 percent remained in the same quartiles of weight, and only 39 percent remained in the same quartiles of total body water (Frisch, Revelle, and Cook 1973).

This finding yielded a method of predicting the age of menarche from the height and weight of a girl at ages 9, 10, 11, 12, and 13 years, and also of predicting the age of initiation of the adolescent growth spurt from the height and weight of a girl at age 8 years (Frisch 1974b).

Regression of age of menarche on height or weight within a quartile of total body water/body weight percent at each age gave the lowest significant standard error of estimate, lower even than when all subjects were combined at each age (Frisch 1974b).

Classification of the subjects by standard height or weight percentiles, or by weight for height percentiles, gave either worse standard error of estimates than classification by total body water/body weight or insignificant results.

The error of prediction by this method is less at all ages, in some quartiles by as much as 65 percent, than by prediction from stage of secondary sex characters (Marshall and Tanner 1969; Zacharias, Wurtman, and Schatzoff 1970), which have a quite variable association with menarche (Marshall and Tanner 1969). The time difference between actual and predicted age of menarche was six months or less for 59 percent of subjects at age 12, 53 percent at age 11, 48 percent at age 10, and 47 percent at age 9 (Frisch 1974b).

It would be useful to classify premenarcheal girls by predicted age of menarche in studies of the endocrinological and growth changes of adolescence. Girls having the same predicted age of menarche should be more homogeneous physiologically and endocrinologically than girls classified by chronological age, as Shock (1943) actually observed for the physiological criteria of oxygen consumption, pulse rate, and blood pressure (Frisch 1974a, b).

Exceptional, Early Maturing Girls

At each age from 9 to 12 years, prediction of age of menarche is better for the heavier girls, who are found in the lowest total body water/body weight quartiles, Q_1 and Q_2 (inversely to the weight quartiles), than for the lighter weight girls (total body water/body weight quartiles 3 and 4). This is because of the exceptional group of early maturing girls (18 percent of early maturers, 9.5 percent of all subjects), who are very short and LIGHTWEIGHT at menarche (mean height 147.8 ± 0.7 centimeters; mean weight 40.9 ± 0.8 kilograms; Table 4; Frisch 1974a, b).

Normally at menarche, the short girls have more weight for their

Table 4.   Weight (mean ± S.E.) at various heights (mean ± S.E.) with increasing age of menarche, and at all ages of menarche. (Categories of height are by rounded standard deviation (6 cm.) from the rounded mean, 158 cm.)

Height category (cm.)	Menarche ≤ 12.9 years		
	No.	Height (cm.)	Weight (kg.)
≤152.0	17	148.6 ± 0.56	40.9 ± 0.84
152.1–158.0	32	155.2 ± 0.32	48.5 ± 1.2
158.1–164.0	37	161.2 ± 0.24	50.6 ± 0.96
≥164.1	9	165.9 ± 0.64	53.4 ± 2.2
All subjects	95	157.4 ± 0.57	48.4 ± 0.71

	Menarche ≥ 13.0 years		
	No.	Height (cm.)	Weight (kg.)
≤152.0	8	146.0 ± 1.8	38.8 ± 1.1
152.1–158.0	26	155.1 ± 0.37	44.8 ± 1.2
158.1–164.0	27	160.7 ± 0.30	48.0 ± 1.2
≥164.1	25	167.9 ± 0.74	51.4 ± 1.1
All subjects	86	159.7 ± 0.78	47.2 ± 0.72

	All ages of menarche		
	No.	Height (cm.)	Weight (kg.)
≤152.0	25	147.8 ± 0.72	40.2 ± 0.69 [a]
152.1–158.0	58	155.1 ± 0.24	46.9 ± 0.87
158.1–164.0	64	161.0 ± 0.19	49.5 ± 0.75
≥164.1	34	167.4 ± 0.59	51.9 ± 0.98 [a]
All subjects	181	158.5 ± 0.48	47.8 ± 0.51

[a]   Differs from mean for all subjects at $P < .01$.

height than do tall girls (Frisch and Revelle 1970, 1971b). Interestingly, however, the fat percentage, 22 percent, of these short, light, early maturing girls at menarche is similar to the fat percentage, 24 percent, found for all subjects at menarche.

The small number of SHORT, LIGHT, LATE maturers (9.3 percent of late maturers, 4.4 percent of all subjects) is also exceptional because late maturers at menarche are usually taller than early maturers (Frisch and Revelle 1970, 1971b). These short, late maturers also have a calculated fat content of about 21 percent of body weight at menarche.

These two exceptional groups of girls may differ genetically in the set point of the hypothalamus pituitary-thyroid regulatory system (Reichlin, et al. 1972), resulting in the normal lean body weight to fat ratio found at menarche and, therefore, the same metabolic rate/kg., but attained at lower weights and heights than are average for the population. The data of Osler and Crawford (1973) on weights at menarche of ambulatory and bedridden patients support this explanation (Frisch, 1974b).

Comparison of the growth and body composition of the short, light, late maturing girls with wild type breeds of animals (Pálsson 1955) suggests that these females may represent the "wild type" primitive female. These slow-growing, smaller individuals would have greater survival ability in times of fluctuating food supply (Pálsson 1955).

Fat Deposition During the Adolescent Growth Spurt and a Hypothetical Scheme for the Synchronization of Body Weight and Menarche

The finding that the prediction of menarche is best when a premenarcheal girl is classified by her total body water/body weight percent, a good indicator of fatness, supports the idea that the relative degree of fatness (in the range of 20–25 percent of body weight) plays a role in determining sexual maturation (Frisch 1974a).

Another finding about body fat during the adolescent spurt is of special interest in considering hypothetical mechanisms for the onset of menarche. Fat increases linearly with increasing lean body weight for all subjects at menarche and at spurt initiation, but at both events fat increases at a slower rate with increasing lean body weight in late maturers than in early maturers (Figure 17). This explains why late maturers have less fat on the average at each event than do early maturers, although they do not differ in lean body weight (Frisch, Revelle, and Cook 1972, 1973). Widdowson and McCance (1960) observed this difference in fat gain between fast and slow growing rats, and it is also found in early and late maturing domestic sheep, pigs, and cattle (Pálsson 1955).

The difference in fat deposition between early and late maturers could be a determinant of early and late maturation. One possibility is that the storage of estrogen in fat depots affects blood levels of estrogen, and/or other steroids, or their secretion rates. Brown and Strong (1965) found differences in estrogen production and metabolism to be a function of body weight, and hence, fat; they suggest that estrogen metabolism may be influenced by factors involved in fat metabolism, including thyroid hormones. A third possibility, which does not exclude the others, is that fat concentration is important in regulating energy balance by the hypothalamus (Hervey 1969, 1971; Kennedy 1953), and thus determines the setting of the gonadostat, which determines the output of gonadotrophins and, therefore, estrogen.

If the number of cells of the adipose tissue in human beings is determined by early nutritional experiences (Hirsch and Knittle 1970) as it is in the rat (Knittle and Hirsch 1968; Knittle 1971, 1972), and if there is an interaction between adipose tissue and gonadal hormones, or meta-

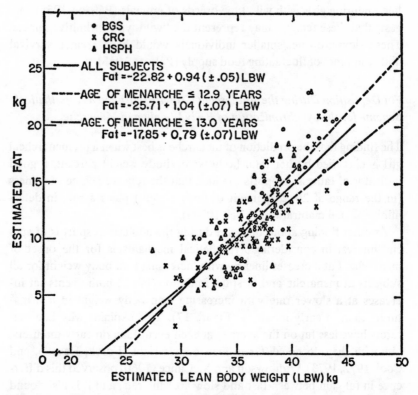

Figure 17.   Fat versus lean body weight (LBW) at menarche for CRC, BGS, and HSPH girls. The slope of the regression line of fat on LBW for early maturers is significantly greater (P < .01) than that of the late maturers. Reprinted with permission from Frisch, Revelle, and Cook (1973).

bolic rate, or both, then early or late maturation might be determined by differences in fat depots established very early (Frisch 1974a).

A hypothetical scheme of the synchronization of body weight and sexual maturation beginning at birth — in very bare outline — could then be as follows: *Weight at birth*, which is determined by the prepregnancy weight of the mother and, also, by her weight gain during pregnancy (Eastman and Jackson 1968), and *food intake of the infant after birth*, determines (1) *the body weight at the time of the deceleration of weight growth*, which is before, or about, age two years in human beings (Figures 1–3). This body weight determines *the level of the hypothalamic restraint on food intake* and the accompanying *onset of lipostatic control*, which determine, at the same age, *the rate of food intake*, which determines (2) *the rate of growth* (Kennedy 1953, 1957, 1969; Kennedy and Mitra 1963; Widdowson and McCance 1960) and (3) the number and size of the adipose cells at about age two years. The rate of growth and size of the adipose tissue would affect the metabolic rate per kilogram body weight (Frisch 1974a).

Rapid growers are fatter than slow growers, and therefore attain the first critical metabolic rate/kg., which triggers the initiation of the adolescent growth spurt, at an earlier age than do the slower growers. The childhood acceleration in weight (Figure 2) at the average ages of 5–7 years may contribute to the attainment of the critical metabolic rate. At this time, or perhaps after rapid growth is initiated (simultaneously or somewhat later), there is a change in sensitivity of the hypothalamus to estrogen; it becomes less sensitive, requiring a higher setting of the gonadostat (Kennedy and Mitra 1963).

The amount of height and weight gained during the adolescent spurt

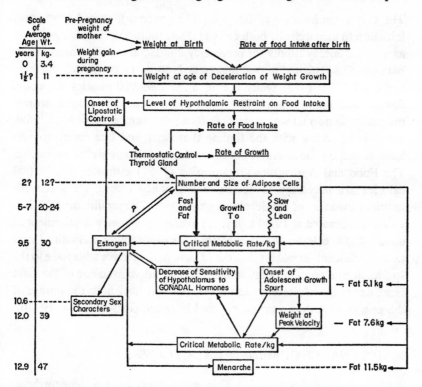

HYPOTHETICAL SCHEME OF THE RELATION BETWEEN BODY WEIGHT, SIZE OF ADIPOSE TISSUE, AND ONSET OF PUBERTY IN CAUCASIAN GIRLS.

Figure 18. Hypothetical scheme for the synchronization of body weight, size of adipose tissue, and sexual maturation in Caucasian girls. Reprinted with permission from Frisch (1974a) in the *Control of the onset of puberty*, edited by M. Grumbach, G. Grave, and F. Mayer. New York: Wiley.

seems to be invariant to rates of growth and independent of previous growth (Frisch and Revelle 1971b). The second critical metabolic size (which may be at two stages — at peak velocity, which almost always precedes menarche, and at menarche) is a signal for a further decrease in sensitivity of the hypothalamus to estrogen, and gonadotrophin levels rise high enough for the ovarian and uterine changes that result in menarche. A positive hypothalmic-estrogen feedback (Kulin, Grumbach, and Kaplan 1972) may be initiated at peak velocity (Figure 18; Frisch 1974a).

Significance of the Storage of Energy During the Adolescent Growth Spurt

The very large increase of fat, 6 kg. (120 percent), gained from spurt initiation to menarche by both early and late maturing girls, is significant as a stored energy supply for pregnancy and lactation. The mean fat for both early and late maturers at menarche is about 11 kg. (Frisch, Revelle, and Cook 1972, 1973), which is equivalent to 99,000 calories. Emerson, Saxena, and Poindexter (1972) found that the caloric cost of a normal pregnancy in normal women is 27,000 calories, regardless of body build, which is in accord with the finding that early and late maturing girls have stored on the average, the same amount of energy by menarche. The Food and Agriculture Organization (1957) estimates that 80,000 calories are necessary to sustain a pregnancy among the less well-nourished women of the developing countries. The requirement for lactation is estimated at 1,000 a day. An average pregnancy requirement of about 50,000 calories would, therefore, allow for about a month's lactation. Adolescent female fat thus could have had selective advantage to the species during times of unfavorable food conditions, and one of the main functions of the adolescent spurt in females may have been the storage of this energy to sustain a pregnancy and lactation (Frisch 1974a, 1974b).

MAINTENANCE OF MENSTRUAL CYCLES

Study of the weights at which girls and women become amenorrheic, and the weights at which they resumed cycles, supports the idea that a stored energy depot is necessary for the maintenance of menstrual cycles and reproductive ability (Frisch and McArthur 1974). By the time height growth is normally completed for all girls, at ages 16–18 years, and weight growth has slowed markedly, about 16 kg. of fat have been stored;

this is equivalent to 144,000 calories. This energy supply would be sufficient to sustain a pregnancy and three months lactation (Frisch and McArthur 1974).

These findings suggest that women who live on marginal diets would have irregular periods and be less fertile, as has been observed (Solien de González 1964), and that poorly nourished lactating women would not resume menstrual cycles as early after parturition as well-nourished women, as also has been observed (Solien de González 1964).

Significance of the Weight Dependency of Sexual Maturation

Irrespective of any causal relationship, the weight dependency of menarche in human beings, as in animals (Monteiro and Falconer 1966; Kennedy 1969), operates as a "compensatory mechanism" for both environmental and genetic variation. The result is a reduction in the variability of body size at sexual maturity, and therefore a reduction in the variability of adult body size. As in many other animals, human body size at sexual maturity is close to adult size (Donovan and van der Werff ten Bosch 1965); weight and height at menarche are 85 percent and 96 percent of adult weight and height, respectively (Frisch and Revelle 1971b).

An example of compensation for poor nutrition is the significantly later age of menarche of undernourished girls compared to controls (Frisch 1972). An example of compensation for genetic variation is the longer time interval of the adolescent growth spurt of normal, slow growing, late maturers (Figure 2), compared to the more rapid advancement from initiation to menarche of the early maturers (Figure 1; Frisch and Revelle 1970, 1971b; Shuttleworth 1937).

Boas noted that the "tempo of growth" was inherited (1935). Thus the well-established genetic component of variation in age of menarche (Tanner 1960) may be in part through the genetic control of growth rate. Tanner (1960) notes that age of menarche is a very convenient measure of "tempo of growth," which is to be expected from the association of menarche with a particular weight, representing a particular body composition.

Different racial groups have different critical weights (Frisch 1972; Frisch and Revelle 1969a; Frisch, Revelle, and Cook 1971). The inheritance of the absolute value of a critical menarcheal weight, independently of tempo of growth, could also be a component of the genetic control of age of menarche (Frisch 1972).

Finally, with or without causality, the regulation of human female size at sexual maturity by the weight dependency of menarche has obvious selective advantages for the species because birth weight is correlated with the prepregnancy weight of the mother (Eastman and Jackson 1968); infant survival is correlated with birth weight (Baird 1945; Douglas 1951; World Health Organization 1961); and low birth weight, particularly at term, is associated with a greater incidence of neurological and physical handicaps (Frisch 1971).

Other Modulating Influences on Sexual Maturation

These observations on body weight do not exclude the possible modulating influences on sexual maturation of other factors for man, or anials, such as light, stress, pheromones (Donovan 1972), or, as was suggested in 1844, sweet music. The latter influence was tested in an admirably direct experiment, recounted by Dr. M. A. Raciborski (1844), Laureate of the Royal Academy of Medicine in Paris in 1844. An orchestra was brought to the elephant cage in the Jardin des Plantes, and there the distinguished musicians played sweet music, including the dance in B minor from Gluck's "Iphigénie en Tauride." The emotional reaction of the two elephants, Hanz and Parkie, to each musical selection was carefully noted: "O ma tendre musette," played solo on the bassoon, moved Parkie to "Les transports les plus passionnés"; Hanz, indifferent to bassoons, was finally overcome by an overture to "Nina," played solo on the clarinet. The experimental results were positive; the elephants matured in 16 to 17 years instead of the normal time of 25 years. An alternative explanation is that elephants in zoos are probably better fed and move around less than those in the wild (Frisch 1973).

FUTURE RESEARCH

It would be interesting to know:
1.   the critical weights of different races and populations, and what percentage they are of adult size;
2.   whether the critical weight of other races, or populations, represents the same body composition of lean body weight to fat as that found in Caucasian North American girls, even though absolute values of these components are different because of differences in adult size (Frisch and Revelle 1969a); and
3.   the relative frequency in different populations of the two special groups at menarche; short, light, early maturers and short, light, late

maturers, the latter most probably representing the primeval type. The routine recording of age of menarche, when height and weight are being followed for girls with abnormally slow or rapid growth, as well as for normal girls, and the recording of the height and weight at menarche, when possible, would provide useful data for investigation of the mechanisms controlling sexual maturation in girls.

REFERENCES

ANDERSON, E. C.
1963   Three component body composition analysis based on potassium and water determinations. *Annals of the New York Academy of Science* 110:189–212.

BAIRD, D.
1945   The influence of social and economic factors on still births and neonatal deaths. *Journal of Obstetrics and Gynaecology of the British Empire* 52:339.

BARNETT, S. A., E. M. COLEMAN
1959   Effect of low environmental temperature on the reproductive cycle of female mice. *Endocrinology* 19:232–240.

BENEDICT, F. G.
1938   *Vital energetics*. Washington, D.C.: Carnegie Institute.

BOAS, F.
1895   The growth of first-born children. *Science*, n.s. 1:402–404.
1935   The tempo of growth of fraternities. *Proceedings of the National Academy of Science* 21:413.

BROWN, J. B., J. A. STRONG
1965   The effect of nutritional status and thyroid function on the metabolism of oestradiol. *Endocrinology* 32:107–115.

BROŽEK, J., F. GRANDE
1955   Body composition and basal metabolism in man: correlation analysis versus physiological approach. *Human Biology* 27:22–31.

BULLOUGH, W. S.
1951   *Vertebrate sexual cycles*. London: Methuen. (Cited in Kennedy and Mitra 1963.)

CAHILL, G. F., JR.
1962   "Adipose tissue metabolism," in *Fat as a tissue*. Edited by K. and B. Issekutz. New York: McGraw-Hill.

CRICHTON, J. A., J. N. AITKEN, A. W. BOYNE
1959   The effect of plane of nutrition during rearing on growth, production, reproduction and health of dairy cattle, I: Growth to 24 months. *Animal Production* 1:145–162.

CRISP, A. H., E. STONEHILL
1971   Relation between aspects of nutritional disturbance and menstrual activity in primary anorexia nervosa. *British Medical Journal* 3:149–151.

DICKERSON, J. W. T., G. A. GRESHAM, R. A. MCCANCE
1964   The effect of undernutrition and rehabilitation on the development of the reproductive organs: pigs. *Endocrinology* 29:111–
118.

DONOVAN, B. T.
1972   Neural control of puberty. *Journal of Psychosomatic Research*
16:267–270.

DONOVAN, B. T., J. J. VAN DER WERFF TEN BOSCH
1965   *Physiology of puberty.* London: E. Arnold.

DOUGLAS, J. H. B.
1951   Health and survival of infants in different social classes. *Lancet*
1:440.

DREIZEN, S., C. N. SPIRAKIS, R. E. STONE
1967   A comparison of skeletal growth and maturation in undernourished and well-nourished girls before and after menarche. *Journal
of Pediatrics* 70:256–263.

EASTMAN, N. J., E. JACKSON
1968   Weight relationships in pregnancy, I: The bearing of maternal
weight gain and pre-pregnancy weight on birth weight in full
term pregnancies. *Obstetrical and Gynecological Survey* 23:1003–
1025.

EMERSON, K., JR., B. N. SAXENA, E. L. POINDEXTER
1972   Caloric cost of normal pregnancy. *Obstetrics and Gynecology* 40:
786–794.

FOOD AND AGRICULTURE ORGANIZATION OF THE UNITED NATIONS (FAO)
1957   *Calorie requirements,* page 11. Rome.

FORBES, G. B.
1972   Growth of the lean body mass in man. *Growth* 36:325–337.

FORBES, G. B., J. B. HURSH
1963   Age and sex trends in lean body mass calculated from K^{40} measurements: with a note on the theoretical basis for the procedure.
Annals of the New York Academy of Science 110:255–263.

FRIIS-HANSEN, B. J.
1956   Changes in body water compartments during growth. *Acta Paediatrica, Supplement* 110:1–67.

FRISCH, R. E.
1971   Does malnutrition cause permanent mental retardation in human
beings? *Psychiatria Neurologia, Neurochirurgia* 74:463–479. (Reprinted 1972 in *Annual progress in child psychiatry and child
development.* Edited by S. Chess and A. Thomas. New York:
Brunner/Mazel, London: Butterworths.)
1972   Weight at menarche: similarity for well-nourished and undernourished girls at differing ages, and evidence for historical con-
stancy. *Pediatrics* 50(3):445–450.
1973   Influences on age of menarche. *Lancet* 1:1007.
1974a "The critical weight at menarche and the initiation of the adolescent growth spurt, and the control of puberty," in *The control of
the onset of puberty.* Edited by M. Grumbach, G. Grave, and F.
Mayer. New York: Wiley-Interscience.

1974b Age at menarche: a method of prediction from height and weight at ages 9 through 13 years. *Pediatrics* 53:384–390.

FRISCH, R. E., J. W. MC ARTHUR
1974 "Menstrual cycles: Fatness as a determinant of minimum weight necessary for their maintenance or onset." *Science* 185:949–951.

FRISCH, R. E., R. REVELLE
1969a Variation in body weights and the age of the adolescent growth spurt among Latin American and Asian populations in relation to calorie supplies. *Human Biology* 41:185–212.
1969b The height and weight of adolescent boys and girls at the time of peak velocity of growth in height and weight: longitudinal data. *Human Biology* 41:536–559.
1970 Height and weight at menarche and a hypothesis of critical body weights and adolescent events. *Science* 169:397–399.
1971a The height and weight of girls and boys at the time of initiation of the adolescent growth spurt in height and weight and the relationship to menarche. *Human Biology* 43(1):140–159.
1971b Height and weight at menarche and a hypothesis of menarche. *Archives of Disease in Childhood* 46(249):695–701.

FRISCH, R. E., R. REVELLE, S. COOK
1971 Height, weight and age at menarche and the "critical weight" hypothesis. *Science* 174:1148–1149.
1972 Components of the critical weight at menarche and at initiation of the adolescent spurt in girls: total water, lean body weight, and fat (Abstract). *Pediatric Research* 6:335.
1973 Components of the critical weight at menarche and at initiation of the adolescent spurt: estimated total water, lean body mass and fat. *Human Biology* 45:469–483.

HERVEY, G. R.
1969 Regulation of energy balance. *Nature* 222:629–631.
1971 Physiological mechanisms for the regulation of energy balance. *Proceedings of the Nutrition Society* 30:109–116.

HIRSCH, J., J. L. KNITTLE
1970 Cellularity of obese and nonobese human adipose tissue. *Federation Proceedings* 29:1516–1521.

HOLLIDAY, M. A.
1971 Metabolic rate and organ size during growth from infancy to maturity and during late gestation and early infancy. *Pediatrics* 47(2):169–179.

HOLLIDAY, M. A., D. POTTER, A. JARRAH, S. BEARG
1967 The relation of metabolic rate to body weight and organ size. *Pediatric Research* 1:185–195.

JOHNSTON, F. E., R. M. MALINA, M. A. GALBRAITH
1971 Height, weight and age at menarche and the "critical weight" hypothesis. *Science* 174:1147–1148.

JOUBERT, D. M.
1963 Puberty in female farm animals. *Animal Breeding Abstracts* 31:295–305.

KENNEDY, G. C.
1953 The role of depot fat in the hypothalamic control of food intake in the rat. *Proceedings of the Royal Society of London*, series B, 140:578–592.
1957 The development with age of hypothalamic restraint upon the appetite of the rat. *Endocrinology* 16:9–17.
1969 Interactions between feeding behavior and hormones during growth. *Annals of the New York Academy of Science* 157:1049–1061.

KENNEDY, G. C., J. MITRA
1963 Body weight and food intake as initiating factors for puberty in the rat. *Journal of Physiology* 166:408–418.

KEYS, A., J. BROŽEK
1953 Body fat in adult man. *Physiological Reviews* 33:245–325.

KNITTLE, J. L.
1971 Childhood obesity. *Bulletin of the New York Academy of Medicine* 47:579–589.
1972 Maternal diet as a factor in adipose tissue cellularity and metabolism in the young rat. *Nutrition* 102:427–434.

KNITTLE, J. L., J. HIRSCH
1968 Effect of early nutrition on the development of rat epididymal fat pads: cellularity and metabolism. *Journal of Clinical Investigation* 47:2091–2098.

KULIN, H. E., M. M. GRUMBACH, S. L. KAPLAN
1969 Changing sensitivity of the pubertal gonadal hypothalamic feedback mechanism in man. *Science* 166:1012–1013.
1972 Gonadal-hypothalamic interaction in prepubertal and pubertal man: effect of clomiphene citrate on urinary follicle-stimulating hormone and luteinizing hormone and plasma testosterone. *Pediatric Research* 6:162–171.

MARESH, M. M.
1972 A forty-five year investigation for secular changes in physical maturation. *American Journal of Physical Anthropology* 36:103–109.

MARSHALL, W. A., J. M. TANNER
1969 Variations in pattern of pubertal changes in girls. *Archives of Disease in Childhood* 44:291–303.

MARTIN, L., J. W. CLARK, T. CONNOR
1968 Growth hormone secretion enhanced by androgens. *Journal of Clinical Endocrinology and Metabolism* 28:425–428.

MC CAMMON, R. W.
1970 *Human growth and development.* Springfield, Illinois: Charles C. Thomas.

MC CANCE, R. A.
1962 Food, growth and time. *Lancet* 2:671–675.

MELLITS, E. D., D. B. CHEEK
1970 The assessment of body water and fatness from infancy to childhood. *Monographs of the Society for Research in Child Development* 35:12–26.

MONTEIRO, L. S., D. S. FALCONER
1966 Compensatory growth and sexual maturity in mice. *Animal Production* 8(2):179–192.

MOORE, F. K., K. H. OLESEN, J. D. MC MURREY, H. V. PARKER, M. R. BALL, C. M. BOYDEN
1963 *The body cell mass and its supporting environment.* Philadelphia: W. B. Saunders

OSLER, D., J. CRAWFORD
1973 Examination of the hypothesis of a critical weight at menarche in ambulatory and bed-ridden mentally retarded girls. *Pediatrics* 51: 675–679.

PACE, N., E. N. RATHBUN
1945 Studies on body composition, III: The body water and chemically combined nitrogen content in relation to fat content. *Journal of Biological Chemistry* 158:685–691.

PÁLSSON, H.
1955 "Conformation and body composition," in *Progress in the physiology of farm animals,* volume two. Edited by J. Hammond. London: Butterworths Scientific Publications.

QUETELET, A.
1869 *Physique sociale,* volume two. St. Petersburg: Issakoff.

RACIBORSKI, M. A.
1844 *De la puberté et de l'âge critique chez la femme.* Paris: Baillière.

REED, R. B., H. C. STUART
1959 Patterns of growth in height and weight from birth to 18 years of age. *Pediatrics* 24(2):904–909.

REICHLIN, S., J. B. MARTIN, M. A. MITNICK, R. L. BOSHANS, Y. GRIMM, J. BALLINGER, J. GORDON, J. MALACARA
1972 The hypothalamus in pituitary-thyroid regulation. *Recent Progress in Hormone Research* 28:229–286.

SHOCK, N. W.
1943 The effect of menarche on basal physiological functions in girls. *American Journal of Physiology* 139:288–292.

SHUTTLEWORTH, F.
1937 *Sexual maturation and the physical growth of girls age 6 to 19.* Monographs of the Society for Research in Child Development 2(5).

SOLIEN DE GONZALEZ, N.
1964 Lactation and pregnancy: a hypothesis. *American Anthropologist* 68:873–878.

STUART, H. C., R. B. REED, *et al.*
1959 Child health and development (Longitudinal studies). *Pediatrics* 24:875–878.

TALBOT, F. B.
1938 Basal metabolism standards for children. *American Journal of Diseases of Children* 55:455–459.

TANNER, J. M.
1960 "Genetics of human growth," in: *Human growth,* volume three. Edited by J. M. Tanner, 43–58. London: Pergamon Press.

1962   *Growth at adolescence* (second edition). Oxford: Blackwell Scientific Publications.
1966   The secular trend towards earlier physical maturation. *Tijdschrift voor Sociale Geneeskunde* 44:524–539.

TISSERAND-PERRIER, M.
1953   Étude comparative de certains processus de croissance chez les jumeaux. *Journal de Génétique Humaine* 2:87–102.

TUDDENHAM, R. D., M. M. SNYDER
1954   Physical growth of California boys and girls from birth to eighteen years. *University of California Publications in Child Development* 1(2):183–364.

VALŠIK, J. A.
1965   The seasonal rhythm of menarche: a review. *Human Biology* 37: 75–90.

VALŠIK, J. A., P. ŠTUKOVSKÝ, L. BERNÁTOVÁ
1963   Quelques facteurs géographiques et sociaux ayant une influence sur l'âge de la puberté. *Biotypologie* 24:109–123.

VAN WAGENEN, G.
1949   Accelerated growth with sexual precocity in female monkeys receiving testosterone propionate. *Endocrinology* 45:544–546.

VAN WIERINGEN, J. C., F. WAFELBAKKER, H. P. VERBRUGGE, J. H. DE HAAS
1971   *Growth Diagrams 1965, Netherlands.* Groningen: Wolters-Noordhoff.

WIDDOWSON, E. M., W. O. MAVOR, R. A. MCCANCE
1964   The effect of undernutrition and rehabilitation on the development of the reproductive organs: rats. *Journal of Endocrinology* 29:119–126.

WIDDOWSON, E. M., W. O. MAVOR, R. A. MC CANCE
1960   Some effects of accelerating growth, I: General somatic development. *Proceedings of the Royal Society*, series B, 152:188–206.

WORLD HEALTH ORGANIZATION (WHO)
1961   *Public health aspects of low birth weight.* Technical Report Service. Geneva.

ZACHARIAS, L., R. WURTMAN, M. SCHATZOFF
1970   Sexual maturation in contemporary American girls. *American Journal of Obstetrics and Gynecology* 108:833–846.

Physical Growth and the Social Environment: A West African Example

D. K. FIAWOO

The hypothesis that Euro-American children have better growth performance than their African counterparts and that such a difference is due primarily to nutrition is no longer new to educators and clinicians in Africa. The few scattered investigations on the continent seem to prove the hypothesis.[1] But beyond this, we know very little about the physical growth patterns of the African child. Only a few figures, even of heights and weights, can be found in the published literature that go beyond the formative period. We need to know what local factors promote and retard growth. The specific objectives of this paper are as follows:

1. to give figures on heights and weights of Ghanaian children;
2. to examine the relative growth patterns of boys and girls; and
3. to compare the heights and weights of children from different environmental situations in Ghana.

METHODS

The height and weight measurements of 4,585 primary-middle school children and 715 Achimota (secondary) school students were collected between 1966 and 1968. The children, wearing uniforms but without

[1] See the references, especially Waddy (1956), Deane and Geber (1964), and Welbourne (1951). The only published material on height and weight growth in Ghana comes from Waddy's survey of children from the Northern Territories. Although the sample is quite large, the limited age range of six to twelve for boys and girls tends to hamper analysis in terms of the development cycles and the relative growth of boys and girls.

shoes, were measured with the help of trained undergraduates of the Department of Sociology of the University of Ghana at Legon. Data were regrouped into bivariate frequency tables and analysis was by the regression technique.[2]

By far the most important factor in the analysis of heights and weights of African children is the problem of accuracy of age. Exact age was calculated for each child from the date of birth and the date of measurement. Unusual care was taken to ensure accuracy. The schedules for the measurements required details of information on age, including evidence of age. Such evidence included inspection of birth certificates, school records and the interviewing of teachers and of parents where necessary. In the villages where recorded ages were few, all the available techniques were used in the assessment of age.

Subjects and their Social Evironment

Five groups of Ghanaian children, plus a small sample of expatriate non-African children, representing different social environments in Ghana were selected for study. With the exception of the international schools, all the Ghanaian children in the selected schools were weighed and measured. Of the former, only half the total number in school were randomly selected.

a.   Achimota school students: This was the only group of secondary school students. Measurements were taken by the medical department of the school.[3] Included in this sample were 227 girls and 488 boys.

Very high standards of secondary school education obtain in the country generally; nevertheless, Achimota School, founded in 1925, has since its foundation enjoyed the reputation of an elite school. Being a residential school with a tradition of good discipline, it was expected that the students would have more than average growth performance.

b.   "Privileged" urban children: These were Ghanaian children attending various expensive international schools at Accra during the period of this study. They included the Accra International School at the Cantonments, Christ the King and the Ridge Church School. These are highly rated schools and very much in demand among the elite Ghanaian families. They are mostly operated by expatriates and the large

[2]   The author is grateful to Dr. Kpedekpo of the Institute of Statistics, Legon, for statistical advice.
[3]   I am grateful to the headmaster and the medical officer-in-charge for their permission to analyze these data and to incorporate them in this study.

majority of teachers are expatriate graduates or holders of high professional certificates.

The results of their Common Entrance Examination[4] from year to year, and their high standard of discipline are said to justify the exorbitant fees paid. The children who patronize these schools tend to come from relatively wealthy or highly educated Ghanaian homes. Included in this sample were 223 girls and 213 boys.

c. Other urban children: These children were drawn from various government and City Council primary-middle schools in the heart of Accra. Their parents live at Accra and the children enjoy the amenities of West African urban life. There were 735 girls and 756 boys in this group.

d. Suburban children: Like the group above, these children were attending various government-approved primary-middle schools, but at the outskirts of Accra, or in suburban areas. All the settlements featuring in this study were within a radius of five to ten miles from the heart of Accra and included Apenkwa, Anumle, Achimota (village) and Alogboshie on the Accra-Nsawam Road.

Large numbers of children attending these schools were drawn from nearby villages of Kisseihma and Christian's Village situated between Legon and Achimota. Apart from Anumle which represents a planned settlement,[5] all these are very primitive communities with the barest minimum of social amenities. The parents of the children are mostly wage earners who commute to Accra, Legon and Achimota School. Only a tiny fraction are full-time farmers. There were 408 girls and 593 boys in this sample.

e. Rural school children: These were attending various Local Authority and Mission Schools in the Tonu (Tongu) Lower Volta District. The selected villages included Tefle, Sogakofe, Sokpoe, Vume and Kpotame. All the villages lie on the main trunk road from Accra to Lome in the Togo Republic. The men are mostly farmers and fishermen; the women assist the men but are also petty traders in their own right (Fiawoo 1961). This group comprised 651 girls and 1,005 boys.

f. Expatriate children: This group was made up mostly of Euro-American children attending the same international schools as the privileged urban children discussed above. Their parents held key positions in international organizations, in government, education, commerce and the diplomatic fields. They included children of university

---

[4] This is an examination conducted by the West African Examinations Council for admission to approved secondary schools.
[5] Anumle represents the staff village of Achimota School.

professors and lecturers, and Syrian-Lebanese children whose parents were very successful traders in Ghana. The sample included 146 girls and 156 boys.

From these group characterizations, the following deductions were made:

1.   Families in the urban area are probably wealthier than those in the rural area and the suburbs.

2.   Urban parents who send their children to expensive international schools are probably better off economically than those who send their children to normal government schools.

If it is further postulated that the physical growth of the child is closely related to parental socioeconomic status, then the following hypotheses are relevant:

1.   Privileged urban children will grow taller and heavier than their normal counterparts in the city.

2.   Other urban children will have better growth performance than their rural and suburban counterparts.

RESULTS

Among 2,568 primary-middle-school boys aged between five and eighteen, there is a marked degree of correlation between age and height, the correlation coefficient being 0.99: the older the boy the taller he grows. The highest point of acceleration is at age fourteen to fifteen which falls within the Ghanaian pubertal age range of thirteen to fifteen.[6] At age eighteen boys are still growing; the mean is 65.6 inches and the range between 57 and 73 inches.

Among 2,017 primary-middle school girls there is almost perfect correlation between age and height ($r = 0.98$), the highest point of acceleration being at age ten to eleven. The curve rises sharply between ages ten and thirteen (see Figure 1). This is not different from the Euro-American pattern, where the highest point of acceleration for girls is between eleven and thirteen (Cole and Morgan 1961). At age fifteen growth declines appreciably and is hardly noticeable at seventeen to eighteen. The mean height at eighteen is 63.4 inches and the range is between fifty-nine and sixty-eight inches.

---

[6]   From various studies conducted at Accra and the Sogakofe district of the Volta Region (unpublished materials).

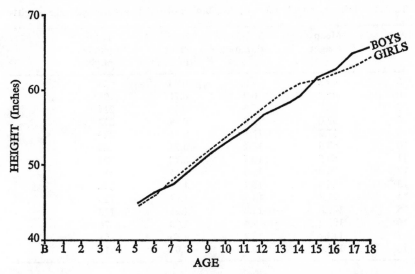

Figure 1.   Relative rates of growth of boys and girls in primary-middle schools

Table 1.   Primary-middle schools: distribution of weight according to age — boys

Age	Mean weight	Standard deviation	Standard error of mean	Total number of boys
5	43.4	3.3	0.63	27
6	43.6	5.1	0.50	104
7	46.0	7.1	0.46	242
8	50.9	7.4	0.47	248
9	55.7	8.4	0.52	261
10	61.0	10.5	0.69	235
11	64.8	8.4	0.57	220
12	71.7	10.4	0.71	214
13	76.3	11.9	0.82	214
14	81.1	10.2	0.72	198
15	92.6	15.0	1.05	203
16	97.9	16.7	1.28	169
17	109.0	15.7	1.32	142
18	114.8	14.4	1.51	91

Relationship between Age and Weight

In Table 1 are shown the features for weight for boys. There is a positive correlation between age and weight (r = 0.98). The highest point of acceleration is at age fourteen to fifteen — the same as for height. The annual gain remains significant at seventeen, and at eighteen the

Table 2. Primary-middle schools: distribution of weight according to age — girls

Age	Mean weight	Standard deviation	Standard error of mean	Total number of girls
5	44.8	4.5	0.90	25
6	45.2	6.9	0.71	95
7	48.0	5.3	0.36	215
8	52.0	9.8	0.59	272
9	57.2	11.1	0.71	243
10	63.5	12.1	0.74	268
11	69.5	10.5	0.70	224
12	78.0	15.4	1.25	151
13	86.6	15.1	1.25	146
14	91.8	13.5	1.22	123
15	100.8	13.2	1.25	113
16	108.2	9.4	1.08	76
17	113.4	13.2	1.86	51
18	117.4	8.0	2.07	15

boys are still growing. At eighteen the mean is 114.8 pounds and the range between 79 and 148 pounds. This wide range is probably suggestive of the varying socioeconomic groups of children featuring in this study.

The growth features for girls are expressed in Table 2. Once again, there is a marked degree of correlation between age and weight ($r = 0.99$). Except for age fourteen, the curve rises sharply between twelve and sixteen years. At eighteen the weight curve is still rising. There is no marked difference between growth in height and growth in weight for girls except that ages fourteen and fifteen (followed closely after age thirteen) stand out as the highest point of acceleration in weight growth, whereas in height, growth begins to decline at this age. This might suggest that growth in weight declines less rapidly than growth in height. The mean weight at eighteen years is 117.4 pounds and the range between 96 and 140 pounds.

Relative Rates of Development for Boys and Girls

Contrary to the Euro-American pattern, Ghanaian girls are heavier and taller than the boys for a considerable part of their growing period, including the elementary school years. In height, boys and girls are almost at par between the ages of five and six — the boys lead by only a tiny fraction of an inch. Between six and seven years the girls catch up with the boys and outdistance them at seven. They maintain the

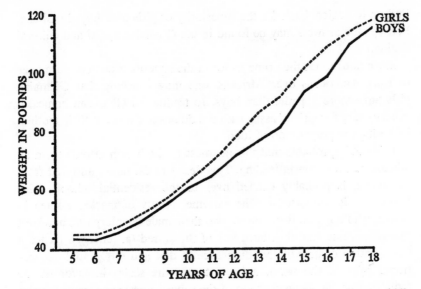

Figure 2.   Relative rates of weight increase of boys and girls in primary-middle schools

lead from seven until fourteen. The boys overtake them at fifteen and maintain the lead for the rest of adolescence.

In weight, the female superiority is even more striking; girls are heavier than boys throughout the growing period, i.e. from five to eighteen.

These represent significant departures from the Euro-American norms where the growth trend shows a tendency for boys to exceed girls in height and weight from birth through the preschool and elementary school years. The girls become physiologically mature two years sooner than boys and thus attain adolescence earlier. This has the effect of carrying them ahead of the boys between eleven and thirteen. By fifteen, however, the boys are back in the lead "when their greater and probably more sustained adolescent spurt begins to take effect" (Tanner 1967: 18). This male superiority is true of height and weight growth. It is significant that the Ghanaian expatriate group is parallel to the Euro-American standard in the relative growth of boys and girls. The Ghanaian rural, suburban and urban groups are well behind this standard.

While there is some physiological explanation for the superiority of girls over boys between preadolescence and early adolescence, there seems to be no such explanation for the overall superior growth performance of boys in the Euro-American pattern. Similarly, one can find no biological basis for the superiority of girls over boys in Ghana. Perhaps the answers may be found in the Ghanaian social and cultural setting.

Since nutrition is the prime factor in the superior growth performance of Euro-Americans over Africans, one may conclude that Ghanaian girls have more appetite than boys. In traditional Ghanaian homes, it is customary for girls to assist with the domestic chores of their mother, including the preparation of food.

It is not improbable that this nearness to the hearth affords them an advantage over boys in feeding. This desire to eat more, nurtured from the home, is probably carried over to the residential schools. This hypothesis is supported by the extreme obesity of market women in Accra, who apparently eat more than their male counterparts, but exert themselves less, and thus burn less of the stored fat (energy). Hence a combination of quantitative difference in diet and differential occupational roles of the sexes, appears to tip the scales in favor of the females. But the whole question of the superior performance of females needs further study.

Individual Group Performance

The Ghanaian growth pattern delineated above represents the average performance of the groups of primary-middle school children discussed above in the introduction. It does not include Achimota School. To a large extent, each group typifies this growth pattern, especially in the case of the relative growth of boys and girls. In the following paragraphs, I examine each group in relation to the others and to the total pattern. It should be borne in mind, however, that each part of the whole is relatively small and that statistical errors are possible in the reckoning of individual group mean.

Tables 3 and 4 show the mean height growth for boys and girls. In the former, Achimota shows a trend of marginal superiority to rural, suburban and urban groups, the differences being mostly between one and two inches. Compared to privileged urban and the expatriate groups, however, Achimota shows consistently inferior performance at eleven to thirteen years, the only age groups where data are comparable. The height growth for girls shows a fairly similar trend.

In weight growth, the pattern is strikingly similar to height: Achimota is generally inferior to the urban "privileged"-expatriate group, but is clearly superior to the rural-suburban-urban group. In weight, how-

Table 3. Achimota and primary-middle schools: distribution of height according to age — boys (mean height, inches)

Age	Rural	Suburban	Urban	Privileged urban	Achimota	Total boys	Expatriate
5	—	—	42.0	45.0	—	27	44.8
6	45.2	43.5	44.6	48.1	—	104	46.3
7	47.1	45.5	46.5	49.2	—	242	48.8
8	49.2	48.0	48.4	51.2	—	248	52.1
9	51.0	49.4	50.3	53.7	—	261	54.4
10	52.0	51.0	52.3	55.4	—	235	55.2
11	53.6	53.7	53.6	57.1	55.5	226	58.1
12	55.9	55.1	56.0	58.4	58.2	242	58.9
13	57.2	56.7	57.4	59.0	58.9	268	59.0
14	58.4	57.9	59.1	—	61.5	278	—
15	60.5	61.9	60.9	—	62.9	291	—
16	62.4	62.1	61.8	—	65.1	239	—
17	64.1	64.4	63.7	—	65.9	201	—
18	65.2	64.7	65.1	—	65.3	147	—

Table 4. Achimota and primary-middle schools: distribution of height according to age — girls (mean height, inches)

Age	Rural	Suburban	Urban	Privileged urban	Achimota	Total girls	Expatriate
5	44.5	43.0	—	44.5	—	25	44.7
6	44.5	43.9	45.9	46.7	—	95	45.9
7	47.1	46.0	48.2	48.4	—	215	49.1
8	49.7	47.4	49.7	51.4	—	272	51.7
9	51.1	48.9	51.3	53.7	—	243	53.3
10	52.7	51.3	53.5	56.0	52.5	269	55.3
11	55.0	53.8	55.6	58.2	58.9	235	59.1
12	56.7	55.0	58.2	61.5	59.7	176	60.7
13	58.8	57.7	59.7	62.7	61.3	181	—
14	59.4	59.0	61.9	—	61.5	182	—
15	61.0	60.8	61.3	—	62.4	140	—
16	62.7	61.5	62.1	—	61.8	104	—
17	61.8	62.3	63.4	—	62.1	74	—
18	63.9	61.5	64.5	—	62.7	25	—

ever, the gap between Achimota and the rural-suburban-urban group is very wide compared to the urban "privileged"-expatriate group.

When the privileged urban is compared with the expatriate the results are very close indeed. In height growth for girls aged five, seven, eight, and eleven the expatriate group has the edge; the Ghanaian privileged urban group is dominant at ages six, nine, ten, and twelve. For the boys, the privileged urban group takes the lead from five to ten. The expatriate group catches up and outdistances it at eleven and maintains the lead up to age twelve. At thirteen the privileged urban group catches up and both groups remain at par.

The same dramatic performance characterizes weight development (Tables 5 and 6). For the boys, the Ghanaian group takes the lead at

Table 5.   Achimota and primary-middle schools: distribution of weight according to age — boys (mean weight, pounds)

Age	Rural	Suburban	Urban	Privileged urban	Achimota	Total boys	Expatriate
5	—	—	35.0	45.9	—	27	45.5
6	40.7	37.9	40.6	51.9	—	104	50.4
7	45.4	42.2	44.0	57.7	—	242	59.4
8	50.5	47.7	48.4	62.2	—	248	66.0
9	55.0	51.1	53.9	69.5	—	261	69.4
10	57.8	54.4	60.2	75.0	—	235	71.7
11	63.5	63.2	63.1	83.2	76.4	226	87.7
12	71.2	68.9	71.3	86.1	85.6	242	91.5
13	76.1	73.5	77.1	88.0	90.4	268	91.0
14	81.1	78.0	83.8	—	102.6	278	—
15	88.7	99.2	92.0	—	109.4	291	—
16	99.2	96.7	102.5	—	122.5	239	—
17	109.9	108.5	111.3	—	125.5	201	—
18	114.8	118.2	121.0	—	124.9	147	—

Table 6.   Achimota and primary-middle schools: distribution of weight according to age — girls (mean weight, pounds)

Age	Rural	Suburban	Urban	Privileged urban	Achimota	Total girls	Expatriate
5	41.5	40.0	43.0	45.7	—	25	44.4
6	40.7	38.2	45.7	49.6	—	95	48.7
7	45.0	41.3	49.7	55.8	—	215	56.6
8	51.6	41.3	52.1	64.1	—	272	65.8
9	53.6	45.9	57.2	72.7	—	243	67.1
10	60.8	54.9	62.6	78.2	67.0	269	74.5
11	67.2	62.9	69.8	88.6	87.9	235	89.7
12	73.4	68.3	83.0	95.5	94.4	176	94.3
13	78.1	81.3	91.1	99.0	108.7	181	—
14	85.0	87.3	99.2	—	111.7	182	—
15	96.3	99.0	103.8	—	116.3	140	—
16	104.5	106.2	109.8	—	121.8	104	—
17	106.8	116.0	118.5	—	120.5	74	—
18	114.7	115.0	127.0	—	122.0	25	—

five and six; it is overtaken by the expatriate group at seven and eight. The privileged urban group recovers the lead at nine and maintains it until ten, when it is again overtaken by the expatriate group which maintains the lead from eleven to thirteen. The same general features characterize the growth for girls.

In height and weight growth for boys and girls, the urban group shows complete superiority over the suburban. But there is an interesting development when urban is compared with rural. While the urban girls are consistently taller and heavier than the rural girls, the rural boys are taller than the urban boys — except for the postpubertal period of seventeen and eighteen; in weight, the rural boys are superior between six and eleven; the urban boys seize the lead from twelve to eighteen.

In effect, urban superiority over rural is not a *fait accompli*; it is questionable in places. The superior development in height among the rural boys is probably due to open-air activities which contribute to a better growth of the long bones.[7] Correspondingly, strenuous farm activities on the part of the rural boys may lead to the burning of much of the stored fat (energy).

Factors Promoting and Retarding Growth

In terms of aggregate growth performance, the six groups featuring in this study may be ranked as follows:
1. expatriate,
2. urban privileged,
3. Achimota,
4. urban,
5. rural, and
6. suburban.

The first three groups show better-than-average growth performance. The children are taller and heavier than the last three.

There is considerable evidence that children from both expatriate and privileged urban groups belong to the highest socioeconomic strata. Their parents are highly educated and hold status positions with corresponding earning power. Such well-to-do parents are better able to afford the balanced diet necessary for growth than their less affluent urban counterparts.

7 Personal communication from Dr. Oracca-Tetteh, a biochemist at Legon.

Achimota school has long ceased to be the preserve of the elite as a result of the fee-free educational policy of the Ghana Government. The selection of students from the "common entrance" pool ostensibly gives a fair chance to all Ghanaians; nevertheless, an unobtrusive selective process operates whereby the students — usually the cream of the pool — tend to come from the well-to-do homes with a relatively long tradition of education.[8] Secondly, Achimota is a residential school with a tradition of good feeding and good discipline. These combined factors tend to encourage better-than-average growth performance.

The urban group represents a heterogeneous body. It includes the middle-range stratum of Ghanaian society and the "working classes." Obviously, some of the children in this group would have excellent growth opportunities, and others would be far less fortunate because of varying parental socioeconomic status. It would be desirable in future growth research to break this group down into two or three discrete components. The results would probably show that the higher the parental socioeconomic status, the better the growth performance in the urban area.

Rural performance in this study reveals that the natural environment, the geographical setting, as well as the occupation dictated by these surroundings may contribute to physical growth.

Finally, the poor suburban growth performance is a clear reflection of the effects of unsanitary surroundings, economic poverty, and gross illiteracy.

SUMMARY AND CONCLUSIONS

The following major conclusions have emerged from this study:

1.   The highest point of acceleration in height and weight growth for boys is at age fourteen to fifteen, and for girls at ten to thirteen.

2.   Girls are bigger and taller than boys for a considerable part of their growing period.

3.   In terms of individual group performance, it has been shown that the higher the socioeconomic group of the child's parent, the better the growth performance. For example:

   a.   "Privileged" urban children perform as well as expatriate children in Ghana and are taller and heavier than the average Ghanaian urban child;

[8]   See Forster (1965: Chapter 7) for a fuller discussion on the relationship between school attendance and parental socioeconomic status.

b.   urban children have better growth performance than their sub-urban counterparts; and

c.   rural children perform better than suburban children; and some-times as well as urban children.

Some of these conclusions, especially the differential growth per-formance of children of different socioeconomic groups, are already familiar in the Euro-American context where periodic measurement of the height and weight of school children has become a regular feature of educational research. While the social strata are less clearly defined in Ghana — and in Africa generally — than in Europe or America, one can safely distinguish between the urban elite and the average urban dweller in terms of education and/or earning power.

Similarly, the distinctions between urban and rural, urban and sub-urban are almost clearcut in the African context. One is likely to find a higher standard of education with a stronger earning power in the urban area. It is the relationship between rural and suburban which needs further study. The relatively permanent village settlement adja-cent to a major road and with clearly defined means of sustenance is certainly superior to a suburban community where members have to eke out an existence; it may even offer a challenge to the urban settle-ment as this study reveals.

Thus, the various groups in this study represent defined socio-economic groups in the African context. The study further reveals that there is some relationship between these groups and the growth per-formance of the children.

The conclusions relating to the growth spurt as well as the superior growth performance of girls over boys need further study.[9] These con-clusions need to be treated as hypotheses which must be tested and retested by successive investigations. The final picture will probably emerge only after years of painstaking field work.

Finally, it is important to stress that the data analyzed in this paper have been collected only from southern Ghana. How far they reflect Ghana as a whole will depend upon future investigations.

[9]   Note that in his study of Baganda children in the vicinity of Kampala, Wel-bourne (1951) observed that girls up to nine years were taller and heavier than the boys, but from twelve to fourteen years they were shorter and lighter. He was unable to comment on the significance of this pattern because of an alleged un-certainty concerning the ages of his subjects.

REFERENCES

COLE, L., J. J. B. MORGAN
 1961   *Psychology of childhood and adolescence*. New York: Holt, Rinehart and Winston.
DEANE, R., M. GEBER
 1964   The development of the African child. *Discovery* 25:1, 14–19.
FIAWOO, D. K.
 1961   *Social survey of Tefle, Ghana*. Child Development Monograph (mimeograph).
 1972   "Puberty and adolescence in Ghana." Unpublished manuscript.
FOSTER, PHILIP
 1965   *Education and social change in Ghana*. Chicago: University of Chicago Press.
GRANT, M. W.
 1951   "The technique for the analysis of heights and weights." Mimeographed manuscript. Applied Nutrition Unit, London School of Hygiene and Tropical Medicine.
GRANT, M.W., G. R. WADSWORTH
 1959   The height, weight, and physical maturity of Liverpool schoolgirls. *The Medical Officer* 102:303–306.
JELLIFE, D. B.
 1962   The African child. *Transactions of the Royal Society for Tropical Medicine and Hygiene* 46:13.
ROBERTS, D. F.
 1960   "Effects of race and climate on human growth as exemplified by studies on African children," in *Human growth*. Edited by J. M. Tanner. Oxford: Pergamon Press.
TANNER, J. M.
 1967   *Education and physical growth*. London: University of London Press.
WADDY, B. B.
 1956   Heights and weights of children in the northern territories of the Gold Coast. *The Journal of Tropical Medicine and Hygiene* 59:1, 1–4.
WELBOURNE, H. F.
 1951   The growth of Baganda children in the vicinity of Kampala. *East African Medical Journal* 28:428.

Some Biosocial Determinants of the Growth, Health, and Nutritional Status of Papua New Guinean Preschool Children

L. A. MALCOLM

Within primitive populations, social and cultural factors determine to a major extent the biological interrelationships between growth, health, fertility, and morbidity patterns. Interwoven with these variables is the impact of poor nutrition which interacts with the infective load in a community to modify and distort the capacity of populations to achieve their potential size, fertility, and life span (Scrimshaw, et al. 1968; Jelliffe 1966; Scrimshaw 1964). Adaptive mechanisms developed by populations to deal with the stresses are both biological and social. I will examine here these interrelationships within the rapidly changing context of the human biology of Papua New Guinea.

The study of growth and development in Papua New Guinea has revealed as diverse a spectrum of growth patterns as has been reported from any country (Malcolm 1970a, 1970b, n.d.). Figure 1 shows the variation in growth rate noted in children aged 0 to 3 years from various populations. The most rapid rates are achieved in urban children (Malcolm n.d.), and especially from families of the members of the Papua New Guinea Defense Force, who are provided with a reasonable income, family allowances, permanent housing, and adequate health services. In these children, weight at 3 months actually exceeds that of the Harvard standards. By contrast, the growth rate observed in the Asai children of the highlands (Malcolm 1970b) is slower than in any other reported population and seems to be related to a deprived nutritional environment, with a low protein intake, poor health services and with limited cultural contact with social changes which have occurred in other parts of the country. The curves between these extremes are from populations whose environmental character-

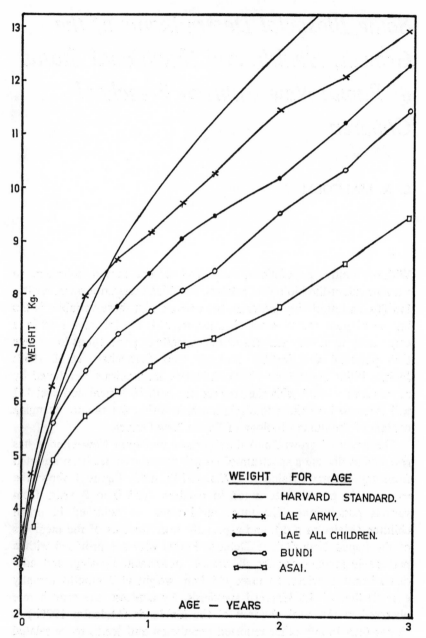

Figure 1.   Weight by age of children from some Papua New Guinean populations compared with Harvard standards

istics exhibit a corresponding spectrum of variation and change.

It will be noted that the shape of the growth curve in all populations follows a similar pattern, but at different levels, with reasonably satisfactory increments for the first few months, followed by a progressive departure from the trend of the European child. Nutritional opinion in the past has tended to regard this pattern, which is typical for developing countries (Jelliffe 1966; Guzman, et al. 1968), as being due to a poor quality, protein-deficient weaning diet. A close examination, however, suggests that deficient total food intake is the more probable explanation. Evidence for this conclusion comes from the comparatively less affected range of height variation, which is a more specific measure of protein intake (Malcolm 1972) and from the changes observed in the skinfold thickness, a more specific indicator of total energy intake. Figures 2 and 3 show the changes in this latter parameter in two Papua New Guinean populations (Malcolm n.d.) compared with that of European children. The New Guinean children from both urban Lae and a typical rural population, Kaiapit, reach a peak prior to 6 months, following which there is a steady fall until the age of 1½ to 2 years. By this time a considerable gap has developed, especially in the triceps area, between European and Papua New Guinean values. Although European norms may not be the most appropriate standards, the changes strongly suggest that total food intake is inadequate and is a major factor determining impaired growth. It cannot be the case that the relatively small needs of the child at this age cannot be met by the available food in any society. A possible explanation, however, may be found in the social and cultural attitudes to child care and feeding. Few observers appear to have asked the obvious but perhaps important questions: why does a mother feed her child; what determines whether a mother feeds her child at a particular time; and what motivating factors operate in child feeding in different cultures?

The Western observer, examining the cultural patterns of primitive people, too often interprets his findings, including child care practices, in concepts familiar to himself and his own cultural background. The Western mother normally feeds her child to satisfy her own preconceptions of the child's needs. In many situations, this concept of need is in excess of the actual need. Feeding is based on a timetable, and success is measured by satisfactory weight gain. Failure to attain certain predetermined goals, either in food intake or weight gain, may lead to distress and anxiety in the Western mother. To the mother in a primitive culture, however, factors determining feeding practice may be quite different. Child-rearing in most Papua New Guinean societies

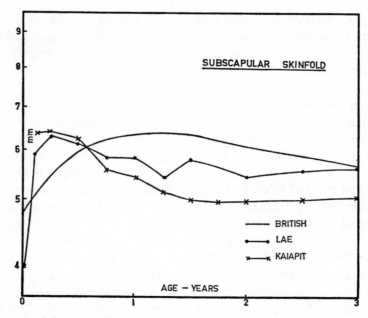

Figure 2.   Subscapular skinfold thickness by age of Lae and Kaiapit children compared with that of British children

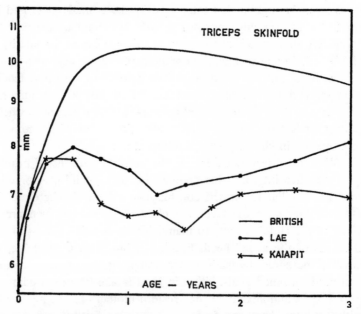

Figure 3.   Triceps skinfold thickness by age of Lae and Kaiapit children compared with that of British children

is permissive and unrestricted, and much of a child's activity such as sleeping, eating, excreting, etc., is determined by the personal choice of the child.

Studies of the mother-child relationship using prolonged, unobtrusive, and unstructured film sequences (Sorenson, personal communication) suggest that child feeding in Papua New Guinea is based almost entirely, and at all ages, even from birth, on the demands of the child. It is the child who determines when and with what he is fed. In the early weeks of life, the breast is immediately available when he cries and is given without hesitation at any time of the day or night. As soon as the infant is old enough to grasp the breast, he will take the nipple himself. The infant is thus capable of satisfying his own needs by his demands with the breast until the age of 6 months. However, beyond this time or in the event of lactational failure, the maternal response to his demands for the food resources immediately available to him appears insufficient to maintain an adequate nutritional intake. It is only later in the second year of life that he becomes sufficiently mobile and vocal to satisfy his needs through his own efforts. A gap therefore exists between the age of 6 months and 1½ to 2 years, during which this demand/permissive type feeding regime fails to satisfy the nutritional requirements of the child.

While this pattern may be interpreted as maternal neglect, it must be emphasized that it is of physical needs only, not of emotional needs. The converse may well be true, however, of Western type feeding and child care patterns. These findings suggest that the quantitative deficit described above may be largely due to a maternal failure to appreciate this demand gap and to fill this gap from whatever food might be available. The different levels within this pattern may be attributable to the different quantitative and qualitative success of continued breast-feeding under different nutritional circumstances (Malcolm n.d.) as well as a better weaning diet and increased awareness of the needs of the child, with socioeconomic improvement.

The importance of the social micro-environment of the child has recently been stressed by Cravioto and DeLicardie (i.p.) as a determinant of development of clinical malnutrition. The quality of maternal care influences, to a major extent, the growth, health, and nutritional status of the preschool child rather than the macro-environmental factors such as food availability and quality which have been the targets of traditional nutrition improvement programs.

The prolonged breast-feeding pattern of Papua New Guinean mothers has been noted with considerable interest by many investigators (Malcolm 1970a, n.d.; Bailey 1964; Table 1). The duration varies from a mean of 1.5 years in urban areas (Malcolm n.d.) to over 3 years in the New Guinean Highlands (Malcolm 1970a). Related to this prolonged period is a consequent variation in the length of the birth interval between successively born children. Studies of urban families indicate that, following pregnancy in the average mother, amenorrhea, presumably lactational, ensues for nearly a year, that conception occurs at 1.25 years, breast-feeding consequently ceases at 1.5 years, and delivery occurs at 2.0 years. A situation of maximum biological fertility therefore exists, restrained only by the prolonged lactational amenorrhea.

Table 1.   Birth interval, duration of breast feeding, and fertility in Papua New Guinean populations

Population	Breast feeding duration (years)	Birth interval (years)	Birth rate/1000
Bundi [a]	3.5	4.0	30
Sepik [b]	2.5	3.3	30–26
New Guinea Is. [c]	—	2.6 → 2.1	40–55
Urban [d]			
Migrant	2.0	2.4	
			60–80
Permanent	1.5	2.0	

[a] Malcolm 1970a.
[b] Sturt and Sturt 1973.
[c] Ring and Scragg 1973.
[d] Malcolm n.d.

By contrast, the prolonged birth intervals of 4 years reported for Bundi mothers (Malcolm 1970a) are also mediated through prolonged breast-feeding, but culturally, not biologically. Throughout much of Papua New Guinea there is, but to a diminishing extent, a prohibition on sexual intercourse during the breast-feeding period (Malcolm 1970a; Ring and Scragg 1973), due to the belief that the semen may poison the breast milk of the mother. This cultural belief may have had a basis in the biological wisdom of previous generations in that it acts to preserve the health of the mother from the stress of too frequent child-bearing, as well as giving the valuable support of the breast milk for the crucial first three years of life.

In a recent study of a Sepik population, Sturt and Sturt (1973) report that this belief is still strongly held to the extent that only 16 births in 512 (3%) occurred with a birth interval of less than 1.5 years between surviving children. Of these 16, 8 were accepted into the family and of the other 8, 1 was starved to death, 3 were adopted out, and in four cases the previous child was either killed or starved to death. Following the early death of a child, however, the average interval was much shorter and was closely correlated with the age at death of a child, an observation also noted by Ring and Scragg (1973).

Throughout many areas in Papua New Guinea, however, this belief is having a diminishing influence with a consequent increase in fertility (Ring and Scragg 1973) and, as indicated above (Malcolm n.d.), has already been abandoned by the urban mother, whose fertility is now determined biologically rather than culturally. The impact of these changes on the health of both the mother and child, however, is apparently not serious at this stage, as the changes have coincided with equivalent socioeconomic improvements which have minimized the potential consequences. Of some concern, however, is the impact of change and increase in the traditional family size of five to six children, which, particularly in urban areas (Malcolm n.d.) is becoming an insupportable burden within the confines of an nonexpanding home and income, and in the rural areas (Ring and Scragg 1973) where population expansion, due to both decreased mortality and increased fertility, is already leading to accelerated urban drift. Change in the attitude toward intercourse during the breast-feeding period in such areas as the New Guinean Highlands, which may be anticipated, and indeed is already occurring, could have a major impact on family size, health, and the limited land resources of people, whose adaptation within the current ecosystem is only just being maintained.

A further factor in the changing health and fertility patterns is the biological length of the menstrual span. In all traditional New Guinean populations the occurrence of the menarche, which is related to growth and protein intake, is delayed, the mean age in most populations ranging from 16 to 19 years (Malcolm 1970a). Marriage occurs some two years later than menarche, with the first child being born at a mean age for the mother of 20 to 24 (Sturt and Sturt 1973; Scragg 1973). Recent studies (Scragg 1973) indicate that late menarche is also associated with both early menopause and earlier cessation of child-bearing, presumably due to the deprived nutritional circumstances of the slow-maturing groups.

Chow (personal communication) has shown from animal experiments that protein deprivation markedly delays the onset of sexual maturity and shortens the total duration of the reproductive life. A shortened menstrual span therefore may be considered as a possible adaptive mechanism to the deprived nutritional environment and the restriction of fertility, with its protein demands for fetal tissue and lactation, to within tolerable limits. On the other hand, improved nutrition and socioeconomic circumstances result in an earlier menarche and later menopause (Wolanski 1972) with a consequent extension of menstrual span and potential fertility.

It is possible that protein malnutrition may also reduce sexual drive and hence make tolerable both the restriction on intercourse during the breast-feeding period and the reported restriction on intercourse for the early months of a new marriage for a Bundi couple (Malcolm 1970a). Reduction in sexual activity has also been noted in animal experiments (Chow, personal communication); but the measurement of such a complex, but perhaps important, biosocial factor in fertility would be most difficult in human populations.

CONCLUSION AND SUMMARY

Biosocial interrelations determine to a considerable extent the patterns of growth, health, and fertility of primitive populations such as those in Papua New Guinea. The typical growth in the weight pattern of the under-three-year-old child is related to a quantitative deficit in the total food intake, which in turn seems to be due to a pattern of feeding care determined more by the demand of the child than any maternal appreciation of the child's food needs. The spacing of children, so important for the maintenance of the health of the mother and child, is determined in traditional societies by social constraints on sexual intercourse during a prolonged breast-feeding period, a constraint which is rapidly disappearing under the impact of cultural change and has entirely disappeared in the urban family, where spacing and fertility are now determined biologically and limited only by prolonged lactational amenorrhea. Fertility is further restricted biologically by protein malnutrition, which both delays menarche and leads to an earlier menopause, and hence to a shortening of the menstrual span and reproductive life. Malnutrition may also have led to a reduction in sexual drive, making more tolerable the cultural constraints on sexual activity both before and early in marriage as well as after child-bearing.

REFERENCES

BAILEY, K. V.
1964 Growth of Chimbu infants in the New Guinean highlands. *Journal of Tropical Pediatrics* 10:3–16.

CRAVIOTO, JOAQUIN, ELSA R. DELICARDIE
i.p. *Ecology of malnutrition: environmental variables associated with clinical severe malnutrition.*

GUZMAN, M. A., N. S. SCRIMSHAW, H. A. BRUCH, J. E. GORDON
1968 Nutrition and infection field study in Guatemalan villages, 1959–1964, VII: Physical growth and development of preschool children. *Archives of Environmental Health* 17:107–118.

JELLIFFE, D. B.
1966 *The assessment of the nutritional status of the community.* W.H.O. Monograph Series 59. Geneva.

MALCOLM, L. A.
1970a *Growth and development in New Guinea: a study of the Bundi people of the Madang district.* Institute of Human Biology Madang, Monograph Series 1.
1970b Growth, malnutrition and mortality of the infant and toddler of the Asai valley of the New Guinea highlands. *American Journal of Clinical Nutrition* 23:1090–1095.
1972 "Anthropometric, biochemical and immunological effects of protein supplements in a New Guinean highland boarding school." Paper delivered at the Ninth International Congress of Nutrition, Mexico.
n.d. "Health and nutrition, growth and development of children in urban Lae, Papua New Guinea." In preparation.

RING, A., R. F R. SCRAGG
1973 A demographic and social study of fertility in rural New Guinea. *Journal of Biosocial Science* 5:89–121.

SCRAGG, R. F. R.
1973 "Menopause and reproductive span in rural Nuigini," in *Proceedings of the Ninth Annual Symposium of the Medical Society of Papua New Guinea*, Port Moresby, July 1973.

SCRIMSHAW, N. S.
1964 Ecological factors in nutritional disease. *American Journal of Clinical Nutrition* 14:112–122.

SCRIMSHAW, N. S., C. E. TAYLOR, J. E. GORDON
1968 *Interactions of nutrition and infection.* W.H.O. Monograph Series 57. Geneva.

STURT, R. J., A. E. STURT
1973 "A study of family health in a Sepik population," in *Proceedings of the Ninth Annual Symposium of the Medical Society of Papua New Guinea*, Port Moresby, July 1973.

WOLANSKI, NAPOLEON
1972 Comment on "Anthropology and population problems," by S. Polgar, et al. *Current Anthropology* 13:255–258.

The Effects of Genetic and Environmental Factors upon the Growth of Children in Guatemala City

FRANCIS E. JOHNSTON, MICHAEL BORDEN, and
ROBERT B. MacVEAN

The study of human growth enjoys a long history in the annals of human biology and of biomedical science. Descriptions of the patterns of development of children and youth may be traced well back into the nineteenth century and may be noted for virtually every racial group. Though there are gaps in the record, it is possible to extract from the literature a considerable amount of information on the morphology, the maturation levels, and frequently, the rates of change of the growing members of our species (Meredith 1969; Krogman 1941).

Despite this mass of descriptive data, we are still largely ignorant of the mechanisms by which the hereditary information carried by the individual interacts with the environmental stimuli and pressures which he or she encounters, in ways which will influence the course of development and ultimately the size, shape, and composition of the adult. Stated more simply, we just do not know whether the range of variation in adult morphology among populations of the world results from primary genetic differences or through the long term response to the environment. The overwhelming majority of studies that cut across ecological and racial boundaries fail to account adequately for the effects of these forces and result only in description without interpretation or explanation.

To be sure, much is known of the degree to which genetic factors may produce developmental variation. Both experimental (Taylor 1968; Hunt 1966) and twin studies (Osborne and DeGeorge 1959; Vandenberg 1962) have demonstrated that hereditary factors markedly affect a wide range of developmental parameters. Likewise innumerable studies have documented the profound effects of environmental stress on human growth and maturation (Frisancho and Baker 1970; Stunkard 1968;

Ekblom 1969; Cabak and Najdanvic 1965).

Such studies, however, present but one side of the picture. By focusing on either genetic factors or environmental pressures, they reveal primarily information on the extent to which human development may be influenced by the one when the other is kept at a constant. While such data are invaluable in establishing the range of response potential in man, we also need to know the extent to which human development is affected in normal populations living in natural ecosystems in which both the genetic and environmental determinants are free to vary.

There have been relatively few studies whose designs permitted any attempts to analyze this problem. Hiernaux's work in East Africa (1963) is an example of a study in a single population, while Roberts' survey of the literature (1969) affords an example of a cross-population analysis; both attempted to account for inherited factors and experienced forces in the development of human morphological variation.

We attempt to address this problem by comparing differences in the growth patterns of two genetically dissimilar samples living in the same ecosystem with differences in the growth patterns of two genetically similar samples living in different environments. Since one sample is used in the genetic comparison and the same one in the environmental comparison, it is hoped that our analysis will shed some light on the degree to which the hereditary determinants of development in that sample may be altered by environmental pressures experienced during development.

MATERIALS AND METHODS

Three groups of children and youth were compared in this study. These samples may be described as follows:

1. *Individuals of Guatemalan descent residing in Guatemala City*. The individuals of this sample are taken from our records of the longitudinal development of growth, maturation, and behavior conducted by the American School (Colegio Americano) of Guatemala City since 1953. This study involves the annual examination of children attending the American School plus four other private and public schools in the city selected to provide a range of socioeconomic levels from high to low. For this particular paper, we have utilized the best longitudinal records of subjects from the American School. This school draws its pupils from the highest socioeconomic levels of the city. Not only do the children enjoy excellent home environments, they also participate in a progressive school program involving systematic medical and dental care, supervised

and well-planned school meals, and a vigorous program of physical activity and exercise. In other words, this sample consists of children, studied longitudinally, who have enjoyed as nearly optimal an environment as is presently possible.

Inclusion in this sample was limited to those children defined as Guatemalan; i.e. all four grandparents were native born and possessed Spanish surnames. The data analyzed consist of the heights and weights from 1,413 examinations (808 male, 605 female) of 148 children who ranged in age at examination from five through seventeen years. This yielded an average of 9.9 examinations per boy and 9.0 per girl; 60 percent of the children (85) were examined at least nine times.

2. *Individuals of European descent residing in Guatemala City.* The individuals of this sample are the offspring of parents who live in Guatemala City and who themselves were born either in western Europe (virtually all from the United Kingdom or Germany) or North America. The children were pupils at the American School and hence come from similar socioeconomic levels; participation in school activities and programming insured further environmental similarity. Though not all of these children were born in Guatemala, most of those in our sample had attended the American School for ten to twelve years. These data consist of the heights and weights at 833 examinations (446 male, 387 female) of 83 children of the same age range as the Guatemalan sample. This sample averaged ten examinations per individual and, in fact, only five were seen less than eight times.

3. *Individuals of European descent residing in the United States.* The children and youth comprising this sample are taken from the records of the longitudinal study of the Fels Research Institute of Yellow Springs, Ohio. Its subjects are drawn from the surrounding, largely middle class, rural population, and enjoy an acceptable level of health, nutrition, and general environmental quality. These data are unpublished and have been made available to us through the kindness of Dr. A. F. Roche. They consist of the heights and weights from 4,651 examinations (2,432 males, 2,219 females) of several hundred individuals. For all three samples, this study yielded a total number of 6,897 examinations.

The analysis of genetically dissimilar groups living in similar environments was accomplished by comparing the patterns of growth in height and in weight of the American School Guatemalan (ASG) and American School European (ASE) samples. Genetic dissimilarity was based on a comparison of the distribution of the ABO phenotypes of American School students classed as either Guatemalan or European by the above criteria; these distributions are shown in Table 1. These two distributions

Table 1. ABO phenotypes in American School students of Guatemalan and European ancestry

ABO phenotype	Guatemalan descent		European descent	
	n	f	n	f
A	50	0.29	50	0.41
B + AB	21	0.12	21	0.17
O	99	0.59	52	0.42
Total	170		123	

chi-square = 7.292, d.f. = 2, p < .05

differ significantly: the deviation of the ASG from the ASE group is in the direction expected, were the Guatemalan children to display significant admixture of Spanish-speaking and Mayan gene pools, namely, more type O and less A, B, and AB.

The analysis of genetically similar groups living in different environments was accomplished by comparing the growth patterns of ASE children with those of the Fels sample. The distribution of ABO phenotypes in the ASE sample did not differ significantly from that established for North American populations of western European ancestry.

The mean height and the mean weight were regressed upon the mean age in a linear fashion for males and females separately. These regression equations, each exhibiting a significant slope, are shown in Table 2. While we recognize that postnatal growth is most accurately represented by complex algebraic functions (Deming and Washburn 1963; Bock, et al. 1973), our analysis dealt with growth after five years of age; from this age to adolescence growth is almost a linear function of age. Therefore, the major source of error associated with our selection of a linear function rests with adolescence.

The regression of mean height or weight upon mean age also ignores individual variability. However, our concern in this report is with group

Table 2. Regression of mean height and weight upon mean age in American School students and in United States children

	Height (centimeters)	
	Male	Female
American School Guatemalan	Ht. = 83.6 + 5.2 (age)	Ht. = 92.3 + 4.2 (age)
American School European	Ht. = 82.7 + 5.4 (age)	Ht. = 92.5 + 4.5 (age)
Fels Institute	Ht. = 75.9 + 5.9 (age	Ht. = 82.8 + 5.0 (age)
	Weight (kilograms)	
American School Guatemalan	Wt. = −4.00 + 3.8 (age)	Wt. = 1.2 + 3.3 (age)
American School European	Wt. = −3.00 + 3.8 (age)	Wt. = 1.2 + 3.5 (age)
Fels Institute	Wt. = −7.86 + 4.4 (age)	Wt. = −1.7 + 3.6 (age)

trends. In addition, the coefficients of variation for both height and weight were similar for all three samples leading us to conclude that individual variability did not affect any comparison differentially.

The regression lines were compared by means of an analysis of covariance (Snedecor and Cochran 1967). This analysis compares the deviation of individual means from the regression lines, one for each sample, with that obtained from a single line using pooled data. Separate F-ratios are obtained for differences between the regression coefficients (i.e. the slopes of the lines) and for the adjusted means (i.e. the elevations of the lines).

Table 3. Mean heights of three samples by age and sex

Age [d]	ASG [a] $\bar{x}$	s	ASE [b] $\bar{x}$	s	Fels [c] $\bar{x}$	s
	Male					
5	112.2	4.3	112.6	5.7	109.6	4.4
6	118.0	4.8	117.8	5.9	116.3	4.6
7	123.5	5.0	123.5	5.8	122.5	4.9
8	128.0	4.9	129.0	6.3	128.6	5.2
9	132.9	5.3	133.7	6.3	134.4	5.4
10	137.9	5.8	138.6	7.0	139.8	5.7
11	142.6	8.0	144.4	7.8	145.1	6.0
12	148.4	8.8	150.1	8.8	150.6	6.6
13	155.6	8.1	156.1	8.5	157.0	7.6
14	160.0	12.5	162.8	8.5	164.7	8.2
15	167.9	6.0	168.3	7.2	171.4	7.5
16	170.6	5.7	172.2	6.3	175.9	6.3
17	172.1	6.0	173.6	6.7	177.8	6.0
	Female					
5	110.8	4.2	113.4	5.7	108.5	4.2
6	117.2	4.9	119.7	6.1	115.2	4.6
7	122.8	5.6	125.0	6.2	121.3	4.8
8	126.9	6.5	130.2	6.4	127.3	5.1
9	132.6	7.2	136.5	7.0	133.1	5.4
10	137.9	8.7	142.0	7.6	138.8	5.9
11	145.0	8.1	148.7	8.7	145.2	6.6
12	149.9	9.5	153.7	7.7	152.0	7.1
13	153.5	9.2	158.9	6.6	157.6	6.5
14	156.1	6.3	161.3	6.0	161.2	5.6
15	155.9	10.1	163.0	5.5	163.3	5.5
16	156.5	6.3	163.1	5.7	163.9	5.3
17	159.2	6.0	164.2	5.1	164.8	5.5

[a] American School Guatemalan.
[b] American School European.
[c] Fels Institute.
[d] For ASG and ASE, mean age = half year; for Fels, mean age = whole year.

RESULTS

The heights, weights, and their standard deviations are presented for each of the three samples by age and sex in Tables 3 and 4; these data

Table 4.   Mean weights of three samples by age and sex

Age	ASG $\bar{x}$	s	ASE $\bar{x}$	s	Fels $\bar{x}$	s
	Male					
5	20.2	2.8	20.0	3.1	18.9	2.3
6	23.0	5.5	22.5	4.8	21.3	2.9
7	24.9	3.7	35.6	5.2	23.7	3.1
8	27.5	4.3	28.7	6.7	26.8	3.9
9	30.0	6.0	31.4	7.5	30.2	5.1
10	33.3	5.8	35.0	9.0	33.7	5.8
11	36.8	7.3	38.9	10.5	37.6	6.8
12	41.4	8.9	43.3	12.0	42.3	8.3
13	46.2	10.1	47.9	12.3	47.5	9.1
14	52.1	10.5	53.6	12.0	54.0	9.8
15	57.8	9.9	58.2	10.5	60.9	10.0
16	60.6	8.4	61.1	9.0	66.2	10.1
17	61.9	11.9	63.2	8.1	68.8	9.0
	Female					
5	19.5	2.9	21.0	4.7	18.1	2.3
6	23.0	4.2	24.2	5.2	20.4	2.8
7	25.2	4.2	26.1	5.6	22.9	3.6
8	27.6	5.8	29.4	6.7	25.8	4.4
9	31.1	6.5	33.3	7.0	29.0	5.3
10	34.6	8.8	36.8	8.5	32.7	6.9
11	40.2	9.2	41.9	9.4	37.2	7.7
12	44.4	10.9	47.2	10.3	42.7	9.5
13	47.3	11.1	52.1	9.4	47.3	9.6
14	51.7	8.1	55.3	9.4	51.9	9.6
15	52.6	12.0	56.2	7.4	54.0	9.1
16	53.8	10.1	56.9	7.9	55.2	10.1
17	56.3	9.6	58.1	6.2	56.1	9.9

may be seen graphically in Figures 1 and 2. For height (Figure 1) the ASG samples are consistently the shortest, though the difference is much more marked in the case of females. The height curves for Fels and ASE females overlap but, in the case of males, the Fels boys are noticeably taller throughout most of the age period than either of the other groups.

Insofar as weight is concerned (Figure 2), the ASG and the Fels females display curves which overlap considerably; the ASE girls are heavier at all ages. Among boys, the curves are very close through the early years of the range diverging thereafter; the Fels boys are the heav-

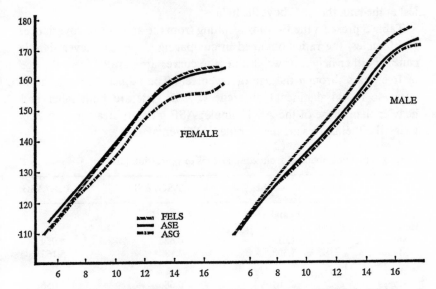

Figure 1. Mean height, plotted against age, in American School children of Guatemalan (ASG) and European (ASE) ancestry, and in North American residents (Fels) of European ancestry

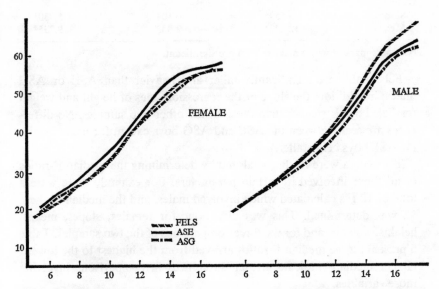

Figure 2. Mean weight, plotted against age, in American School children of Guatemalan (ASG) and European (ASE) ancestry, and in North American residents (Fels) of European ancestry

iest at the end, the ASG boys the lightest.

Table 5 presents the F-ratios resulting from the analysis of covariance. For females, the ratios obtained in comparing slopes are never significant for either height or weight; i.e. the curves are parallel from the age of five years through the age of seventeen. The adjusted means, however, do reveal significant differences. ASE girls are both taller and heavier than those of the ASG sample; ASE girls are heavier than Fels girls, who themselves are heavier than ASG females.

Table 5.   F-ratios obtained from comparisons of regression lines

	Fels/ASE	ASG/ASE	Fels/ASG
Females			
Height			
Slopes	1.414	0.682	4.054
Means	2.308	7.180*	5.163*
Weight			
Slopes	0.261	0.686	1.056
Means	4.299*	8.950*	0.528
Males			
Height			
Slopes	12.482*	1.380	17.800*
Means	12.652*	5.728*	39.289*
Weight			
Slopes	5.559*	0.104	5.830*
Means	12.827*	2.032	9.255*

Numbers marked with an asterisk (*) are significant.

Fels males are significantly taller and heavier than ASE or ASG males; in addition, the slope of the regression lines of height and weight for Fels boys is steeper than those of the other two samples. No differences are seen between the ASE and ASG boys except for mean height, the ASE boys being taller.

These data were further analyzed by determining the median F-ratios of all those involved in certain parameters. For example there were a total of 12 F's calculated which involved males, and the median of these 12 was determined. This was also done for females, slopes, means, heights, weights, and for the three comparisons of the two samples. Table 6 presents these median F-ratios arrayed from the highest to the lowest. Higher medians indicate greater differences in comparisons involving those variables.

With respect to the question of hereditary versus environmental effects, Table 6 demonstrates that the comparison involving genetic contrasts in a similar environment, ASG/ASE, yielded lower F-ratios than the comparison involving environmental contrasts with similar genetic backgrounds, Fels/ASE. In other words, the curves of children, whether for height, weight, male or female, raised in a common environment are closer, despite genetic differences, than are the curves for children raised in different environments and whose genetic backgrounds are similar. Furthermore, the curves of children who were raised in different environments AND whose genetic backgrounds are different are the most divergent.

Table 6. Ranked median F-ratios

Variable	Median F-ratio
Males	7.543
Means	6.454
Fels/ASG	5.497
Heights	5.446
Fels/ASE	4.929
Weights	3.166
Females	1.861
ASG/ASE	1.706
Slopes	1.361

Other observations of interest are indicated by Table 6. F-ratios involving comparisons of male curves are larger than are those involving females, as indicated by higher medians. In fact, the male median is the highest of the nine shown.

The median F-ratio for means is higher than that for slopes, the latter value being the lowest of the nine. That is, the slopes of the curves differ far less than do the means. The median F-ratio for height comparisons is somewhat higher than that for weight, though the differences are small and both medians fall near the center of the array.

DISCUSSION

These data suggest that environmental factors are responsible for greater differences between samples than are genetic differences, where the conditions resemble those which exist in our comparison of Guatemalan and North American children. Our evidence is based on the greater similarity of the curves of children who have lived most of their school years in a common environment, yet who display significant genetic differences, when compared with the curves of genetically similar children who have lived their school years in differing environments.

The relevant environment factors cannot be identified from our data, though it seems certain that they do not relate to health or to chronic undernutrition, since all samples have been drawn from socioeconomic levels characterized by favorable conditions for child development. Differences in the composition of their diets may play a part, as may different activity levels. Other possible factors must include the climatic differences between the two geographical areas; the tropical climate of Guatemala City with little seasonality and considerable time spent outdoors contrasts with the much greater temperature variation and seasonality of Ohio. Only further research can determine the factors in question.

The plasticity of human morphology in response to different environments has, of course, been a matter of record for decades (Boas 1940; Kaplan 1954; Eveleth 1966; Eveleth, et al. 1969; Hulse 1957; Froelich 1970). However, the role of these differences, over and against the role of genetic differences, is still incompletely understood. Our data suggest that environmental factors, which vary within an acceptably normal range, may be more important than genetic variation between populations, in producing growth variation; and that subtle, chronically experienced, and not easily perceived differences, associated with particular ecosystems, may be a major source of morphological differences among adult populations.

REFERENCES

BOAS, F.
  1940 "Changes in the bodily form of descendants of immigrants," in *Race, language, and culture*. By F. Boas, 60–75. Toronto: Free Press.
BOCK, R. D., H. WAINER, A. PETERSEN, D. THISSEN, J. MURRAY, A. ROCHE
  1973 A parameterization for individual human growth curves. *Human Biology*, 45:63–80.
CABAK, V., NAJDANVIC, R.
  1965 Effect of undernutrition in early life on physical and mental development. *Archives of Disease in Childhood* 40:532–534.
DEMING, J., A. H. WASHBURN
  1963 Application of the Jenss curve to the observed pattern of growth during the first eight years of life in 40 boys and 40 girls. *Human Biology* 35:484–506.
EKBLOM, B.
  1969 Effect of physical training in adolescent boys. *Journal of Applied Physiology* 27:350–355.

EVELETH, P.
1966   The effects of climate on growth. *Annals of the New York Academy of Sciences* 134:750–759.

EVELETH, P. B., J. A. DE S. FREITAS
1969   Tooth eruption and menarche of Brazilian-born children of Japanese ancestry. *Human Biology* 41:176–184.

FRISANCHO, A. R., P. T. BAKER
1970   Altitude and growth: a study of the patterns of physical growth of a high altitude Peruvian Quechua population. *American Journal of Physical Anthropology* 32:279–292.

FROELICH, J. W.
1970   Migration and the plasticity of physique in the Japanese-Americans of Hawaii. *American Journal of Physical Anthropology* 32:429–442.

HIERNAUX, J.
1963   Heredity and environment: their influence on human morphology. A comparison of two independent lines of study. *American Journal of Physical Anthropology* 21:575–589.

HULSE, F. S.
1957   Exogamie et hétérosis. *Archive Suisse d'Anthropologie Génétique* 22:103-125.

HUNT, E. E.
1966   "The developmental genetics of man," in *Human development.* Edited by Frank Falkner, 76–122. Philadelphia: Saunders.

KAPLAN, B.
1954   Environment and human plasticity. *American Anthropologist* 56: 780–800.

KROGMAN, W. M.
1941   *Growth of man.* Tabulae Biologicae 20.

MEREDITH, H. V.
1969   *Body size of contemporary groups of eight-year-old children studied in different parts of the world.* Monographs of the Society for Research in Child Development 34(1).

OSBORNE, R. H., F. W. DeGEORGE
1959   *Genetic basis of morphological variation.* Cambridge: Harvard University Press.

ROBERTS, D. F.
1969   Race, genetics, and growth. *Journal of Biosocial Science,* supplement 1:43–67.

SNEDECOR, G. W., W. G. COCHRAN
1967   *Statistical methods* (sixth edition). Ames, Iowa: Iowa State University Press.

STUNKARD, A. J.
1968   Environment and obesity: recent advances in our understanding of food intake in man. *Federation Proceedings* 27:1367–1373.

TAYLOR, C. S. ST.
1968   "Genetic variation in growth and development of cattle," in *Growth and development of mammals.* Edited by S. A. Lodge and G. E. Lanning, 267–290. New York: Plenum.

VANDENBERG, S. G.
1962 How "stable" are heritability estimates? A comparison of heritability estimates from six anthropometric studies. *American Journal of Physical Anthropology* 20:331-338.

Biographical Notes

JEFF BEAUBIER (1939–   ) has degrees in anthropology from Stanford and the University of North Carolina, one in Epidemiology from the School of Public Health, and another in Asian Studies from the East-West Center. He has lectured at several universities on topics related to his research interest, causal factors in longevity. He is an NIH Fellow at the Duke University Medical Center.

JEAN BENOIST (1929–   ) is a native of Lyon, France, and has an M.D. degree from Lyon and a D.Sc. from the University of Paris. His present appointment is at the University of Montreal where he is Professor of Anthropology. His chief interest has been the study of biocultural dynamics in human populations and its implications for population structure, genetics, and health. He has done field research on human populations in French Canada, the West Indies, and the Indian Ocean. In 1968 he was awarded the Prix Broca by the Société d'Anthropologie of Paris.

MICHAEL BORDEN (1946–   ) received his undergraduate degree from the University of Arizona and has done graduate work at the University of Texas and Temple University where he is currently a Ph.D. candidate. He is also a research assistant in pulmonary diseases at St. Christopher's Hospital for Children in Philadelphia, Pennsylvania. His research interests include child growth and development and respiratory physiology with emphasis on cystic fibrosis.

EDWARD JOHN CLEGG (1925–   ) graduated in medicine from Sheffield University in 1948 and obtained his doctorate in medicine in 1964. He has taught at the Universities of Liverpool and Sheffield and is at present Reader in Human Biology and Anatomy at the latter. He has worked on the biology of high altitude peoples and of island populations.

MICHAEL H. CRAWFORD (1939–   ) was born in Shanghai, China. He was educated in China, Australia, and the United States, receiving his Ph.D. at the University of Washington in 1967. He has taught at the University of Washington, University of Pittsburgh, and is presently an Associate Professor in the Department of Anthropology, University of Kansas. His chief fields of interest have been the anthropological genetics and demography of Mexican, Irish Tinker, and Italian populations. He is co-editor of a book on anthropological genetics.

GAIL DAVILA (1944–   ) was born in Seattle, Washington, and has a B.A. degree from Antioch College in Economics and International Relations. She also attended the Universidad de Concepción, Chile. She is currently a Research Associate at the Fels Research Institute where she has participated in numerous studies of child growth and development.

DZIGBODI K. FIAWOO (1926–   ) was born in Ghana. He received his undergraduate degree from Cornell University, his M.A. from Columbia University, and his Ph.D. from Edinburgh University. He was a postgraduate Research Associate at the Laboratory of Human Development at Harvard University (1961–1962) and a Senior Commonwealth Fellow at Cambridge University's Centre of African Studies (1970–1971). He was also a visiting lecturer at the Centre for West African Studies, Birmingham University, Birmingham, England. He is Senior Lecturer (Acting Head) of the Department of Sociology, University of Ghana, Legon, Ghana. He has done research on child development in Ghana, as well as on traditional religion and social change, with special reference to the Ewe-speaking people, and is currently National Director of a Ghana Government Project on the Young Child, sponsored by UNICEF.

EDWARD F. FOULKS (1937–   ) received his M.D. degree from McGill University and a Ph.D. in Anthropology from the University of Pennsylvania. He is currently Associate Professor of Psychiatry and Anthropology at the University of Pennsylvania. His major research interests are in the areas of psychoanalysis and cross-cultural psychiatry. In 1973 he received the John Gillin Prize from the American Anthropological Association for his study of arctic hysterias of the North Alaskan Eskimo.

A. ROBERTO FRISANCHO (1940–   ) did his undergraduate work at the National University of Cuzco, Peru, and received his doctorate from the Pennsylvania State University. He is Associate Research Scientist of the Center for Human Growth and Development and Associate Professor of Anthropology at the University of Michigan. His research specialties are growth, adaptive physiology, and biocultural adaptation of Latin American populations.

ROSE E. FRISCH (1918–   ) is a Research Associate at the Harvard Center for Population Studies, Harvard School of Public Health, and at the Children's Hospital Medical Center, Harvard Medical School. She has published extensively in the field of her major interest, the synchronization of adolescent physical growth and sexual maturation in girls and boys, and its implications for human fecundity. Her undergraduate work was at Smith College and her graduate work at Columbia University and the University of Wisconsin, where she received her doctorate in Physiological Genetics. She is a Guggenheim Fellow (1975–1976) and Lecturer in the Department of Population Sciences, Harvard School of Public Health.

H. HUGH FUDENBERG (1928–   ) received his undergraduate degree from U.C.L.A. and his M.D. from the University of Chicago. He is currently Chairman, Department of Immunology, Medical University of South Carolina, Charleston, South Carolina. He is an internationally recognized authority in the field of immunology and has studied all aspects of the field. He is a member of the expert advisory panel on immunology to W.H.O. He received the Pasteur Medal from the Institute Pasteur in Paris in 1962 and the Robert A. Cooke Memorial Medal from the American Academy of Allergy in 1967. He is on the editorial boards of *Blood, Vox Sang., Biochemical genetics, Clinical and Experimental Immunology, J. of Immunology, Immunochemistry, Amer. J. Hum. Genet., Transfusion and Clinical Immunology and Immunopathology.*

D. CARLETON GAJDUSEK (1923–   ) was born in Yonkers, New York. He received his undergraduate degree in biophysics from the University of Rochester and attended graduate school at the California Institute of Techology in physical chemistry. His M.D. degree was awarded by

Harvard Medical School. His research interests and major publications have been on the pathogenesis of chronic and persistent viral infections of man, studies on child growth and development and disease patterns in primitive cultures (the Americas, Africa, Middle East, Central Asia, Far East, and Oceania), human population genetics, and theory of notation and coding in the study of neurological patterning and learning. In 1963 he received the E. Mead Johnson Award from the American Academy of Pediatrics for his pediatric research in primitive cultures, and in 1974 was elected to the National Academy of Sciences. Since 1961 he has been Chief of the Central Nervous System Studies Branch of the National Institute of Neurological Diseases and Stroke, National Institutes of Health, Bethesda.

RALPH M. GARRUTO (1943–) was born in Binghamton, New York. He received his undergraduate degree from the Pennsylvania State University in zoology, and his doctorate in anthropology (human biology) from the same university. From 1970–1972 he was selected as a National Institute of General Medical Sciences pre-doctoral trainee in human biology. His chief research interests and publications have been in environmental physiology and genetics, hematology, and the study of disease patterns in isolated human populations (Oceania, South America). Since 1972 he has been a Staff Fellow with the National Institutes of Health, National Institute of Neurological Diseases and Stroke, the Central Nervous System Studies Branch.

H. WILLIAM HARRIS, JR. No biographical data available.

MARY L. HEDIGER (1950–) did her undergraduate work at Bryn Mawr College where she received a B.A. degree with honors in Anthropology. She is currently working on a Ph.D. degree in physical anthropology at the University of Pennsylvania. She holds a training grant from the National Institute of Dental Research.

JEAN HIERNAUX (1921–) was born in Huy, Belgium, and received an M.D. degree from the University of Brussels and a Diploma in Tropical Medicine from the Institute of Tropical Medicine in Antwerp. He was named Agrégé de l'Enseignement Supérieur by the University of Brussels and Docteur d'État en Sciences by the University of Paris. At present he is Director of Research at the Centre National de Recherche Scientifique in Paris. His major research interest and publications have been in the physical anthropology and the human ecology of Africa, a subject on which he has published two books, *La diversité humaine en Afrique Subsaharienne* and *The People of Africa*. He has been named an Honorary Rector of the State University of the Congo.

FRANCIS E. JOHNSTON (1931–) received his B.A. and M.A. degrees from the University of Kentucky and his Ph.D. in Anthropology from the University of Pennsylvania. From 1966–1968 he held a special Postdoctoral Fellowship from the National Institutes of Health. He has published research articles on human growth and development, genetics, and demography and is author of a book on human microevolution. At present he is Professor of Anthropology at the University of Pennsylvania.

SOLOMON H. KATZ (1939–) received his Ph.D. in Physical Anthropology from the University of Pennsylvania in 1967. He is currently Associate Professor of Anthropology at that university. His primary research interests are in the areas of human biology and adaptation.

KENNETH A. R. KENNEDY (1930–) did his undergraduate and graduate work at the University of California, Berkeley, receiving his Ph.D. in 1962. Presently he is Associate Professor of Anthropology, Asian Studies (South Asia Program) and at the Division of Biological Sciences (Section of Ecology and Systematics) at Cornell University. His research interests in paleodemography and skeletal biology have taken him to India and Sri Lanka where he has directed a number of archaeological excavations. Laboratory research of prehistoric skeletal remains from South Asia has been carried out by the author at the British Museum (Natural History), London, as well as at various institutions in Paris, Vienna, Berlin, and Basle. In addition to monographs and articles on the study of prehistoric man in South Asia, he has recently published a collection of essays and readings with the late Theodore D. McCown on the topic of human phylogeny.

GABRIEL WARD LASKER was born at York, England, and educated in the United States. After two years in China he entered graduate study at Harvard where he received his Ph.D. in 1945. Since then he has been on the faculty of the Department of Anatomy at Wayne State University with brief leaves for field research (in Mexico and Peru) and to teach anthropology elsewhere. He has been President of the American Association of Physical Anthropologists, Chairman of the Council of Biology Editors, and is Editor-in-Chief of *Human Biology*. He is author of numerous journal articles and a textbook in physical anthropology.

ROBERT V. MACVEAN.   No biographical data available.

LAURENCE MALCOLM (1929–   ) is a New Zealander and graduated from the Otago Medical School in Dunedin in 1953. He has held posts in public health administration in Papua New Guinea from 1957–1974 and more recently was head of the Health Planning Unit of the Department of Public Health involved in the preparation of the first National Health Plan for the country. His research interests include child growth and development, nutrition, community biology, community health, and planning and evaluation of health services. He is a Fellow of the Royal College of Physicians, Edinburgh, a Fellow of the Australian College of Health Administrators, and a Member of the Faculty of Commonwealth Medicine.

RICHARD B. MAZESS (1939–   ) was born in Philadelphia, Pennsylvania, and educated at Pennsylvania State University where he received his B.A. and M.A. degrees. He holds a Ph.D. from the University of Wisconsin. At present he is Assistant Professor of Radiology at the University of Wisconsin-Madison. His research has been in the area of body composition, especially bone, and its relationship to environmental adaptation, growth and aging, and nutrition.

JOHN McDANIEL (1942–   ) received his undergraduate degree from Washington and Lee University and his M.A. and Ph.D. in Anthropology from the University of Pennsylvania. He is currently Assistant Professor of Anthropology at Washington and Lee University. His major research interest is the relationship between culture and disease and his research has been done in Latin America.

E. DAVID MELLITS (1937–   ) received his undergraduate education at Johns Hopkins University. He did graduate work in statistics at the University of Rochester and completed his graduate study at the Johns Hopkins School of Hygiene and Public Health where he earned an Sc.D. in 1965. He is currently Associate Professor in the Departments of Pediatrics and Biostatistics at Johns Hopkins. His major interests is in the application of statistics to biomedical research.

HUGUES PICOT (1934–   ) was born in Fougères, France, and holds an M.D. degree from the University of Paris where he also received training in human biology. He taught parasitology and tropical medicine at the University of Paris for a number of years and has studied the epidemiology of human parasites in West Africa. Since 1971 he has been Director of the Laboratory of Epidemiology and Environmental Hygiene at St. Denis on the French island of Réunion, a post which has furthered his interest in the role of social and human factors in the endemnicity of intestinal parisites.

D. F. ROBERTS (1925–) graduated from the University of Cambridge and subsequently taught and did postgraduate work there. He taught in the University of Oxford for a number of years and, during this period, undertook intensive fieldwork in the Southern Sudan and in West Africa. He is currently Head of the Department of Human Genetics in the University of Newcastle upon Tyne, a department which he brought into being.

ALEXANDER F. ROCHE (1921–) completed a medical course, M.B., B.S., at the University of Melbourne and subsequently received a Ph.D., D.Sc., and later M.D. After teaching courses in gross anatomy and conducting the Growth Unit with the Department of Anatomy at the University of Melbourne, he moved to the Fels Research Institute in 1968. His main interests are physical growth and development.

FRANCISCO MAURO SALZANO (1928–) was born in Cachoeira do Sul, Brazil, and received his undergraduate degree from the Universidade Federal do Rio Grande do Sul and graduate degrees from the Universidade de São Paulo (Ph.D.) and the Universidade Federal do Rio Grande do Sul (Priv. Doc.). His present appointment is at the Instituto de Biociências, Universidade Federal do Rio Grande do Sul where he is an Associate Professor in the Department of Genetics. He has published widely in the field of human population genetics and has done much original research on the genetics of South American Indians. He became a member of the Brazilian Academy of Sciences in 1973.

JORGE SANCHEZ (1938–) graduate from the University of Cuzco, Peru, where he is currently Associate Professor of Anthropology. His research interest is in the area of biocultural adaptation of Andean populations.

MOSES S. SCHANFIELD (1944–) received his undergraduate degree from the University of Minnesota in Anthropology and graduate degrees in Anthropology (M.A.) from Harvard University, and in human Genetics (Ph.D.) from the University of Michigan. His research has been on the distribution of immunoglobin markers in human populations, and their relationship to disease as a possible selective role. He is currently the Director of the Reference Laboratory at the Milwaukee Blood Center, Milwaukee, Wisconsin.

WILLIAM ARTHUR STINI (1930–) received his undergraduate and graduate education at the University of Wisconsin where he earned his Ph.D. degree in 1969. He is currently Associate Professor of Anthropology at the University of Kansas. His main area of interest is human adaptation to environmental stress, especially the effects of nutritional deprivation on the growth process. He has done research on the growth of poorly nourished children in Latin America and experimental work on the effects of malnutrition in laboratory animals.

PHILLIP V. TOBIAS (1925–) was educated at the University of the Witwatersrand, Johannesburg, where he obtained his basic degrees (B.Sc., B.Sc. Hons.), a medical degree (1950), a Ph.D. in cytogenetics (1953) and a D.Sc. for his paleoanthropological contributions (1967). For the past 30 years he has been associated with the Witwatersrand University Anatomy Department and in 1958 he became Head of the Department, a position he still holds. He has been a Visiting Professor at Cambridge University (1964), is a Fellow of the Royal Society of South Africa, a Fellow of the Linnean Society (of London), British Association medallist, and recipient of the Simon Biesheuvel Medal, the South Africa Medal, and the Senior Captain Scott Medal. He is the author of numerous articles and books on a number of aspects of human biology (especially paleoanthropology). He was a member of the International Committee for I.B.P. (Human Adaptability) from its inception, was a founder-Council member of the International Association of Human Biologists, and founder and first President of the Institute for the Study of Man in Africa. He serves on the Editorial Boards of a number of scientific journals published in Britain, the U.S.A., and South Africa.

LINDA VALLEROY (1950–) received her undergraduate degree in sociology and anthropology from Swarthmore College. Presently, she is studying in the doctoral program in anthropology at the University of Pennsylvania and working at the W. M. Krogman Center for Research in Child Growth and Development at the Children's Hospital of Philadelphia. Her primary research interests are physiological adaptability and child growth and development.

TULIO VELASQUEZ (1930–) graduated from the School of Medicine of the National University of San Marcos in Peru. He is Professor of Physiology of the Instituto de Biología Andina of the University of San Marcos. His research interest is respiratory physiology.

ELIZABETH S. WATTS (1941–) was born in Atlanta, Georgia, and received her undergraduate education at Tulane University. She obtained a doctorate in physical anthropology from the University of Pennsylvania and returned to Tulane University where she has been a member of the anthropology faculty since 1968. Her main field of interest is physical growth and development of human and non-human primates. She is Secretary-Treasurer of the North American Section of the Society for the Study of Human Biology.

JOSEPH S. WEINER (1915–) was born in Transvaal, South Africa, and received his undergraduate education at the University of Witwatersrand. He obtained his M.A. degree at Hertford College, Oxford, his D.Sc. from the University of Oxford, and was named Member of the Royal College of Surgeons and Member of the Royal College of Physicians at Saint George's Hospital, London. His research has been in human paleontology, where his major publications are on the Swanscombe find and the Piltdown forgery, and in human population biology where he has contributed many papers on skin color, morphology, and climatic adaptation. He is currently Professor of Environmental Physiology at the University of London and has been awarded the Rivers Memorial Medal of the Royal Anthropological Institute.

HENRY C. WOMACK (1938–) did his undergraduate work at Alcorn A and M and holds an M.S. degree in Biology and a Ph.D. in Anatomy from Wayne State University. He is currently Assistant Professor of Physiology and Health Science at Ball State University. His major research interest is in human body composition, especially variations in body fat distribution.

Index of Names

Index of Subjects